LOGIC AS A HUMAN INSTRUMENT

LOGIC as a Human
Instrument _____

by

Francis H. Parker

HAVERFORD COLLEGE

and

Henry B. Veatch

INDIANA UNIVERSITY

HARPER & BROTHERS, PUBLISHERS, NEW YORK

To JOHN WILD
in gratitude and affection

CONTENTS

A PREFACE FOR TEACHERS

"What, another logic textbook!" Such will undoubtedly be your immediate reaction as you first open this newly arrived book and catch a glimpse of the title that is being sent you for your examination. And what will you do then? Already we can see you, with that look of bored resignation on your face, tossing the torn wrappings into the wastebasket with one hand and with the other reaching down to the dusty lower shelf of your office bookcase, there to deposit this most recently proffered textbook in the small space that still remains at the end of a whole row of poor, faded predecessors, alike unopened and unread. Yes, such is the dismal fate that usually awaits logic texts nowadays at the hands of hardened, textbook-sated professors.

Now, if there were only some way that we could open your eyes and unstop your ears to our confident protest, "But this book is different!" Yet what good would this do? It would only provoke the cynical rejoinder, "That's what they all say."

Just the same, suppose you stop for a moment and consider: What is it that the ordinary textbook in logic these days aims at achieving, and what is the student supposed to derive from the study of such a text? At once, the obvious answer that suggests itself is that the purpose of an undergraduate course in logic is to acquaint the student with various and sundry logical techniques. Very well, but just what does a mastery of such techniques have to do with philosophy, and why should they be studied in a so-called philosophy course? For it may be presumed that most logic courses are still offered in philosophy departments, be it for better or for worse.

Does this last question perhaps make you feel rather more hard put to it to find a ready answer? What is there particularly philosophical about logic courses nowadays? And are not logic textbooks with real philosophical content rather conspicuous by their absence?

Why should this be? Is it necessary that logic first take a vow of philosophical poverty before it can rightly become logic? It would hardly seem so. Indeed, if logic is to be relevant to human knowledge and life, it would rather seem that the logician must constantly have a regard both for the real that is to be known through the use of man's logical instruments and also for the peculiar way in which such instruments function so as to enable men thereby to acquire knowledge of the real. And surely there could not be found any more perennial and proper concerns of philosophy than being and knowing. Hence must not logic, by its very nature, be a thoroughly and radically philosophical discipline?

How, then, is one to explain the curious current divorce of logic from philosophy? One reason might be the extraordinary complexity and intricacy of the techniques that have been developed by modern mathematical and symbolic logicians. In consequence it is not surprising that one should find among not a few contemporary logicians a fascination with the proliferation and manipulation of seemingly infinitely varied and complex logical forms and structures, apparently merely for their own sakes. Questions as to why and how such forms are logical—i.e., as to why and how they are fitted to function in human knowing—tend to be brushed aside as comparatively unimportant and "philosophical," and hence as not really pertinent to the serious business of textbook logic.

But surely the price paid for this conversion of logic into no more than a mathematician's delight in abstract forms and structures is ruinously high. For will not the critical student come to think of logic, when so conceived, as no better than an ingenious and intricate irrelevancy? True, if he has taste and talent for symbol manipulation, he may find such logic fun. But will he feel that there is much point to it? Will he feel that the study of it has given him much of an insight into the means and devices of human cognition? Indeed, one is often struck by the fact that the pedagogical situation with regard to modern symbolic logic today is in many ways not unlike the situation that prevailed for so long in connection with so-called Aristotelian and Scholastic logic. For in the latter tradition, it will be remembered, it was customary simply to posit the subject-predicate form of the proposition, or the generic-specific ordering of concepts, or the syllogistic form of arguments, as being things which the student simply had uncritically to master and learn how to manipulate. But as to the why of the subject-predicate form, or the reasons for genera and species, or the point of the syllogism—these were matters that the student was never told about and that the instructor himself perhaps never even thought about. Little wonder that under such circumstances logic came to be regarded as largely an affair of mechanical manipulation. And has not a strictly comparable situation come to prevail today, except that the manipulations are much more complicated and the mechanisms to be learned much more intricate and difficult?

Nor will it do to defend the almost exclusive formalism of so much of modern logic merely on the ground that its seeming irrelevancy to our natural human concern to understand the logical procedures of our thinking and reasoning is due simply to the desire of such a logic to order and systematize what in everyday use and practice are but helter-skelter and hit-and-miss procedures. Thus it is not infrequently said that modern systems of symbolic logic are to be compared to the everyday logical practices that we all use, much as

Euclidean geometry is to be compared to the actual practices of surveying and measuring that are in common use. Yet such a comparison is really not apposite. For while geometry did succeed in systematizing the actual practices of surveyors, and in making clear why such practices were reliable and actually worked, modern symbolic logic often tends to distort and to repudiate, and generally fails to systematize, many of those everyday practices which we know for certain are quite rational, but which somehow do not lend themselves to systematization according to the self-appointed canons of symbolic logic. One need only mention by way of illustration such things as the so-called nonformal inferences, the counter-factual conditionals, the "referring use," as Strawson calls it, of ordinary subject terms in propositions, the relations in opposition between categorical A, E, I, and O propositions, etc. Indeed, the disparity between what is recognized as logically permissible by the standards of the symbolic logicians and what is recognized as logically permissible by the standards of ordinary human reason has become so great and so glaring as to cause a contemporary French logician to broach the question of whether there may perhaps be a necessary and an irreconcilable divergence between the logical and the rational.[1]

No, there would seem to be no denying the fact that the formalism of the symbolic logicians, quite as much as that of so many of the traditional Aristotelian logicians, has had the effect of rendering logic, as it is taught to students, at once nonphilosophical and practically irrelevant. At least it is irrelevant for us as human beings, whatever it may be for computing machines. But what about the various reactions against such formalism—reactions like those of John Dewey some years ago and more recently those of the latter-day Oxford partisans of ordinary language? Will these reactions, especially the later ones, have the effect of once more restoring philosophic content to logic and of rendering it humanly significant and meaningful to students? Well, it is perhaps still too early to judge what will be the consequences for the teaching of logic of these newer fashions in the theory of logic, which hold that the ultimate standards of logical correctness are simply the everyday uses of ordinary language, and not at all those esoteric and artificial uses which it was once the fashion for logicians to invent and then to canonize in austere and forbidding treatises like *Principia Mathematica*, et al.

Yet we are far from being sanguine over these developments. To be sure, an intensive effort to direct the students' attention to the actual logical uses of ordinary speech may well have the effect of once more making logic seem humanly relevant and practically significant. But so long as no attention is paid to the philosophical grounds for the various logical uses in ordinary speech, such uses will surely strike the student as being mere

[1] "Logique et Raison," by R. Blanché in *Annales publiées par la Faculté des Lettres de Toulouse*, 3me Année, Facicule 5, November, 1954.

historical and cultural accidents, without philosophical intelligibility. The question is bound to arise: Why is it that these uses have the efficiency they seem to have, and what is it about them that enables them to function in their roles as instruments and media of human knowledge?

In fact, it has long been customary in the more elementary logic courses in this country to eschew philosophical questions, not because of an exclusive preoccupation with abstract logical forms, but rather from an almost opposite preoccupation with concrete cases and examples. And one wonders whether the current interest in the uses of ordinary language may not resolve itself, so far as the teaching of logic is concerned, into a renewed popularity of logic courses whose primary concern is with the inculcation of "correct thinking" or "critical thinking" or "practical thinking," etc. All of which, of course, is fine so far as it goes. But again, what is there that is properly or distinctively philosophical in all this? And is it not legitimate at least to raise a question as to what the value is of merely acquainting students with logical procedures and techniques, be they abstract or concrete, so long as one does not also strive to give the students some understanding of the philosophical grounds and import of these logical tools and procedures?

At any rate, such is the purpose of this book: to present logic to students in such a way as to make it apparent that logic is an integral part of philosophy and can serve as a valid and proper introduction to philosophy.

Now this does not mean that we have tried to write a book of the sort one would ordinarily expect a philosophical logic to be—that is to say, a book in which little or no attention is paid to the so-called formal part of logic and to the various techniques governing the construction and manipulation of such forms. No, for we have tried to do justice to the formal part of logic, even utilizing wherever we could the symbolic techniques of modern mathematical logic. At the same time, our concern has been constantly to explain why these forms are as they are and what their "intentional"[2] function is—i.e., how they are peculiarly fitted to enable us, when we use them, to "intend" and come to know things as they really are. Only when viewed in this light can such forms be recognized as being properly *logical* forms, as contrasted with the almost limitless variety of forms and structures that may be invented by the mathematical imagination.

Or to explain the stress and emphasis of our book in a slightly different way, we might say that our aim has been to present logic as being simply semantics. Unfortunately, this latter term has become somewhat à la mode these days, with the result that its meaning may be as empty as it is fashionable. Yet if one accepts Morris' characterization of semantics as the study of "the relations of signs to the objects to which the signs are applicable,"[3] there is certainly a

[2] On the meaning of this term see below, pp. 13–14.
[3] *Foundations of the Theory of Signs*, University of Chicago, 1938, p. 6.

sense in which the philosophical presentation of logic which we are here attempting may be called semantics. For as we have repeatedly insisted, our concern is not with so-called logical forms just in themselves and *in abstracto*, so to speak. On the contrary, such an abstraction, we feel, is vicious, and inevitably leads to a confounding of logic with mathematics. For as we see it, logical forms, in contrast to the constructions of mathematicians, are precisely such forms as by their very nature are adapted to being of and about other things, and which for that very reason are the natural instruments for our human knowledge of objects. Hence it seems to us that logic cannot be other than semantics and that the study of logic cannot fail to take account of how and why our logical instruments function "intentionally" as they do.

It's true, of course, that semantics nowadays is often thought of as involving the study of the relations of various artificially constructed languages to the objects which such languages are designed to signify. But this sort of thing is of no concern to us in the present book. For while such languages may perhaps be constructed, and while they may be of use for various specialized purposes in physics or in economics or in behavioristic psychology or in the setting up of computers or what not, still, underlying all these artificial languages and serving as the necessary medium for them all, it would seem that there must be the natural and non-artificial logic of human beings just as such—a logic which is ordered not to the specialized cognitive concerns of scientists or technicians or other specialists but rather to the universal human concern of understanding the real. Accordingly, it is precisely this human logic, if you will, or this humane logic, or logic considered as a universal human organon, that is the object of investigation and exposition in this book.

Now strange as this project of a human or humane or humanistic logic may sound, will it lessen or will it only serve to compound the strangeness if we hasten to explain that a human logic is none other than a logic correlated to our actual human world? After all, as human beings we do live in a common everyday world of men and things—of beings that simply are and exist, that not only are but are what they are, with their own characteristic natures and traits, that act and are acted upon, and whose being and behavior both are and are intelligible in and through real causes. It is to the cognition of just such a world of everyday human experience that our various human logical tools are adapted—definitions, syllogisms, universal concepts, affirmative and negative propositions, inductions, relations of opposition, etc.

"Oh," we can hear you protest, "who cares about this old-fashioned, common world of everyday experience? Has it not been completely discredited and displaced as a result of the totally different world picture that is presented to us by modern science, particularly modern physics? And may it not

be presumed as well that a logic that is adapted to a knowledge of the everyday world of human experience must now give place to a logic adapted
to the altogether different purpose of getting to know the esoteric world of
modern physical science?" In reply, we may freely admit that we are anything
but insensitive to the criticisms implicit in such questions. What's more, we
might also admit, with certain reservations, that so long as one remains
within the context of the elaborate mathematical constructions and theories
of modern physics a logic which is wholly adapted to the intentional function
of enabling us to come to know things in terms of what they are essentially
—and through their causes, and in their very acts of existing—would appear
to be strangely out of place and irrelevant, for the very reason that mathematical theories of physics seem quite unconcerned with such things as causes,
essences, substances, acts of existing, etc.

Be all this as it may, it would scarcely follow that either our human world
or our human logic appropriate to the understanding of such a world should
be regarded as discredited and displaced. Quite the contrary; even the most
sophisticated scientist cannot wholly avoid being a human being, as well as
a scientist. And as a human being he will find himself, quite as much as the
rest of us, immersed in an everday world of things living and nonliving, of
friends and enemies, of birth and death, of joy and sorrow, of beauty and
ugliness, of change and permanence, of intelligibility and mystery. Not only
that, but as an inhabitant of this world of common human experience our
physicist can scarcely keep himself from thinking and reasoning and trying
to understand simply in the manner of a human being qua human. Thus he
will want to know what this is, and whether that is, and why something else
is; in other words, his concern will be with essences and existences and
causes. But such cognitive concerns will be served, we suggest, only by a
human or humanistic logic of the sort we are here trying to present.

Such then being our thesis and our project for a humanistic logic, how do
we propose to execute it? A glance at the rather detailed topical outline
in the Contents should answer this question. The three main parts of the
book follow the rather traditional division of logic into concepts, propositions, and arguments, each of these being an indispensable instrument that
human beings find themselves quite naturally employing in their efforts to
understand their human world. Moreover, in accordance with our program
of trying always to bring to light the philosophical grounds and import of
specific logical techniques and devices, it will be noted that under each of
these three main parts the first several chapters are devoted to a philosophical
explanation of what in reality the particular logical tool in question is especially
adapted to enabling us to get to know, as well as of how that tool is particularly
adapted to its specific cognitive purpose. There then follow chapters devoted

to an exhibition of the formal properties of the tool in question, as well as the various ways in which it tends to be employed in the context of everyday language.

It may appear at first glance that our project of presenting logic in both its formal and its philosophical aspects is overly ambitious, in that considerably more material is contained in the book than students can readily master in a single semester course. Nevertheless, for some years we have tested and retested this material in our classes both at Haverford College and at Indiana University and have found that it is by no means impossible for students to cover this much material in a single semester. At the same time, we recognize that at different institutions an elementary logic course will serve a rather different curricular purpose. Consequently, we should expect that in adapting the book to their particular uses different instructors will find rather different combinations of chapters suitable to their purposes. For instance, as mere suggestions we might offer the following two alternative minimum programs for a one-semester course in logic. The alternatives are based upon whether an instructor wishes to stress the technical, practical, formal-linguistic side of logic or is more interested in having his students concentrate on the theoretical and philosophical side of logic.

For the former purpose, the following combination of chapters might suffice as a minimum:

Introductory, Chapter 1.
On concepts, Chapters 5 and 6.
On propositions, Chapters 10, 11, 12, 13, and 14.
On arguments, Chapters 20, 21, 22, 23, 24, 25, and 26.

For the latter purpose, the more theoretical and philosophical, the following might do:

Introductory, Chapter 1.
On concepts, Chapters 2, 3, and 4.
On propositions, Chapters 7, 8, 9 (sections 9.1 and 9.2), 10, 12, and 13.
On arguments, Chapters 15, 16, 19, 20, 25, and 26.

Again, be it noted that these suggestions represent no more than the barest minimum in the way of reading assignments, which the particular instructor would presumably wish to supplement with further assignments according to his own interests and emphases. Thus, by way of example, one will note that in neither of our proposed reading lists were Chapters 17 and 18 included, even though in many ways these might be regarded as among the more important chapters of the book. However, these chapters treat of certain of the standard criticisms of both deductive and inductive inference, criticisms which constitute some of the central issues of modern philosophy. And yet, being criticisms, they are perhaps not indispensable to the bare exposition of deduction and induction. For this reason they were omitted from both lists of minimum assignments.

Finally, our acknowledgments are due to a number of colleagues who by their suggestions and criticisms, as well as by their steady encouragement, have greatly aided and furthered our enterprise. Professor Robert Jordan of the University of New Hampshire has used the book in a preliminary mimeographed version and has offered a number of comments that we have found exceedingly helpful. Also, Miss Joan Ogden, formerly a graduate student at Indiana University and an instructor at the University of Missouri, has made several suggestions regarding our treatment of the square of opposition. But more particularly we stand in debt to Professor Samuel M. Thompson of Monmouth College. He has not only used the book and given us the benefit of his reactions but most generously put at our disposal a quantity of original logical materials which he has worked out during his many years of experience in teaching logic. We are also grateful to the Haverford College Faculty Research Fund for assistance with secretarial work.

FRANCIS H. PARKER

HENRY B. VEATCH

September, 1958

INTRODUCTION

CHAPTER 1

WHAT IS LOGIC?

1-1   THE SUBJECT MATTER OF LOGIC

Finding yourself enrolled in a logic course—by requirement, to be sure, and not by choice—you may ask yourself, "What's this going to be about, anyway?" After all, when you enroll in an astronomy course, you can pretty well guess what it will be about: the stars. A botany course will, you suppose, have something to do with plants. A course in marketing will be about just what it says. But what will a logic course be about?

Now it's not as if the word "logic" were altogether unfamiliar. You have doubtless on any number of occasions made remarks to this effect: "I just don't see the logic of his position," or "He has a very logical mind," or perhaps even, "All women are illogical." Still, if faced directly with the question "Just what sorts of things will be studied or investigated in a subject called 'logic'?" you may well find yourself rather at a loss for a ready answer.

Perhaps you might hazard a guess that logic will have something to do with thinking or reasoning. Nor would this be altogether incorrect. Yet no sooner do you make such a suggestion than a fairly obvious objection will probably occur to you, an objection which should pretty well indicate why it could not be entirely correct to say that thinking or reasoning is the subject matter of logic. For what about psychology? Will it not claim that thinking and reasoning must properly fall within its domain? If the only subject matter to which logic can lay claim should turn out to be thinking and reasoning, it is not hard to imagine that imperialistically-minded psychologists will promptly start boasting that logic is, after all, no more than a rather insignificant department of that vast and lordly domain which they have recently staked out with the high-sounding title of "the science of behavior." All of which might be eminently satisfying to the psychologists but is an exceedingly bitter pill for the logicians! And since this, after all, is a book written by professors of logic, you can reasonably assume that any account of logic which would simply expose it to eager expropriation by psychology just will not be tolerated in the present context.

Very well, then. If we are to understand logic as having something to do with thinking and reasoning, and yet in such a way as not to involve any confusion with psychology, we might perhaps proceed on a somewhat different tack.

3

Suppose someone were to ask you quite bluntly, "Just what is the point of thinking or reasoning anyway?" or "Why do you ever try to think or reason things out; where is that supposed to get you?" No doubt the bluntness of the question might take you somewhat aback. After all, considering how much time and effort—yes, even how much thought itself—you may have expended in trying to avoid thinking, to be confronted thus with the question of why you should ever bother to think is perhaps a rather shattering experience: "Why do you, or why does anyone, ever do any thinking? Just what is the purpose of thinking or reasoning?"

If you have now begun to recover your composure but are still somewhat nonplused by the question, it may only be because the answer is so obvious and unsophisticated. For isn't the point of thinking and reasoning simply to gain knowledge and understanding?

No sooner is this said, however, than we hear your cynical reply, "If the purpose of thinking be the attainment of knowledge, it is not a little ironical how often that purpose seems to end only in frustration!" True enough, it is certainly undeniable that human thinking is sometimes unsuccessful in this regard. Nor is this surprising, for it stands to reason, as one might say, that one's thinking or reasoning will not be successful or fruitful unless one goes about it in the right way—unless one goes about it logically. For there are clearly *means* and *methods* of thinking, there are various *tools* and *instruments*, various *devices* and *techniques*, that have to be employed in thinking and reasoning if such thinking is to be fruitful—i.e., if it is to lead to anything like knowledge and understanding.

With this we can perhaps begin to see in a rough sort of way just what it is that the study of logic will be concerned with. It will be concerned not with the psychological acts and operations of human thinking as such but with the methods and techniques and instruments which must be employed in thinking, if such thinking is ever to lead to knowledge. Or looked at a little differently, logic itself is the means or the technique which, when we observe it and use it, insures that our thinking will be correct and valid and, so far as possible, even true.[1] Thus it was that the title which eventually came to be given to the

---

[1] Many logicians would deny that logic has any concern with the truth of the conclusions we draw, its proper interest being only in whether these conclusions have been drawn validly, i.e., in whether they have followed logically from the premises. These logicians would argue that to know whether a statement is true or not one must know whether it corresponds to the facts, and so one must know these facts as well. On the other hand, to know whether a conclusion follows or does not follow from its premises requires absolutely no knowledge of facts or of the real world at all; instead, all that is necessary is the mere recognition that the conclusion is either undeniable or deniable when taken in conjunction with its premises. And this recognition, in turn, requires only a knowledge of logic, whereas to know whether one's statements are true requires a different sort of knowledge—scientific knowledge or knowledge of facts.

Now unquestionably, there is merit in such a way of understanding logic. Yet we feel that

logical writings of Aristotle, who first systematically formulated what we now know as logic, was the Greek word *organon*,[2] which means literally "tool" or "instrument." Thus it is too that, defined in terms of its purpose, logic is simply *the tool or instrument of human knowledge*.

1–2   THE MAIN TYPES OF LOGICAL INSTRUMENTS

Very well, then, supposing that logic, as distinguished from other sciences, has to do precisely with the various tools and instruments of human knowing, let us pause to consider briefly and in a preliminary sort of way some examples of human cognitive tools. For no sooner does one speak of instruments of knowledge than we all tend to think immediately of such forbidding objects as telescopes, microscopes, computing machines, cloud chambers, and what not else. This reaction only serves to show how sophisticated we all are in this scientific age—so sophisticated, indeed, that we sometimes miss altogether the more simple and elementary facts of life. And such is the case here, for while it is certainly true that microscopes, X-ray machines, cloud chambers, etc. are instruments of knowledge, they are nevertheless cognitive instruments of a rather different sort and of a much less fundamental and rudimentary kind than properly logical instruments. We sometimes forget that before men are scientists they are human beings; and even after they become scientists some few of them manage to remain human beings. Moreover, simply as human beings men are capable of at least some knowledge and understanding, quite independent of thè rather specialized and artificial modes of knowing associated with the various special sciences. Besides, when scrutinized more closely, most of the scientific instruments that we are familiar with are not so much instruments of knowledge in the strict sense as they are instruments for providing us with additional materials to be known. A telescope or a microscope or a fluoroscope extends our field of vision enormously, enabling us to see things which we should never have seen simply with the naked eye. Nevertheless, our vision thus extended, it still remains for us to know, in the sense of understand, what

---

it often leads to a certain oversimplification regarding the characteristic function of logic. After all, the only reason one desires one's arguments to be valid is that one's conclusions may thereby have a better chance of being true. Accordingly, logical tools must surely be regarded as devices that are used in the interests of attaining truth and not merely as gauges of validity. Likewise, coming at the matter from the other direction—that of science and factual knowledge generally—it may be safely said that no scientist, and for that matter no human being, ever achieves any factual knowledge of any kind save through the use of logical instruments. At the same time, we should be the first to acknowledge that for such a scientific knowledge of the facts something more is needed than a mere knowledge of logical tools and how they are used.

For further discussion pertinent to this issue, see pp. 283–284.

[2] According to W. D. Ross this title did not come into current use until as late as the sixteenth century. Cf. his *Aristotle*, Methuen, 3rd ed., 1937, p. 20, note 6.

we have been shown or have seen. And this is where our ordinary, everyday, human, logical instruments become not only relevant but absolutely indispensable.

What and where are these so-called everyday human logical instruments? Can't we exhibit a few of them to public view, so that it will be just a little clearer what we are talking about? Of course we can, and yet to the end of doing so we must beg you first to submit to the indignity of trying to become just as naïve and receptive of the obvious as you possibly can. To begin with, suppose you ask yourself the simple question: "Is it possible for me ever to come to know or understand anything about anything whatever without having at least some idea or notion of what it is that I am dealing with?" The answer is "No," of course. But note that already you have stumbled across one of those everyday logical tools or instruments that is altogether indispensable for us if we are to know anything at all. It is the instrument of the so-called "idea" or "notion," or as the logician is more likely to call it, the "concept" or the "term."

Now don't bother to ask yourself yet just what an idea is. Goodness knows, this is one of those loose, viscous, slippery words of which everyone knows the meaning, but no one can quite say what it is. There will be time enough and to spare later on for a really careful determination of the meaning of "idea" or "concept." For the present, it is enough if you simply recognize that whatever ideas may be, it is simply a fact that there can be no knowledge of anything without our having at least some sort of idea of what the thing in question is.

Having got this far, the next step becomes obvious too. For while ideas or concepts are certainly indispensable instruments of knowledge, they aren't the sole instruments. Thus you can have any number of ideas you like: "fat," "eternity," "logic," "higher than," "evanescent," "dull," "fortitude," "green," "parallelogram." Still, these would hardly constitute knowledge in the usual sense of the word. Indeed, one could multiply one's ideas almost *ad infinitum;* they still would not suffice for knowledge. What else is needed? Well, suppose, to take a very simple example, a friend of yours had the notion of "dull" and also the notion of "logic." He still would not have arrived at the awful truth that logic is dull, until he combined his ideas in a certain way. And what is that way but simply such a one as will make his ideas susceptible of truth or falsity? In other words, the notion of parallelogram just in itself is neither true nor false. Nor is the notion of "logic," or of "dull," or of "angiosperm." Not only that, but even in combination such concepts do not necessarily become true or false. For instance, suppose someone were to ask you, "Fat men whom Caesar trusted—is this true or false?" The question cannot even be answered. On the other hand, were one to say, "The men were fat whom Caesar trusted," you might be somewhat puzzled as to just what was meant, if you hadn't read

Julius Caesar recently; but at least you would be presented with something which could presumably be regarded as either true or false.

Accordingly, to use the logicians' terminology, one might say that, in addition to having concepts, we must also order and combine our concepts in *propositions.* For save through the medium of propositions, concepts are neither true nor false, and as such will not suffice for knowledge. Or to put it just a little differently, we might say that just as one cannot know anything about anything unless one has some sort of idea or concept of the thing in question, so also one cannot possibly know anything about anything unless one formulates a proposition in regard to it, stating whether the thing in question is thus and so, or what is true of it. In other words, the cognitive instrument through which we come to know whether or not a thing is thus and so is simply the logical proposition. Nor is there apparently[3] any way for us human beings to attain knowledge in the sense of truth except through the use of propositions.

There is a third logical tool which is quite as common and quite as indispensable as concepts and propositions. This is the tool or instrument known as argument or demonstration. Its role is in many ways the easiest of all to understand. Suppose you have the ideas both of logic and of "something that is a waste of time." Suppose, too—which is certainly not hard to imagine—that you have even gone so far as to formulate—to be sure, only tentatively—the proposition "Logic is a waste of time." Still, do you really know this for a fact; are you quite sure? After all, a proposition, as we have seen, is the kind of thing that is susceptible of either truth or falsity. But in a given case, which is it? Is it true or is it false that logic is a waste of time? The mere concepts in themselves and the mere proposition in itself do not suffice to answer this question one way or another. One must look for some evidence of the truth or falsity of the proposition. And to advance evidence for or against a proposition is nothing more or less than to adduce an argument in its support or in refutation of it.

Thus in the present case you might say, "I talked to my fraternity brothers and they told me that logic was a waste of time; therefore I believe it is true." Or you might say, "Any subject that concerns itself only with thoughts and words and not with tangible facts, testable in the laboratory, is a waste of time."

Here are a couple of arguments advanced in support of the truth of the proposition "Logic is a waste of time." Now whether they are good arguments or not and whether they actually do succeed in proving that logic is a waste of

---

[3] This statement is in a sense too sweeping. One might cite the knowledge of a religious mystic, or the sort of knowledge that comes through art—indeed, intuitive knowledge generally. Such is certainly not necessarily a propositional knowledge. Nevertheless, for purposes of this book we need not concern ourselves with these presumably extra-logical types of knowledge.

time are, of course, somewhat delicate questions on which we should perhaps discreetly draw the curtain, at least for the time being. Yet be they good arguments or bad, they are arguments, and as such they illustrate well enough how readily and even inescapably this sort of tool comes to hand in the everyday business of seeking to know and understand.

1–3 LOGIC AND LANGUAGE

At this point a bright idea may suddenly occur to you. "Oh," you will say, "I begin to get what you mean by all this high-sounding talk of logical tools and instruments. When you come right down to it, what are these tools—concepts, propositions, and arguments—but ordinary words and sentences ordered and arranged in various ways? Logic itself, when looked at in this way, appears to be nothing more than a matter of ordinary grammar and language. Thus when it is argued that one cannot possibly come to know or understand anything unless one has some sort of idea or concept of it, does this amount to any more than saying that one can't possibly know anything without naming it and using words to describe it? And similarly, when it was argued that mere concepts alone do not suffice for knowledge, but must rather be combined in propositions, was not this but a disguised way of saying that mere words alone, whether in isolation or even in combination, just don't make complete sense? Instead, they must first be placed in sentences in order to make up a 'complete thought,' as the grammarians might say, or in order to become susceptible of truth or falsity, as the logicians might prefer to say. In other words, what is logic but mere grammar? And similarly, when it is said that logic is no less than the organon itself of human knowledge, why could not this be interpreted as meaning that logic is an instrument of knowledge in precisely the same sense as language is?"

Whether or not the suggestion that logic be simply identified with language is entirely true, it is certainly illuminating.[4] For one thing, as we shall have occasion to see later, language is important not merely as a means or instrument for the communicating of knowledge; it has in addition a role to play in the

---

[4] The tendency to equate logic with language is quite widespread among contemporary logicians. The reason for this would appear to be twofold. For one thing, linguistic entities like words and sentences can to a certain extent be regarded as behavioral phenomena and hence as much more amenable to empirical investigation than such things as thoughts and ideas. For another thing, many recent English philosophers and logicians have come to feel that the various uses of words and expressions in ordinary language have a certain ultimacy and autonomy which warrant their being studied for their own sake. Hence in this latter view logic becomes not so much the norm and standard in terms of which ordinary ways of speaking and arguing are judged and corrected as just the other way around. The logician is supposed to regard it as his principal task to understand ordinary linguistic usage and to consider that all of the so-called special and artificially designed logical languages are really no more than *ad hoc* deviations from the norm of customary, everyday use.

very achieving of knowledge itself.[5] Furthermore, to compare logic with language serves a useful purpose in pointing up the characteristic way in which logic functions as an instrument of knowledge. Just as we tend to take the instrumentality of language more or less for granted, frequently giving it scarcely a thought and seldom worrying much about perfecting our use of it as an instrument, so it is with logic too. That's one of the reasons why, as we noted earlier, we are likely to think of the instruments of knowledge as the artificially contrived instruments of the scientists rather than as such rudimentary and natural instruments of knowledge as concepts, propositions, and arguments. These latter, just like our linguistic tools, we tend simply to take for granted and seldom bother about really trying to understand or master.

Nevertheless, while logic and language are thus closely parallel, it seems clear that they cannot be identical. Compare the word "house" with the word *"Haus"* or *"maison."* Regarded simply as words, there is no doubt that the English expression is different from the German, and the German from the French; they are, in short, three different words. Yet all three do have one and the same meaning, or very nearly so. Or to put the same thing in another way, the three words, though different as words, nevertheless all convey the same idea or concept. On this basis, then, one seems compelled to distinguish between words considered simply as linguistic or grammatical entities and their meanings or the ideas and concepts which they are intended to convey. Moreover, the logician is interested in the meanings or the concepts which the words express, and only indirectly in the words or linguistic expressions themselves.

A like contrast may be drawn between sentences and propositions. Thus compare:

He laid the book on the table.
Er hat das Buch auf dem Tisch gelegt.

The grammatical structure of each of these, considered simply as sentences, is somewhat different from that of the other. Yet they both say pretty much the same thing. Or to put it in a way a little better suited to the purposes of logic, one can say that both sentences are designed to express the same truth or signify the same proposition. Indeed, given the multitudes of different languages, there must be an enormous number of ways of expressing this same truth or proposition through sentences each with a different syntactical structure. But logic, in contrast to grammar and linguistics, is concerned with the intended proposition and its structure, not the various sentences and their structures, or at least not directly.

Accordingly, just as it is necessary to distinguish the logical tools and techniques that are employed in thinking and reasoning from the thinking and reasoning themselves, so also it is important to distinguish logical entities like

[5] See pp. 20–22.

<u>concepts, propositions, and arguments from the grammatical and linguistic devices that are employed to express and communicate them.</u> In other words, logic is no more identical with grammar and linguistics than it is with psychology.

1-4 THE MAIN OBJECTS OF LOGICAL INSTRUMENTS

Let us pause a moment to take stock of at least some of our results thus far. Apparently it has required no more than a simple, unsophisticated reflection upon our everyday human experience to make us conscious of three types of logical tools or instruments, corresponding more or less to certain obvious linguistic devices, which, quite undeniably, we do in fact use in our normal human efforts to gain an understanding of ourselves and our world, and which, equally undeniably, we could in no way dispense with. For just how could any one of us possibly know anything at all without forming some sort of concept of that which we know, and without formulating at least some propositions about it, and without constructing various arguments in support of our propositional assertions in regard to it? Yet even so, our preliminary account of these three main types of logical tool or instrument which we human beings use for purposes of knowledge is inadequate in at least one major respect. For is it not essential to an understanding of any tool or instrument that we recognize not merely *that* it is used and *how* it is used, but also *why* a tool of that particular type should be adapted to its particular job? Granted that in our efforts to know we do in fact use instruments such as concepts, propositions, and arguments, just why do we? What is there about these particular instruments that fits them for the peculiar and respective functions which they are presumably supposed to perform in the everyday business of cognition?

The Three W's and Their Corresponding Objects. If you have ever been around small children and had a chance to observe the development in their speech and attitudes, you will know that they go through various "stages." Indeed, perhaps the easiest way for parents to rationalize some instance of particularly unpleasant behavior on the part of their child is to say, "Oh, this is just a stage he's going through." And of these stages there are two which are especially noticeable and interesting: the "what" stage and the "why" stage.

About as soon as the child learns to talk, he appears to the proud parent to be little more than a bundle of "what" questions: "What's this?" "What's that?" and so on. A little later he still appears to the proud but now tiring parent to be a bundle of questions, but they have now changed from "What?" to "Why?" "Why do birds fly?" "Why do men smoke?" "Why does it snow?"—and so on *ad nauseam.*

What is the child looking for in each of these questions? What kind of answer

What - nature or essence → concept (word)
Why - reason or cause → argument/demonstration (position)
Whether - existence → proposition (sentence)

What Is Logic?   11

does he want? When he asks, "What's that?" the answer will be, "a dog," or "rain," or "mud." A "what" question calls for a "what" answer—an answer which reveals *what* the thing in question is, its nature or essence or character. One of the objects of knowledge, then, is the "what" of things—their *nature* or *essence*.

When a child asks "Why?" he is looking for a reason, explanation, or cause. "Why do birds fly?" "*Because* they have wings." "Why do men smoke?" "*Because* it gives them enjoyment." A "why" question calls for a "why" answer—an answer which reveals the reason or cause of the thing in question. Thus a second object of knowledge is the "why" of things—their *reason* or *cause*.

Contained implicitly in these "what" and "why" questions, and often made explicit, is a third type of question, a question which is perhaps not quite so noticeable because its answer is usually already assumed. When the child asks, "What is that?" contained implicitly in his question is a further question: "*Is* that something?" "*Is* there anything there?" and an assumed answer: "Yes, there *is* something there." When he asks, "Why do birds fly?" the further question, "*Do* birds fly?" and its assumed answer, "Yes, birds *do* fly," are present as silent determinants. This question as to *whether* something *is* such and such is often tacit, especially in children, because their questions usually concern things which are immediately sensed and whose "whether" is therefore beyond question. Hence "whether" questions usually increase as our minds extend themselves beyond immediate sensation, and consequently as we mature. But even in children the question is often explicit: "Is it raining outside?" "Do dogs go to heaven?" "Is Santa Claus real?"

What kind of answer does this third question, the "whether" question, demand? We would probably answer by saying: "Yes, it *is* raining outside," or (if we are cruelly frank), "No, Santa Claus *is not* real," or (if we are perplexedly honest), "I don't know whether dogs *do* go to heaven or whether they don't." The key word here is the "*is* word"—"is" or some equivalent. In short, a "whether" question calls for an answer concerning the *existence, reality,* or *factuality* of something. Thus a third kind of object of knowledge is the "whether" or *existence* of things.

These three questions—"What?" "Why?" and "Whether?"—are natural and inescapable for us; one could hardly imagine a day passing without their being asked in some form or other. That they seek three kinds of object—a characteristic, a reason, and a fact—is also clear and natural, though perhaps somewhat less explicit. When we express the situation in ontological terms and say that the mind intends three aspects of reality—*essence, cause,* and *existence*—you are likely to say, like Monsieur Jourdain, "Is *that* what I am seeking to know?" "But still," you will add, "I see the connection."

Thus the objects of knowledge are phases of the reality about us, and these objects are of three types. There is the "what" of things, their essence or nature, which we seek to know when we ask the question "What?" There is the "whether" of things, their existence or nonexistence, which we seek to know when we ask the question "Whether?" And there is the "why" of things, their cause or reason, which we seek to know when we ask the question "Why?"

The Three W's and Their Corresponding Instruments.   But now note how these three different kinds of object of knowledge, or three W's as we have called them, are precisely correlated with and actually determine the character of the three different logical tools. "What is that?" "Rain." The tool for knowing a "what" or essence is a *term* or *concept*. "Is it raining?" "It *is* raining." The tool for knowing a "whether" or existence is a *proposition*. "Why is it raining?" "*Because* the mountains have lifted warm, moist air and it has cooled, so as to make the temperature and dew point converge, and whenever this happens it rains." The tool for knowing a "why" or cause is an *argument* or *demonstration*.

Furthermore, since language in its cognitive function is designed to convey knowledge, there will necessarily be three different types of linguistic tools corresponding to the three different types of logical tools and to the three W's. If you are asked *what* this is you are reading, you will say: "a book," or "a page," or "logic," or "a page of a logic book." The linguistic tool corresponding to a concept and to a "what" is a *word* or *phrase*. If you are asked whether or not this is a logic book, you may answer: "Yes, it is (or at least claims to be) a logic book." The linguistic instrument corresponding to a proposition and to a "whether" is thus a *sentence*—usually, but not always, a declarative one. And finally, if you are asked *why* this is a logic book, you may reply: "Because it is a book which is explicitly concerned with the universal instruments of human knowledge, and any book with this explicit concern is a logic book." If this reply were expanded linguistically it would read something like this: "All books explicitly concerned with the universal instruments of human knowledge are logic books. This is a book which is explicitly concerned with the universal instruments of human knowledge. Hence, this is a logic book." Thus the linguistic tool corresponding to an argument and to a "why" is an integrated *group* of sentences—often a paragraph. These parallels between the objects of knowledge and the logical and linguistic instruments of knowledge may be summarized as follows:

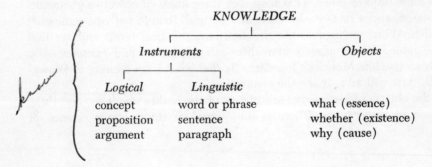

KNOWLEDGE

	Instruments		Objects
	Logical	*Linguistic*	
	concept	word or phrase	what (essence)
	proposition	sentence	whether (existence)
	argument	paragraph	why (cause)

1–5 SIGNS AND SEMANTICS

Before we proceed to the main business of logic, which is a detailed investigation of each of these three logical tools and how they work, we must stop to consider a certain general feature that pertains to all three of them and that really more than any other single feature fits them to function as properly logical tools or instruments of knowledge.

The Intentionality of Knowledge. The most fundamental feature of knowledge—and indeed of all awareness—is that it is always *of* or *about* something other than itself. We have an experience *of* war, a feeling *of* pain, a concept *of* a triangle. We make propositions *about* bodies gravitating, and arguments *about* the interior angles of a triangle equaling two right angles. All awareness, all consciousness, all knowledge, is about something other than itself. It *tends into,* or *intends,* something distinct from itself. For this reason this most fundamental trait of knowledge is called its "intentionality." All knowledge is "intentional"; every piece of knowledge is an "intention."

It is obvious at once that the word "intention" has here a somewhat unusual meaning, for we ordinarily use the word to pertain to acts of will or purpose. Indeed, intentions are the things which, when they are good, pave hell, as Dr. Johnson remarked, and, when they are dishonorable, are what we must warn our daughters against. Yet this does not mean that the word is here being given a meaning which is absolutely different from its usual meaning. The moment we stop to think about it, we can see present in acts of will the very same *of* or *about* structure which we have noted in instances of knowledge. You have the intention *of* studying, for example, or the purpose *of* making friends. Furthermore, it is not difficult to see that willing and purposing are "intentional" precisely *because* they contain a cognitively "intentional" element. You can have the *purpose of* being courteous, for example, only when you have some *knowledge of* what courtesy is.

Thus the most basic trait of knowledge is its intentionality—the fact that it is always *of* or *about* something other than *itself*. And this trait sharply distinguishes instances of knowledge from other things. Your concept of a triangle, or your proposition about its interior angles, is *of* or *about* the triangle; but the *triangle* isn't of or about anything—it is just itself. So intentionality is the distinguishing feature of all items of consciousness, and the most basic general characteristic of knowledge.

This being so, the instruments involved in knowledge must also be intentional. Our knowing tools, like knowing itself, must be revelatory, disclosive, meaningful. That is to say, the instruments by which we know reality must of necessity be *significant* of reality. In brief, then, all cognitive instruments are *signs*. But what is a sign? This question belongs specifically to the science of semantics (from the Greek *sema*, "sign"), but an understanding and use of logic requires some knowledge of the nature of signs. What, then, is a sign?

1–5.1   Definition of "Sign"

We can see at once that every sign refers to something of which it is a sign, and does so in such a way as to stand for or substitute for that thing. A sign may be said to be *that which is representative of something other than itself.*

We say "where there's smoke there's fire," that is, that smoke is a sign of fire. Or we say that a red and white striped pole is a sign of a barber shop, or that the word "rain" is a sign or symbol[6] of rain, etc. In every such case we see that for a person to recognize a sign for what it is is for that person to be led cognitively by the sign to something different from the sign itself, namely, that which the sign signifies—its signatum. For instance, the trained physicist, Becquerel, recognized that certain impressions left on a photographic plate were significant of something else, other than the impressions themselves; that is, the impressions signified to him the radioactive character of uranium. So also if a person fails to recognize this pointing characteristic of a sign, he may know many of the characteristics of the sign as a thing itself, but he will not know that which it represents; he will not see its significance or meaning.

Thus every sign is representative, and representative of something *other* than itself. Though there is a saying that "the Indian sign" of rain is that it is "gray all 'round and still pouring down," we would certainly think it strange to say that "rain is a sign of rain," however much the grayness of the sky may be. Though an individual may represent himself in a court of law, he is not thereby a *sign* of himself. The signatum, though perhaps similar, is always a distinct existent; it is always really distinct from the sign.

1–5.2   Natural and Artificial Signs

Besides being representative of something other than itself, every sign represents *its* particular signatum, some certain thing rather than any other thing. Why should this be so?

Why should smoke signify fire rather than, say, the evolution of man? Why should a fossil imprint signify a certain extinct species of fish? Or why should a red and white striped pole signify a barber shop rather than a candy shop? The answer, you will say, is that there must be in each case some underlying *connection* between the sign and what it signifies. *For every relation of a sign to its signatum there is another relation which underlies and justifies the particular relation of significance in question.* This justifying relation we shall call the *foundation-relation.*

---

[6] We are here using the word "sign" as just defined—that is, in the broadest sense so as to include what are sometimes called symbols. The term "symbol" we shall use for what we shall later call an "artificial" sign.

A natural sign is one whose foundation-relation is natural. Why does smoke signify fire rather than something else? Because smoke, the sign, is the *effect* of fire, the signatum, and fire the *cause* of smoke. In the same manner rosy cheeks (when they are natural!) signify health because the former are produced by the latter. Conversely, a cause, either total or partial, may sometimes signify its effect. Thus carpenters at work, or stacks of lumber and bricks, or an architect's blueprints (causes) may each signify the construction of a building (effect).[7] In both cases the justifying foundation-relation is a natural cause-effect relation. The sign signifies its signatum because the two are in nature causally connected.

Why does a fossil imprint signify a certain species of fish rather than something else? Because the fossil is *similar* in appearance to the extinct fish—and in this particular example the sign *is* similar to the signatum because the signatum (the extinct fish) was the *cause* of the sign (the fossil). Likewise a picture reminds you of a loved one because it is a likeness of the loved one, and Tweedledum brings Tweedledee to mind because they really look alike. Thus the foundation-relation may be one of natural *similarity*, either alone or in combination with a causal relation.

Furthermore, the foundation-relation of similarity may sometimes be a similarity of *relations* rather than of things or properties, and in this case the sign situation is what we call a *metaphor.* For example, light sometimes signifies truth, as when we say "Truth is light, or like light." Here there is clearly no real similarity between truth and light themselves, but there is a similarity between the *relations* which each bears to something else. The relation between truth and the knowing mind is like the relation between light and the object it illuminates. Many other examples of such metaphorical signification may come to your mind: when you see a lion you may think of a king, since the lion (supposedly) is to the other animals as a king is to his subjects; or when you see a sunny sky you may think of a smile, since the sun illuminates the sky as a smile illuminates a face.

In such cases as all of the foregoing where the foundation-relation is quite natural and real and not "made up" or artificially contrived by a human mind, the signs in question are called *natural signs.* Causation is certainly the most common of foundations for natural signs, but similarity and possibly other relations such as propinquity or spatial or temporal contiguity also give rise to natural signs.

An artificial sign is one whose foundation-relation is artificial. A red and white striped pole might seem to be more similar to peppermint candy than to barbering—even though barbering used to (and perhaps too often still does, financially if not physiologically) involve the letting of red blood to run down white skin. Nor does there seem to be much causal connection between the

[7] These are examples, respectively, of efficient, material, and final causes.

pole and barbering. Why then does the red and white pole signify a barber shop rather than something else?

It does so simply because our culture, in its customs and habits, conventionally associates the two, probably owing to an original arbitrary act of inventive genius on the part of some individual in the past (which act, however, may have been motivated by some vague natural resemblance). It is for the same reason that three balls signify a pawnshop, and that the word "rain" signifies rain. When the foundation-relation is not a natural connection but rather a connection imposed by human artifice, convention, custom, or habit either by an individual or by a group, the sign is called an *artificial* or arbitrary or conventional sign. When such artificial signs are specially contrived, we call them "symbols."

Thus signs, on the basis of differing foundation-relations, are either *natural* or *artificial*. Consider words and linguistic devices generally. We have already seen how linguistic tools are in many respects very like logical tools. It should also be apparent that words are signs. Very well, then, are such linguistic instruments natural signs or artificial signs? At first you might be inclined to say that they are both, and you might readily think of examples of words that are onomatopoetic or ideographic. When spoken, such words as "ring," "honk," and "bowwow" are somewhat similar in sound to the whole or a part of what they signify, yet they are still conventional and artificially constructed. So also the Chinese and ancient Egyptian written languages are almost entirely ideographic, the written characters being similar in appearance to their signata, more so originally than in their developed forms—for example, the Chinese character for "move from place to place" involves a picture of a foot.[8] But no matter how much language may be based on original similarities between words and things, it is always and invariably specifically devised to perform a certain function and thus is always essentially artificial or conventional. Thus any sign is connected with its signatum either entirely naturally or at least partly artificially. In the first case the sign is natural, and in the second case artificial.

1–5.3 Material and Formal Signs

In addition to these differences in signs brought about by the foundation-relation, signs differ with respect to the sign-relation itself. In order to see this, we must now look more closely at the sign-relation proper.

Material signs are "signs-plus." The signs we have so far considered are smoke, fossils, barber poles, and written and spoken words. In all these cases the sign is a sign and also something else, namely, an entity in its own right. If you are asked, "What is smoke?" you may say, "It is a sign of fire," or you

---

[8] For an interesting and amusing attempt to show that all language is natural, see Plato's *Cratylus*.

may say, "It is the gaseous product of combustion." Your double answer indicates clearly that all the signs we have mentioned are double-natured; each is a sign *plus* a thing of a certain kind in its own right. Or more succinctly, each of the signs we have so far mentioned is both an entity and an arrow: it is an entity with a certain nature of its own in virtue of which it points like an arrow to something else—its signatum. Thus a fossil is a rock of a certain shape, a barber pole a red and white striped piece of wood, a written word a pattern of ink, and a spoken word a configuration of air vibrations—*in addition* to the fact that each is also a *sign of* something other than itself. Such a "sign-plus," which has a nature of its own in addition to its signifying nature, we shall call a *material* sign.[9]

Since a material sign is significant in virtue of its own peculiar nature, that nature must itself be known *first, before*[10] its significance or signatum can be known. And this real nature which must first be known includes also its relations to other things, and especially its foundation-relation—its similarity or causal or artificial connection—to the thing which it signifies. Before you can know that the gray, gaseous phenomenon signifies fire, you must first know that it is smoke, and not steam, or breath, or heat waves, and that it is an effect of fire. And before you know the meaning of the word "ichthyophagy," you must be able to identify it as *that* word rather than the word "ichthyology," must know that it is a word in the English language, and must know at least something of the artificial stipulation which produced its meaning. In short, material signs must first be known in their own right before their significance can be known.

Formal signs are "signs—period." Are all signs material ones? Not if anything representative of something other than itself is called a sign, for what about ideas? If someone walks up to you and says, "I've got an idea," your immediate reply will doubtless be, "What *about?*" If he should then say, "About? About? It's not about anything; it's just an idea," you would probably start listening for a report of an escape from the local asylum. As we have already seen, the basic trait of all awareness is its intentionality—its being about something other than itself. You have a sensation *of* something blue, a memory image *of* last summer, a concept *of* energy, or a proposition *about* the viciousness of war. Hence such ideas are representative of things other than themselves and are therefore signs. But are they material signs? Are they signs-*plus?* Do they have natures or

---

[9] In the classical account of signs given by John of St. Thomas in his *Ars Logica*—an account which we have followed rather closely here—material signs are called "instrumental" signs. We prefer the expression "material sign," however, because the expression "instrumental sign" is redundant and unilluminating since all signs are instrumental, because the term "material sign" provides a more meaningful contrast with the corresponding term "formal sign," and, finally, because all material signs are material or physical entities.

[10] The priority may in some cases not be a *temporal* priority, but it is always a *cognitive* priority.

characteristics of their own apart from their significance? Or put differently, do you first have to know the characteristics of your idea and only *afterwards* know what the idea is of or about?

Clearly not. Just to *have* an idea is to know what it is an idea *of*. Of course you have to *have* the idea, but you do not have to *know* the idea before you know what it's about. Hence ideas—images, concepts, propositions, etc.—are not material signs. They do not have traits which must be known before their significance is known. They are not *means*—things which *have* meaning. They are themselves meanings; they are signs and nothing but signs: "signs—*period.*" Such "signs—period," which have no nature other than their signifying nature, are called *formal* signs; their very nature or form is significance.

A formal sign, then, is one whose very form or nature is simply to represent or mean or signify something other than itself. Formal signs, it is true, can themselves be turned into objects or signata so that a study can be made of the characteristics of their formal significance. Indeed, this is just what we are doing right now. But the important point to be noted here is that when we do make a formal sign—some idea—the object of our study, it ceases to be a sign and becomes instead a *signatum* of *another* formal sign—*another* idea. Thus formal signs are significant only when in *use*, though their formal significance can itself be studied. An analogy may make this clearer.

Perhaps you are wearing a pair of glasses as you read this page. If so, and if you are really reading these words, you do not see the lenses of your glasses. Yet it is through or by means of those lenses that you see the printed words. In short, the lenses reveal something other than themselves while at the same time not revealing themselves.

Now turn your attention to the lenses. Notice that just in order to see them you must take them off. If you do so you see them—their glassiness, concavity, and perhaps a few specks of dirt or some fingerprints—but you no longer see the printed words on this page, or at any rate you no longer see them clearly.

Furthermore, in seeing the lenses of your glasses you are using *other* lenses, the lenses in your eyes; and while you are using your eye lenses you do not see *them.* Perhaps the point is now clear without your taking the next gruesome step: plucking out one eye and seeing its lens with the other eye lens which you do not see. In brief, then, spectacles present only other spectacles, never themselves.[11] And here the ambiguity in the word "spectacle" is significant: both the glasses and what they present are "spectacles."

The glasses in the analogy are ideas or formal signs, and the eyes in the analogy are ideas or formal signs *of those* ideas or formal signs. Ideas, when

---

[11] This is oversimplified. With both spectacles and ideas one is *vaguely,* or perhaps even only *unconsciously,* aware of the instrument while using it to be clearly and consciously aware of something else. But in any case, to make the instrument into an object is to destroy its actual instrumentality, even though it remains an instrument potentially.

in use, are nothing but revelatory or significant of something other than themselves.

And when they are themselves revealed or signified, they are so revealed by other ideas which are themselves not revealed. Thus formal signs are the most efficient of instruments for the simple reason that they are *nothing but* instruments. They are both purely diaphanous and also evanescent. If you can imagine having a pair of invisible glasses which pop on your nose to give you perfect vision when you need it, and yet which disappear at bedtime without your having to put them away, and yet which, finally, make themselves visible when, in a scientific or curious mood, you wish to examine them, then you will have some idea of what ideas are like. The carpenter at the close of his day must take time to put his tools away, but the mind's tools simply disappear when not in use and yet immediately reappear when they are needed. Ideas, then, are tools and nothing but tools, signs and nothing but signs: "signs—period," *formal* signs.

While a material sign is always *different* from (though sometimes similar to) its signatum, the nature of a formal sign is always precisely, identically the nature of its signatum. This is simply another way of saying that a formal sign has no other nature than its signifying nature. But if a formal sign is, in its nature, identical with the nature of its signatum, how can it even be a sign? For a sign, according to our definition, is always of something *other* than itself.

The answer lies in the qualification "in its nature." Formal sign and signatum are identical in *nature* or *character*, but not in their *status* or *condition*. In the formal sign the nature or character exists in the status or condition of a pointer; in the signatum it exists in the condition of an independent being which happens to be *pointed at*. And this difference of state or condition is sufficient to preserve the difference or otherness which must obtain between any sign and its signatum.

Formal signs are necessary. We have considered the nature of formal signs. But what role do they play in the cognitive process? Are they truly indispensable? The easiest way to see the answer to this question is to try to eliminate them, leaving only material signs, and see what happens. What will happen, interestingly enough, is exactly the same sort of thing that we found in an earlier context would happen if one tried to make do with only linguistic entities like words and sentences, to the complete exclusion of more properly logical tools like concepts and propositions. Somehow, the very use of language was found to presuppose such logical meanings and instruments. And so likewise with material and formal signs.

A material sign, we have seen, has a nature of its own which must first itself be known before its significance can be known. But how can this nature itself be known? If it can be known only through *another*, prior material sign, then the peculiar nature of that *prior* material sign must itself first be known as it really is in order that its significance and signatum can be known. Then if this prior material sign can be known only through *another* material sign, the same difficulty arises again, and so on. Thus if we had only material signs we would be in an infinite regress in which we could never know even any material sign, let alone any signatum.

You will doubtless say immediately that such an infinite regress is senseless and unnecessary because the nature which makes the material sign significant is known immediately without the use of any other sign. Agreed. At some point there must be an idea which reveals the nature of a thing identically, exactly as it is. But this is just the point. An idea which reveals something other than itself identically as it is without first having to be known itself is exactly what is meant by a formal sign. Thus formal signs are always necessary to any knowledge. Material signs are often a *necessary* condition of knowledge, but they are never sufficient.

Linguistic signs are necessary. One very important matter remains to be straightened out. It may be admitted that there must be formal signs as well as material signs. Likewise, it may be admitted that when the distinction between formal and material signs is applied in a specifically logico-linguistic context, it is the logical tools and instruments that function as formal signs, and the linguistic instruments that function as material signs. But having shown the necessity, for purposes of knowledge, of such things as formal, logical signs, are we equally clear as to just what the role is of material, linguistic signs? All along we have insisted upon the close connection between language and logic, as well as upon the need for distinguishing carefully the one from the other. Just how does language function alongside of logic in the business of human knowledge?

Of course, the obvious answer to this question is that language is necessary for the *communication* of knowledge. This is due directly to the fact that we humans are physical (though psychophysical) beings who are therefore spatially and temporally separated. In so far as we are physically separate, communication demands a physical bridge between us; and language in its various forms is just such a bridge—however possible it may be that there are also nonphysical means of communication in so far as we are psychical.

But in addition, language is necessary even for the very *formulation* of knowledge in individual thought. We human beings think in terms of images; and of the images we possess, only verbal ones have the purity and singleness characteristic of the ideas that make up our knowledge. As you look at this page, you have a concrete visual image brimming with a profusion of undistinguished traits. If, however, you now abstractly attend to just one of those traits, say the shape, what concrete sensory image can you use to formulate and express that single trait? If you analyze your experience carefully, you may find before your mind's eye a faint white rectangle suspended as if drawn in the air, or you may find a kinesthetic image of your arm making the motions required to draw the figure, or, finally, you may find a tactual image of smooth, straight sides and sharp, square corners. These sensory images have certainly left behind some of the traits of your original sensation of this page, and are therefore better able than the original to express the abstract shape. But are they entirely adequate? Have they left behind *all* other traits save the shape?

Your answer, after careful consideration, will doubtless be "No." You find that your visual image of the ethereal, free-floating figure still has in it some sort of color—perhaps the white of chalk or the blue-gray of smoke—its lines have a certain thickness and grain, the whole figure has some sort of visual location, etc. So also your kinesthetic and tactual images are impure: they contain such additional traits as motion, texture, location, etc. Thus these images still contain a number of different traits or characteristics which are quite accidental to the shape as such; they are still impure. How, then, can they serve to convey or signify just the shape, all alone, which is the object of your idea?

They cannot. And it should not take much reflection to see that no natural sensory image could have the purity and singleness to express a trait in its purely abstracted state. How can we get an image which is adequate to express such an abstract characteristic?

If we can't find one naturally we can make one artificially. And such an artificial sensory image, specially contrived to convey or signify the abstract idea of a single trait or characteristic, is a *word*. What concrete sensory image do you have to convey the abstract nature of the shape of this page? The word "rectangularity." The meaningful message which is borne by the word "rectangularity" excludes all the other traits which we saw to cling so tenaciously to any natural sensory image—such traits as color, texture, location, etc. Its message is therefore simply or just rectangularity. Hence it can adequately convey the abstract idea where natural images cannot. In having visual or auditory or kinesthetic or tactual images of the word "rectangularity"—as a word, that is, as a sign—we have at once an idea of the abstracted isolated characteristic, rectangularity.

In forming words, therefore, we are attempting to reduce to a minimum the multiplicity of traits which characterizes natural sensory images. In short, a word is an ideal sensory image. It is a natural sensory image artificially idealized and purified of all accidental accretions and thereby qualified to convey or signify a single abstract trait.

A word, nevertheless, still signifies only materially; it is still only a material sign since it is a mark or sound in its own right with certain properties of its own which are quite different from the properties of its meaning or signatum. In spite of the purity or singleness of its significance, it is still not pure and single in the way in which an idea or formal sign is, for the latter is nothing but significant of its signatum, rectangularity. Moreover, the word is also an artificial sign since its significance depends essentially on an arbitrary human act. And since this is so, its significance will vary in place and time, whereas the idea or formal sign is as constant as the pure characteristic or trait, such as rectangularity, with which it is identical in nature. This means that few words, if any, achieve the cognitive ideal of signifying just one thing, because different linguistic customs will attach more or less different meanings to them. Very specifically contrived languages such as mathematical language, however—languages which are usually called "artificial" as distinct from the so-called "natural" languages such as English—come close to this ideal of singleness of signification. But ambiguity of language always remains in some degree, and it will have to be a topic for our study in Part I of this book.

Thus language is necessary for both the formulation and the communication of knowledge. Of course, we use language for other purposes too, such as expressing our feelings, issuing commands, and performing ceremonies. It is doubtful whether any single function of language ever occurs entirely alone. Almost every linguistic expression has a number of purposes, though the complete spectrum of living language goes from the extreme of almost pure scientific discourse (e.g., mathematics) to the extreme of almost meaningless grunts and groans. Even so, it is possible for purposes of analysis and study to abstract some single function without distorting the purpose of the language, so long as the existence of the other functions is not thereby denied. And this is precisely what we shall be doing throughout our study of logic. Since logic is the organon of human knowledge, we shall be concerned with only the cognitive use of language—with language as an instrument in the knowing process. Thus in learning the techniques of logic you will constantly need to abstract from linguistic expressions just their cognitive or logical function.

1–5.4   Summary and Diagrams

Logical instruments are then most basically signs, and a sign is whatever is representative of something other than itself. Such representation is due to an underlying foundation-relation which may be either natural or artificial, thus justifying either a *natural* or an *artificial* sign. Furthermore, such signification may be either *mediate*, through a prior knowledge of the sign's own peculiar nature, in which case the sign is a *material* one, or *immediate*, through a formal identity of sign and signatum, in which case the sign is a *formal* one. A chart may help to clarify this double classification:

	Signs	
	natural	artificial
material	smoke, thunder, etc.	barber pole, language, etc.
formal	ideas	

That all formal signs are natural—that none of them is artificial—is clear from the fact that awareness is a natural phenomenon, where the connection between ideas and objects cannot be artificially contrived. These three different sign situations might perhaps be diagramed as follows, where the solid lines indicate natural connections and the broken lines artificial ones:

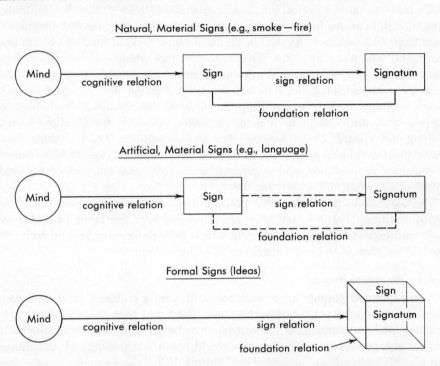

Although natural material signs often have an important place in the acquisition of knowledge, the signs most important—even necessary—to the cognitive process are ideas and language, formal signs and artificial signs. These two sets of cognitive instruments we may call, respectively, the logical instruments and the linguistic instruments. What are logical instruments? They are signs, and more specifically they are natural formal signs. But there are also other ways in which we may regard logical instruments, and to those we shall now turn.

1–6 THE ONTOLOGICAL STATUS OF LOGICAL INSTRUMENTS

We opened this chapter with what must have struck many of you as a sensible sort of question: "What is logic about anyway?" Now that we have tried to answer the question, at least in a preliminary way, you may perhaps be experiencing a few doubts as to whether the answer makes quite as much sense as the original question. Even so, we hope that you now have some idea of what is meant by the notion of logical tools or instruments of knowledge, as well as what some of these various kinds of logical tools are. However, one thing may have occurred to you and caused you no little perplexity. You may say, "To me a tool or an instrument has always been a thing rather like a hammer or a waffle iron—a usable, physical instrument. Somehow, these strange logical tools, even though I can see how and why they are tools in a sense, nevertheless don't seem to be like ordinary physical or material objects. What kind of objects are they? And where are they too? That is to say, just where and how do things like concepts, propositions, and arguments exist? Presumably they aren't like ordinary, material, tangible, natural objects. A concept, for instance, doesn't weigh anything. It doesn't have shape or physical dimensions. Indeed, even to suppose that the concept or idea of the color yellow is itself yellow seems nothing but absurd. Or to suppose that the proposition 'Oil is lighter than water' itself weighs 50 pounds, or 1½ ounces, or 40 tons just doesn't make sense. If concepts, propositions, and arguments apparently aren't a part of the real world at all, what and where are they?"

These questions pertain to what philosophers call the "ontological status" of logical entities. That is to say, they are questions as to the being or reality of such entities, as to the precise sense in which such things may be said to be or exist. What then is the ontological status of logical entities?

1–6.1 Beings of Reason

As exasperated parents know only too well, young children (and doubtless even old ones!) have lively imaginations. They find that the world of their ordinary physical contacts is too restricted to be an adequate abode for their restless energies. Hence they live in a world composed not only of *real* things but also of *"pretend"* or *"make-believe"* things. If Sally's playmates are too few or too uninteresting, she may also find an imaginary friend who, unlike her real friends, is always coöperative and always interesting. And if her real cat or dog is sometimes too tired or bored or tame to keep her occupied, she may find more exciting creatures lurking around the house—tigers in corners, lions under tables, elephants on the lawn. Ordinarily Sally is able to keep those two kinds of associates pretty well distinguished; she has her "real" friends and her "pretend" friends. Sometimes, however, the line of demarcation blurs a little so that it becomes rather difficult to distinguish between her "pretend pretend" friends, her "pretend real" friends, and her "really real" friends.

We adults, of course, never confuse the two—or at least if we do someone else will be happy to remind us of the distinction, perhaps tapping his forehead with a queer look if we get too forgetful. Though Hamlet on the stage may seem as real as anyone else, we remember after the play that he is, after all, only a fictional character. And when we stop to think about it we realize that

real beings - triangle, book

beings of reason - concept of triangularity
if accidents book
size, color, rectangularity, etc..

What Is Logic? 25

Hamlet, unlike the sun or the great nebula in Andromeda, would not even exist if it had not been for the creative genius of Shakespeare in the past and the minds of all his devotees in succeeding generations. We see that "what there is" thus falls into two camps: what there is *really, apart from anyone's thinking it, and what there is *mentally,* dependent upon somebody's *thinking* it.* We see, in short, that there are two kinds of beings: *real* beings and "beings of *reason,*" *entia* and *entia rationis,* as they have been called.

Real beings are those beings which are independent of their being thought about—those whose existence and nature are in no way dependent upon someone's thinking them thus and so. This does not mean that all real things are independent of *minds,* for minds themselves are real and so are their various activities. It does mean that all real beings are independent, in their nature and existence, of their being thought *about,* that they have a place in reality not dependent upon the fact that they may or may not happen to be objects of thought or desire. Your thoughts as you read this are mental and they depend for their existence and nature upon your mind. But both your thoughts and your mind, once they come into existence, continue to exist whether or not anybody, including yourself, thinks *about* them—whether or not they become objects of thought.

Being an object-of-thought, however, means being dependent upon thought for existence and efficacy; and objects-of-thought or beings of reason have on this account also been called "*objective*" beings, that is, things which have only "*object*-ive" existence—though this sense of "objective" must be carefully distinguished from its more usual sense.[12] Thus beings of reason are cognitive parasites; they derive what substance they have from the real thinking and knowing activities which are their hosts. And such a distinction between real beings and beings of reason is vital to any realistic outlook on life—to any view which believes in a real world existing independently of thought.

The realm of real beings, then, is the realm of things which exist independently of being thought. They are the goals or objectives of the cognitive process and are also its outer, independent termini in so far as that process is successful. But they are not parts of that process or instruments of the activity of knowing. Since logic is the study of just such instruments, however, the realm of real beings is not the concern of logic but of such various sciences as physics, psychology, economics, and history.

Does this mean that logic is concerned with the whole realm of beings of reason? Should we now be studying Hamlet, Pogo, and Greek mythology? Hardly. These areas of fiction would seem rather to fall within the subject

---

[12] Today the word commonly refers to things as they are in themselves independently of being thought, in contrast to "subjective." In its original and literal sense, however, it meant just the opposite: the character of being an *ob-ject,* thrown before the mind. We are here using the word in this original sense.

matter of the various creative arts. This means that within the domain of beings of reason we must distinguish the merely fictional from those which are the concern of logic. The distinction between *logical* and *fictional* beings of reason can be seen in two ways.

In the first place, though logical entities are not themselves the real beings which we seek to know, they are nevertheless instrumental in the knowing of such beings, whereas fictional beings are not. Although you would certainly be startled to meet a concept, or a proposition, or an argument walking down the street, these beings are indispensable in your *knowledge* that anything is or is not walking down the street, or in your knowledge of anything whatsoever. Elves, Lilliputians, and centaurs, however, you can certainly get along without and still know real things quite well; no matter how entertaining such fictions may be in themselves, they are not indispensable to the cognitive process. They could not be formal signs, for they have peculiar (to say the least!) natures of their own. Hence even if they were signs, they would have to be material signs; and they therefore could not be logical instruments. To know anything requires a concept of its essence, a proposition about its existence or nonexistence, and an argument concerning the reasons for this fact; it certainly does not require the manipulation of mythical monsters. Thus logical entities, though not themselves real beings, are essentially instrumental in the knowledge of anything, including real beings.

Since logical entities are instrumental for our knowledge of the real, they differ from fictitious beings, in the second place, by having a *foundation* in reality even though they are not themselves real. Though you still do not experience a concept coming down the street, there is something about the being you do meet, say John Jones, which permits and even requires that you *use* a concept if you are to understand him. To understand what J. Jones is requires the concepts "man," "friend," "good-looking," etc. Thus logical entities, while not themselves real, are reflections of the real, whereas fictitious entities are not. Though the two parts of a mermaid have, respectively, a delightful and an edible counterpart in independent reality, the mermaid herself, unfortunately, is a pure mental creation; she does not, as a mermaid, reflect anything in the domain of the real. Logical entities are therefore beings of reason *with a foundation in reality,* while fictions are beings of reason without any such foundation.

But if logical entities as formal signs are identical in nature with their real signata, what is there about them which sunders them ontologically from their signata to place them in a separate realm of being—the realm of beings of reason? The answer, as we have earlier mentioned in passing, is that the *state* or *condition* of logical entities (formal signs) remains diverse from that of their signata, thus enabling them to satisfy the definition of a sign, even though their nature or character is identical. This condition or state which occurs only in cognition makes them beings of reason. Their <u>nature or character is indiffer-</u> <u>ent from that of their signata, but their status as formal signs of their signata</u> <u>renders them existent only as inseparably bound up with objects of thought.</u> An example may help make this clear.

Before you now is a real thing—this book—which, even though it was originally produced by brains and hands, now continues to exist even if no one happens to be aware of it, even if—as will doubtless be the case—it spends the rest of its life gathering dust in some dark corner of a library stack. As a real being it has certain properties in its own right—color, size, shape, weight, density (both physical and intellectual, perhaps), etc. These properties belong to it prior to and quite apart from your being aware of them.

But now notice: when you know these properties, a strange thing happens to them. The real rectangularity of the book and its really being a book, for example, become *concepts* of rectangularity and book. They also become, respectively, a *predicate* and a *subject* in a proposition: "This book is rectangular." Moreover, the togetherness of these two traits in the proposition may in turn become a *premise* or a *conclusion* in an *argument*. The book which in its state as a real being exists as an integrated physical thing comes, in the process of your knowing it, to be torn into a multitude of parts such as bookness, rectangularity, weight, color, texture, etc. Yet all the while it was never *really* torn apart at all, but slumbered on oblivious to its own logical disintegration. In the same way it becomes, through your knowing it, a subject or predicate, middle term or major term, while all the time remaining really quite unchanged. This disintegrated state of the book and these new, strange properties do not belong to the book-in-itself as a real independent being at all. They belong to the book rather *only* in so far as it is a *book-which-happens-to-be-known,* only to the extent that it is an object of knowledge. But they do belong to the book; it is the very same thing, the book, which has both of these states or conditions. Your *concept* of the book is a concept of the *book.* Thus one and the same thing or trait may exist in two quite different ways: as a real, independent being and as a being of reason.

It is the job of logic to study the behavior and various properties which things take on cognitively, not really, just in order to be known. Logic, in short, is concerned with beings of reason rather than real beings. New York City is a physical entity in its own right. As such it has various real properties—being large, noisy, exciting, etc. But it is also the terminus of the New York Central Railroad. As such it has other properties: it appears in a timetable, it is the goal of commuters, etc. It is not really a part of New York City to be in a timetable or in a commuter's mind; it is a property belonging inherently to the timetable or the mind and is bestowed only extrinsically and cognitively upon the city as an object of thought or scheduling. So also things in reality, while having various inherent properties in their real state, acquire by extrinsic rational addition in the cognitive process certain other properties which appertain to them only in so far as they are known, and belong inherently only to the minds that know them. These various properties of the cognitive state of things are the concern of logic. Logical instruments are thus beings of reason. A diagram, though in certain respects misleading, may help to make this clear:

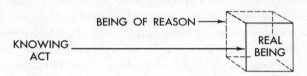

1–6.2   Second Intentions

We have seen that the basic trait of knowledge is its intentionality, and that all cognitive instruments are therefore intentions—that they are signs, that they are *of* or *about* or represent something other than themselves. A different formulation of the ontological status of logical instruments as beings of reason can be gained by seeing that logical entities, unlike real beings which are always the initial or primary object of our intentions, become objects only with an additional or secondary intention.

To use an earlier analogy, if you are wearing glasses as you read these words, you do not see the glasses (the lenses) but only the words and the page. You see other things with or through your glasses, but you do not see them. Thus your first intention is of the page; the page is the object of your first intention. But if you now remove your glasses and intend them, you have a second and different intention, even though you still intend the glasses by means of other instruments, your eyes. Your second intention is of the instruments of your first intention.

The word "intention," furthermore, has a significant though confusing ambiguity. Like so many English words ending in "tion" it may signify the *operation* or the *object,* the *means* or the *end,* the intending or the intended. The word "delegation," for example, may refer either to the act of delegating or to the persons delegated; "The audience witnessed the delegation of great power to the delegation from Indiana" illustrates both senses of the term. Thus in our earlier analogy your glasses are a second intention (intended) of a second intention (intending), your eyes.

The same is true of knowledge. Our minds in knowing are first directed toward the world of real, independent beings, and we are not aware of the instruments and operations in which that knowing consists. Real beings, then, as objects of knowledge are our primary objects of attention and intention; they are *first* intentions, and all of their real properties are called first intentional properties. But when in reflection we turn to the instruments involved in this primary intention, we make them objects of a *second* intention; they are thus *second* intentions, and all of their peculiar properties are known as second intentional properties. This is true of all those features which things come to have just in so far as they are known—such properties as being a concept or a subject or a predicate. That is, the properties belonging to the cognitive status of things, to the status of things as formal signs, are second intentions. This, of course, is not true of material signs like words, since they are real beings with real properties of their own in addition to being signs. Like a pair of glasses, formal signs, though they are involved in our knowledge of reality, are themselves objects only of second intention. Logical instruments, then, are not only beings of reason; they are also second intentions.

The practical point of this second intentional status of logical instruments is to realize that increased proficiency in knowing the real world requires a temporary withdrawal from the real world—like interrupting your reading to clean your glasses—to those instruments and techniques without which no knowledge of the real world is possible. This is the job of logic as a study. But logicians, like Plato's philosopher-kings, must then return to the "cave" of the real simply because the very meaning of the things which concern them in their withdrawal is to signify or reveal the real.

Summary. Enough by way of cursory introduction to the subject of logic. It is to be hoped that you may by now have some feeling for the sorts of things logic is about, viz., the tools and instruments of knowledge with which all human beings are more or less naturally endowed and which presumably are quite indispensable if men are ever to know things for what they are, and whether they are, and why they are. Being nothing but intentions or meanings or formal signs, logical instruments have a peculiar ontological status. Indeed, you have now seen just why and how they do not exist in the way in which ordinary physical objects do, but rather as mere beings of reason and objects of second intentions.

Accordingly, the bare introductions having been made, it remains for you to try to get to know these various logical instruments somewhat more intimately and individually. Before you are through, you should find yourself on quite familiar terms with concepts, propositions, and arguments all three—a cheerful prospect, no doubt. And so to the business in hand.

all propositions and concepts are formal.

EXERCISES

Which type of sign (natural formal, natural material, or artificial material) is each of the following?

1. a stop light
2. the word "light"
3. the concept "light"
4. thunder
5. a smile
6. hand-shaking
7. litmus paper
8. the sensation of blue
9. hieroglyphics
10. a fossil
11. The proposition "Now is the time for all good men to come to the aid of their party."

PART I

THE CONCEPT

3-15-22

CHAPTER 2

CONCEPTS AND CATEGORIES

Essences as Objects of Concepts. Having seen in a general way what logic is, as well as what are some of the main types of cognitive tools or instruments that are studied in logic, it remains for us actually to study these logical tools singly and in detail. The first such tool or instrument to be considered is the sort of thing which might be named indifferently "idea," "notion," or "concept." This is the instrument that enables us to get to know or recognize the natures or essences of things, the "whats" of things.

Suppose that in order to convince yourself of the peculiar role of concepts in knowledge, as well as of their indispensability to knowledge, you tried to imagine what it would be like attempting to gain knowledge or understanding of something without having any notion or idea of that thing whatever. It is simply impossible: one cannot know or understand anything, save in so far as one gets some inkling of what it is, i.e., the kind of thing it is; and this is but to say that one must have some sort of idea or notion or concept of the thing— i.e., of what it is.

Still you may be puzzled to know just what these strange-sounding natures or essences are that are supposed to be the objects of logical concepts, and that we are supposed to apprehend in things through the medium and instrument of logical concepts. What are some examples of them? How may they be classified, etc.?

We might remark at the outset that since an essence is that which is grasped or apprehended in and through a concept, any concept or idea will necessarily be the concept or idea of a nature or essence.[1] Thus we have ideas of green, of hydrogen, of rectangularity, of dishonesty, of houses, of happiness, of writing paper, of logic, etc., etc. Every one of these things, since it is a something of

---

[1] It should be recognized that we are here giving the terms "nature" and "essence" a much more extended sense then they have customarily had in the main tradition of philosophical realism as it has come down from Aristotle. Nevertheless, for purposes of this textbook, it seemed unnecessary to distinguish between the natures and essences of things in the more precise sense and all the various traits, characteristics, features, attributes, etc., that things may be said to have in the broadest and most general sense. Accordingly, throughout this book we shall use "nature" or "essence" as roughly synonymous with "characteristic," "trait," or "attribute."

which we have a concept or idea, is a nature or essence, in the sense in which we are using the term.

Or look at the matter this way. Each of these examples of a nature or essence might be regarded as an answer to the question "What?" For example, "What is this?" "Green." "What is this?" "Logic." Et cetera. In other words, as we have already noted, the nature or essence of things might be regarded as simply the "what" of things.

But no sooner are natures and essences characterized in this way than there would seem to be nothing at all that isn't a nature or essence, or isn't a "what" of something or other. Can you think of anything that isn't, in some sense or other, the what of something? "Smooth," "true," "pterodactyl," "15 inches long," "helium," "God," "magnificent," "worn," etc.—each of these, and for that matter any other term that one can think of, presumably means something or stands for something; and *what* it means must be just such a "what" or essence. How could it be otherwise, since anything *what*ever cannot but be some "what" or other?

Put it this way. Anything whatever, in order to be or to be real, must be something. And what it is is simply its nature or essence or "what." The essence of a thing is that which constitutes it and makes it to be the kind of thing it is. Or as we might say, it is in virtue of its essence that anything whatever—fish, rough, similarity, engineering, or *what* not—is what it is. The essence just *is* the "what." Hence just as *what* this is is not *what* that is, so also the essence or nature of this thing is not the essence or nature of that: brown is not black; a circle is not a square; nor, indeed, is brownness as such what a circle is or what a square is.[2] No, these are all different, are so many different *kinds* of things. In short, as we suggested at the beginning of the paragraph, the essence is what makes a thing to be the kind of thing it is, just as it makes it to be what it is.

Classification of Essences: The Categories. This suggestion as to the different kinds of things may provide us with a clue to the ordering and classifying of essences. For that things are different in kind means simply that what one thing is is not what another is. And the "what" of a thing, as we have seen, is simply its essence or nature. Accordingly, any classification of things or beings into their basic kinds will *ipso facto* be a classification of the "whats" or natures or essences of things, in virtue of which they are of this kind or of

---

[2] Of course, even though a circle cannot be a square, it might well be brown; and this might seem to indicate that the "what" or essence of one thing might be the "what" or essence of something else. Nevertheless, the principle is not really violated, after all, for although a circle might be brown, it could not possibly be brownness. On this, see below, pp. 128–129. In another sense, too, it would seem to be not only possible but even common for the essence of one thing to be the essence of another. Thus *what* I am is a human; but this is *what* you are too. Here, however, we are dealing with things which, far from differing in kind, are of the same kind or essence. See below, p. 118.

that. Since our concern at present is with trying to get a somewhat better understanding of that which is apprehended in and through concepts, or of the objects of concepts, or of what concepts are concepts of, we can do no better perhaps than to ask ourselves directly: What are the different kinds of things there are in reality? This is nothing but a question as to the different "whats" or essences of things; and the "whats" or essences of things are precisely what concepts are concepts of.

Traditionally, ever since Aristotle, the inquiry into the basic kinds of things has been known as a search for the *categories.* The very word "category" has taken on the meaning of a basic kind or division or classification of things. Our present question simply becomes the question: What are the basic categories of being or reality?

Doubtless the first answer that occurs to you will be along some such lines as these. "The basic kinds or types of things?" you will say. "Surely these must be something like the old-fashioned division into animal, vegetable, and mineral. For what could be more all-embracing as a classificatory scheme? Must not anything whatever be either animate or inanimate, and if animate, either plant or animal?"

True, such a classificatory scheme may not be altogether up to date. Yet it will do well enough for purposes of illustration. Besides, it is a scheme that is in fairly common use. Universities, for example, in their course offerings, still customarily distinguish between biological sciences and physical sciences, and within the biological sciences between botany and zoölogy. Nevertheless, despite the currency and familiarity of this way of dividing all things into either animate or inanimate beings, it is still not a sufficiently broad and all-embracing scheme really to include all of the various kinds of things there are. How would one fit into the scheme such things as, say, the quantity two-feet-long, or a relation such as similar-to, or the color yellow, or an activity such as sewing? Is sewing an animal, a vegetable, or a mineral? What about two-feet-long? Obviously, there is something wrong here. Our classificatory scheme just does not seem meant to include things of this sort.

Yet things of this sort are things; they are beings, quite as much as hydrogen atoms, conifers, human beings, water molecules, etc. The color yellow certainly is something. So is the relation of similarity, or the activity of sewing. But clearly, if these are things, if they are and are realities in some sense or another —not only that, but if these are legitimate objects of concepts, and hence legitimate "whats"—then obviously any adequate set of categories must be such as to make possible their classification among the kinds of things there are.

2–1   THE DISTINCTION BETWEEN SUBSTANCE AND ACCIDENT

Accordingly, in order to deal with things like sewing, similarity, and two-feet-long, we suggest that in the list of basic categories a distinction should be made between nature and essences that are *accidental* and those that are *substantial*. What does this mean? In answer we need only point out that in our common human experience of things we recognize, the minute we reflect a bit, that there are on the one hand things that are able to exist in themselves, so to speak, and on the other hand things that are able to exist only in other things. Take the color yellow. Could there possibly be such a thing as yellow, or could yellow exist, without there being something that was yellow? That is to say, yellow is apparently the kind of thing that can only be or exist *in* something that is yellow or has this color.

Likewise, it is obviously quite impossible for an activity such as sewing to take place or to exist all by itself and in itself. Quite the contrary. Before there can be sewing, there must needs be something or somebody that is doing the sewing. In fact, it is rather amusing to try to picture to yourself a feverish activity of sewing going on, with no person or thing doing the sewing. True, it might be an enormous boon to laundrymen, housewives, and especially bachelors. But unhappily this is just the kind of thing that cannot be—at least not in the real world, however appropriate it might be in a Lewis Carroll world of fantasy.

What goes for things like yellow and sewing goes also for our other examples —two-feet-long, similar-to, etc. Imagine encountering a length which was not the length of anything at all! Or imagine similar-to without there being anything that was similar, or anything that it was similar to. No, in all these cases we are dealing with things (essences or "whats") which cannot exist by themselves, or in themselves, but must needs be in or of other things. For this reason they have traditionally been called accidents, which means literally that which "falls to" or "befalls" another.[3]

On the other hand, if we turn our attention from accidents such as yellow, two-feet-long, sewing, etc., to the things that are yellow or are two feet long or that do the sewing, it immediately becomes obvious that we have to do with a very different kind of thing or "what" from accidents. Indeed, of anything that is yellow or that has a certain length or that is engaged in an activity such as sewing we may say that it is a *substance,* which means literally that it "stands under" or upholds or supports accidents.[4] For instance, it may be a leaf that is yellow, or a stone that is two feet long, or a seamstress that is doing the sewing. In each case, we recognize a distinction between that which has the accidents, or characteristics, and the accidents or characteristics which thus "fall to" or pertain to it.

Moreover, just as it would seem to be of the very nature of an accident to be in or of something else, viz., a substance, so also it would seem to be of the nature of a substance not to be in or of anything else, but to be simply in itself.

[3] From the Latin *ad*, "to"; *cadere*, "fall."
[4] From the Latin *sub*, "under"; *stare*, "stand."

It is true, of course, that a leaf (substance) that is yellow (accident), for example, will presumably be the leaf of some tree, and it may well be *in* my hand or *on* the ground, etc. Yet clearly, the leaf is not in or of another thing in the same way that the yellow is in the leaf. For one thing, the fact that the yellow is in the leaf means that we can say that the leaf is yellow. But the fact that the leaf is in my hand does not mean that we can say that my hand is the leaf. In fact, prepositions such as "in" and "of" are simply equivocal in these two contexts.

The point is that a substance can never be in another in the way in which an accident is in a substance. For an accident is in or of a substance as "falling to" it or being a characteristic of it. But a substance is never a characteristic of anything else. Rather it is precisely the sort of thing that other things are accidents or characteristics of. And this is just what is meant by saying that it is a *substance, or that it exists in itself and not in another*.

In setting up categories of the major types or kinds of things that there are, then, we must distinguish the categories of accident from the category of substance. For accidents just aren't the same kind of "what" that substances are. As a matter of fact, our earlier suggested classification of things as animal, vegetable, or mineral was an attempted classification of substances only and hence must be regarded as entirely inadequate, since it leaves accidents out of account altogether.

2-2   THE VARIOUS CATEGORIES OF ACCIDENT

No sooner do we decide to recognize accidents as well as substances among the basic kinds of "whats" or essences than we must also recognize that accidents themselves are of a number of irreducibly different kinds. Sewing and being two feet long, for instance, would seem to be altogether different kinds of things. In fact, they are as different from each other as either of them is different from the sort of thing we have called a substance. Accordingly, just as the category of substance must be distinguished from the categories of accident, so also various categories of accident must be distinguished from one another.

Unfortunately, the list of the categories of accident is not one of which we can be too certain. Aristotle suggested a list of ten categories (including substance), but even for him the list was tentative. Nor is the reason for this uncertainty hard to discover. After all, if one is trying to set up basic categories for all of the fundamental types and kinds of things, it is only wise to be somewhat tentative about it. It is entirely likely that a further familiarity with the mysterious "ins" and "outs" of reality may disclose new types or kinds of beings and necessitate the addition of further categories. Not only that, but some types may be seen to be reducible to others, etc. With due apologies for its tentativeness, we suggest the following as a fairly plausible list:

Substance

Quantity
Quality
Relation
Time
Place
Activity
Passivity

2–3   THE PERTINENCE OF THE CATEGORIES TO LOGIC

Now for purposes of logic alone, as contrasted with metaphysics and the philosophy of nature, it is perhaps not necessary to discuss and defend each of these categories in detail. Nevertheless, the general utility and plausibility of the scheme as a whole stands in need of further illustration.

As we have reiterated so often, these categories are supposed to be a classification of all the different kinds of things there are. Consequently, if we ask what any being or thing or entity whatever is, in the final analysis we will come down to saying that what it is is either a substance or a quantity or a quality or a relation or an activity, etc.

Take our earlier example of yellow. This is certainly something. But what is it? Well, it's not a substance certainly. But is it an activity, or possibly a relation or a quantity? Hardly. No, being a color, yellow is the kind of thing we call a quality. As such, it is different from two-feet-long, which is obviously the size or quantity of something. Again, what is the thing we call sewing? It is an activity. On the other hand, things like molecules, human beings, leaves, granite, amoebae, etc., since they are obviously not qualities of anything or quantities or activities or what not, are simply substances.

In other words, of anything whatever, supposing that we want to know what it is, and supposing our list of categories to be complete, we may say that it is either a substance or a quantity or a quality or a relation, etc. In this sense the categories are unmistakably a classification of the "whats" or essences of things. Moreover, since, as we have seen, ideas and concepts are always of something and since what they are of are "whats" or essences, it follows that any concept one may have must perforce be the concept of a substance or of a quantity or of a quality, etc. And so it is that the categories, though strictly speaking they represent a classification of real beings,[5] nevertheless become at least indirectly pertinent to logic. For they may be regarded as a classification of *that which*, or better of those things which, we come to know in and through the use of the logical instrument of concepts.

---

[5] For this reason the categories might be said not to pertain properly to logic, this being concerned only with beings of reason. Cf. above, pp. 24–28.

2–4 CURRENT SKEPTICISM CONCERNING SUBSTANCE

Despite the fact that any list of the categories of accident will tend to be somewhat tentative and uncertain for the reasons we have suggested, there would seem to be no doubt as to the validity and even inescapability of the basic distinction between substance and accident. For the whole of our human effort to understand reality seems hinged on the fact that accidents inhere in substances, that certain types of entity are such as to exist only in other things called substances which are never mere characteristics of other things. The activity of walking, for instance, just is a different sort of thing from the person who does the walking. Or the size of a thing just is different from the thing that is of that size, however true it may be that size must be the size of something and that things—at least in the natural world—must have some size or other.

But despite the seemingly obvious validity of this distinction between substance and accident, as well as of the mutual dependence of the one on the other, the whole doctrine has come in for sharp criticism in modern philosophy —so much so, in fact, that this deeply ingrained human intellectual habit of regarding accidents as somehow inhering in substances is now largely sneered at as being "dated" and no longer à la mode.

Needless to say, a philosopher like Bertrand Russell represents the height of fashion in such matters, and in his customarily lucid and winning way he offers simply to usher the distinction between substance and accident off the philosophic stage altogether. Thus he says:

> There is a notion that an instance of walking, as compared with Jones, is unsubstantial, but this seems to be a mistake. We think that Jones walks, and that there could not be any walking unless there were somebody like Jones to perform the walking. But it is equally true that there could be no Jones unless there were something like walking for him to do. The notion that actions are performed by an agent is liable to the same kind of criticism as the notion that thinking needs a subject or ego. To say that it is Jones who is walking is merely to say that the walking in question is part of the whole series of occurrences which is Jones. There is no logical impossibility in walking occurring as an isolated phenomenon, not forming part of any such series as we call a "person."[6]

It is somewhat difficult to know just what Lord Russell means by "logical impossibility" here. Whatever he may mean, one cannot help wondering whether it is quite so easy to conceive of walking as "an isolated phenomenon" —i.e., as taking place without there being any thing or person that does the walking. Indeed, one might almost be tempted to suppose that what is ap-

[6] From *The Analysis of Mind.* See *Selected Papers of Bertrand Russell,* Modern Library, n.d., pp. 355–356.

parently so easy of conception for a Nobel Prize winner and a noble lord is presumably much more difficult for the rest of us. Be this as it may, even if we could manage to conjure up in our fancy or imagination a strange figment of walking without having anything doing the walking, still so far as the real world goes our ordinary experience assures us that such things simply cannot be.

Modern Science as Supposedly Justifying Such Skepticism.   Nevertheless, even though it is easy simply to laugh off the current philosophical fashion of skepticism with respect to substance, we cannot afford to disregard entirely the grounds and reasons for the skepticism. One such ground particularly deserves mention, and that is that much of modern science, especially modern physics, seems altogether indifferent to substances. Indeed, the more modern physics submits to an ever increasing mathematization, the more dispensable substances would seem to be. It is as if the physicist were coming to be concerned only with the mere correlation of quantities with each other in mathematical formulas, and not at all with the things which the quantities might be supposed to be quantities of.

The history of the famous, or perhaps infamous, notion of a luminiferous ether might be a case in point. In its origins there is no doubt that this so-called ether was thought of as the substance underlying the supposed wavelike motion of light. After all, it would seem that one could no more have a wave-like motion without there being a something that was thus moving in waves than one could have an activity such as walking without there being a something that was walking. Accordingly, ether came to be regarded as the substance which supports such wave motion.

Listen to the story of this strange substance as told by Louis de Broglie:

> Since light waves traverse empty space without difficulty, it is not matter which transmits them. What then is the carrier of these waves, what medium is it whose vibration constitutes the light vibration? Such was the question that was asked of the protagonists of the wave theory. In order to answer this, they imagined a subtle medium, the luminiferous ether, distributed throughout the entire universe, filling all the empty spaces and impregnating material bodies.[7]

De Broglie then traces the history of this concept of an ether-substance as it developed later in the theories of electromagnetism. Eventually, as he says, "in the electromagnetic theory, one can very well say no more about an ether":

> It is enough to consider the properties of empty space as being defined at each point by two vectors, the electric field and the magnetic field. The theory then takes on that abstract aspect which so often characterizes the theories of modern physics:

[7] *The Revolution in Physics,* Noonday Press, 1953, p. 50.

it becomes in essence a system of equations. This abstract aspect of the electromagnetic theory is particularly evident in the form which Hertz gave to it sometime after Maxwell. Nevertheless, a great many physicists of this period still felt the need of giving a prop to the electromagnetic field, to consider it as a state of something. Great efforts were made, notably by Lord Kelvin, to obtain a mechanical representation of electromagnetic phenomena with the help of tensions and deformations in the ether, but these representations were never completely satisfactory and ended by falling into discredit. Since then the ether has served only as a hypothetical medium of reference which permits us to define systems of coordinates with reference to which the equations of Maxwell are valid in their ordinary form. Even when reduced to this modest role, the ether still proved troublesome: the electrodynamics of bodies in motion based on the idea that the ether can serve to define the axes of absolute rest, was a complicated doctrine which, at last, was shown not to be in accord with the experiment. The theory of relativity has cleared up this situation by taking the lead in completely abandoning the notion of ether.[8]

In Defense of Substance.   This account of the luminiferous ether is significant for our present purposes in a number of respects. For one thing, it confirms the fact of an almost irresistible bent of the human mind to try to find a substance in which certain observable accidents can exist. Indeed, if the mind cannot *find* such a substance, it seems almost constrained to invent one. How else are we to interpret the fact that physicists, when pressed as to the substance of the light waves, "imagined," as De Broglie says, the luminiferous ether? How else are we to interpret the fact that even after the notion of a luminiferous ether seemed discredited many physicists "still felt the need of giving a prop to the electromagnetic field, to consider it as a state of something"?

For another thing, this story of the concept of the ether shows that this almost irresistible bent of the human mind to find a substance for accidents is nevertheless resisted, at least sometimes. Specifically, this seems to have happened in the case of the ether, and the circumstance under which it happened is apparently that of an extreme mathematization of physical theory. As De Broglie puts it, "the theory takes on that abstract aspect which so often characterizes the theories of modern physics: it becomes in essence a system of equations."

Very well; how is this situation in modern physics to be interpreted? Are we to suppose in the light of it that the apparently natural bent of the human mind to find a substance as a support for accidents is, after all, only a superstition, and that in reality there just aren't any substances underlying accidents, but only a correlation of accidents one with another? Such presumably is the view of a man like Bertrand Russell. Yet even among scientists and philosophers of science this view is far from being received with unanimity, not to say satisfaction, nowadays, however much it does seem to be currently in the ascendancy.

[8] *Ibid.*, pp. 54–56.

Thus the late distinguished French philosopher of science, Emile Meyerson, goes right to the heart of the matter when he asks bluntly:

> Now is an object anything but a group of phenomena?[9] And since these phenomena are all ruled by laws, is not what we call an object simply a group of relations conformable to the law? One can immediately render obvious the truth of this proposition by observing that we only know an object by its properties,[10] and that each property in particular can be so formulated that the statement is a law. What is sulphur? It is solid,[11] yellow, melting at 114° C., boiling at 448° C., producing by combustion a gas well known under the name of sulphurous anhydride, etc. Now in saying: Sulphur is yellow in color, sulphur melts at 114° C., etc., I incontestably state laws. How does it happen that I stipulate the immutability of laws in time and not that of objects?[12]

Having thus stated the issue, Meyerson goes on to resolve it in favor of a doctrine that recognizes the reality of substance. He even insists that recognition of the reality of substance is constantly presupposed in physical science and gives meaning and intelligibility to the whole program of scientific research:

> When I say that sulphur melts at 114° C., that it boils at 448° C., or that it is combustible, it is clear that these are phenomena which cannot be observed unless the temperature is high—that is to say, they cannot be observed if the ordinary conditions cease to exist. Without doubt we indeed assume that to this phenomenon which will only be produced under determined circumstances, there corresponds, even in sulphur at an ordinary temperature, *something*—a thing badly defined, however—not showing itself constantly, but being apt to show itself, as is plainly indicated by the grammatical form of the terms when we say that sulphur is *fusible* or *combustible*. It is not, then, an actual quality, but a *faculty*, and, if we refer to what has been said previously, it is clear that all the properties which we attribute to substances are only faculties of this kind, all manifesting themselves only under determined conditions and apt to be modified if these conditions happen to change.[13]

Moreover, whatever may be the reservations of the physicists with respect to a classificatory scheme involving substance and accident, it would certainly seem that in the biological sciences the realities there encountered fall quite

[9] Phenomena, as the word is used here, amount to no more and no less than what we have chosen to call accidents.

[10] "Properties" here = "accidents" in our sense.

[11] Meyerson's actual words, as rendered in the English translation, are "a solid substance." However, we have altered this to "solid" on the ground that this does not change Meyerson's meaning, and at the same time it guards against a natural misunderstanding that would arise if the word "substance" were used, particularly against the background of our whole present discussion of "substance."

[12] "Objects" here = "substances" in our sense. *Identity and Reality*, Macmillan, 1930, pp. 39–40.

[13] *Ibid.*, pp. 40–41.

neatly into place under the heads of the various categories. For instance, consider the following account of the matter as given by a contemporary biologist:

> Nevertheless, if we consider the movement and methods of the Inductive Sciences it seems clear that for them the things of Nature are still suspended in the primordial framework of the Aristotelian categories. To these correspond certain irreducible questions inductive science asks about things. Everyone will not concede that all these questions are irreducible. It has always been possible to find philosophers to oppose this view, but like other fundamental elements of the Aristotelian doctrine, it seems, as Bergson has conceded, to be part of "la Métaphysique naturelle de l'esprit humain."

> Consider, for example, the procedure in the descriptive branches of the Inductive Sciences. The botanist describing a new plant assumes, implicitly, that he is dealing with a real, self-contained entity forming the subject of his description, and thus assumes it to be a *substance*. He measures his specimen and gives its *dimensions*. He describes its colour, its shape, the character of its leaves and flowers, in a word, its *qualitative* or specific attributes. He notes its place in the flora, its relation to other organisms. He mentions the *date* on which he discovered it, the *spot* in which it grew, its *position*, its *activities*, and the effect exerted on it by other living things. All of these several points appear to him to be necessary and irreducible elements in his description.[14]

Apparently, then, the issue in regard to substance is by no means a dead letter even within the context of modern science itself. Yet for our purposes the whole dispute over the scientific usefulness and legitimacy of the notion of substance is at once misplaced and irrelevant. For logic, as we have seen, is most properly and most basically to be thought of as simply the instrument of *human* knowing—that is to say, of human beings simply qua human, and not necessarily in their more specialized capacities as physicists or biologists or radio technicians or what not. And certainly, just as a human being, and in his ordinary day-to-day existence of talking with friends, going out for a walk, making a purchase at the drug store, reading a newspaper, casting his vote in the elections, etc., even the most sophisticated of modern physicists lives in a world of people and things which have various characteristics and attributes, act upon one another in various ways, and undergo manifold changes as a result of the various influences that operate upon them.

In other words, your real world and ours—and the real world of the physicist, too, in so far as he is a human being—would seem to be quite unmistakably and ineradicably a world of substances, of substantial people and things. And while it may be convenient, and indeed even necessary, within the somewhat rarefied context of scientific research, and for the specialized and restricted purposes of that research, to dispense with the category of substance and to employ, say, only the categories of relation, time, and quantity, still this in no

[14] W. R. Thompson, *Science and Common Sense*, Longmans, Green, 1937, pp. 57–58.

way invalidates or enables us to dispense with the category of substance so far as the real world of everyday human existence is concerned, the world to which the scientist himself must inescapably return, even from his most recondite researches, and in which he has to live as a human being.

For human logic, accordingly, there is no escaping the fact that one of the things we come to know through the use of the cognitive instrument of the concept must needs be what we have here designated by the ancient term "substance."

EXERCISES

Identify the category to which the signatum of each of the italicized words or phrases belongs:

1. "The Jarabe *Tapatio* is *danced* in *theatres, cabarets, secular fiestas,* and *rodeos.* It always *awakens* a *joyous response* with *hand-clapping* for the 'Diana.' If there are *many young men* in the *audience,* they *whistle* and *yell.* It is *irresistibly gay, beating* its *rhythm into* the very *blood.*" (*Guadalajara Tourist News*)
2. "*Early in the Spring of 1848,* Miles and his *brother Andrew combed southern California* for the *best horses they* could *find.* As *later events proved,* the *Goodyears acquired horses full* of *endurance* and *stamina.*" (R. M. Denhardt, *The Horse of the Americas,* University of Oklahoma Press, 1948, p. 144)

CHAPTER 3

CONCEPTS AS UNIVERSALS

3–1 UNIVERSALS AS PRODUCTS OF REASON

Having tried in the foregoing section to gain a somewhat better idea of the natures or essences of things that are the objects of concepts, we must now turn our attention to concepts themselves, in order to see just what there is about them that fits them for their peculiar intentional function of intending the "whats" or essences of things. So far in Part I we have done little more than remark that concepts are *universal,* and that they involve the *abstraction* of natures or essences from the concrete particular objects in which they exist. Let us now consider more carefully what we are to understand by universality and abstractness.

Concepts are universal, we say. But just what is universality? Literally, to be universal means to be "one with respect to many" (*unum versus alia*). And interpreted in a logical context, this means that concepts, while in a sense meaning one thing, nevertheless are applicable to many things. For instance, the concept "triangle" certainly means just one thing, viz., the nature or essence of triangularity, yet this same concept is applicable to any number of different things: to any and every possible triangle that is, was, or shall be. There is no triangle, that is to say, but that it is a triangle, i.e., but that one and the same concept "triangle" is applicable to it and signifies what it is.

Getting at the same thing a little differently, we might say that a universal concept intends or signifies something that is common to many different things. For instance, individual triangles are certainly different from one another: the one may be scalene and the other isosceles; the one may be drawn with white chalk, the other with green; the one may be large, the other small; the one may be a drawing in sand, the other an outline of a triangular plot of ground, etc. Yet they are all triangles. So also with any other concept you can think of —yellow, hydrogen, molecule, gravitational pull, or what not. Thus are not even different patches of yellow unlike each other? They differ in shade, in size, in location, etc. But they are all alike yellow.

Moreover, it is precisely the concept that intends or gets at this one in many, this common element in diverse things. It is not in sensory perception that we recognize a one which is thus common to many. Imagine two triangles, the one isosceles, the other scalene; the one drawn on the blackboard, the other on paper; the one two inches from apex to base, the other two feet. Clearly, these two would not look alike, being different in color and size and shape; they wouldn't feel alike, and doubtless if we could hear, taste, or smell them, they wouldn't be alike in these respects either. Yet we readily recognize both of them as triangles. For this a different cognitive faculty must be brought into play besides sensation.

Or put it this way. Consider that common element that all particular triangles may be said to share in: triangularity. What does it look like? The question is absurd, simply because such a common or universal element would not have any "look" about it. For any triangle that we see must be of a particular color and a particular size and a particular shape, etc. But that which is common to all triangles has no particular color and no particular size and no particular shape, etc. Hence we could not possibly see it, or feel it, or taste it, or touch it, or sense it in any way. It can only be grasped intellectually—viz., in and through the sort of thing we call a concept.

Why Universality Is Indispensable in Knowledge.   Granted that universal concepts can be achieved only in rational or intellectual cognition and not in sensory cognition, still we may ask why such universals are so important and even indispensable in knowledge. *That* we must employ such universals is perhaps obvious. Put it to the test yourself: can you possibly say or think what anything is without using universals? "Red," "angiosperm," "logic," "fifty feet wide," "sea serpent"—all these are concepts through which we attempt to understand what various things are. But they are all universals: each signifies something that is common to any number of different possible particulars.

Still, why are such universal concepts so necessary for knowledge? Almost at once a fairly obvious answer suggests itself to this question: universal concepts are necessary because they effect a quite indispensable economy in the business of knowledge. Imagine how hopeless would be the task of cognition if we could use no general terms or concepts at all. Instead of employing the one term "men" to apply to all men, we should have to consider each individual separately, and as if he had nothing in common with any other men. Or suppose that a chemist could not talk about hydrogen, for example, at all, but had to treat each bit and parcel of hydrogen as if it were utterly different and diverse from every other, and as if what were true of one particular bit of hydrogen would not be true of the next one. Yes, the situation would be even worse than this. For even to speak of *what* would be true of just one bit of hydrogen would be ruled out in such a case, since to think or say what is true of anything necessarily involves the use of a universal concept.

Nevertheless, however much universal concepts may contribute in the way of economy to our knowledge, their contribution would be quite irrelevant and even misleading if the realities which we seek to know through the use of concepts were not themselves sufficiently similar to permit. of a description of many by one concept. Thus it must needs be shown that precisely through universal concepts and only through universal concepts are we able to discern something in things and in reality which otherwise we should never be able to recognize, and being ignorant of which we should never know things as they really are.

What is this feature or aspect of things which we are able to apprehend only in universal concepts and which cannot be grasped in sensation alone? We have already given the answer: it is no less than the natures or essences of things that are apprehended in universal concepts. Thus anything whatever that can in any sense be said to be or to exist not only is, but is something—i.e., it has a certain determinate nature, and is what it is and not something else. However, it is precisely this "what" of a thing, its determinate nature or essence—what it is, in short—that is the object of a universal concept and that can be apprehended only by means of such an instrument. In other words, without universal concepts we should quite literally not be able to know what anything is at all.

Why and How Universality Is Brought About by Abstraction.   Moreover, the reason such concepts are universal is that they are products of abstraction; and what abstraction means literally is to extricate something, to separate or draw it out, or even to drag it out (cf. the Latin *ab,* "from" or "out of," and *traho,* "to draw" or "drag"). Nor is it hard to see why abstraction is necessary for the apprehension of the essences or "whats" of things. Obviously, in any concrete material object[1] of knowledge there will be any number of "whats" or essences. Suppose that you are holding an ordinary lead pencil in your hand. What can you say about it? You can say that it is a pencil, of course, and perhaps also that it is yellow, that it is seven inches long, is made of wood, has

---

[1] The expression "material object" is used advisedly here. For in speaking of a material object of knowledge, one does not necessarily mean a physical object, or an object that has material properties in the literal sense. No, "material object" is here used in contrast to "formal object." And the reason for such a contrast is that many philosophers and logicians in the realistic tradition (e.g., people as different as John of St. Thomas and John Locke in the seventeenth century, or Santayana and Maritain in the twentieth century) have found in ordinary experience that the objects of our knowledge seem to be in a certain sense twofold or double-phased. First, there are the *natures* or essences of things, which are the *immediate* objects of our knowledge. Second, there are the *things themselves* of which they are the natures, which things themselves are the *mediate* objects of our knowledge. The immediate objects (natures) are called technically the *formal objects* of knowledge. The mediate objects (things themselves) are called the *material objects* of knowledge. The material objects of knowledge are thus the *real things* which we know, and the formal objects of knowledge are those *intelligible aspects (natures or forms) through* which we come to know them. In other words, the material object of knowledge is *what* we know, and the formal objects of knowledge are what we know about it. What you know, for example, is this book (material object); and you come to know it *through* its stable natures such as "book," "logic," "difficult," etc. (formal objects).

a hexagonal surface, is in your hand, is smooth to the touch, etc. Now each one of these features is a determinate "what" or characteristic; yet all pertain to the same concrete, particular object.

Note, however, that though all these "whats" pertain to the same thing, every one is quite different and distinct. There is nothing about the nature or essence of pencil as such that requires it to be yellow, or about the color yellow that requires it to be the color of a pencil. Likewise, the characteristic of being seven inches long is certainly not the same as that of being in your hand, and vice versa. Moreover, for a proper understanding of the pencil as it really is, each of these "whats" or traits must be distinguished from the others with which it is fused and merged in the concrete, material object.

But what cognitive faculty is it that can do this distinguishing and dis-criminating? It can't be sensation. For the senses present us with just the con-crete fusion, or confusion, of many different traits and "whats." For instance, as you look at a pencil held out in front of you, what you see may be a long, narrow, yellow surface, of a certain size and hue and shape. Yet there is nothing about the nature of yellow color as such that requires it to be of that shape, or even of that particular shade and hue. This sort of discrimination, however, the senses do not make. Instead, the intellect is required to distinguish and sepa-rate out and abstract the color from the size, and the size from the shape, and all three from the fact that the thing is a pencil, and so on for all the various other traits.

In short, without the intellect there will be no abstraction, and without abstraction there will be no discrimination of "whats" or essences, and without a discrimination of these various "whats" one simply will not be able to recog-nize anything for what it is.

Another interesting consequence of this abstraction of natures and essences from their concrete setting in material objects is that once they are thus ab-stracted the concepts of them will perforce be universal. For after all, what is it that makes this particular pencil this one and not something common to all pencils? Is it not precisely the fact that the nature or essence "pencil"—which as such can be shared in by any number of individuals—is in this particular instance individuated and merged with any number of other traits and essences? As a result, this pencil is not just any pencil, but a yellow one; and not just any yellow pencil, but one that is seven inches long and is in your hand and has six sides etc.; etc. Accordingly, in so far as the nature or essence of pencil is abstracted from all these other traits of size, location, color, etc., and considered alone and in itself, quite naturally the concept of it will then be universal: it will be the nature of pencil as such that is being considered and not just this particular pencil; hence the concept of such a nature will be applicable to any number of different individuals—viz., to all individuals that may be said to have such a nature.

3-2   THE PROBLEM OF UNIVERSALS[2]

Unfortunately a difficulty suggests itself at this point. Universal concepts are means of economy in human cognition, and they are also instruments for the apprehension of the very "whats" and essences of things. Indeed, only in and through universal concepts is it possible for us to recognize what anything is at all. But does this mean that the very "whats" and essences of things themselves are universal, just like the concepts through which they are apprehended? Alas, whichever way we answer this question, we find ourselves beset with difficulties.

True, when the issue is thus first presented in this bold fashion, it no doubt seems about as pedantic and academic as anything could possibly be. And yet just think about it a little.

The Position of Extreme Realism and Its Difficulties.   Suppose that the natures and essences of things are universal in fact and in reality. In a way, this would seem plausible enough in the light of our foregoing discussion, even if in itself it may strike you as a point of very little consequence. Thus we insisted that if universal concepts were to be reliable instruments of knowledge it was not enough to show that they were sources of economy in cognition. For if things themselves were not really susceptible of the sort of cognitive economy that universals contribute, then the use of universals would appear to distort rather than reveal the true nature of things. Accordingly, we argued that any "what" or essence of anything, if it is really to be recognized and known, must be abstracted and separated out from all the other natures and traits and characteristics with which it is associated in the concrete material thing. But the minute it is thus abstracted and analyzed out of its concrete context, it thereby seems to lose all that tends to individuate and particularize it—i.e., to make it this particular bit of yellow rather than yellow as such, or this particular human being, rather than human nature as such, etc. In other words, as a result of abstraction a nature or essence becomes universal and as such is the proper object of a universal concept.

But if a nature or essence becomes universal when considered just in itself, must that not be because it *is* universal in fact and as it really is in itself? This, indeed, is the alternative that we wish first to consider, viz., that the natures and essences of things are themselves universal in fact and in reality, or that universals are real things actually existing *in rerum natura*. Such a philosophical doctrine has traditionally been known as *realism*, the name signifying simply that in its view universals are regarded as being real things—in fact, just as real as particulars, if not more so. However, in order to distinguish this sort of

[2] For excellent accounts of this issue, cf. Etienne Gilson, *The Unity of Philosophical Experience*, Scribner's, 1937, Part I, Chap. I; and John Wild, *Introduction to Realistic Philosophy*, Harper, 1948, pp. 449 ff.

realism from the realistic position which we are presenting in this book, we shall henceforth always refer to the former as *extreme realism.*

Well, what is the matter with extreme realism? First of all, there is something downright fantastic about it. For can one believe that in addition to this, that, and the other human being there is also such a thing as human nature just as such? Indeed, as one of the ancient critics of Plato once quipped, "Horses I see perfectly well, but horseness I do not see!" And more seriously, would not all of us recognize that whatever exists always seems to be a particular individual thing, never a universal? It is triangles that exist in the real world, not the abstract essence of triangularity. Likewise, where in the world of actual things has one ever encountered greenness just as such and in the abstract? Is it not always this particular green that we find actually existing?

Another and perhaps even more serious difficulty with extreme realism is this: If human nature, for example, is *one*, then how can there possibly be *many* human beings? After all, the whole point of the theory is that it stresses the unity and sameness of every nature or essence. Just as the concept yellow is supposed to be the same, whether it be applied to this yellow or that, so also the nature or essence of yellow is supposed to be one and the same whether in this particular yellow patch or in that. All yellows are supposed to be equally yellow, and all men equally human, and so on for all the other natures and essences.

Yet how can this be? If human nature, for example, be something which Joe Doakes has, then how can you claim to have it too? Presumably, the only way in which many individuals can share in one thing is for each to have some part of it. So it is when men share the wealth or share their food or share a house. But certainly men can't share their human nature in this way. For human nature isn't a quantitative sort of thing of which you have a little bit, and Joe Doakes another, and John Doe another, etc. However, if human nature cannot be divided up, how can many of us be said to have it or to share in it? The irritating thing is that it is so obviously true *that* we are all human and *that* we all possess human nature; yet *how* can we possibly do so!

The Position of Nominalism and Its Difficulties.   Little wonder that in the light of difficulties of this sort many philosophers have rejected realism altogether. After all, they say, why must one suppose that universals are real and actually exist in the real world? Why not consider that it is only our terms and concepts that are universal, but not things themselves? To be sure, we human beings cannot get along without using universal notions and general terms. But that does not mean that there necessarily have to be actual universal things or entities corresponding to our notions and ideas.

This philosophic position has traditionally been known as *nominalism.* And the reason for the term (from *nomen*, "name") is that in contrast to the extreme realists, who hold that universals are all real, the nominalists hold that universals are mere names, or at best mere concepts or ideas, to which nothing corresponds in reality. Thus they would agree: merely because the name "man" has three letters, we should certainly not suppose that the things so named, viz., the real man, must have three letters too; likewise, why should we suppose that because "man" is a common noun or universal concept the thing that is grasped by such a concept must itself be common and general and universal?

All this sounds plausible enough, but difficulties immediately suggest themselves. For one thing, if there is no universal, common human nature—to use the same example again—in which all human beings share, how can we possibly call all men by the same name, "man"? Certainly, if we use the same word or concept to describe them all, it would seem that there would have to be something common to them all, or something in respect to which they are all alike or all resemble each other; otherwise they could not legitimately be brought under the same heading or subsumed under the same concept.

And if the nominalist retorts that using the term "man" to describe all men is but a convenient shorthand device of the human mind, but one that is in no wise to be taken as indicating anything about the real character of the entities considered, the same difficulty reasserts itself. Either there is something about a group of particulars that enables us to treat them as all alike, or there is not. If there is, then our use of one concept to describe them all is thereby rendered legitimate, but at the same time nominalism is refuted. If there is nothing really in the particulars that enables them to be considered as similar, then there is no ground or basis whatever for using a common name or common concept to characterize them all.

Besides, would not anyone have to admit that all human beings really are alike, at least in some respect? It is undeniably true that all of us are human beings really and in fact. But if men really are alike and really do resemble one another, they must be alike and similar in respect to something. And what could that something be save human nature? In short, if any two things are alike really, then there would seem to have to be a real attribute or nature or characteristic or trait or "what" in respect to which they are alike. But this is just what the nominalist tries to deny. How can he, without seeming to fly in the face of the most obvious of facts?

Or we might pose the nominalist's dilemma in this way: either he recognizes the legitimacy of common names, in which case it would seem impossible for him not to concede that there must be something really common in things; or he tries to renounce the use of common names and universal concepts altogether—but this is tantamount to intellectual suicide. We have already had occasion to call attention repeatedly to the absolute necessity and indispensability of universals in knowledge. One simply cannot say what anything is without using universal concepts. Not only that, but the task of cognition would be laborious to the point of impossibility if each individual had to be regarded as absolutely different from every other, and if what was true of one could never be taken as indicating what might be true of another. No, there is no getting around the fact that, whichever way you take it, nominalism is an utterly untenable position.

3–3   SOLUTION OF THE PROBLEM:[3] MODERATE REALISM

If both nominalism and extreme realism are untenable, we would seem to have landed in an impasse indeed. What is one to do? On the one hand, universals seem absolutely necessary for the intelligibility of things; on the other hand, the reality of things forces us to recognize that everything that is is particular. Thus extreme realism, in its determination to save the intelligibility of things, seems to fly in the face of the real facts of nature. And extreme nominalism, in its determination to stick to the concrete particulars of the real world, seems unable to account for the intelligibility of these same particulars. Or again, in emphasizing the obvious unity of groups and classes of things, extreme realism finds itself unable to explain their multiplicity; and nominalism, in insisting on the undeniable multiplicity of things, finds itself wholly unable to account for their unity.

Is there no alternative, then, to either extreme realism or extreme nominalism? Apparently not, for either universals really exist or they don't, and that would seem to be an end to the matter. Nor can one attempt to evade the issue by just not raising it. For human beings do use universal concepts and general terms and common nouns in their effort to understand the vast multiplicity of real things. And they do recognize that the incredible numbers of real particulars are somehow united in groups and classes and types and kinds of things. The issue is there, ready-made for us, whether we choose, ostrich-like, to disregard it or not.

Very well, let's face the issue and let's face it by trying to find some third alternative between realism and nominalism. Such an alternative, we believe, can be glimpsed, if one will but scrutinize a little more closely the peculiar character of the so-called natures or essences which, as we have seen, are the formal objects of our universal concepts. Already we have had occasion to note[4] that these natures and essences are capable of a sort of dual existence at one and the same time. The essence of "man," for example, is able to exist both

---

[3] The solution of the problem here proposed is certainly implicit in Aristotle. However, it was the Arabian philosopher Avicenna who probably was the first to spell it out explicitly and in detail. Avicenna's solution, in turn, formed the basis for the masterly discussion of the whole issue which is to be found in St. Thomas Aquinas' little treatise, *On Being and Essence*. Cf. the translation by A. A. Maurer, Pontifical Institute of Mediaeval Studies, 1949, Chap. 3.

[4] See pp. 26–27.

physically *in rerum natura* and at the same time intellectually or intentionally as an object before the mind, i.e., as an object of a concept. Moreover, as we were careful to point out, it is one and the same nature or essence which exists in these dual states or conditions.

But right here, perhaps, we have the solution to our difficulties and a way out of the impasse of nominalism and extreme realism. For what pertains to a nature or essence as it exists really *in rerum natura* will presumably be somewhat different from what pertains to it as it exists intentionally and in its condition of being an object before the mind. Specifically, we may say that it is only in the latter state or condition, i.e., as an object of a concept, that the nature or essence is universal, whereas, as it exists *in rerum natura*, it will be thoroughly individuated and particularized.

Thus human nature as it exists in this and that and the other human being is without question radically individuated. After all, your human nature is not Adolf Hitler's, but yours. True, you may be said to be like Hitler, and like every other human being for that matter, in that you are all men. Yet this certainly does not mean that you have the same identical essence, in the sense that you are essentially the same, and hence only a superficially different person from Hitler or any other man.

On the other hand, when such a nature or essence as that of man has been abstracted and separated intellectually from its individuating conditions, and so brought before the mind as an object of a concept, in this state or condition it will necessarily be abstract and universal. In individual men, human nature will be not abstract but concrete, not universal but particular; but as abstracted and separated from the concrete, individuating conditions of its existence in the real world, it will be abstract and universal.

In other words, in this view, which we shall term simply realism, or *moderate* realism, one agrees with the nominalist and disagrees with the extreme realist in insisting that universality is not in things, but only in the mind. On the other hand, in disagreement with nominalism and in agreement with extreme realism, the moderate realist insists that there really is something in reality which is apprehended in universal concepts and which yet is not just the particular as such, viz., the nature or essence which is present in the particular and makes it to be what it is. By such means the moderate realist both guarantees the knowability or intelligibility of things and at the same time avoids having to hypostatize in the real world any mysterious, abstract entities of the sort of universals.

It must be admitted that the moderate realist accomplishes these objectives at a price which to many may seem too high. Nor is there any point in trying to hide or conceal what the necessary payment is. It is this: In order to be able to maintain that a nature or essence is universal in the mind, but particular in things and in reality, the moderate realist must contend that in itself a so-called nature or essence is neither one thing nor many. This does sound paradoxical, to say the least.

But look at the matter in this way. According to the realist, the nature or essence which makes things to be what they are is really there, but it is multiple and diverse. That is to say, it really is multiplied and diversified and individuated in things. On the other hand, the nature or essence through which the many particulars come to be understood, is, in the mind or as an object of a concept, one and the same. That is to say, one and the same concept "man," for example, applies to or describes this man and that and the other.

Consequently, if in itself and intrinsically the essence "man" or "human nature" were necessarily one and the same, then it could never be multiplied and diversified in things. And correspondingly, if in itself and intrinsically an essence such as human nature were necessarily many and diverse, then it would be quite impossible for it to be one and the same in its condition of being an object of a concept. There is no alternative but to recognize that, considered just in themselves and as such, natures and essences are neither one nor many.

Nor is this so altogether implausible when we consider how natures or essences are capable of a dual existence. The very same essence, say yellow, can exist both physically in things and intentionally before the mind. Accordingly, we must recognize that, considered just in itself and as such, a nature or essence is neither something physical nor something intellectual or intentional but rather something that is capable of existing in either state. So now we must recognize similarly that natures and essences, precisely because they are capable of existing either in the mind or in things, cannot as such be either one or many.

CHAPTER 4

THE STRUCTURE OF CONCEPTS

4-1 CONCEPTS AS RELATIONS OF IDENTITY

Having thus attempted what to many may seem a rather cavalier *"veni, vidi, vici"* with respect to the vexed question of the reality of universals, we must now return, briefly and by way of conclusion, to the question of universality in concepts. In the preceding section we sought to fix universality in concepts and concepts alone. And in still earlier sections we tried to give some idea as to just what the universality of concepts involves—how it is indispensable for purposes of human knowledge, how it is attainable only in intellection and not at all in sensation, etc.

Still, we are not finished with this topic entirely. For when we say that a concept is universal, what do we mean? So far we have merely said that for a concept to be universal means that while it signifies one thing it is nevertheless applicable to many. Moreover, in the light of the foregoing section we can now add that the *one* thing which a concept signifies is always a nature or essence, and the *many* things to which it is applicable are the many particulars which have that nature or essence. All of this is true, but not sufficiently precise and definite. We still need to know what the structure of a universal concept is—a structure that makes it possible for one to intend through it the natures or essences of things.

As a matter of fact, it is not uncommon for logicians and philosophers generally to suppose that universal concepts are veritable atoms, without complexity and without structure. As over against this, we should like to insist that concepts are intrinsically complex and structured. Specifically, we suggest that they are relations, and, more specifically still, that they are relations of identity. Further, it is precisely because of their peculiar relational character that they are able to perform the distinctive intentional function which it is theirs to perform.

Very well, then, let us consider typical concepts such as "man," "yellow," "hydrogen," "equal to," etc. How and in what sense may these be regarded as relations of identity? They may be regarded as relations simply because in each case what is involved is nothing more nor less than a relation between an abstracted nature or essence and the particulars or individuals from which it has been abstracted and to which it is applicable.[1] Moreover, they may be regarded as relations of identity because in each case the abstracted essence is simply what the relevant particulars or individuals are, and the relation of a thing to what it is would seem to be none other than a relation of identity, albeit of a rather special kind.

For instance, "man" is a universal "what" abstracted from the particular human beings in which human nature exists. At the same time, "man" is what each individual human being is. That is why, as we have so often reiterated, although it signifies one thing, a concept is nonetheless applicable to any number of different things. We might even say that any concept has a double significance or meaning: primarily, it means a certain "what" or essence; secondarily it means the individuals that have such a "what." Later we shall deal with this double meaning or significance by saying that every concept has both *comprehension* and *extension*.[2]

Nor is that the only feature of concepts that becomes readily explicable, once they are regarded as mere relations of identity. In addition, it explains how and in what sense a concept is a universal, an *unum versus alia:* it is the "one" which the "others" are; it is the relation of identity that holds between an abstracted essence and the particulars that have that essence.

Likewise, for a concept to be a relation of identity is altogether consonant with that feature which, as we saw,[3] pertains to all logical entities and distinguishes them from ordinary real beings. For logical entities are mere beings of reason and as such cannot exist independently of human cognitive activity. But clearly, a relation of identity can be no more than a being of reason. For in fact and in reality nothing is ever separated from itself and then related back to itself by a relation of identity. It is only reason that can effect such a separation and reidentification. Specifically, too, in the case of concepts it is the very "what" of a thing—what it is—that is separated by abstraction from the thing itself and then related back to it. But where in reality does one find a separation between what a thing is and that thing itself, not to mention a relation of identity between them? No, all this is unmistakably the work of reason and intelligence.

Moreover, this particular work of reason and intelligence is precisely to the end of knowledge and understanding. It may be remembered from our earlier discussions[4] that besides being mere beings of reason logical entities are recognizable by a further and even more distinctive criterion: they are intentions or

---

[1] The individuals or particulars to which the abstracted essence is related by a relation of identity must be thought of as including not merely all such actually existing individuals but all possible or all conceivable individuals of this kind.

[2] See below, pp. 57–61.

[3] Above, pp. 24–28.

[4] See above, pp. 16–23.

formal signs. Accordingly, no sooner does one recognize that it pertains to the very nature of concepts to be relations of identity than their character as intentions and formal signs immediately becomes evident.

Thus concepts are precisely those instruments through which we intend the "whats" of things. And be it noted that the last three words are important in this context. For it isn't just things that we intend through concepts, but their "whats" or essences, the kinds of things they are. Likewise, it isn't just "whats" or essences that we intend, but the "whats" or essences of things. But what could be more adapted to the performance of this intentional function than that peculiar relation of identity which a concept is—viz., the relation between an abstracted essence and the various possible particulars that might have such an essence? This is the instrument through which we come to apprehend the "whats" of things.

4–2 COMPREHENSION AND EXTENSION OF CONCEPTS

Since the universality of concepts consists in the fact that they are relations of identity between an abstracted nature and the individuals which possess it, it follows that there are two aspects in the significance of every concept. The signified nature or essence itself, or rather its structure or constituent notes, is called the _comprehension_ of the concept; and the classes, types, and individuals which possess that nature make up the _extension_ of the concept. The ideas of comprehension and extension are important for later use, so you should take pains to gain an accurate understanding of them now.

The comprehension of the concept "man," for example, is the set of traits which constitute human nature—what it means to be human. And the extension of the concept "man" consists of all men, initially all types of men such as Caucasian, Mongoloid, etc., and American, English, etc., and ultimately of all individual human beings, such as Richard Roe and Dorothy Doe. These two complementary aspects of conceptual meaning are sometimes called _intension_ (not to be confused with intention) and _extension,_ or _connotation_ and _denotation,_ or _description_ and _application,_ respectively. Later we shall learn how to formulate the comprehension of concepts as _definitions_ and how to analyze the extension of concepts in _divisions._

Our description of extension requires, however, one important qualification. The extension of a concept consists of all things which _could possibly_ be characterized by the comprehension of that concept, as well as those which happen actually to be so. Thus the extension of the concept "animal" includes dragons and mermaids, centaurs and Martians, as well as horses and men. This is true because, as we have seen, a concept by itself signifies only a _what_ and never its _whether,_ only an essence and never the existence or nonexistence or type of existence of that essence. Such utterances as "snow," "phlogiston," "canals on Mars," and "square root of minus one" convey in themselves no inkling as to whether or not such things actually exist. For all your *concept* is concerned, Martian canals may or may not be real.

Another way of making the same point is to note that concepts alone are neither true nor false. To intend existence, to answer a "whether" question, to assert something with truth or falsity a second logical tool is needed, the proposition. The proposition that "Martian canals are real" is true or false, but the concept "Martian canals" is not. True, we may convey existence and non-existence, truth and falsity, without explicitly using propositions, as when we utter a term with a certain intonation. Thus "Martian canals!" and "Martian canals?" may tend to assert and to question, respectively, their existence. But in such cases propositions over and above the concepts are implicit in the intonations.

With concepts alone, therefore, we are restricted to mere "whats." Thus the extension of any concept consists of all *possible* or *conceivable* classes, sub-classes, and individuals possessing the comprehended traits—all the past, present, and future instances of the nature as well as all those which could but never will see the light of day at all.

The Inverse Variation of Comprehension and Extension. *As the comprehension of a concept increases, the extension decreases, and vice versa;* this has been called "the law of the inverse variation of comprehension and extension." It means simply that the more we qualify something the less it applies to, and the less we qualify something the more it applies to. Thus "organism" applies to everything that "animal" does, and more, because "animal" is a particular qualification of the broader concept "organism." Only the inorganic world is excluded from the extension of "organism"; more is excluded and less included in the extension of "vertebrate organism"; still fewer things are "mammalian vertebrate organisms"; and as we increase the comprehension even further by the addition of such traits as "canine," "domesticated," "long-eared," "long-haired" and "short-legged," we find that progressively fewer things can satisfy the demands of our characterization. If, finally, we further increase the comprehension by the addition of the traits "nervous" and "irritable," the society for the prevention of cocker spaniels may be relieved to know that fewer still could embody this essence.

Nevertheless, you may well point out that the extension of "irritable, nervous, short-legged, long-haired, long-eared, domesticated, canine, mammalian, vertebrate organism" still, unfortunately, includes an infinity of individuals, no matter how rich the comprehension may be, since the extension of a concept consists of all possible types and individuals answering the description, and since it is at least possible or conceivable that there be an infinite number of things which fit the above description. Here it must be noted that the words "increase" and "decrease," "more" and "less" in our remarks refer not to numbers of individuals but to numbers of groups or classes, each of which, as a true universal, contains an infinite number of possible individuals. Thus "square" extends over an infinite number of possible individuals, and so does "parallelogram." Still "parallelogram" extends over or applies to more groups and classes than "square" does, for the former covers an infinity of rectangles and rhombuses as well as the infinity of squares. If the notion that one infinity can be larger or smaller than another seems odd to you, just remember that the numbers 10 and 1 each contains an infinite number of fractions and yet 10 is larger than 1.

Thus the law of the inverse variation of comprehension and extension means simply that the more we say the less we say it about, and the less we say the more we say it about. This is reflected in the quip that the scientist knows more and more about less and less while the philosopher knows less and less about more and more. The relation of comprehension and extension is like that, though it doubtless falls short of the ultimate scientific and philosophic situations of knowing everything about nothing and nothing about everything, respectively.

It is often objected, however, that the law of the inverse variation of comprehension and extension is no law at all because it has exceptions, because it is possible to vary the comprehension of a concept without affecting its extension. This is most obviously true when the terms added to the comprehension of a concept are ones like "being," "entity," "existent," "thing," "one," etc. For instance, there are just as many rational animal beings or rational animal things as there are rational animals, period. Such terms have traditionally been called *transcendentals* since their application transcends even the categories, themselves the most general divisions of reality. Everything whatsoever, be it actual or possible, real or fictitious, past, present, or future, must in some sense be a being (note the significance of this redundancy) or thing and be one thing—even a multiplicity is one multiplicity. Since such transcendental terms are absolutely universal in their scope, they are already tacitly included in the comprehension of every concept so that their explicit mention does not really add anything new and therefore does not change the extension of that concept.[5]

Other more ordinary terms explicitly added to the comprehension of a concept may also already be implicitly contained therein.[6] The addition of the qualifying trait "male" to the comprehension of the concept "Harvard undergraduate" does not reduce the number of members of that illustrious institution because "male" is already implicit in the definition of "Harvard undergraduate."

Finally, the citation of another type of example as violating the law of the inverse variation of comprehension and extension is based on the failure to

[5] Cf. pp. 84–86.
[6] Such may be *properties*, which are treated on pp. 63 and 121–125 below.

observe our earlier stressed point that extension, as an aspect of *conceptual* meaning, comprises possibilities only and never actualities. It is sometimes maintained, for example, that "The extension of the term 'university professor' is the same as the extension of 'university professor older than five years.'"[7] Although it might be argued (wrongly, we think) that the trait "older than five years" is already tacitly included in the term "university professor" and that there is therefore really no increase in the comprehension at all, it is more important to note that the example is based on the assumption that the extension of a concept includes only actually existent instances of the nature in question. It does happen to be true as an actual matter of fact, actions to the contrary notwithstanding, that there are no university professors aged five or younger, but it is still conceivable or possible that there might be, unless such possibilities were ruled out by the definition of "university professor." But in that case, again, "older than five years" does not really add anything to the comprehension, for it is already implicitly contained within it. Hence the extension of the concept "university professor over five years of age" *excludes* the *possible* university professors *not* over five and is therefore smaller than the extension of the concept "university professor" alone.

This question also essentially involves the question of just what is entailed in the definition of "university professor"—just what is present, that is, in the comprehension of the concept "university professor." Tools for solving this part of the problem will be discovered later when we come to definitions. But it is important to reëmphasize the other part of the question now: the extension of a concept comprises all *possible* instances of the comprehended nature. If this is remembered, and if the change in the comprehension is a genuine one, really adding or subtracting traits not already tacitly included or excluded, then the traditional law of the inverse variation of comprehension and extension holds good. Concepts are blind to all existential distinctions. To see once again that extension cannot mean the actual, real existence of instances of the comprehended nature—though actual instances are included as possible, since everything that is actual is also possible—one need only note that if this were the case every concept would be true, since what every concept intended would actually exist as intended, and error and falsehood would then be impossible.

Having examined at some length the nature and relation of the two aspects of conceptual meaning, we must turn to a consideration of the ways in which concepts are related to each other on this scale of increasing extension and decreasing comprehension. These ways have traditionally been called the predicables, because they are also the different ways in which one concept is predicable of another in a proposition. As predicables we shall meet them again

[7] Cohen and Nagel, *Introduction to Logic and Scientific Method,* Harcourt, Brace, 1934, p. 33.

when we come to propositions.[8] But as relations among concepts they are of vital importance in general in coming to understand what we mean and in particular in learning how to make good definitions.

4-3   RELATIONS AMONG CONCEPTS: THE PREDICABLES

The five predicables, we shall see,[9] are *genus, differentia, species, property,* and *accident*. Genus and species are the technical terms for *general* and *specific kinds,* respectively. To be the genus of another concept is to have greater extension and less comprehension than that other concept. And to be a species of another concept is to have smaller extension and greater comprehension. Thus "animal" is a genus of "man," and "man" is a species of "animal." A genus is a more general type that generates more specific types of that same general type. However, since individuals, such as Hitler, are not *kinds* of things at all, they are never either species or genera. Hitler is not a species of man (unless "Hitler" is used to mean a certain kind of human being, as when one says, "He's a regular Hitler!"), but "man" is the species to which Hitler belongs.

Genus and species are relative concepts, but they are relative to certain absolute limits. The broadest or most general kinds of things possible are, we have seen, the categories: substance, quality, quantity, relation, time, place, activity, and passivity. Above these no distinctions in *essence* or *nature* can be made among things—although it is still possible to make certain higher existential distinctions.[10] Hence the categories are the highest kinds of things there are, and they are therefore known as the *summa genera,* each of them being the *summum genus* for all those many species which fall under it as its specific types. At the other extreme, at the extreme of minimum extension and maximum comprehension, we find the most specific kinds of things, the least species or *infimae species,* as they are called, each of which is an *infima species* or most specific possible type of some category or summum genus. Just what species are indeed the most specific ones is a more difficult question which we do not need to consider here. But for purposes of illustration let us say that "man" is an infima species of the category or summum genus "substance." The next concept greater in extension than "man," let us say "animal," is the nearest or *proximate* genus of "man"; and "vertebrate" and "organism" are more *remote genera.* "Animal" and "plant" are *coördinate* species of "organism" since those two types are divisions of "organism" at the same logical level. And any species of any species of a given genus is known as a *subspecies* of that genus; thus "vertebrate" and "invertebrate," "mammal" and "reptile," etc., are subspecies of the genus "organism."

[8] Pp. 118–125 below.
[9] Pp. 118–125 below.
[10] The types of *designation,* discussed on pp. 131–136 below.

Concepts are varied in extension and comprehension by the addition or subtraction of some note or trait. This note or trait the addition of which increases the comprehension and decreases the extension is called the *specific difference,* or *differentia,* and its addition to any given concept generates a species of the original concept, which original concept becomes, in turn, the genus of that generated species. Thus "sentient" when added to "organism" is the differentia of the species "animal"; it is the difference between the coördinate species "animal" and "plant." And "rational" is the differentia whereby "man" is in turn a species of "animal," coördinate with the species "brute animal" and a subspecies of the remote genus "organism." This interrelation of genus, species, and differentia, and their relation to the inverse variation of comprehension and extension, may perhaps be made clearer with a graph:

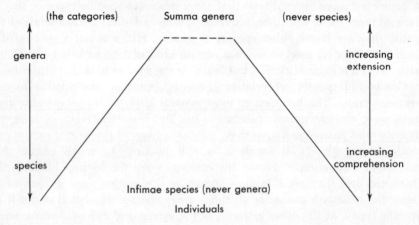

Thus a species is generated by adding a differentia to a genus. The differentia is always essential to the species simply because a species is an *essence* signified by a *concept.* Here it is extremely important to avoid confusing an essence or nature with the existent individuals which possess it. Consider for example the two following expressions:

> "Man" is "the rational animal."
> Men always or usually cook their food.

In the first case we are speaking about the *essence* "man" and the *concept* which signifies it, and we are saying that that essence is a species of the genus "animal" and different from its coördinate species in virtue of the differentia "rational." In the second case we are talking about individual *existents* which embody the essence "man," and we are saying that these individual existents happen also, usually or always, to embody the essence "cooking food." *Men* may, or may not, happen to be cooks, but *man* is not *cook.* A given essence simply is that essence and not another thing. Thus in citing the genus and differentia which make a given essence the species that it is, we must be most careful to cite notes which are intrinsic or constitutive of that essence itself—which are essential to it—and not ones which are extrinsic or non-constitutive of that essence even though they may happen to characterize the same actual individuals.

So no essence is any other essence. Still, some essences are necessarily connected in such a way that one can be inferred from another, while others are not. Thus "triangle"—closed plane figure (genus) with three angles (differentia)—is necessarily connected with "having interior angles equal to two right angles" so that either can be obtained or inferred from the other. But "white" is not necessarily connected with, and therefore cannot be obtained from, either of these essences. When we deal with propositions and their intention of existence we shall see that essences which are necessarily connected with other essences belong to the predicable *property* or *necessary accident*, while those which are not necessarily connected with another essence but merely happen to characterize the same individuals as that essence belong to the predicable *contingent accident*.[11] The important thing to remember now is this: To give the difference between one species and others in the same genus you must cite a trait intrinsic or essential to that species or essence rather than an extrinsic or nonessential one, even if that extrinsic one should be necessarily connected with the species in question.

Besides varying in the degree of their comprehension and extension, terms also vary in many other ways. Thus terms may be *general* ones like "man," signifying many individuals, or *singular* ones like "France," signifying only one individual. Further, general terms may be either *collective* ("team") or *distributive* ("man") according as they signify these individuals collectively as a group or separately as individuals. And they may be either *concrete* like "man," referring to individuals, or *abstract* like "humanity," referring to an essence. Again, they may be *substantive* like "man," referring to substances, or *attributive*[12] like "tall," referring to attributes of substances. And they may be *simple* ("man") or *complex* ("red-headed man") according as they signify a single essence or a union of essences. And so on. The tremendous richness of our logical and linguistic tools makes it impossible to give a complete catalogue of all the varieties of terms, and it is fortunately also unnecessary for our present purposes.

Summary of the Nature and Function of the Concept. We have now completed our examination of the nature and function of the concept. That which is known by the concept or term, the first logical instrument, is an essence, trait, or characteristic which functions as an answer to some "What?" question.

[11] Pp. 121–125 below.
[12] These two types of terms are traditionally called *absolute* and *connotative*, respectively. Cf. note 3 in Chap. 9.

Essences as grasped by concepts are abstracted from existence; the question of whether or not they exist requires a further logical tool, the proposition, to which we shall turn in Part II. The perennial classifications of the most basic "whats" or essences are known as the categories, and among these the most important which thought and language demand is the category of substance, or thing. That by which essences are known is the universal concept, a relation of identity between a given essence in its abstracted, mental state and the very same essence in its concrete, individuated, real state. This duality or relationality in the structure of universal concepts is the ground for the two aspects of meaning which belong to every concept: (1) the comprehension, or comprehensional meaning, which is the set of traits or notes comprehended in the essence itself, and (2) the extension, or extensional meaning, which is the set of all possible instances of the conceived essence. In the case of all ordinary (non-transcendental) concepts, comprehension and extension are related inversely: the greater the comprehension the lesser the extension, and vice versa. Finally, moreover, concepts are related to each other on the scale of increasing comprehension and decreasing extension as being species of broader concepts and genera of narrower ones.

With this theoretical background of the structure of the concept, we must now turn to the practical question of its uses on the road to knowledge. Here our first task must necessarily be that of the identification and clarification of concepts, the detection and elimination of ambiguity.

CHAPTER 5

CONCEPTS IN USE:
AMBIGUITY AND DIVISION

Having gained some theoretical understanding of the nature of concepts, let us now turn to the task of learning to make them clear. The first question we naturally tend to ask, as we have seen, is the question "What?" What is justice? What is logic? Since all such concepts as "atomic energy," "justice," and "logic" possess both comprehension and extension, any complete answer to a "what" question will involve two operations: *defining* or analyzing the term's comprehension and *dividing* or analyzing its extension.

But before we can even begin to define or divide a concept we must know what concept it is which we need to define and divide. We must, in short, first *identify* our meanings. Nor is this always an easy task, for our concepts are formulated and communicated in language, and language is notoriously slippery. As we saw in our discussion of signs, concepts are natural formal signs, one in nature with their signata, while words are artificial material signs, physical entities with peculiar traits of their own whose connections with their signata are as tenuous as the shifting whims of the human will. This means that there is seldom if ever a direct one-to-one connection between a word and a concept, and this absence of clear, direct verbal-conceptual connection is known as *ambiguity*.

5–1 AMBIGUITY AND THE IDENTIFICATION OF CONCEPTS

It is all-important, in the first place, to remember that ambiguity is a disease of *words*, not of concepts. If it is true to say that most if not all words are ambiguous in some degree, just because their connection with their meanings is artificial, it is also true that no concept is ever ambiguous. A concept, as a formal sign, is nothing but revelatory of its particular signatum. Hence to *have* a concept is to be aware of what it signifies. A concept with two or more meanings is two or more concepts, for concepts are themselves meanings. Though you may not know whether the *word* "pen" in this sentence refers to the concept of a writing instrument or to the concept of an enclosure, your concept of a writing instrument is just that, and so also is your concept of an enclosure. Words are ambiguous; concepts never are. Hence our task will be to discover the precise, unambiguous concept which a given word is being used to stand for. Our ideal will be to assign every word to one and only one concept.

5–1.1　Types of Ambiguity[1]

Since human beings can engage in verbal duplicity in as many ways as they can create and use language, the varieties of ambiguity are manifold. Still, the more usual varieties may be classified under three main headings: (1) *equivocation,* or semantic or verbal ambiguity, where the ambiguity attaches to a single word or phrase;[2] (2) *amphiboly,* or syntactic or sentential ambiguity, where the ambiguity is due to the syntax or particular arrangement of words and phrases in a sentence; and (3) *accent,* or inflectional and contextual ambiguity, where the ambiguity arises from the intonation, facial expression, gestures, or general context in which the utterance occurs.

Equivocation. The manufacturer who advertises that "our cheeses are handled by dealers all over the country" is unfortunately unaware of the fact that "handle" can mean not only "to merchandise" or "to sell" but also "to lay hands on"—as when a parent says "Don't handle things!" to his child. The verbal identity may in other cases be merely a sameness in sound, the written symbols differing; that is, the ambiguous word may be a phonic homonym of another word. Witness the old saw: "The boy climbed up the tree with a bear behind"—though here "behind" is also equivocal. Nor need the ambiguous word be exactly similar to another word; the contrary is the case in malapropisms and loose or bad puns. Consider the following news article, for instance:

---

[1] Metaphorical and analogical terms are frequently thought to be ambiguous, but this belief rests on a confusion of logic with language. In the statements "St. Francis was a *good* man," "That's a *good* steak," and "He's a *good* safecracker" "good" is not ambiguous but analogical. The reference of the word is perfectly clear, but what the word refers to is a complicated relational structure, the relation of fitness or appropriateness to extremely diverse things. The same is true of metaphorical terms. "A tree whose hungry mouth is pressed against the earth's sweet flowing breast" is not ambiguous, and any treatment of metaphorical language as ambiguous would destroy all poetry and most literary prose. On this interpretation the treatment of analogy and metaphor belongs to metaphysics and esthetics, not to logic; and in any event our task here is simply to clarify our language whether it be literal, metaphorical, or analogical, although metaphorical and analogical terms will not be subject to proper definition. For a clear elementary account of metaphor see Monroe Beardsley, *Practical Logic,* Prentice-Hall, 1950, Chap. 4. For a logico-metaphysical treatment of analogy see Henry Veatch, *Intentional Logic,* Yale, 1952, pp. 97–105. And for excellent metaphysical treatments of analogy and metaphor see James F. Anderson, *The Bond of Being,* Herder, 1949, and John Wild, "Introduction to Metaphysics" (mimeographed), pp. 6–23.

[2] Though "ambiguity" and "equivocation" are roughly synonymous in popular speech, we shall follow the usual logical custom of using the word "equivocation" to refer to a particular species of ambiguity.

The lady owner of a canine veteran of World War II said last night she would be glad when the use of the searchlight in front of a Broughton street theater was discontinued.

"My dog," she sadly related, "went through the war and its nerves are in bad shape. Every night when the light swings back and forth in the sky my dog sees it and begins whelping."[3]

A puppy litter a night would doubtless set an all-time record, but anyone who sees the similarity of "whelp" and "yelp" sees also that this was not meant. Even misspellings may often occasion equivocation: "I say that sex, in its purist form, must be explained in biological terms," wrote a student in an essay.

Not all equivocations are so trivial or humorous, however. Consider the problem posed by the following statement from a student's essay: "If the government makes a law which is contrary to a particular individual's personal tendencies, the decision to break that law is with the individual." Is the writer saying that the individual should break the law, or not? The answer depends on the particular meaning assigned to the expression "is with."

Amphiboly.   An ad in a daily paper read as follows: "FOR SALE: Antique desk suitable for lady with curved legs and large drawers, also mahogany chest. Please write E. L. Brown, Box 5150 Metropolitan Station, Los Angeles 14."[4] In this example none of the individual words is ambiguous—at least not to any important degree. Rather the ambiguity attaches to the expression as a whole, and it is due to the *arrangement* of the words and phrases—in this case a misplaced modifier. Ambiguity which arises from the arrangement, grammar, or syntax of words in sentences is known as amphiboly. Amphiboly is so common as to be found even in the best circles: for example, if you look carefully at p. 129 of this book you will find an amphiboly.

Syntactic ambiguity may have many different causes. In addition to misplaced modifier amphibolies exemplified above, ambiguity may arise from uncertainty as to what part of speech a particular word is in a given sentence. Note for example the following headline: "DUODENAL ULCER DRUG ON MARKET."[5] Is "DRUG" the subject of the tacit verb "is" or a predicate noun? If subject, we get: "Duodenal ulcer drug is on the market"; if predicate noun, then "Duodenal ulcer is a drug on the market." Notice also that the expression "drug on the market" is equivocal. Furthermore, uncertainty concerning the antecedents of pronouns and relative clauses can cause amphibolies. When it is asserted that "Happiness is the only life, and without it one cannot live," is it happiness or is it life that one cannot live without? And punctuation, especially the use of commas, is a frequent cause of amphiboly. "There is only one reality, God and all other things might be considered manifestations of this single reality,"

---

[3] Savannah (Ga.) *Morning News,* reprinted in *The New Yorker.*
[4] Reprinted in the *Journal of the American Medical Association,* Sept. 19, 1953.
[5] In the New York *Herald Tribune,* reprinted in *The New Yorker.*

wrote a student in a philosophy paper. Is God a part or the whole of reality? If the comma present after "reality" is supposed to be a semicolon or period, we have one answer. But if a comma or semicolon is intended after "God," then we get a different one.

Amphiboly can of course occur in combination with equivocation. An editorial was once headed, "HUME WRONG"—an expression which a philosopher might interpret as an abbreviation for "Hume is wrong," where "wrong" is an adjective. But anyone familiar with the political events of that period would understand that the headline is a proper name rather than a statement. Again, consider the following news note: "Formerly of Long Beach are Dr. and Mrs. C. L. Doolittle. They are making their home with their two-year-old son in Corral de Tierra."[6] Here two puzzling questions arise: Is their son with them or not? If we place a comma after "home" and after "son," then he is; but if we place a comma only after "home," then he is not. And in the second place, is the home the property of the parents or of the son? A double meaning in our customary usage of the word "with" permits either interpretation.

Accent. As the name indicates, accent is a change or addition in meaning brought about by emphasizing some particular aspect of an expression while deëmphasizing the other aspects. Such emphasis may be vocal, as in the case of the midwestern farmer who rationalized his perjury by quoting from the Bible: "Thou shalt not bear false witness against thy *neighbor*." Or it may be graphic, as in the case of the use of italics. In general, any of the factors involved in the total communication situation—facial expression, gestures, etc.—may introduce ambiguity into the language used.

The varieties of accent are legion, but a couple of forms may be noted. *Innuendo* is one such common form. "Oh, no! She didn't steal it!" is given a meaning precisely opposite to its literal one by an ironic or sarcastic tone of voice. Another form of accent is known as *special pleading*. This consists in an exclusive emphasis upon the points which are especially favorable to the speaker's or writer's own case at the expense of those which are unfavorable. A third form is the *fallacy of selection*, which is committed when words or sentences are lifted from their total context in such a way as to alter their meaning without the reader's or listener's being any the wiser, unless he has chanced to meet the original. It should be noted, finally, that accent in many of its forms does not so much result in an ambiguous expression as in the production of a relatively new, unambiguous expression which is different from the original or non-accented expression in certain important ways.

5–1.2 The Elimination of Ambiguity: Verbal Definition

With this background concerning the nature and types of ambiguity, we are now in a position to apply our knowledge toward the goal of eliminating

---

[6] From the *Salinas Californian,* reprinted in *The New Yorker.*

ambiguity so as to identify the conceived essence which is to be analyzed. In eliminating ambiguities in everyday life we all follow some sort of procedure more or less unconsciously, but we can be more thorough and accurate in this task if we make that procedure explicit and exact. When explicated and systematized, our ordinary procedure for the elimination of ambiguity is probably something like the following:

1. State the expression in which the ambiguity occurs.
2. Identify, as specifically as possible, the factor—the word, phrase, punctuation, etc.—which is responsible for the ambiguity. (This step is usually the most difficult one, for we are often aware of the fact that an expression is ambiguous without being able to say why it is.)
3. Formulate the relevant alternative meanings of the ambiguous expression. [The ambiguous expressions will sometimes also have meanings which are clearly excluded by the context. The separation of meanings can be sharpened by labeling them with different numbers, such as "pen-1," "pen-2," or perhaps better by including an identifying word or phrase in parentheses: e.g. "pen (writing)" and "pen (enclosure)."]
4. Restate item 1—the original expression—now substituting the alternative meanings to yield two or more unambiguous expressions.

Let us apply this procedure to an example.

The following item from a story in *True Confessions* was reprinted in *The New Yorker:* "He told it well—it had been funny when it happened, and it was still funny, to Father as well. I hadn't heard him laugh so heartily since Mother died." Since we do not normally associate laughter with death, we suspect that something is wrong in the last sentence. So in step 1 we state that sentence:

1. I hadn't heard him laugh so heartily since Mother died.
Then:
2. "since"
3. "since-1"—"since before"
   "since-2"—"since the time that"
4. I hadn't heard him laugh so heartily since before Mother died.
   I hadn't heard him laugh so heartily since the time that Mother died.

The handling of such simple examples as this may not require us to make our procedure very explicit, but having some such systematic procedure will help us in less obvious or more difficult cases.

The Analysis of Identified Concepts.   Thus the first step in understanding what we mean is to *identify* the "what," the essence, which we are conceiving. And this step requires the recognition, and frequently the elimination, of ambiguity by the formulation of alternative meanings signified by the same words. Once we have pinned down the concept signified by a given word, our next step in coming to understand what we mean is to analyze the structure of that identified concept. Such analysis may be of either the extension or the comprehension of the concept. In the first case we are engaged in *division* or *classification;* in the second case we are engaged in *definition*. Both are attempts to answer the question "What do you mean?" or "What is that?"— division and classification by giving instances or examples and definition by citing traits or characteristics.

"But wait!" you may say. "Didn't you say earlier that merely to have a concept is to know what it means, in the sense of apprehending its signatum, since every concept is a formal sign?" True, we did; but we also suggested that the comprehension and extension of any concept consist of the total structure of that concept and not merely of the aspects that we are explicitly aware of. Here a concept is like a jigsaw puzzle: its many pieces are apprehended either not at all or else very indistinctly after they are put together so as to merge into a single picture. This difference between having an idea and thereby knowing vaguely or in general what one means, on the one hand, and being explicitly aware of all that is implicitly involved in that idea, on the other hand, can also be made very clear by just considering a couple of examples. You probably figure rightly that you could recognize a human being whenever you should see one, but does this mean that you know all the races, nationalities, types, and groups of human beings that there are, or—*mirabile dictu!*— can recite the names of all the people who ever did, do, shall, or could live? Or, to turn from a division of the extension to a definition of the comprehension of a concept, how would you define "left" in the expression "She is left-handed"? True, you've known which is your left hand since you were five or six, and in that sense you know what "left" means; but do you know what it means in the sense of being able to cite the definitive structure of that meaning?

It is to this task of exhibiting the extensional and comprehensional structures of our concepts that we must now turn. Let us first consider division, the analysis of extension.

5–2   DIVISION AND CLASSIFICATION: THE EXTENSION OF CONCEPTS

When children—and frequently even adults—ask us what a certain term means, we usually find that our answers are more easily understood, and often even more easily given, if we state them as examples. What does "metropolis" mean? Well, it means such things as New York, Philadelphia, Chicago, and London. What is communism? It's what's going on in Russia and China. Or instead of naming the examples of the term in question we sometimes point them out with a gesture. When a child asks his father, "What is lightning?" his father may take him outside, point up to the sky, and answer: "There! That's what lightning is!" Explaining the meaning of a term by citing examples from its extension is sometimes thought of as a type of definition. When the examples are named the answer is often called by logicians a *denotative definition,* and when the examples are directly pointed out the answer is sometimes called a *demonstrative definition.* Since such answers cannot properly limit or define the term, however, and since they are concerned with its extension rather than with its comprehension, they are not properly definitions at all. They are, however, genuine attempts to explicate the meanings of terms, albeit rather inchoate or preliminary ones; and they are the first steps toward the goal of logical division.

The extension of a concept, we have seen, includes all the species, subspecies, infimae species, and ultimately all the possible individuals to which that term applies. When the process of analyzing the extension of a term is a *descending* one, from the concept to its instances—from "man" to "American" to "John," for example—the process is known as *division.* When it is an *ascending* one, from the instances to the concept—from "John" to "American" to "man," for instance—it is called *classification,* the placing of an item into a class or kind. Thus division and classification are two inverse dimensions of one and the same process: the relating of a concept to the items in its extension.

Rules for Adequate Division (or Classification). The rules for division and classification, like those for eliminating ambiguity, are simply exact and explicit formulations of the procedures which we naturally and unconsciously tend to follow. Since the object of division is to exhibit the extension of a term, there is one basic rule which must be followed:

1. The rule: *The extension must be exhibited according to exactly one principle of division* (fundamentum divisionis).

The principle of division, or *fundamentum divisionis,* is simply the standard in terms of which the various species of the generic term to be divided are separated from each other. In dividing the term "building" (or in classifying buildings), for example, we may use as our principle of division *function* (homes, schools, churches, business, etc.) or *architectural style* (Colonial, Victorian, Byzantine, contemporary, etc.) or *structural material* (brick, stone, frame, metal, etc.), and so forth. It is perfectly proper to use different principles of division in different divisions, but not more than one principle should be used in any one division. And each such division should be carried out exhaustively. But the reasons for these two caveats can be seen more clearly by considering two corollary rules which are implicitly contained in the one general rule:

2. Corollary rules:

a. *The divisions or classes must be jointly exhaustive.* This means simply that any analysis of the extension of a concept should be an analysis of the *whole* of the extension, rather than merely of a part of it. A classification of climates into hot and cold ones would violate this rule, for temperate climates would be omitted. Such a division or classification is said to commit *the fallacy of incomplete division* (or *classification*). This rule does *not* mean, of course, that every last item in the extension of the concept must be mentioned, for this is impossible since there is an infinite number of (possible) individuals falling under the concept. It means rather that all *of the coördinate species* at some level of abstraction or other must be cited—the level being determined by the principle of division.

b. *The divisions or classes must be mutually exclusive.* This means that there should be no overlapping of classes so as to include any item more than once. A division of sports into team, individual, and outdoor would violate this corollary rule, for sports which are both team and outdoor, such as football, are counted more than once. Such a division is said to commit *the fallacy of cross-division* (or *cross-classification*).

Since the specific rules a and b are corollaries of the one general rule, any division or classification which violates the general rule will also violate one or both of the corollary rules. Thus a division of cities into large and small violates corollary a as well as the general rule, for the two classes are not jointly exhaustive of all cities. There is no cross-division, however, provided that the principle of division is clear and definite, for the same city cannot (in the same respect) be both large and small. A division of animals into vertebrates, invertebrates, and mammals, while satisfying corollary a, violates corollary b as well as the general rule, for the classes "vertebrates" and "mammals" are not mutually exclusive. Finally, a classification of vehicles into land, water, and passenger violates both corollaries in violating the general rule: more than one principle of classification is used and neither of these principles is carried out exhaustively, so the division commits both the fallacy of incompleteness and the fallacy of cross-classification.

The point, in short, is this: Once you begin a division or classification according to some particular principle you must finish it by that principle instead of switching to another. Consider, for example, the shifts in the following classification of books: poetry (according to form), fiction (according to content), texts (according to purpose), octavos (according to size), Spanish (according to language), and red (according to color). The application of more than one principle always and necessarily results in the fallacy of cross-division, provided that the division is complete, and it usually does even when the division is not complete. Again, and finally: Every division or classification which violates either of the corollary rules will also violate the general rule, and every one which violates the general rule will also violate either or both of the corollary rules.

Subdivision and Superclassification. We have seen that the extension of any concept comprises all of the various types and kinds of things possessed of the given essence and even, ultimately, all the possible individuals of that nature. We also saw that these various types and individuals form a scale of abstraction from individuals through infimae species, proximate genera, and remote genera up to the summa genera, the categories.[7] We may therefore now see that division and classification may occur at various levels on this scale. A division of living substances into plants and animals, for example, occurs at a higher level of abstraction than a division of living substances into vertebrates, invertebrates, angiosperms, and gymnosperms. And a classification of John, Joe, and Jane as human beings takes place at a lower level of abstraction than their classification as organisms.

We may, moreover, not only divide something into its kinds but also divide those kinds into their kinds, and those kinds into their kinds, etc., just as we may also classify classes of things, and classes of classes, etc. These processes may be called, respectively, _subdivision_ and _superclassification_. The ascending process of classification may start at any level short of the summa genera, from the ultimate individuals on up, and proceed to any level including that of the summa genera. The descending process of division may start at any level from the summa genera on down to but not including the infimae species and proceed through the infimae species but fall short of the individuals. This is so because the individual is logically indivisible, and also because any division _into_ individuals would have to be incomplete in view of their infinite number. A chart may help make this clear:

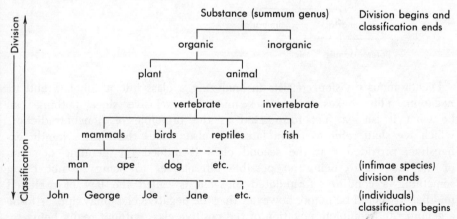

Different numbers and types of classes and different levels of abstraction might of course have been obtained in this chart by the application of different

[7] See p. 62 above.

principles of division, but this simple example will perhaps suffice to illustrate the extent and limits of division and subdivision and classification and superclassification.

Dichotomous and Nondichotomous Division. Saying what ought to be done is usually easier than actually doing it, and division and classification are not exceptions. Divisions should be exhaustive and exclusive—this is clear and evident. But it is much more difficult to abide by these rules in actual practice. There is, however, one easy way to insure the mutual exclusiveness and joint exhaustiveness of the classes at any given level. This way is simply to divide the given class into one kind of thing and everything else that is not of that kind. Thus the term "book" may be divided into "red" and "non-red," or "English" and "foreign." This type of division is called *dichotomy* because it consists in cutting a class into two parts. The most famous historical example of dichotomous division is the "Tree of Porphyry," Porphyry being a Neoplatonist logician of the third century A.D.:

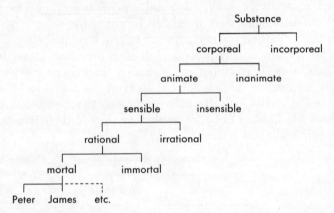

Dichotomous division consists in analyzing a class into a subclass and its negation. This makes the classes mutually exclusive since nothing can be what it isn't—a fact formulated as the principle of noncontradiction, which we shall refer to again later.[8] It also makes the classes jointly exhaustive, provided that the second class is indeed the genuine negation of the first, there being no possible alternatives to being or not being something—a condition formulated in what is called the law of excluded middle.[9] It should be noted, however, that the negative class may appear to be a genuine and complete negation of the positive class without really being so.

[8] P. 116.
[9] Both the law of noncontradiction and the law of excluded middle have been attacked at various times throughout their history, as have most laws; but the nature of these attacks need not concern us here.

To divide people into kind and unkind ones, for example, is to produce an incomplete division, for some people are neither kind nor unkind; the complete negation of "kind" would be "not kind" or "non-kind."[10]

Yet in spite of the relative ease with which dichotomous division satisfies the rule, it is susceptible of two defects. In the first place the negative class does not so much tell us what we know about the extension of the concept as what we don't know. To know that something is noncorporeal, for example, is not to know very much about it, although many words which are literally negative have come in time to have very positive meanings: "irrational," "faithless," and "unfortunate" are examples. And in the second place it may well be the case that the most significant divisions of a concept are more than two in number. Thus a zoölogist may find it more helpful to divide "vertebrate" into "mammal," "fish," "bird," and "reptile" than into "rational" and "irrational." This question, however, is one which lies outside the province of logic; and in many a case a dichotomous division may well be the most significant one after all. Dichotomous division is sometimes criticized, finally, on the grounds that the negative class may have no members, since the only requirement for membership in it is absence of the traits present in the positive class. It might be said, for example, that in the division of "mammal" into "hairy or warm-blooded" and "lacking hair and warm blood" the negative class has no members at all, for all (actual) mammals have either hair or warm blood. If you here reminded us that it is *possible* for there to be mammals without hair and without warm blood, since this is not excluded by the comprehension of "mammal"; if you insisted that there can be no distinction between actual and possible instances so far as concepts alone are concerned, you would be quite correct.

Outlining.   One extremely useful instance of division is outlining. Of course outlining is the division of a whole body of thought into its constituent ideas rather than a division of a term into its instances, but still it involves the same principle: the clarification of thought by analyzing it into its divisions. In outlining a book, for example, we first break it up into chapters, then into sections, then into paragraphs, and finally into sentences. Though outlining, like division proper, may be conducted according to various principles, the principle we usually use in order to understand the interrelations of the parts is the principle of inference or sequence. We first state any definitions that may be present, then any assumptions or premises, and finally the conclusions—which in turn may of course become premises for further conclusions. If you will but recall your high-school excursion into Euclid, for instance, you will see that mathematics offers us in its structure the most nearly perfect examples of outlining. Since good outlining actually involves a knowledge of the principles of inference or reasoning, however, it goes beyond the logic of concepts to the logic

[10] Various kinds of negation will be discussed in connection with propositions. See especially pp. 174–179 and 196 below.

of argument; and when we later analyze arguments we will be engaged in outlining.

What then do we mean by our concepts? One answer which gives one dimension of conceptual meaning is division and classification—the citing of examples, the analysis of the extension of a concept. The other answer presenting the other dimension of conceptual meaning is definition, and to it let us now turn.

EXERCISES

1. Identify and eliminate any ambiguities in the following:

a. "For serene contentment and relaxation, sip a drink from a coconut while listening to the plaintiff music of the mariachis in the tree-shaded plaza in the center of town." (*Guadalajara Tourist News*)

b. "The Duke yet lives that Henry shall depose." (Shakespeare, *Henry VI*, Part II, Act I, sc. 4)

c. Would you rather a lion ate you or a tiger?

d. "So Feline Hater (letter Dec. 29) 'cannot stomach those sneaky, slinky monstrosities.' They have a good and sad reason for being suspicious, because of persecutions by cruel creatures like himself and dogs, who want to exterminate every creature they don't happen to like—just like Hitler.

"My heart aches as I see only a few of them anymore, and they slink around after dark, looking scared and starved, and especially if they have a thin kitten following them.

"The dogs where I live are not all confined to 'yards and basements.' They are running the streets menacing people who dare to walk the streets and leaving their filth around.—Feline Champion." (from the letters column in a newspaper)

e. "RHODESIA PLANS OPEN WAR ON FLY CARRYING ELEPHANT" (from the Montreal *Star*, reprinted in *The New Yorker*)

f. "Vac., Inc., was a Terran corporation supplying the vacuum of space for use in laboratory research. At its plant on Luna, it manufactured its product by welding two duralloy hemispheres lip to lip and thus sealing a vacuum inside the globe they formed.

"One container in a shipment to the University of Venus proved to be defective. The University sued for damages resulting from the sudden failure of the built-in valve. . . .

"Attorneys for the defendants asked for dismissal of the suit on the grounds that a vacuum was *nothing*, and that when both parties to the action had stipulated the loss of a vacuum, the plaintiff in effect admitted losing nothing. In support of this contention, attorney for the defendants exhibited the advertising slogan of Vac., Inc., 'Nothing—but the best!'

"Attorney for the plaintiff countered the dismissal motion by stating that if this were true, then the defendants were confessing to giving nothing in exchange for good hard cash. However, attorney for the plaintiff argued, no absolute vacuum exists in all space, there being a minimum of twelve molecules per cubic foot in the emptiest reaches. Therefore, she claimed, there is nothing in the Universe which one might name 'nothing.'

"That last statement, attorney for the defendants replied scornfully, was self-contradictory. 'Nothing' *exists*, he said; the space *between* the molecules is 'nothing.'

"Quickly, attorney for the plaintiff exclaimed that now her learned opponent was arguing on the side of her client by agreeing that 'nothing' is something. At this point the judge wearily recessed court. . . . As soon as the court reconvened, the judge asked if either party objected to the swearing in of a panel of semanticists. There was no objection. . . . The majority decided that a vacuum is 'something.'

"The judge denied the defendants' motion for dismissal, heard the case, and found for the plaintiff. He awarded to the University 40 million credits. But legal expenses and the adverse publicity bankrupted Vac., Inc.

"It paid nothing." (Edward Wellen, "Origins of Galactic Law," *Galaxy Science Fiction*, April, 1953, pp. 91–92)

g. Which day is really Sunday? "As now contemplated, calendar revision would be unjust discrimination against minorities and would jeopardize the economic security of many. Its advocates propose to omit the 365th day of each year, plus leap year day, from the weekly cycle in order to effect a uniform unvariable calendar. The breaking of the weekly cycle would be of grave importance. The present week has remained intact in its transition from Jewish to Christian practice.

"The breaking of the traditional week would cause established days of weekly worship to wander through the new week. The first year the true Sunday would be on Saturday of the false week, and the next year it would fall on Friday. Thus it would continue endlessly its nomadic course through the proposed new calendar week. This perpetual shifting of the day of worship would bring confusion and distress alike to Christian, Jew, and Mohammedan. The conscientious religionist would be forced to choose between his religious convictions and the calendar. The two would always remain discordant.

"By being obliged to observe a different day of the week for religious devotion each year, many conscientious individuals would be faced with economic insecurity. An employee would be forced to lose his income on the working day upon which his Sabbath occurred, together with the loss of income on the Sunday of the man-made week. Parents would be forced to choose between sending their children to school or to religious service on the real day of religious observance. The loss of one day would be detrimental to the students. Should half the teachers observe the true day of worship while the other half kept the false day, when would our schools be in session?—J. Melvyn Clemons, Pastor, Chestnut Hill Seventh-day Adventist Church." (from the letters column of a Philadelphia paper)

h. "When an act is intrinsically good, good in itself, then that act belies absolute goodness, or ultimate goodness." (student paper)

    i. "The leanings of the slave group should be towards conformity and mediocracy." (student paper)

    j. "Princeton claimed a foul on the play but the referee, Frankly Stumped, settled the question with a flip of a coin." (from *The N.Y. News,* reprinted in *The New Yorker,* Jan. 23, 1954, p. 82)

    k. "I would like to remind those responsible for the treatment of tuberculosis that Keats wrote his best poems while dying of this disease. In my opinion he would never have done so under the influence of modern chemotherapy." (from a letter in the *Lancet,* British medical weekly, reprinted in *The New Yorker,* Mar. 6, 1954, p. 98)

    l. "WENCH FOR SALE—Complete with rope. For further information call 3081 Rivesville." (advertisement in the Fairmont *West Virginian,* reprinted in *The New Yorker,* Mar. 6, 1954, p. 104)

    m. "Four Good Ways to Barbecue Yourself." (circular from the *American Home,* reprinted in *The New Yorker,* Apr. 17, 1954, p. 34)

    n. "SUMMER RENTAL: Five room house with wood paneling plus small guest and garage in rear. Unfurnished. $80. per month. Tel. 1933-J-3." (advertisement in the Princeton [N.J.] *Town Topics,* reprinted in *The New Yorker,* June 12, 1954)

    o. "It won't be a real New England clam chowder unless you put your heart into it." (New England *Homestead,* reprinted in *The New Yorker,* June 12, 1954)

    p. "Although slightly hazy around the city this afternoon, weather bureau officials claimed that no fog was imminent." (Hartford [Conn.] *Times,* reprinted in *The New Yorker,* May 15, 1954, p. 90)

    q. "DAVID B. WOODRUFF JOINS STAFF TO TEACH JUVENILE DELINQUENCY." (headline in Adult Education Newsletter, reprinted in *The New Yorker,* May 15, 1954, p. 110)

    r. "GUEST FOR LUNCH ONE WAY TO SOLVE EATING PROBLEM" (headline in the Providence *Bulletin,* reprinted in *The New Yorker,* May 8, 1954, p. 72)

    s. "DOCTOR COMPILES LIST OF POISONS CHILDREN MAY DRINK AT HOME." (headline in the Sacramento *Union,* reprinted in *The New Yorker*)

    t. "These things are all but a small part of the great Reality, or God." (student essay)

    u. "So Clean! Clothes washed in Tide come out of your rinse tub—the Cleanest Clothes in town—cleaner than any woman can get with any soap of any kind!" (legend on a box of soap)

    v. I shall lose no time in reading your manuscript.

    w. "*Alice:* Would you—be very good enough—to stop a minute—just to get—one's breath again? *White King:* I'm *good* enough, only I'm not *strong* enough. You see, a minute goes by so fearfully quick. You might as well try to stop a Bandersnatch." (Lewis Carroll)

    x. A gorilla is more like a man than a chimpanzee.

    y. Women alone are excluded from the club dining room.

2. Divide (or classify) the following: forms of government, types of art, the sciences, personality types, the forms of life, the subject matter of your major field of study.

3. Outline the following selection:

"Relations in the strict sense, which actually belong to the category we are studying, fall into three major groups: the equiparent, the mutual, and the non-mutual relations. The first (equiparent) is founded on the intrinsic, formal structure of things and always possesses a similar *converse* relation. Thus, similarity is an equiparent relation, for if A is similar to B, B is also similar to A. Mutual relations are founded on efficient causal action. They possess a converse relation which is dissimilar. Thus, *invader-of* is a mutual relation. The converse of this relation, *being-invaded-by*, is dissimilar. Finally there are non-mutual relations founded on extrinsic, formal causation which have no converse at all. Thus the idea of this chair is really related to the existent chair, its extrinsic, formal cause. Of course we speak of the chair as being known. But this is a purely logical relation set up by the mind which corresponds to no real accident in the thing known. The chair does not suffer even the slightest accidental alteration when it is known. If so, it could never be truly known as it actually is. Many important relations, such as *picture-of* and *being-the-object-of-desire*, are non-mutual." (John Wild, *Introduction to Realistic Philosophy*, Harper, 1948, p. 350)

4. Evaluate the following divisions (classifications):
   a. Schools: technical, professional, public, private, and liberal arts.
   b. Criminals: born, habitual, professional, occasional, and emotional.
   c. Books: textbooks, novels, plays, poetry, and first editions.
   d. Transportation: land, sea, air, mechanized, and commercial.
   e. Forms of government: aristocracy, timocracy, oligarchy, democracy, and tyranny. (Plato, the *Republic*)
   f. Climates: temperate, hot, cold, dry, wet.
   g. Sports: team, individual, indoor, outdoor, and professional.
   h. Vertebrates: mammals, birds, reptiles, fish, and quadrupeds.

4-5.6²

CHAPTER 6

CONCEPTS IN USE:
DEFINITION

Examples do convey something of the meaning of a concept, and they are especially valuable psychologically for they bring us nearer to concrete sensory experience. Good divisions do even more to express what we mean by a certain concept. But any explication of meaning in terms of extension alone is bound to be imperfect and less than ideal because we would not be able to justify the examples as such unless we could also cite the definitive traits which the things must embody in order to be examples. Examples are always relative to and dependent upon what they exemplify. In the very same way division and extensional meaning are relative to and dependent upon, and hence logically posterior to, definition and comprehensional meaning. Our goal of knowing clearly what our concepts mean will be properly or completely achieved only when we are able to define them, to exhibit the comprehended structure which makes individual instances truly instances. Definition, then, is our present task.

The word "definition," like many words ending in "tion" (e.g., "intention") refers both to an operation and to a result. Definition as an operation means literally the setting of limits or boundaries to something, and definition as a result or product refers to that something as bounded. In English sentences the definition (sometimes called the *definiens*) is ordinarily signified in writing by the right-hand expression. The word or concept which is to be thus bounded, determined, or defined is called the *definiendum*, and in written English sentences it is normally signified by the left-hand expression. If we say, for example, that "man is the rational animal," "man" is the definiendum and "rational animal" the definition or definiens.

6–1 VARIETIES OF DEFINITION

The varieties of definition are as legion as our classifying ability is ingenious: "persuasive definitions," "recursive definitions," "definitions in use," "implicit definitions," etc. However, we shall here consider only three main types of definition (aside from the so-called denotative and demonstrative definitions which we have seen to be instances of division[1]): *verbal, conceptual,* and *real.* Each of these types of definition may be either explicit or implicit, depending on whether or not it is stated as a definition or left to be inferred from the context. It is frequently the case in common speech that the definition of a word or concept is clear from the context and that it is therefore unnecessary to define it explicitly. Furthermore, mathematical systems often employ implicit definitions, leaving the basic concepts as "primitives" whose meanings are determined by the axioms of the particular system. But since it is possible to explicate any implicit definition, and since good implicit definitions have the same characteristics as good explicit ones, we shall confine ourselves to a consideration of the latter.

The definiendum or left-hand expression either may be merely a word or phrase, as in our procedure for the elimination of ambiguity, or may signify a concept and essence. In the first case we have a *verbal* or *nominal* definition, in the second case a *conceptual* definition. The definition (definiens) or right-hand expression of course always signifies a concept in the case of conceptual definitions, but in the case of verbal definitions it may signify either a concept or merely a linguistic entity. Sometimes it is difficult to tell whether a word is being defined in terms of a concept or merely in terms of another word, but the context usually makes this clear.[2] When a conceptual definition—the comprehension of a concept or the structure of an essence—is introduced into a proposition and asserted to exist in some fashion, then we have a *real definition*.[3] Since real definitions are predicates in propositions, we shall discuss them later.[4] Still, a word concerning their relation to conceptual definitions will be helpful at the present time.

Conceptual and verbal definitions as instruments for understanding just what we mean, in contrast to asserting that what we mean is thus and so, are, like the concepts and words which they analyze or stipulate, neither true nor false; they just are what they are. Still, the proposition which asserts a given definition as the conceptual or verbal meaning of a certain definiendum will be true or false, according as the definition is or is not in fact the conventional or natural significance of the definiendum. But the definitions which may thus be asserted in propositions are *themselves* neither true nor false, for they are simply "whats," not "whethers," concepts or phrases rather than propositions or sentences. Thus " 'Triangle' means 'three-sided plane figure' " is either true or false, but "three-sided plane figure" is not. Definitions are not true or false but they are, as we shall shortly see, good or bad, adequate or inadequate,

[1] P. 71 above.

[2] It is sometimes advisable to introduce special notations such as " " for concepts and ' ' for words, but this seems unnecessary for our present purposes.

[3] What we have here called a "conceptual definition" is sometimes called a "real definition."

[4] E.g., on pp. 118–120 and 228–232 below.

according as they more or less accurately present the meanings of their definienda. In short, concepts exist, and there are therefore truths which may be asserted about them even though the concepts themselves never assert any existence or truth. This latter function belongs exclusively to the proposition.

Though common language often confuses a definition and the assertion of its existence in a proposition by using the connective "is" in both cases, logicians try very carefully to keep them distinct. Toward this end it will be helpful to use "is" only as a propositional connective, as a sign of existence, and "means" or "signifies" as a definitional connective, as expressing, that is, the relation between a definition and a definiendum. Thus "Man *is* the rational animal" is a proposition whose predicate is a real definition: this proposition is the instrument for asserting the existence of this kind of being, the tool for answering a "whether" question. But " 'Man' *means* 'rational animal' " is a proposition whose predicate is a verbal or conceptual definition; this proposition is the instrument for asserting a truth about meanings (linguistic or conceptual), the tool for answering a "what" question. Since real definitions involve propositions, they need not concern us now; but we must proceed to examine verbal and conceptual definitions in more detail.

6–2   VERBAL DEFINITIONS

In verbal definitions we cite a concept, or a word or phrase, or both, as the equivalent of some given word or phrase. Whether the meaning which is cited as the definition of the word in question is itself a linguistic or a conceptual entity is sometimes difficult, but often unimportant, to decide. Since words are artificial signs, they do not inherently or naturally or "really" mean anything. And since they do not of themselves mean anything, any definition of them asserts merely their artificial connection with certain concepts or other words either in the past, as in the case of *dictionary* or customary definitions, or in the present, as in the case of *stipulative* or specially contrived definitions.

Dictionary Definitions.   We look in dictionaries to discover, not what words "really" mean, but what most people have *used* them to mean in either the recent or the remote past. If this were not the case there would be no reason for revising dictionaries. As it is, however, there is always a gap between even the most up-to-date dictionary and living language.

Another limitation of dictionary definitions is the fact that they frequently give us, not an analysis of the meaning of the word in question, but rather only another word whose customary usage is the same, or approximately the same, as that of the definiendum. Such definitions are called *synonymous,* since the definition is a synonym, or partial synonym, of the definiendum. They are also sometimes called bi-verbal definitions, because both definiendum and definition are linguistic entities. A forceful example of the limitations of synonymous definitions is offered by bilingual dictionaries. If an English-speaking person wishes to find out what a pomegranate is, he is not greatly aided by being told in an English-Spanish dictionary that it means "*granada*," even though the two words, while in two different languages, are synonymous. Even in a single language the inquirer is often stymied, at least temporarily, by synonymous definitions. "Gourmet," for example, means "epicure," and you are enlightened if, but only if, you know what "epicure" means. If you don't you will have to look it up too, and if you do you are told that "epicure" means "connoisseur." Again, this is instructive only if you are familiar with the meaning of "connoisseur." If you aren't and have to look it up also you are told, finally, that "connoisseur" means "a critical judge, one competent to act or pass upon."[5] This last definition passes beyond the synonymous stage—though its adequacy, especially as a definition of "gourmet," is another matter and one to be tested by rules we shall soon introduce. Thus whenever we use a synonymous or biverbal definition we are saying in effect: "I don't know, or don't care to know, what concept the word 'x' signifies, but at any rate it means the same thing that the word 'y' means."

Stipulative Definitions.   Perhaps you have found yourself in the situation of being unable to put your finger, or tongue, on a word suitable to express an idea you have in mind. If you have and you were ingenious and a little daring, you probably made up a word on the spot. Such a linguistic creation is a *stipulative definition*—the assignment of a meaning to a mark or sound which has, at least to its creator's knowledge, either no previously assigned significance at all or else a different meaning from the one which he is stipulating. Stipulative definitions are therefore simply creations of artificial material signs. They express decisions, acts of will, rather than any real connection. Wherever new or uncommon ideas are being utilized, or wherever it is important to formulate and communicate a clear and precise meaning as in many of the sciences, stipulative definitions play an important role. Whenever one gives a stipulative definition one says in effect: "We are (or I am) now deciding to let the symbol 'x' mean y, or whatever the symbol 'y' means."

Such are two types of verbal definition—the assignment of meanings to words. But this was the task to be accomplished in the procedure for the elimination of ambiguity, a task which was only preparatory, we saw, for the analyzing of our concepts. To this job we must now return and as we do so we reach our final goal: the formulation of conceptual definitions.

6–3 CONCEPTUAL DEFINITIONS: THE COMPREHENSION OF CONCEPTS

A conceptual definition, we have seen, is a complex term which signifies or reveals the comprehension of a concept. But here additional qualification is

[5] From Webster's *Giant Illustrated Approved Dictionary*, World Publishing Co., 1949.

necessary, for it is unnecessary if not impossible to list the whole of the comprehension of any concept. Must we in defining "squirrel," for example, say "bushy-tailed, fur-covered, pointed-eared, chattering, nut-gathering, arboreal, mammalian, vertebrate, etc., etc., living substance"? Surely not. What is needed is rather a clear relation of the conceived essence to other similar essences and at the same time a sharp demarcation of the conceived essence from all these other similar ones. In other words, conceptual definition is simply the determination of the precise boundaries of a meaning. But how is this to be done? Well, we all know more or less how it is done for we do it more or less consciously every day. Here, as before, our logical rules are only exact, conscious formulations of tools which we all unconsciously use. And in conceptual definitions the relevant tools are ones with which we are already familiar: genus and differentia.

1. *General rule for conceptual definition: The definition should consist of the proximate genus and the differentia of the definiendum.* Thus conceptual definition may be regarded as the descriptive location of an essence on the scale of abstraction[6]—the scale of increasing comprehension and decreasing extension—by means of its genus or general kind and its differentia or specific difference from its coördinate species. But this means that only those concepts are definable which have a higher genus and a specific difference. Hence concepts at the two extremes of the scale of abstraction—the broadest, most inclusive concepts on the one hand and the least inclusive or singular concepts on the other—are not conceptually definable, though they may be verbally defined or characterized.

The broadest, most inclusive concepts are conceptually indefinable simply because they have no higher, or broader, genera to which they can be assigned. This is obvious in the case of transcendental or analogical concepts like "being."[7] For how could there be a higher or broader genus to which "being" could be assigned? If there were, such a genus would have to include within its scope things other than being, from which the beings would then be differentiated, just as the genus "animal," for example, includes within its scope animals other than men, from which in turn men are differentiated by definition. But what things other than being could possibly be included within a genus? Anything other than being would not be a being at all, would not be anything, would be just nothing; it would not be, in other words. Accordingly, there could not possibly be a genus higher than being, for the simple reason that being includes anything and everything whatever.

Granted that there is no genus higher than being, may we then regard "being" as itself the highest genus, under which the various categories[8] such

---

[6] See the chart on p. 62 above.
[7] See p. 59 above.
[8] See pp. 34–38 and 61 above.

as "substance," "quality," "quantity," etc., may be included as species, and in terms of which they may be defined? Unfortunately, this won't work either. True, a so-called transcendental term such as "being" is more inclusive than a category like "quantity," for there are certainly a lot of other kinds of beings or things in the world besides quantities. Yet we cannot say that "being" is a genus in the proper sense of the word, because there is no differentia that could be added to "being" so as to differentiate the sort of being that a quantity is, say, from the sort of being that a substance is.

But why not? Surely this prohibition seems arbitrary and far-fetched. Nevertheless, just stop and think: How could something be "added to" being so as to differentiate one kind of being from another? If "being" is all-inclusive, as we have just seen that it must be, there is literally nothing whatever that could be added to it which it does not already include, which is not itself already a being. By way of contrast, consider a genus such as "animal." Obviously, one can add a differentia to it, say, "rational," so as to define the species "man." And the reason such a differentia can be added to "animal" is that that differentia is not itself an animal. Thus "rational" or, if you will, "rationality" is not itself an animal; it is not a species or kind of animal, as is "man," for example. To be sure, a rational being is an animal. And "rational" when added to "animal" determines or defines a certain kind of animal. Yet we would never say that "rational" was itself an animal.

On the other hand, when it is "being" that we are considering, as contrasted with an ordinary genus like "animal," any differentia that we might try to add to "being" must itself be a being. Indeed, any differentia that we could ever try to imagine or think of that wouldn't itself be a being of course wouldn't be anything; there just wouldn't *be* any such thing.

Apparently, then, for the very reason that "being" (or any other so-called transcendental term, for that matter) is quite literally and absolutely all-inclusive, it cannot be a genus any more than it can have a genus. That is to say, just as there cannot be any genus above "being," simply because being includes everything, so also "being" cannot itself be a genus above other things, and, curiously enough, for the same reason. For being all-inclusive, "being" cannot therefore be inclusive in the way in which ordinary genera are inclusive; since it is all-inclusive, there is nothing whatever that could be added to a transcendental term like "being" in the manner of a differentia. For what is there that is not already a being, that is not already included within "being," and that therefore could be added to it, as something not already there?

This is not to say that we do not or should not speak of kinds of being or types of being, or should not speak of distinguishing or even of differentiating these various kinds from others. We can't help doing this. Nor is there any harm in it, so long as we keep in mind that, however we may speak of it, the fact remains that "being" and the other transcendental concepts do not behave like ordinary genera and hence can neither be defined themselves nor be used to define other things.

Note that one interesting consequence of "being" 's not being a genus is that the categories, "substance," "quality," "quantity," and the like, are indefinable. For the only way they could be defined would be as species or kinds of being (or of one of the other transcendentals). But since "being" is not a genus and does not admit of a differentia, the categories are simply indefinable. They are, in short, *summa genera* or highest genera. Indeed, it stands to reason that at least some of our concepts must be indefinable; otherwise, one concept would be defined in terms of another, and that in terms of another, and that of another, and so on, with the result that we should be in an infinite regress. If this is to be avoided, the process must come to a stop somewhere in certain summa genera which, themselves indefinable, are nonetheless the ultimate grounds of all our definitions. Such highest genera, or indefinable grounds of all definition, are, as we have seen, the categories.

Moreover, just as the most inclusive concepts, like the transcendentals on the one hand and the categories on the other, are incapable of being defined, so also the least inclusive concepts—viz., singular concepts—are indefinable. And they too are indefinable because they have no proper differentiae or specific differences. Hitler may be characterized as "the German corporal who became the Nazi dictator" or "the cruelest man who ever lived," but such descriptions cannot lay bare Hitler's very individuality. The reason is that an individual is not an essence at all—though it *has* an essence—and any essential trait we assign to it could possibly also be realized in another individual. True, all concepts are universals and signify essences, but a singular concept signifies that essence only secondarily and is primarily devoted to intending an individual which possesses the essence. This indefinability of singular terms is also indicated by the fact that in everyday speech we simply do not ask for definitions of them. "*What* is the *meaning* of 'Hitler'?" is clearly a phony question; instead we say, "*Who* was Hitler?" But only "whats" are conceptually definable, and singular terms do not primarily refer to "whats."[9]

So the definiendum of a conceptual definition must always be a species, and the definition consists of the genus and differentia which make that the species which it is. "Man" (species) means "rational (differentia) animal (genus)," for example; and "neutron" (species) means "uncharged (differentia) particle of matter (genus)." Note carefully that when the definition is a good one there is really no difference between the definiendum and the definition, between the species and its genus and differentia, for the species simply is the combination of the genus and differentia and the genus and differentia simply are the very kind and particular character, respectively, of the species. The difference

---

[9] The problem of the nature of the individual (note the paradox in this expression) is an extremely vexing one but it falls outside the scope of this book.

between definiendum and definition is only a difference between two different acts of awareness, and their respective concepts, of one and the same essence, seen now as an unanalyzed whole and now as a structured complex. Definiendum or species presents the essence as a simple unity; definition, or genus plus differentia, presents the very same essence as a whole of parts.

It is also important to observe that the general rule for conceptual definition requires that the genus be the proximate genus rather than a remote one. This is to prevent confusion of the definiendum with another subspecies of the same remote genus. Suppose, for example, that we should define "square" as "equilateral (differentia) plane figure (remote genus)." Our definition would then also cover other things, such as equilateral triangles and rhombuses, for they have the same genus and the same differentia. But if instead of a remote genus we cite in our definition the proximate genus of the species or definiendum, the confusion disappears: "square" (species) means "equilateral (differentia) rectangle (proximate genus)."

How can we be sure that we do in fact have the proximate genus and the specific difference of a given species or definiendum? Here we will be aided by several working corollaries of the general rule for conceptual definition—corollaries which we all use as everyday rules of thumb.

2. *Corollary Rules for Conceptual Definitions:*

a. *Definitions should not be too broad.* A definition which is too broad includes other concepts in addition to the definiendum and is therefore not a definition of, or limitation to, the definiendum as one particular concept at all. The definition of "circle," for example, as "a figure all of whose points are equidistant from a given point" also includes any arc of a circle as well as spheres and is therefore too broad. Too great breadth is usually caused by citing a remote rather than the proximate genus, as in the case of our earlier definition of "square" and the definition of "circle" just given. To exclude spheres and parts of circles from this latter definition we should have to restrict the genus to the more proximate one, "closed, plane figure." Being too broad is perhaps one of the more frequent defects of definitions.

b. *Definitions should not be too narrow.* A definition which is too narrow excludes some of the items in the extension of the definiendum and is therefore, again, not a definition of *that* concept at all. The United Statesian's definition of "American" as "citizen of the United States of America" is too narrow for it excludes Canadians, Mexicans, South Americans, etc., who also fall in the extension of the concept "American." Just as too great breadth is usually caused by citing a remote instead of the proximate genus, too little breadth is usually caused by having too restrictive a differentia, by citing as the differentia what is in fact the differentia of a species or subspecies of the definiendum. Thus a species of "American" is indeed "citizen of the United States of America," but the latter is narrower than the former.

Concerning these first two corollary rules in general, we can note that what they together require is that the definition exactly coincide with the definiendum, having neither a smaller nor a greater extension. This requirement holds good simply because, as we have seen, definiendum and definition are signs of the very same essence, and every essence must have exactly that range or extension which it does actually have. Moreover, certain definitions violate not only one but both of these rules. The definition of "glass," for instance, as "something one can see through" turns water into glass as well as transforming glass bricks into some other material. Indeed, in this definition there is really no genus at all (though "one can see through" serves, very inadequately, as a differentia), for "something" is a transcendental term and therefore not a possible genus. Since everything whatsoever is something, we do not say what *kind* or *genus* of thing glass, or anything else, is by saying that it is a something.

Thus the first two corollary rules are satisfied when and only when the definition applies to *all* possible instances of the definiendum and *only* to those. If the definition does not apply *only* to instances of the definiendum, it is too *broad*. If it does not apply to *all* instances of the definiendum, it is too *narrow*. Thus "animal that washes its food" is too broad a definition of "man," and "English-speaking animal" is too narrow (and possibly also too broad, if parrots "speak"). But " 'man' means 'animal that laughs' " would seem to be, as the baby bear's bed seemed to Goldilocks, just right.

"Wait a minute!" you may object. "What about the laughing hyena? Doesn't he make this definition too broad? And for that matter what about some of the sourpusses we have all known who never laugh? Don't they make this definition too narrow? The same goes for a lot of the other definitions of man which people are always handing out: 'Man is the rational animal,' 'Man is the featherless biped,' etc., etc. Everybody knows that there are one-legged and even no-legged humans, and also that such unfortunate scoundrels as Huck Finn's friends, the Duke and the King—not to mention many elegantly coifed ladies—get feathered. And finally, what about idiots and imbeciles and all the people who populate our asylums? Such people are hardly rational, not to mention most of the rest of us in our weaker moments. So isn't it impossible for any definition really to be coextensive with its definiendum?"

Many people say not, and some of them, unfortunately, get out of this difficulty by what we might call "the method of convenient reclassification."[10] A person who has always been taught that "Catholic" means "authoritarian, superstitious, and generally bad," for example, may find it easier to reclassify certain apparent exceptions than to give up his stereotyped definition. If such a person should become well acquainted with Danny O'Riordan, for instance, and then be told that Danny is a Catholic, he is likely to say: "Oh, no! Danny's

[10] For an interesting account of this all too frequent attitude, see S. I. Hayakawa, *Language in Action,* Harcourt, Brace, 1941, esp. pp. 155–159.

a good guy! He may be a member of the Catholic church, but he's not *really* a Catholic (authoritarian, superstitious person)."

May we then apply the same method to the above definitions of "man" as "laughing animal," "featherless biped," "rational animal," etc., retaining some or all of them as good definitions by insisting that hyenas don't really laugh, that apes are really quadrupeds, and that amputees, humorless people, and idiots are not really human at all? We may, of course, but this does seem a little high-handed. But if we don't do this must we therefore concede the claim that it is impossible to find a definition which is completely coextensive with its definiendum?

Apparently so, *if* what we mean by the above definitions is that all men always *act* rationally, or actually have two feet, or never wear feathers, or are never gloomy. But a little reflection will show that this is not in fact what we do mean when we proffer such definitions. No, what we mean to assert is that man is naturally, or by nature, rational, two-footed, featherless, or possessed of the ability to laugh. And we back up this claim with our common-sense distinction between an *activity* such as thinking, laughing, or walking—which an individual may or may not exercise[11] and the *essence* or *nature* which tends to produce that kind of activity if nothing intervenes. "Act your age!" we often say, and all such expressions reflect this natural distinction between *being* something and *acting* that way—between being human and acting humanly, between being rational and acting rationally, between being one's age and acting one's age. If "'Man' means 'rational animal,'" for example, is a good definition, then everything that is human must be the *kind* of thing which *would* act rationally *provided* no other forces prevented it from so doing. Thus we all recognize that there is no contradiction in saying that a responsible (in nature) person is acting irresponsibly, that a human being like Hitler can be inhuman (in activity), or even that an idiot can be rational in essence while being irrational in activity—else why do we not treat idiots like animals?

Now definition is an analysis of the *nature* or *essence* or *possibility* signified by a *concept*, not a *proposition* about the *activities* or conditions of *actual individuals*. For this reason we have used the word "means" to express definitions while we use the word "is" to express propositions. Hence a definition is coextensive with its definiendum when the nature or essence signified by the former is coextensive with the nature or essence signified by the latter— whether or not the conditions and activities which tend to follow from each of these essences actually exist. Of course, it is often extremely difficult to tell whether or not a certain essence is really present in individuals which lack an activity which that nature tends to produce—do congenital idiots really possess a rational nature?—or in individuals which apparently possess one of those

[11] Thus these activities fall under the category of activity, which is an accident, in our list of categories on p. 38 above.

activities but lack others—does the apparent laughter of the hyena spring from a real sense of humor? Yet this distinction between essences on the one hand and activity or condition on the other seems to be natural and inescapable; and no matter how difficult the task may be, we always keep trying to discover the real nature or "what" of the thing in question.

Thus it is certainly possible, though admittedly often difficult, to have definitions which are coextensive with their definienda, so long as we remember not to confuse a nature or essence with the actual conditions and activities which that nature may or may not happen to generate when it is realized in actual individuals.

c. *Definitions should be essential (fundamental or basic).* In the light of what has just been said, the first two corollary rules seem to be satisfied by the following definitions:

> (1) "Man" means "rational animal."
> (2) "Man" means "animal with a sense of humor."
> (3) "Man" means "naturally featherless biped."

But are all three of these definitions equally adequate just because each of them satisfies the first two rules? We wouldn't ordinarily think so, for the second one seems to tell us something more fundamental about the nature of man than the third one, and the first one would seem to reveal something still more basic than either of the others. It seems to be more essential to the nature of man that he be rational than that he have a sense of humor or that he tend to be born with two legs and no feathers. And if this is so, then the first one is a better definition than the second or third, even though all three satisfy the rules concerning the breadth of a definition.

Central to this issue is a distinction which we have touched on[12] and which will be discussed in more detail when we come to the theory of the predicables:[13] the distinction between *differentia* and *property*. We have seen that a differentia is a trait inherent in an essence and distinguishes that essence from others. Hence a differentia of a thing is constitutive of the very essence of that thing. A property of a thing, on the other hand, is a trait which always follows from and accompanies the essence of that thing. Thus a property of Tweedledum is that he invariably accompanies Tweedledee (in the imagination of Lewis Carroll), and a property of man is, let us say, that he is born with the ability to laugh. But Tweedledee's constant presence is not constitutive of the very being of Tweedledum, nor would risibility seem to be as close to the essence of man as rationality—for we can laugh *because* we can rationally perceive incongruities. Thus "rational animal" would seem to be a better definition of man than "animal with a sense of humor" because rationality would

[12] Pp. 62 and 63 above.
[13] Pp. 122–125.

seem to be the differentia and risibility only a property of man. But we could be wrong about this because it is often difficult or impossible to tell whether a given trait is essential or merely a property, and, in many cases, knowing what a thing is like is as good as knowing what it really is. Hence a definition in terms of a thing's properties may be as good as one giving its essence. Still, when our goal is to understand the very essence of a thing, a definition giving that essence is better than one giving a property of the thing, no matter how universal and necessary that property may be. Thus all other things being equal, a definition should be as fundamental or basic as possible; it should present the very essence of the definiendum by citing its true differentia.

   d. *Definitions should not be circular or synonymous.* If we are told that "sorrow" means "That which is experienced by a person in grief," we do not feel greatly enlightened, for "grief" is simply a synonym for "sorrow." Whenever the whole or part of the definition is wholly or partly synonymous with the definiendum, the definition is said to be circular. All those verbal definitions which, in our earlier discussion, we labeled "synonymous" are circular. They can aid us in identifying a concept which is or ought to be analyzed in a conceptual definition by giving us more familiar verbal signs for that concept, but they always return the concept to us unanalyzed.

   Thus circular definitions are not so much poor conceptual definitions as not conceptual definitions at all. How clear an idea of the good life, for example, do we get from the following deliverance found in a student essay? "What then is the good life? To live the intense life, to put one's powers to the best possible use—that is the good life. But what is the best possible use: To improve being, to make the world a better place to live in." For "good" in the definiendum we are given at least three synonyms: "best," "improve," and "better." Not all instances of circularity are so simple. Indeed, it is sometimes extremely difficult to decide whether or not a given definition is circular. Try this one: "Right" (as in "right-handed") means "the direction which is to the east of a person facing north." Is this definition circular or not? This time it is much more difficult to say, but it probably is since any definition of "east" and "north" would probably involve, either directly or indirectly, the relation "to the right of." But we could be wrong here, and that is exactly the point.

   e. *Definitions should not be unnecessarily negative.* Though we tend to believe in these troubled days that "peace" means just "the absence of war," we may still wish to know just what it is that is present when war is absent. Such definitions as this which state what the definiendum is not rather than what it is are called *negative definitions.* Our earlier example of man as "the feather*less* biped" is a partially negative definition.

   Negative definitions, like negative divisions, are in general poor on two counts. In the first place, they do not present any positive analysis of the definiendum, although we can often infer more or less of that positive comprehension. Thus to define "Republican" as "U.S. Citizen who is against the New and Fair Deals" fails to tell us what this U.S. citizen is *for*, although we can infer something of his positive platform indirectly if we know the definitions of "New Deal" and "Fair Deal." In the second place, negative definitions are very likely to be too broad, since there are usually many other things which are like the definiendum in not being thus and so. Many Democrats, for example, were against the New and Fair Deals.

While not forgetting these deficiencies of negative definitions, it is most important to emphasize at the same time the word "unnecessarily" in the above rule. Some concepts must receive a negative definition simply because what they intend is negative. Consider, for instance, the following definition: "Death is the term applied to an injury involving the loss of life of the injured."[14] "Loss" makes the definition negative, but is there any way to make it positive? Probably not, for such alternatives as "cessation of heart beat" also involve negative terms. All such concepts involving negation, privation, absence, or lack (e.g., "darkness," "shadow," "nothing," etc.) must be defined negatively simply because the definiendum is negative in meaning.

f. *Definitions should not contain ambiguities or metaphors.* Since the aim of our procedure for the identification of the concepts signified by words was the recognition and elimination of ambiguity, it should be obvious that ambiguous language has no place in conceptual definition. Ambiguities in definitions are not always so apparent as in the case of the schoolboy's definition of "equator" as "a menagerie lion running round the earth and through Africa";[15] and the context often indicates the intended meaning, as when "semicircle" makes clear the intended meaning of "chord" in the definition of "diameter" as "the chord of a semicircle." But ambiguous definitions do require that the user give, implicitly or explicitly, a verbal definition of the ambiguous term, as when one goes on from the last definition to add: "I mean 'chord' in a mathematical sense." Specially humorous examples occur when the definiendum is made ambiguous by offering as its definition the definition of a word similar in sound or appearance, as when "acrimony" is defined as "another name for marriage" or "sinister" as "unmarried woman."[16] But such cases are usually not troublesome. In general, ambiguous definition is simply a reversion to the state wherein verbal definitions are called for.

Nor should conceptual definitions contain metaphorical or figurative language. It may be enlightening to refer to architecture metaphorically as frozen music, but to say that "architecture" means "frozen music" is to give a poor definition, since architecture is not intrinsically, essentially, or literally either frozen or musical. A more serious instance of metaphorical definition occurs

[14] From *The Bureau of Labor Statistics Bulletin,* #667, reprinted in *The New Yorker.*
[15] From the *Reader's Digest,* section edited by Alexander Abingdon.
[16] *Ibid.*

when societies or institutions are thought of as organisms or machines. Thus the seventeenth-century English philosopher Thomas Hobbes defines the state, "that great Leviathan," as "an artificial man . . . in which the sovereignty is an artificial soul, as giving life and motion to the whole body."[17] The achievement of non-metaphorical definitions of basic concepts is a fundamental aim of all the sciences.

Epigrams are frequent and humorous examples of ostensible definitions which essentially involve ambiguity or metaphor. To say that "an agnostic is a person with no invisible means of support"[18] is humorous as well as enlightening in its analogy, but in imparting exact information it falls far short of the dictionary definition: "agnostic," "one who neither affirms nor denies the existence of a personal deity." (Note also that this definition is one of those which is necessarily negative.) So also Santayana's characterization of "spirit" as "a lyric cry in the midst of business" does more to convey Santayana's materialism and pessimism than to exhibit the structure of that concept. The use of ambiguous and metaphorical definitions, like the use of synonymous ones, is simply a return to the stage prior to the possession of exact verbal definitions, the stage where the required task is the identification of concepts to be defined.

g. *Definitions should not be obscure.* A noted psychologist defines "happiness" as follows: "Neurologically the word happiness indicates the extent to which the innate and acquired components of sensori-motor function approach an optimum relationship between the antagonistic processes of individualization and socialization so that the movements of the individual are contributing directly or indirectly to larger and more complex electron-proton aggregates or larger and more complex social organizations."[19] This may be an excellent definition of happiness from a neurological point of view, but to most of us it is obscure, and perhaps even unintelligible, simply because we are not familiar with the words and concepts used in the definition. The fact that any such definition can be obscure to one person and not to another indicates that obscurity is more a psychological defect than a logical one, a defect in the person rather than in the definition itself. Inasmuch, however, as the definitions embodied in language are intended to communicate as well as to formulate the comprehension of concepts, it is important that definitions be expressed in terms which are as familiar to the reader or listener as possible. When we are presented with an obscure definition we are forced to ask for another definition —of one or more of the words or concepts in the original definition. And unless the next definition is presented with less obscurity than the first one, we may find ourselves involved in a well-nigh endless task.

[17] *The Leviathan,* Introduction, first paragraph.
[18] James B. Reston.
[19] A. P. Weiss, *A Theoretical Basis of Behavior,* R. G. Adams, 1925, p. 127.

There are doubtless other logical corollaries and peripheral desiderata for conceptual definitions, but these are the most important ones. Let us now list them in summary form:

Rules for Conceptual Definitions:

1. The general rule: The definition should consist of the proximate genus and the differentia of the definiendum.
2. Corollary rules:
    a. Definitions should not be too broad.
    b. Definitions should not be too narrow.
    c. Definitions should be essential (fundamental or basic).
    d. Definitions should not be circular or synonymous.
    e. Definitions should not be unnecessarily negative.
    f. Definitions should not contain ambiguities or metaphors.
    g. Definitions should not be obscure.

Summary of the Concept.   We have now completed our investigation of the first logical tool, our tool for discovering the "whats" of things, the concept. That which is grasped by a concept is a nature or essence; in order for us to apprehend a nature freed from all the individuating circumstances which cling to it in reality, our concepts must be universal. As a universal every concept has two dimensions: its comprehension or internal structure and its extension or realm of applicability. Furthermore, every general concept is related to every other by the predicables, and all concepts are ordered on a scale of abstraction from individuals to the ultimate categories. When we try to clarify our concepts the first thing we must do is to identify them by eliminating the ambiguities from the language we use to express them and by formulating verbal definitions. Once we have identified our concepts we may analyze them by exhibiting both their extensions in divisions and classifications and their comprehensions in conceptual definitions. Only thus can we understand clearly and precisely the "what" that we mean. But the "what" is only one part of knowledge, and the concept is only the first logical tool. We must now turn to an examination of the second logical tool: the proposition.

EXERCISES

Evaluate the following definitions (by the rules for conceptual definitions):

1. "Coed" means a woman attending an institution of higher learning. *broad*
2. Darkness is the absence of light. *negative   adequate*
3. "For Nietzsche, 'good' seems to signify the rather vague term 'power.' This 'power' appears to include non-conformity and freedom, but I think Nietzsche had in mind primarily 'the ability to select or create values,' particularly values that will tend to make an individual 'enjoy only what is good for him.'" (student essay)   *circular*

4. "An act is good when it does not insult, harm, or degrade any person or his beliefs, or the welfare of the people." (student essay) *F*

5. An idea is an incipient laryngeal articulation supplemented by certain visceral reverberations. *F* *obscure*

6. "Righteousness—a convenient force to encourage you not to disobey the law." (student essay)

7. "To be is to accept being." (W. E. Hocking) *metaphorical*

8. Evil means the privation of any proper perfection. *mere · neg.*

9. "Subjectivity consists of not looking at a problem objectively, that is, not looking at it from the materialist viewpoint. . . ." (Mao Tse-tung, *On Contradiction*, p. 24)

10. Duration is the continuous progress of the past which gnaws into the future. *metaphorical*

11. "I would define a fact as a statement about an empirical concept whose reality can be proved by experience or reflection on experience." (student essay) *F*

12. An American is a United States citizen who is against communism. *F*

13. "Network: anything reticulated or decussated at equal intervals, with interstices between the intersections." (Samuel Johnson, *Dictionary of the English Language*) *obscure   but actually circular*.

14. Propaganda means any attempt to influence the opinions of others.

15. A cause is the invariable antecedent of any event. *broad*

16. An eclipse is the shadow of the moon upon the earth.

17. An automobile is any vehicle driven by an internal-combustion engine.

18. Nothing means whatever is not something.

19. A fundamentalist is one who believes in the credibility of Scripture and the edibility of Jonah.

20. Learning is the modification of behavior.

21. Conscience is an inner voice that warns us someone is looking.

22. Usury is the summary name for all kinds of extortion.

23. Capitalism is that system of industrial organization which develops large-scale production.

24. "A gentleman is a man whose principal ideas are not connected with his personal needs and his personal success." (W. B. Yeats)

25. Faith is the substance of things hoped for, the evidence of things not seen. (St. Paul)

26. A politician is a man who sits on a fence with his ear on the ground.

Happy Easter

PART II

THE PROPOSITION

CHAPTER 7

PROPOSITIONS AND THE
EXISTENCE OF ESSENCES

7-1 CONCEPTS AND PROPOSITIONS CONTRASTED

Concepts, though indispensable as instruments of knowledge, are scarcely sufficient. As evidence, one need only consider a hypothetical situation like the following. Suppose that an acquaintance were one day to accost you with some such utterance as this: "Green, to the left of, harmful, parallelogram, swimming." Certainly something is definitely wrong with this picture. But what? If the acquaintance were a modern poet, you might imagine that, so far from anything being wrong, actually everything was in order, though in what order you might not be too sure. And if you yourself were a psychiatrist, you might find the utterance exceedingly revealing. But the ordinary listener, as well as a more ordinary speaker, would doubtless set down the utterance as just plain nonsense.

Yet is it just nonsense? After all, each of the words uttered has a meaning. Not only that, but it might be presumed that in being uttered each of the words conveyed a meaning or an idea or a concept to you as listener. Indeed, as we have already seen,[1] a concept is simply a meaning or an intention of a "what" or essence. Nevertheless, the present example would seem to indicate quite clearly that an utterance may still in a sense be meaningless, even though it involves nothing but quite meaningful concepts.

What further instrument of meaning, then, is required over and above concepts? Or, since we have thus far spoken of instruments of knowledge rather than of meaning, the present issue might be stated in this way: Concepts are certainly instruments of knowledge. This much we established in Part I. It is through concepts that we come to apprehend the "whats" of things. Yet to one whose knowledge consisted only in concepts of green, to the left of, harmful, parallelogram, swimming, and what not else—to him something would still be decidedly lacking so far as knowledge is concerned. Specifically, for all his knowledge of "whats" such a person would still not know *whether* anything

[1] See above, p. 33.

was this or that; he would not know *that* it was thus and so, or that it was at all; in fact, he would not even know that these various "whats" were in any sense what things *are* in fact or in truth.

Put very simply, this inadequacy or insufficiency of concepts as regards meaning or knowledge might be summed up in the rather obvious consideration that concepts as such are incapable of being either true or false. Thus the concept of the color green is neither true nor false; nor is the concept of the harmful; nor even the complex concept of a harmful green color. On the other hand, the *proposition* "The color green is harmful" is the sort of thing that by its very nature is susceptible of truth and falsity. For that matter, even such a statement as "The parallelogram is swimming," however foolish it may sound, is still not nonsense in the way in which our originally considered utterance was nonsense. On the contrary, it is a proposition, and as such is presumably false, whereas the mere concepts "parallelogram" and "swimming" and even "swimming parallelogram" cannot even be false, much less true.

Apparently, then, what made the earlier cited "green, to the left of, harmful," etc. seem like nonsense is simply the fact that these concepts were not integrated into propositions. And as mere concepts outside of propositions they were able to tell us neither *whether* any thing is, nor *that* it is, nor even what it *is* in fact and in truth. In short, it is only in and through propositions that such a thing as a *true* knowledge of actual *fact* becomes possible.

7–1.1   The Metaphysical Distinction of Existence from Essence

Suppose it be conceded, then, that in addition to concepts that get at the "whats" or essences of things we also need propositions to get at the "whether" or existence of these same things. Yet even though it be obvious that *knowing* the "what" is not the same as knowing the "whether," is it equally obvious that in *reality* itself the "what" is not the same as the "whether"? Nor must one imagine this to be a merely academic and irrelevant question. For we have already observed[2] how distinctions in the logical instruments of cognition must needs be grounded ultimately in some sort of distinction within the reality that thus lends itself to being cognized. Not only that, but even from the point of view of general common sense one might wonder whether the question "what?" and the question "whether?" are in truth aimed at really distinct and different features of the real world that is presented to us. And if so, what are these distinct features and what is the nature of the distinction between them?

Such questions, though perhaps trivial and innocent in appearance, bring us right smack up against one of the most fundamental metaphysical principles ever to play a role in Western thought—the principle of the distinction between essence and existence. Unhappily, this principle has proved to be a most vexa-

2 See above, pp. 10–12.

tious one in the history of philosophy.[3] But happily for us it is a principle not very difficult to grasp, at least not for beginners! For does it not seem obvious that if our knowledge of the "what" or essence of a thing does not give us any indication of whether that thing actually exists or not, it must be because in the thing itself its existence is somehow other than its essence?

Illustrations of the Distinction.   Test this out in terms of your own familiar everyday experience to see if the principle be not borne out in fact. Here are some random examples. Take a Euclidean triangle. Is it not true that a mere concept of such a thing and a mere recognition of the kind of figure this one is do not as such tell us whether there are any Euclidean triangles actually existing? For suppose that our space were radically non-Euclidean in character. In such a case, there might not be any triangular shapes or figures to be found anywhere. Even so, we would still be able to know what such figures would be like if there should ever be any. In other words, a mere knowledge of a thing's "what" conveys no information at all as to whether such a thing actually exists or not.

Or for another illustration, consider human beings. Now we all know what they are and we also know that they are. Yet is there anything necessary about the existence of human beings? That is to say, is there anything about the very nature or essence of man that would make it necessary for human beings always to have existed and always to continue to exist? Of course not. Whether we believe man to have been created, or to have evolved out of lower forms of life, or both, we certainly recognize that men have not always existed. And as for their continued existence, it need hardly be remarked that, in this age of atomic warfare and suicidal death wishes on an international scale, it is not only conceivable but even disturbingly likely that the day will come when the race of men shall simply be no more.

Now the point of the illustration, as of the preceding one of the triangle, is this: It focuses our attention directly on the fact that there is nothing about the nature or essence of either man or triangle that in any sense necessitates that such things should be. Their essence is not the same as their existence. Nor, in consequence, must a knowledge of what such a thing is—a triangle or a human being—be confused with a knowledge of the fact that it is.

Moreover, what is true of man and of triangle turns out to be equally true of any and everything in the whole range of our experience of the world about us. For there is nothing there but that on inspection its existence turns out to be somehow other than and distinct from its essence. Suppose we take the

[3] Some recent historians of philosophy have insisted that the first thinker to bring this distinction between essence and existence clearly into focus was St. Thomas Aquinas. Indeed, Professor Gilson has maintained that St. Thomas was not merely the first but the only thinker to appreciate the real import of this distinction. Cf. Etienne Gilson, *Being and Some Philosophers*, Pontifical Institute of Mediaeval Philosophy, 1949; *The Christian Philosophy of St. Thomas Aquinas*, Random House, 1956.

atomic and subatomic particles of matter. As is well known, the older physics used to insist that atoms were such as to be neither created nor destroyed. Hence it might be presumed that they always had existed and always would exist. But would not this mean that their existence was indistinguishable from their essence—indeed, that by their very nature atoms were incapable of not existing?

Hardly. Even if it be conceded that atoms always have existed and always will exist, the interesting thing from the point of view of metaphysics is that there is no absolute necessity that there be atoms. Quite the contrary; it is entirely conceivable that the very order of nature itself might have been entirely different from what it is—might have been, in short, an order of nature not involving atoms at all. To be sure, supposing the order of nature to be what the older physicists said it was, its material structure would be atomic and its ultimate atomic particles would be both ingenerable and indestructible. But there is nothing necessary about this; the entire order of nature itself is no more than contingent, it being always conceivable that some other order might have been the one which finally came to prevail. In short, there is nothing about the "what" or essence of any determinate order of nature that necessitates its existence or makes it inconceivable that it might never have been.

Perhaps this last point might be made clearer by referring to our earlier example of the triangle. We might say that, by its very nature or essence, *if* a triangle exists, then the sum of its angles must be equal to two right angles. Yet this by no means implies that any triangle actually does exist. So also we might say that *given* a certain type of natural order, it would perhaps be necessary for its ultimate atomic constituents to be of a nature such that they could be neither created nor destroyed. But note the hypothetical element in the phrase "given a certain type of natural order." There is nothing about the essence or "what" of an order of nature that necessitates its being. True, *if* it should be, then certain necessary consequences would follow; but *that* it should be in the first place is not anything that is necessitated by the mere nature or essence of that order considered as such.

Apparently, then, any and every example that we choose confirms the same truth: The fact of a thing's existence is never comprised within its "what" or essence. Quite the contrary; throughout the whole order of the universe, no matter what the thing in question may be—fish or fowl or good red herring, the color red, the age of the earth, or a relation of equality, substance or accident, matter or spirit, fact or fiction—in every case the *fact that* such a thing is is something quite distinct and different from *what* it is: existence is never the same as essence.

Of course, this does not mean that essence may not be related and even ordered to existence. Indeed, these are precisely the kinds of things essences are: they are *what* comes into being when anything does come to be, and they are *what* exists in so far as there is any existence. In this sense, essences or "whats" may be regarded as so many "possibles" with respect to existence: they are ordered to being as that which is merely able to be to its actual being or as that which exists only potentially to its actual existence. Hence existence may be said to be the crown or perfection of essences and even their goal. At the same time, and for this very reason, existence is other than the essences which are perfected by it. Yes, even in so far as any essence actually is and does exist, it does not do so simply by virtue of itself and in its own right. Its existence always comes to it, so to speak, from the outside and must be caused in it and bestowed upon it by something other than itself. Never is the existence of any finite being simply the same thing as its essence.

Kant's Illustration. This last point was brought out somewhat differently but nonetheless strikingly by the great German philosopher Immanuel Kant.[4] For he raised the question "What precisely is the difference between a hundred real dollars and a hundred merely imaginary dollars?" That there is a difference is, of course, a matter of often painful obviousness to the ordinary college student. And even the multimillionaire financier or big-time government spender, while he might consider the difference rather trifling, would surely have to acknowledge, if pressed, that there was some sort of difference between real money and imaginary. But what is it?

Unfortunately, this latter question is not so easy to answer, at least not for a philosopher, however much the economist may treat it as calling for no more than a mere sleight of hand. Quite apart from economics, the question is in many ways the fundamental one of metaphysics or ontology. Just what is it that essences or possibilities acquire when they are said to come into being or to begin to be or to exist? And just what is it that they lose when they cease to be or to exist?

Now Kant did not venture to answer this question directly. But he did bring out one rather significant feature about it, and that is that in a certain sense the question itself is somehow improper or perhaps even "phony." For no sooner does one ask *what* it is that essences or possibilities take on or acquire when they come to be or to exist than one immediately implies that the existence of things, or the fact that they are, is just like any other "what" or essence. It's as if existence were no more than a mere additional characteristic or attribute which things come to "have" just as soon as they come to be, in much the same manner as they may be said to acquire learning or whiteness or height or heat as soon as they come to be learned or white or tall or hot, etc. In short, existence is treated as if it were just another essence.

Kant put his foot firmly down on all such nonsense. He insisted that existence

<hr>

[4] *Critique of Pure Reason,* translated by Kemp Smith, Macmillan, 1933, Second Part, Second Division, Chap. III, Section 4, "The Impossibility of an Ontological Proof of the Existence of God," esp. B 626–629.

just is not a characteristic or attribute of things—that is, in any way comparable to other characteristics or attributes. For instance, if we be asked what a chiliagon is, we might answer that it is a plane figure, that it is enclosed by right lines, that it has 1000 sides, etc. But suppose we add that the chiliagon actually exists or that there are such things as chiliagons. Is it true that existence is just another characteristic pertaining to the nature or essence of a chiliagon *in the same way* as, say, having 1000 sides pertains to its essence? No, for the question as to whether a certain type or kind of thing exists always presupposes that the kind of thing we are considering already is completely the kind of thing it is—i.e., that it is what it is, or is of such and such a nature or essence. Hence existence could not be a part of a thing's "what" or essence, nor could it be just one among the many characteristics of a thing, because it is precisely concerning a thing with a certain determinate "what" or essence and having *all* the characteristics that essentially pertain to it that we ask whether it exists or not. Existence, in other words, is outside the essence and hence is not one of the characteristics of the "what" at all.

Transposing this metaphysical principle of the distinction of essence and existence to our present logical context, we may say that no matter what it is that we may conceive, and the essence of which we may apprehend, it is still quite possible and conceivable that such a thing not be or exist. Hence, any answer given to the question "what?" still leaves open the question "whether?" Moreover, just as a special logical instrument, viz., the concept, seemed requisite for the apprehension of the essence or the "what," it may be presumed that a different logical instrument is required for intending existence or the "whether."

Summary: Concepts as Intentions of Essences; Propositions as Intentions of Existence.   The discussions of the foregoing sections have left several loose ends dangling which now must needs be gathered and tied together. First we tried to point out that simply as a matter of fact mere concepts alone do not suffice for knowledge, that they have to be integrated into propositions, and that the significant thing about propositions is that they somehow bring concepts to bear upon reality and actual fact in such a way as to become susceptible of truth or falsity. Then we turned our attention away from strictly logical entities, like concepts and propositions, and proceeded to consider a certain basic metaphysical principle that pertains to real things as they actually exist in the world: the principle that the existence of such things is something quite different from their essences, that the fact that something is or exists is quite different from what it is. It was suggested by way of conclusion that, just as concepts are the proper instruments for apprehending the "whats" or essences of things, so also must there be an appropriate instrument for the apprehension of existence; and that latter instrument might be presumed to be the proposition.

Bringing together these two sets of conclusions, we can now understand in the first place why concepts just in themselves do not suffice for knowledge and are even in a sense meaningless. For any knowledge which falls short of being a knowledge of things as they are or as they exist, or at least as they are ordered to the act of being or existing—any such knowledge is not a genuine or complete knowledge. Knowledge must by its very nature be a knowledge of fact and of things as they are, the reason being that save insofar as things are and are real and are ordered to the very act of being they are nothing at all.

In the second place, just as it should now be clear that the concept must be supplemented by the proposition because the latter intends the very act of being or existing, so also we can now understand why the proposition, as that which is susceptible of truth or falsity, is the proper instrument for the intention of existence. For truth means simply conformity to that which is or to things as they are. Hence since the proposition is susceptible of truth or falsity, it is an instrument adapted to the intention of things in their very being and act of existing.

7–1.2 Difficulties with This Contrast

Even though superficially this correlation of concepts with essences and propositions with existence, and likewise this attempt at understanding the proposition as simply an instrument for the intention of existence, may seem at least plausible, there are still a number of difficulties to be straightened out. The first difficulty might be put very bluntly thus: Are not concepts capable of an intention of existence after all? For instance, can we not perfectly well form a concept of existence just as we can of white or human being or parallelogram? Furthermore, are not our concepts often, if not usually, concepts of real things? In Chapter 3 we described how concepts were derived by abstraction from sensory awareness. But in sensory awareness it is actually existing things that are presented to us. Accordingly, many of our concepts must surely be concepts of existent essences.

Answer to the Second Difficulty. In response to these difficulties, we may begin by first admitting that our concepts for the most part are certainly concepts of existing essences. Yet this admission by no means entails the consequence that one might suppose.

Consider a different but nevertheless somewhat analogous case, that of the relation between sensory cognition and rational cognition. Now as we have seen in our earlier discussion of concepts,[5] the so-called natures or essences of things cannot be apprehended through the senses, but only through reason and intelligence. At the same time, this does not preclude the possibility that all knowledge must at least begin in sensation. Not only that, but the very same material object, the formal aspects of which are grasped only by the intellect, may itself be an object that is directly presented to the senses, and with which

[5] Cf. above, pp. 45–48.

we become acquainted only through the senses. The point here is, as one might say somewhat metaphorically, "the senses in such a case bear a message (namely, the intelligible natures or essences) which is only meaningful to, and decipherable by, reason or intelligence."[6]

So analogously in the present instance it might be said that, while in and through concepts we apprehend the "whats" of real existing objects, it is not through the concepts just as such that we are able to recognize the being and existence of these "whats" in fact and in reality. It is only in and through propositions that we achieve the latter type of recognition.

In confirmation of this it might be well to recall our earlier remarks on the real distinction in fact and in being between essence and existence. For even with respect to actually existing things in the world about us—men, trees, charges of electricity, spatial relations, hydrogen atoms, etc.—it is invariably the case that what each of these things is is quite different from the fact that it is. Consequently, in becoming aware of these realities as both being and being what they are, our apprehension of the "what" cannot be simply indistinguishable from our apprehension of the "that." Concepts may suffice for the former; but for a recognition of the fact that something *exists,* or that it *is* what it is really and in truth, a proposition is necessary.

Answer to the First Difficulty.   What of the objection that we can perfectly well form a concept of existence? Yes, we can quite readily conceive of something as actually being or existing. Is not this, then, a decisive point in refutation of the contention that it is only in propositions that we are able to recognize that something in fact is or exists?

Hardly. In the first place, be it noted that the mere idea or concept of existence, like every other concept, is abstract and universal, whereas anything that actually is or exists never exists merely in general or in the abstract. Hence the mere abstract concept of existence is never that through which we recognize the actual being of some concrete particular object.

But no sooner is the point made in this way than the same objection presents itself in a little different form. When it is a question of the actual being or existence of some object—say a certain buckeye tree—is it not entirely possible for us to form a concept of such a tree as actually being or existing, in contrast, say, to the concept of such a tree as nonexistent? Indeed, it would seem that "existing" can be combined with "buckeye tree" to form a complex concept, in precisely the same manner as, for instance, "tall" or "sickly" or "full-grown" or what not. Thus we might form the concept of an existing buckeye tree, just as we might form a concept of a full-grown buckeye tree.

But already the answer to this objection has doubtless suggested itself. For consider the complex concept "a real or existing buckeye tree." Is not this like

---

[6] Professor Gilson employs this metaphor in *Réalisme thomiste et critique de la conaissance,* J. Vrin, Paris, 1939, p. 218.

our earlier examples of the concepts "parallelogram," "swimming," "to the left of," or even "swimming parallelogram"? Certainly none of these latter is susceptible of truth or falsity. But neither is the concept "existing buckeye tree." Indeed, even though we can perfectly well form a concept of a buckeye tree as actually existing, in the sense that we simply think of it as existing, this mere concept by no manner of means tells us that or whether such a tree actually does exist. Accordingly, generalizing this point, we may say that although there is a sense in which one may entertain in mere concepts the idea of an essence as existent (or as nonexistent), for the intention of the fact that such an essence exists really one must use the instrument of the proposition.

7–2 THE TWO MAIN TYPES OF PROPOSITIONS

Thus far in the present chapter we have had much to say about that which is intended in and through propositions, viz., the act of existing. Also we have tried to show at some length just how this act of existing cannot be intended through concepts but requires a proposition as the instrument of its intention. In short, the distinctive function of the proposition is precisely the intention of existence.

What exactly is a proposition? Granted that it has the intentional function that we have attributed to it, what is it? What sort of structure does it have that enables it to perform its characteristic function? By what criteria may we recognize it? As yet we have said nothing in answer to questions of this sort. True, in trying to illustrate how propositions perform an intentional function which mere concepts cannot and do not perform we cited several examples. However, the only really distinguishing features of our examples of propositions would seem to have been that they were complete, declarative sentences, as contrasted with mere words. But this is a grammatical and linguistic distinction and hence presumably not a distinction proper to logic as such.

Even so, the contrast between sentences and words is not wholly irrelevant to an understanding of the contrast between propositions and concepts, and thus to an understanding of the nature of propositions. Items of language like words and sentences are but conventions for the expression and communication of concepts and propositions. In fact, the old-fashioned way of characterizing a sentence is to say that it expresses a complete thought. But what is a complete thought if not a proposition? That is to say, propositions are "thoughts" in which our ideas or concepts of essences and "whats" are actually brought to bear on reality, i.e., are recognized as being what things *are* in fact—thus becoming susceptible of truth or falsity. Accordingly, any declarative sentence, being an expression of a complete thought, is a sign of a proposition and hence can be used to illustrate the peculiar function of propositions as contrasted with mere concepts. At the same time, the structure of the sentence being a purely conventional thing, it quite patently varies from language to language. In contrast, the "complete thought" or proposition which is able to be expressed in all sorts of different ways and different languages will presumably have the same structure in all, a structure determined by the natural exigencies of its peculiar intentional function.

Our immediate concern, then, is to try to determine what this natural structure of the proposition is, in contrast to the purely conventional structures of sentences. No sooner is such a question raised than its answer would already seem to be implied by what we have said thus far. For have we not been at great pains in the immediately foregoing sections to point out how the real world in which we exist and which we seek to know and understand is made up of essences that have actually come to be or exist? And have we not also insisted that essence and existence are altogether different and distinct principles of being—so much so in fact that a mere apprehension of an essence or "what" in no wise indicates whether things of such a sort or essence actually exist or not?

If it be through concepts that essences are intended and through propositions that the existence of essences is intended, the structure and composition of propositions would appear to be strictly determined: On the one hand, any proposition must needs contain concepts signifying the "whats" or essences of things; and on the other hand, it must contain some other element that indicates whether or not these essences actually exist. On this basis the structure of propositions would seem most properly exhibited in examples like the following.

> Hydrogen *exists.*
> There *is* such a thing as the color green.
> God *is.*
> Trees *exist.*
> There *are* members of the Communist party.

Each of these propositions contains a concept of an essence or "what"—hydrogen, the color green, God, trees, members of the Communist party. In addition, each proposition contains what might be called an existence-intending element, which in the English sentence is expressed by some form of the verb "to be" or "to exist." Here is a possible pattern or structure for propositions that on its face at least is quite patently adapted to the performance of the proposition's peculiar kind of intentional function.

Nor is there any doubt that propositions of this type—*existence propositions* as they are called—are perfectly legitimate and common. Nevertheless, they are not the only or even the most common type. In addition we constantly encounter and employ propositions which are adapted not so much to indicating merely that something *is* or exists in fact but rather to indicating that something *is thus and so* or has in fact such and such characteristics. Just as we can formulate propositions of the type "Hydrogen exists" or "There is such a thing as the color green," so also we can employ propositions of the type "Hydrogen is an element" or "The color green is located between blue and yellow in the spectrum."

Notice that in each of these types of proposition there is something that one is considering or concerned to know about—viz., hydrogen or the color green—and also something that one professes to know about it—viz., that it is or exists in the one case, and that it is thus and so (an element or located between blue and yellow in the spectrum) in the other case. That which one is concerned to know about in either type of proposition may be called the *subject* of the proposition, and that which one is concerned to know about it—either that it is or that it is thus and so—may be called the *predicate.* Accordingly, the forms or structures of the two types of proposition may be presented symbolically in the following ways.

In the case of the existence proposition, we may let S stand for the subject which the proposition is about; and since in the case of such propositions the only thing that the predicate of the proposition intends or signifies is merely that the S is or exists, we may represent the predicate simply by a form of the verb "to be" or "to exist." Thus the form or paradigm for existence propositions becomes:

"S is" or "S exists" or "There is, or exists, an S."

In the other type of proposition we are concerned to know not merely that S is or exists but that it is thus and so. That is to say, the predicate in such propositions is supposed to intend not the mere fact that S is but also what the S is really and in fact. Consequently, while we may again let S stand for the subject of the proposition just as before, the representation of the predicate must this time be more complicated. True, since the proposition is designed to intend what S *is*, we would do well to retain the existence word "is" in our formal representation of the proposition's structure. Nevertheless, inasmuch as the predicate intends not the mere fact that S is but also what it is, we might let P stand for this "what." Thus we come out with the following paradigm:

S is P.

Now in contrast to existence propositions, propositions of this latter type have come to be known as *subject-predicate* propositions. Consider the following:

This sheet of paper is white.
Faulting is a fracture in the earth's surface.
The incommensurability of the sides of a square and its diagonal was a source of profound concern to the ancient Pythagoreans.
Human nature is capable of being changed for the better.
Trees are a comparatively late form of planetary life.

Note how in each case there is something one is talking about or concerned to know about, viz., the subject—e.g., this sheet of paper, faulting, the incommensurability of the sides of a square, etc. But also there is something that one is saying about it or that one recognizes it as being, viz., the predicate—e.g., white, a fracture in the earth's surface, etc.

A Note on Terminology. Unhappily, neither the term "existence proposition" nor the term "subject-predicate proposition" is too felicitous. After all, existence propositions, quite as much as subject-predicate propositions, have predicates; and subject-predicate propositions, quite as much as existence propositions, intend existence. Nevertheless, inasmuch as in the so-called existence propositions one is concerned with intending merely the fact that something is, whereas in subject-predicate propositions one intends not merely that something is but also what it is, the expression "subject-predicate proposition" is designed to point up the fact that here one has the further concern of knowing what an existent thing is.

To sum up, then, we may say that logical propositions, which are our human instruments for the intention of existence, may be of either of two main types: (1) existence propositions, in which our concern is with knowing that a certain "what" (essence) is; (2) subject-predicate propositions, in which our concern is with knowing what a certain "that" (existing entity or thing) is. The structure of the former may be represented by "S is," that of the latter by "S is P."

Cognitive Functions of the Two Types of Propositions.[7]　Having established both that there are two main propositional types and what each of these types is, our next business is to try to determine which of the two is the more usual and useful instrument. Of course, each is useful in its own characteristic way; yet it would seem that the occasions of our needing to use S–P propositions are much commoner and more frequent than the occasions on which we need to use existence propositions. In order to see just why, it will be wise for us to try to fix somewhat more precisely the differing cognitive situations with which we are confronted on the occasions when we need to use the one rather than the other type of propositions.

Thus, on the one hand, there is that initial and primary cognitive situation in which every human being finds himself, the situation in which one is presented through one's senses with a world of real existing things. In such a situation the proper cognitive question would seem to be, "What are these?" or "What is this?" That is to say, in such a situation we want to know what the things are that are presented to us as being and existing. Derivatively, and following the doctrine of the categories,[8] we may want to know how large these beings are, or where they are, or what they are doing, or what is happening to them, or in what relation they stand to other beings, etc.

[7] The major portion of this section repeats, with only a few minor changes in wording, an earlier discussion of the same topic by one of the authors. See Veatch, *Intentional Logic*, Yale, 1952, pp. 162 ff.

[8] Above, pp. 34–38.

To every such question the proper answer will have to be formulated in a subject-predicate proposition, i.e., a proposition that tells what a given thing is, or, derivatively, where it is, or how large it is, etc. In other words, in such a context there can be no question of whether a thing is, the fact of its existence being simply given in sense in the first place; rather one's cognitive concern is directed toward trying to understand *what* such a given being is.

On the other hand, the existence of many things is not and sometimes cannot be given to us directly in sense. Accordingly, we may inquire *whether* they are or not; and to such a question the proper answer will quite naturally be in the form of an existence proposition. Moreover, in explanation of how such a cognitive situation arises, we need but point out that, in contrast to the representations of the external senses proper, all other images, as well as all concepts, are representations only of what might be. That is to say, a mere consideration of what is thus intended in such images and concepts does not indicate whether these objects of intention actually exist *in rerum natura* or not.

To consider just concepts for the moment, it is true, as we have seen,[9] that concepts are abstracted from sense experience. Moreover, abstract concepts are nothing but relations of identity to the individuals from which a given nature or essence has been abstracted and in which that nature or essence can alone exist.[10] Nevertheless, once the nature or essence is thus abstracted and in consequence is made to stand in a relation of identity to the items of its extension, it is impossible to tell from the concept alone whether or not such individuals are actually existing here and now or, for that matter, whether or not they ever have existed or ever will exist. As a result, questions as to whether there ever were dinosaurs, or whether there is such a thing as hydrogen, or whether irrational numbers are real, etc., become meaningful questions. And the existence propositions which are the proper answers to them become likewise meaningful: "Dinosaurs did once exist," "There is such a thing as hydrogen," "Irrational numbers do not exist," etc.

In short, the differing intentions of subject-predicate propositions and existence propositions may perhaps be briefly characterized in this way: In subject-predicate propositions one recognizes the existence (in some sense or other) of the object of one's intention as being given, and one goes on to declare *what* this object is; in existence propositions one begins simply with an intention of an essence as signifying possible objects, and one goes on to declare *whether* such possible objects actually are. In the one case, the existent being given, one proceeds to determine what it might possibly be; in the other case, starting from a possible "what," one proceeds to determine whether there is any existent answering to it.

Moreover, with respect to these two types of cognitive situation, one need

[9] See above, pp. 47–48. Cf. also pp. 280–281.
[10] Cf. above, pp. 55–57.

only consult one's own experience to recognize that the former is by far the commoner one, it being both the primary and the more natural situation for a human being to find himself in. After all, human knowledge must certainly begin in experience; it must also continue in experience if it is to grow and advance, it being through experience that we human beings are constantly presented with new facts to be comprehended and understood. The initial, as well as the most commonly recurrent, human cognitive situation would seem to be the one in which our senses confront us with things that are, and the cognitive challenge is one of trying to get to know what these things are that are. Or to express the same thing directly in terms of the structure of a proposition, the more common cognitive challenge would seem to be one in which we are concerned to know regarding a certain given subject, S, just what it is, viz., P.

On the other hand, the existence proposition is adapted for use in the much less common human cognitive situation, the situation in which mere essences are considered just as such and in abstraction from, and even in indifference to, their existence in the real world. The existence proposition becomes relevant when one asks, concerning mere abstractions and mere possibles, *whether* they actually exist or not, or even whether they are able to exist or not.

It must be admitted that in the context of much recent science, and particularly to the extent to which science is dominated and determined by mathematics, the existence proposition has come to play a rather significant role. For it is precisely in the domain of mathematics that the human mind is most given to the consideration of abstract essences and possibles. The modern mathematician can offer to the empirical scientist any number of the most elaborate conceptual schemes and intellectual constructs of varying possible types of order, which he, the scientist, then proceeds to use as hypotheses, testing them and trying them out, in order to see whether this one or that one fits or works. Viewed simply in this light, the scientific procedures of testing and verification may be said to involve primarily the use of existence propositions, i.e., propositions in which one is concerned merely with knowing whether a given essence or conceptual pattern actually exists in the real world or not.

Whatever may be true of the unusual and somewhat esoteric cognitive situation of the modern scientist, or at least physicist, certainly for the human being simply qua human, and with reference to his common human concern to know and understand, the subject-predicate proposition is the more usual propositional instrument. Through its use one comes to know what this is and what that, or what is true of this or true of that. Accordingly, in our subsequent discussion of propositions we can effect a certain economy by confining ourselves almost entirely to an examination of subject-predicate propositions, mentioning existence propositions only incidentally and in so far as their behavior deviates from the standard of the S–P proposition.

CHAPTER 8

PROPOSITIONAL IDENTITY
AND THE PREDICABLES

We have thus far considered briefly both what the function of the proposition is—viz., the intention of existence, or, more accurately, the intention of essences as existing and in their very acts of existing—and what the two main types or varieties of propositions are. It still remains for us to examine in more detail the actual structure and form of these two types of propositions, and particularly of subject-predicate propositions. For as we have seen in the sections immediately preceding, the S–P form of propositions is not a purely chance or arbitrary thing. Rather it is, or at least is supposed to be, wholly adapted to the performance of a distinctive kind of intentional function. Yet reality is intricate and varied, to say nothing of being distressingly elusive. Accordingly, our intention and cognition of it must be correspondingly subtle and adaptable. Is the common subject-predicate form of propositions an adequate instrument of such intention, and if so, how?

8–1 THE NATURE OF PROPOSITIONAL IDENTITY[1]

Identity in Propositions and in Concepts. Faced with these questions, we can do no better than to begin with an examination of the basic structural rela-

[1] For those who are familiar with, or are interested in, modern mathematical or symbolic logic, it might be well to remark that it is precisely with respect to this matter of propositional identity that classical realistic logic, as derived from Aristotle, differs most profoundly from symbolic logic, as developed, say, in the *Principia Mathematica* of Whitehead and Russell. In the latter sort of logic, no regard is paid to the peculiar and distinctive relation of identity that holds between the subject and predicate terms of a proposition; the structure of the proposition is quite differently conceived by the symbolic logicians. Not only that, but many of the criticisms which the symbolic logicians have leveled at traditional logic are quite wide of the mark, largely because this relation of identity has been so thoroughly misunderstood.

This is not to say that Aristotle himself explicitly recognized the relation between subject and predicate as being a relation of identity in just this sense. And even among the logicians of the Middle Ages the distinctive character of this relationship would appear to have been more hinted at than fully developed. For a somewhat more elaborate treatment of the whole issue, cf. Henry Veatch, *Intentional Logic,* Yale, 1952, Chap. V.

tionship in the proposition, the relation of S to P or of P to S. What sort of relation is this? In answer, we might remind ourselves of the answer that was given in Part I to the question "What is a universal concept?"[2] It was found that a concept is simply a relation of identity of an abstracted "what" or essence to its possible individual instances. In addition, it was found that such a relation of identity was a distinctively logical or intentional relation. For one thing it was a mere being of reason or thing of the mind; and for another its whole being and character were such as to be adapted to the intention of something other than itself.

Perhaps analogously then, the S–P relation in a proposition may turn out to be a relation of identity as well. And so it does. For how better can one characterize this relation of S's being P, i.e., of a subject's being what it is, then to call it a relation of identity? It is also easy to see how this relation of identity which constitutes the proposition is, in a certain sense, but the natural fulfillment of that relation of identity which constitutes the universal concept. For as we saw, a universal concept such as "man," for instance, is nothing but the abstracted "what" or essence of its appropriate individuals, standing over against them in a relation of identity. In the real world, however, no essence ever thus exists apart from its individuals; rather it can only exist in them, or perhaps better, "of them," it being the very "what" or essence of these individual existents. Accordingly, the work of the proposition is to overcome, so to speak, this separated or abstracted condition of the essence, which has been brought about by the abstracting intellect, and to reidentify this "what" with one or more of the individuals which actually and in fact are such a "what" or have such an essence. For example:

> Smith is a man.
> All Americans are men.
> These creatures are men.

The proposition may be viewed as reidentifying a "what" or essence with the individuals in which it really exists and from which it has been abstracted by the intellect. On the other hand, and complementing this way of viewing the proposition, a universal concept, because it is an abstracted essence standing over against the items in its extension in a relation of identity, may be viewed as just the kind of thing that lends itself to being predicated of its individuals in a proposition. For this reason a necessary property of any universal concept is this property of being *predicable* of the items in its own extension.

True, being or reality, as that which one seeks to know or understand through this use of propositions, is, as we have already remarked, complex and elusive. One can find examples of propositions which certainly serve to get at some aspect of the real but at the same time do not seem—at least superficially

[2] Above, Chap. 4, esp. section 4.1.

—to involve this sort of simple identification of an abstracted essence with the individuals in which it exists. Such apparent exceptions and deviations from the norm we must consider later. For the present, let us merely say that the original and rudimentary propositional form would seem to be one in which an abstracted essence, P, is reidentified or reintegrated with an existent subject or subjects from which it has been held apart by the abstracting intellect. By such means the mind is able to recognize an individual subject both for *what* it is and for what it *is*.

The Relation of Identity as Both a Being of Reason and an Intention or Formal Sign.   Not only does the proposition resemble the concept in being a relation of identity, but in addition this relation of identity which constitutes the proposition may be seen to resemble that which constitutes the concept in being both a being of reason and an intention or formal sign. That it is only a being of reason may be recognized as soon as one stops to consider that in the real world of nature there is no such thing as a relation of predicate to subject. One may find there relations of cause to effect, of greater to less, of buyer to seller, of copy to original, of place to place, of before and after, but never a relation of predicate to subject. Nor is the reason for this hard to find. For as we have already seen with respect to concepts, no essence ever exists in reality in abstraction from its instances;[3] but so also no essence in reality ever has to undergo an operation of being reidentified with its instances. After all, if in reality it is never separated from its instances, there is no way in which in reality it could ever go through a process of being reidentified with them. In other words, the relation of identity between S and P in a proposition is not a real relation at all, but only a work of reason.

Likewise, the subject-predicate relation is a thoroughly intentional one, its whole character being adapted to the intending or disclosing of something other than itself. Once again, the subject-predicate relation resembles in this respect the intentional relation of identity in the concept. For the relation of identity of an abstracted essence to its instances is wholly adapted to the disclosure or intention of the "whats" of things. And now we may see that the relation of identity which constitutes the proposition carries this intentional function of the concept one step further not just by disclosing the bare "whats" of things but by disclosing them as the "whats" that things actually *are* in fact and in reality.

Consider for a moment the simple fact that in a sense the goal of all our efforts to know and understand—in science, in history, in philosophy, in religion —is simply to arrive at a recognition of what things are really and of what is true of them in fact and in their very being. How else can one ever come to such a recognition of a thing for what it is, save in terms of its abstracted "what," which is then applied to and reidentified with it? But this involves nothing

[3] Above, p. 54.

more nor less than a relation of identity between S and P in a proposition. It is considerations such as these that serve to drive home the fact of the radical and inescapable intentionality of the simple S—P propositional structure.

8–2 THE PREDICABLES

All this may have sounded plausible enough: There is no way human beings can ever come to know what things are save by using an instrument which simply propounds that a given S is what it is, viz., P. Moreover, thus to say that S *is* P is simply to relate S to what it is by a relation of identity. Indeed, were it not for the fact that it is a relation of identity, we could never say that S literally *is* P.

Yet, when we think about it a little, does there not seem to be something rather dubious about this notion of a relation of identity? What does it mean to say that two things are identical? Must it not mean that they are simply the same? And if they are the same, that could only be interpreted as meaning that there really is no difference between them. And if there is no difference between them, the two things that are found to be identical thereby turn out to be not two at all but simply one and the same.

Nor is it hard to see what the import of such considerations must be, so far as the propositional form S is P is concerned. For if it be a genuine relation of identity that holds between S and P, that must mean that P really is no different from S. But if P is not really different from S, then we ought not to use a different symbol. Instead of S is P, our propositional form should be S is S. In other words, the propositional structure turns out to be really no more than a bare, empty tautology.

The same embarrassing conclusion may be reached by approaching the matter from another direction. Everyone is familiar with that basic principle of being, the so-called law of noncontradiction: A thing cannot both be and not be at one and the same time and in one and the same respect; and derivatively, a thing cannot both be this (i.e., have a certain attribute or characteristic) and not be this (not have that characteristic) at one and the same time and in one and the same respect. On the basis of this principle, we all recognize that a thing cannot be other than itself; it cannot be some other thing or something that it is not. A tree can be only a tree, not a porcupine; the book in front of you cannot be the wall behind you; and you yourself can be only yourself, not someone else.

Very well, then, on the basis of the law of noncontradiction, how could one possibly assert that one thing, S, is another thing, P? Indeed, if P be other than S, then there is no way of stating that S is P (i.e., that S is non-S) without contradicting oneself. Apparently, then, a respect for the law of noncontradic-

tion must lead us to the same conclusion in regard to the structure of propositions that we were led to through our earlier analysis of the relation of identity:
The form of a proposition must be S is S, not S is P.

We might put the conclusion in the form of a dilemma: either the proposition
will have the form of a mere tautology or it will be self-contradictory. That is,
in a proposition, either one must confine oneself to asserting no more than
that S is S or one will simply contradict oneself and assert something equivalent
to S is non-S.

This difficulty in regard to propositions is ancient. Indeed, it was the very
one that Antisthenes liked to throw in the face of his fellow Greeks. Thus he
would argue, "How can you say that a cow is white, for a cow is one thing and
whiteness another? Hence to say that a cow is white is equivalent to saying that
a cow is not a cow—a contradiction." Nor did Antisthenes' difficulty die with
him. In various forms and versions it has continued to plague philosophers
and logicians right down to the present day.

Of course, if Antisthenes were right, his argument would have serious implications not just for the theory of the proposition here defended but also for
human knowledge and human communication generally. For certainly if we
are to attain real knowledge we cannot permit ourselves to fall into contradictions. But if we accept the alternative of tautology, we would scarcely seem to
be much better off. Imagine the predicament you would be in if you were constrained to use only propositions of the form S is S. You could not even say,
"This book is dull"; you could only say "This book is this book." It's true, of
course, that occasionally a poet wants to say some such thing as "East is East
and West is West." Or a businessman might want to defend the indefensible by
insisting that business is business. But more usually, we are concerned to know
not whether the East is merely the East, or business is business—we know that
much already—but rather whether the East is resentful of the West, say, or
whether business is in fact independent of moral and ethical restrictions, etc.
In other words, for purposes of any genuine cognition and understanding, we
must be able to make statements of the form S is P, and not mere tautologies
like S is S. Yet how can we do this in the face of arguments like that of
Antisthenes?

This challenge is not easily dealt with. To be sure, it is always possible to
dismiss the whole of Antisthenes' difficulty as merely so much sophistry and let
it go at that. But arbitrary dismissal is not analysis and refutation. Yet if we
are really to get to the root of the trouble, we must be reconciled to pursuing
a long and even roundabout course. For, instead of beginning straight off with
a lot of arguments to show that the relation of S to P is a relation of identity
after all, we must first face up to the fact that S and P are unquestionably different. More specifically, they are different in meaning. Whenever we say that

some subject or other, viz., S, is thus and so, viz., P, the concept S and the concept P just don't mean the same at all.

Test this out for yourself. "My pen is green"—certainly the concept "pen" does not have the same meaning as "green." "Necessity is the mother of invention"—here again, "necessity" certainly does not mean the same as "mother of invention." And the same will be true of any other proposition you choose (except for such as are mere tautologies): "Hydrogen is an element"; "Washington was the first President of the U.S."; "The sum of the angles of a triangle is equal to two right angles."

Our preliminary task, then, before we can hope to show that S and P are related by identity, is to show the various ways in which the meaning of the predicate concept may differ from that of the subject, and vice versa. And this brings us to the ancient, but currently neglected, doctrine of the *predicables*.

8–2.1   Essential Predicable Relationships

Species to Individual.   To introduce yourself to this doctrine, you have but to ask yourself: "If I am going to say what something is or what is true of it, what are some of the different ways in which I may do it?" One way would most certainly be that which is most immediately adapted to that sort of cognitive situation which, as we suggested earlier,[4] would seem to be the original and rudimentary one that propositions are designed to take cognizance of. This is the situation in which a given, existent individual is recognized for what it is essentially. Thus propositions of the following type might be said to intend situations of this sort:

> This is green.
> That is a parallelogram.
> Khrushchev is a human being.

Here we might say that a predicate concept of a "what" or essence is applied directly to an individual having just that essence and being just such a "what." Note, however, that even though in such propositions we are recognizing the very "what" or essential nature of a given individual, still the predicate concept does not have the same meaning as the subject. For instance, "human being" certainly does not mean the same as "Khrushchev." Otherwise, none of the rest of us could be considered human, but only Khrushchev.

Genus to Species.   Now consider a somewhat different situation. This time the predicate will be supposed to signify the "what" not of an individual but of an essence or nature itself. Just as we can ask concerning a given individual, say Khrushchev, what he is, so also we can ask concerning the very nature or essence of that individual what it is. For example, "What is man (or human

---

[4] Above, pp. 110–112.

being)?" or "What is green?" or "What is a parallelogram?" In answer, we come out with propositions such as this:

> Man is an animal.
>   (*or* Men are animals.)
> Green is a color.
> A parallelogram is a plane figure.

Here again, the predicate concept certainly has a different meaning from the subject, even though it is designed to signify the "what" of the subject, i.e., what it is.

Yet for our present purposes the important thing to note is that in the second set of propositions the predicate differs from, and hence is related to, the subject in a rather different way from that which prevails in the case of the first set of propositions. In the first set we were trying to state what certain individuals are essentially; in the second, what certain natures or essences are essentially. Hence in the first set the predicate differed from the subject as a "what" or essence from an individual; in the second, as the "what" of an essence from the essence itself.

Moreover, from our study of concepts[5] we know that the "what" of any essence is always to be understood in terms of a genus and differentia. Nor is there any mistaking the fact that in our second set of propositions "animal" is regarded as being the genus of "man," "color" the genus of "green," and "plane figure" the genus of "parallelogram." Accordingly, we may sum up the whole foregoing discussion by saying that in the second set of propositions the difference and hence the relation of predicate and subject is that of genus to species, whereas in the first set the difference and hence relation is that of species to individual.

Differentia to Species.　Nor need we stop here. For if it is possible for a predicate to differ from and also be related to its subject as genus to species, it would presumably also be possible for a predicate to stand over against its subject as differentia to species. After all, in our discussion of concepts[6] we pointed out how a concept was to be defined through its genus and its difference. That is to say, one indicates the general kind of thing one is dealing with and then seeks to differentiate it from other things of the same kind. But this being so, it is obvious that, just as a genus may be predicated of a subject as its species, so also may a differentia. For instance, using the same subjects as in the examples just preceding, we might this time predicate of them their differentia:

> Man is rational.
> Green is located between blue and red in the spectrum.
> A parallelogram has all four sides parallel.

[5] Above, pp. 83–94.
[6] *Ibid.*

From these explanations and illustrations we might now set forth three main varieties of predicable relationships, i.e., of ways in which predicate concepts may differ from their subjects and yet at the same time express what their subjects are. In the traditional doctrine of the predicables, these three ways are designated simply as follows:

1. Genus—the P is related to the S as its genus.
2. Differentia—the P is related to the S as its differentia.
3. Species—the P is related to the S as its species.

8–2.2 Accidental Predicable Relationships

Now we must turn our attention to a very different type of predicable relationship. Contrast the two following propositions.

> Human beings are animals.
> Human beings are some of them bald.

In the former proposition the predicable relationship is simply that of a genus to its subject. But what about the latter? If you study it a little, you will see that a markedly different type of predicable relationship is involved. For one thing, in the second example the predicate would scarcely seem to express the "what" of the subject. At least it does not express it in the same sense as does the predicate in the other proposition. If one were to ask, "What is a human being?" one would hardly suppose that the answer "A human being is bald" would be altogether apt. To be sure, being bald is what certain human beings are cursed with perhaps, but it is hardly what they are. Or at least, it is not what they are in the sense in which their being animals is what they are, i.e., in the sense of pertaining to their very "what" or essence.

This last remark provides a key to the whole problem. For we must simply recognize that, while some predicates express the essence of the subject, other predicates do not state what the subject is essentially but only what it is extrinsically and by accident, so to speak. To revert to our examples, while it is perfectly, even if unhappily, true that some men *are* bald, still the quality of being bald is not of the essence of human nature. Indeed, there is nothing about human nature as such that necessitates a man's being bald; otherwise all would be bald instead of just the unhappy chosen few. On the other hand, being of the animal kingdom certainly is of the essence of man—at least if the recognized views of contemporary naturalists are correct. Similarly, that man should be rational is certainly a part of his very nature, for what is it that is distinctive of human nature and differentiates human beings from other members of the animal kingdom if not intelligence or rationality? And as for the proposition that Khrushchev is a human being, this is designed to state what Khrushchev is essentially. His nature or essence is that of human being, as contrasted with that of a dog, a tadpole, a blade of grass, a stream of water, or what not.

In other words, just as we use some predicates in order to signify what the subject is essentially, so we use others to signify what the subject is accidentally or extrinsically. Should one say, "Green is my favorite color," it is certainly not to be understood that the mere fact that green happens to be favored by a particular individual is of the very essence of green. Quite the contrary; green would still be green regardless of whether that particular person favored it or not. On the other hand, we could hardly say that green would still be green even if it ceased to be a color, or if it ceased to be located at such and such a place in the spectrum. No, for being a color, or being located where it is in the spectrum, expresses the very essence of green itself, so that without it green would not be green—it would not be what it is.

The Contrast Between Contingent and Necessary Accidents.[7]   Very well, supposing that it be admitted that, in addition to those predicable relationships in which the very essence of the subject is expressed, there are others expressing what is but accidental to the subject and comes to pertain to it only extrinsically and, so to speak, from the outside—supposing this to be correct, still we must make a further distinction between two main varieties of predicable accidents. For sometimes in coming to recognize what a subject is accidentally, we find that some of the accidents, even though they do not tell us what the essence itself is, do nevertheless signify features and characteristics

---

[7] The word "accident" here may no doubt cause not a little perplexity and confusion. For this same word, which is here being used to characterize one of the ways in which a predicate may be related to its subject, was earlier used, in connection with concepts (see above, pp. 35–38), to characterize all of the several categories other than that of substance. Needless to say, the meaning in the two cases is quite different. But unfortunately this ambiguous terminology has become so fixed in logical tradition that we felt it unwise to change it.

However, even though the term "accident" is an ambiguous one, it is not hard to recognize a connection in meaning between the use of the word in the context of concepts and its use in connection with propositions. Thus, so far as the categories are concerned, "accident" signifies such things as are not substances but rather "fall to" or inhere in substances—things like quantities, qualities, activities, etc. But somewhat similarly, so far as predicable relationships are concerned, that relationship is called "accidental" in which the predicate signifies not what is of the essence of the subject but rather what "falls to" the subject, as it were extrinsically and from the outside.

Of course, the main difference between the two uses is that a "category-accident," if we may call it such, is a certain kind of real being which stands in a real relationship to a substance; a "predicable accident" involves only a relation of reason or a purely logical relation of predicate to subject. There is a further and derivative difference, in that category-accidents can only "fall to" or be accidents of substances. On the other hand, since a subject term in a proposition does not have to signify a substance necessarily, but can signify a being in any category whatever, it is quite possible that a predicate term may be accidentally predicated of a subject, in the sense that what it signifies is outside the essence of the subject and hence accidental to it, even though the subject term does not stand for a substance at all.

that are necessarily connected with the essence and hence inseparable from it. On the other hand, other accidental predicates signify characteristics of the subject which merely come and go, and which in this sense might be said merely to happen to the subject. They have no necessary connection with the subject or with what it is essentially. As examples of the latter type of accident —the so-called separable or contingent accidents—we have but to recall the illustrations we have already used: "Green is my favorite color" or "Some men are bald." In each of these propositions, what the predicate signifies has no necessary connection with the essence of the subject. Thus that certain men are bald is in no wise necessitated by the mere fact that they are men—else we should all be bald. True, there are reasons why these particular unfortunates are so afflicted; yet the point is that it is not their human nature alone and as such which is responsible.

But consider the following proposition: "Men are morally responsible." Here we may suppose that we have a proposition intended to express the relation of a necessary accident to its subject. That is to say, the presupposition of the proposition is that there is something about human nature, something about the essence of man as a rational and intelligent creature, let us say, that makes him morally responsible. True, we do not believe that moral responsibility is the very essence of man; and yet it follows from that essence and is necessarily determined by it, in such a way that the predicate "morally responsible," even though it be not essential, is still related to its subject as a necessary accident.

Take a somewhat more old-fashioned example, but one which will do quite well for purposes of rough-and-ready illustration: "A triangle is such that the sum of its angles is equal to two right angles." Certainly, the predicate here is necessary to the subject in the sense that you could not possibly have a Euclidean triangle without this characteristic. At the same time, the predicate could hardly be said to represent the nature or essence of triangularity itself. Rather, it is *because* a triangle is the kind of figure it is, viz., a three-sided figure, or because it has the nature or essence that it does have, that the property of having the sum of its angles equal to two right angles comes to pertain to it. In other words, the predicate term in the above proposition, though not expressive of the essence itself of the subject, nevertheless is expressive of what is necessarily associated with that essence and derivative from it. Hence we say that such a predicate is related to its subject as a necessary accident.

Difficulties with the Notion of Property or Necessary Accident. Unhappily, it must be admitted that there are many features of this predicable relationship of necessary accident (or "property," as it is often called—i.e., the *proprium* of the subject or that which is proper to it or appropriate to it) that superficially at least would seem to reflect most unfavorably upon its usefulness. For one thing, it is often urged that there is no way of distinguishing in specific concrete cases between necessary accidents and differentiae. Thus if such accidents are held to be necessarily connected with their subjects, in the sense that they are proper and peculiar to them, then why may they not serve perfectly well to differentiate the essential natures of their subjects from those of all others? For instance, to take the case of that property which triangles have of the sum of their angles being equal to two right angles, obviously this is a characteristic which pertains necessarily to *all* triangles and *only* to triangles. Hence why may it not serve just as well to differentiate triangles from other figures as does the alleged differentia of three-sidedness?

For that matter, a modern mathematician might well say that he could quite easily define a Euclidean triangle as a rectilinear plane figure having the sum of its angles equal to two right angles, and then from this he could show that three-sidedness would be necessarily derivative and deducible. He would say that there would be just as much warrant for doing it this way as for our suggestion that three-sidedness be regarded as the differentia, and the sum of the angles being equal to two rights as the property. The one is no more original, and the other derivative, than the other way around. Nor would the one seem to be any more "essential" than the other. It all seems to be but a matter of arbitrary choice or convention.

Moreover, so far as the things of the physical world are concerned, most modern scientists would doubtless say that any such thing as a distinction between differentia and property, or between what is of the very essence of the thing and what is only a necessary accident, is quite irrelevant and useless for purposes of scientific knowledge. Consider the proposition "Silver melts at $960.5°$ C." What possible difference does it make whether we consider the predicable relationship here to be one of differentia to subject or of property to subject? And even if we could show that such a distinction did make some sort of difference, how could we determine in this particular instance whether the predicate "melting at $960.5°$" was a differentia or a property?

These are some of the objections and difficulties that have been raised with respect to the notion of property or necessary accident as one of the predicables. In reply, we shall point out that, so far as the modern natural sciences and also mathematics are concerned, there are perfectly good reasons why the predicable relationship of property should seem irrelevant and unnecessary within the context of these disciplines. For one thing, it may be presumed that so far as the things of the physical world are concerned we have not yet succeeded in gaining too clear an understanding of their essential natures. Hence it is little wonder, and even altogether legitimate, that in such a context we should rely entirely on the properties of things in order to distinguish one kind of thing from another. Thus one chemical element may be distinguished from another in terms of their respective atomic weights. True, we may not know what there is about the respective essences of these elements that determines them to have the weights they do have. Yet in a sense it isn't too important to the chemist perhaps to know this, since for all practical purposes he can differentiate the elements quite well in terms of their differences in weight.

As for mathematics, the tendency in modern mathematics has been—whether justified or not we do not presume to say—to regard the objects of mathematics as not in any sense real natures and essences but only arbitrary and conventional constructions. Accordingly, if the things one is dealing with be mere mental or intellectual constructions, then obviously it makes no difference whether one construct them according to one order of essential and accidental (i.e., necessary accident), or its reverse. It is simply a matter of decision and convention.

Nevertheless, whatever may be true of the particular contexts of mathematics and the natural sciences, certainly in the broader context of human knowledge generally, the predicable relationship of property to subject, as distinguished from that of differentia to subject, is most important. To put it very simply and perhaps even naïvely, the human intellect naturally seeks to understand the *ways* of things in terms of the "whats" or essences of things. Thus to go back to our earlier example, why is it that silver melts at the temperature at which it does? Surely this must be because of something about the very nature of silver. Or why is it that human beings exhibit such traits as moral responsibility, aptitude for religious worship, capacity for making and constructing artifacts of the most ingenious and varied kinds? Surely it must be because human beings are the kind of beings they are—i.e., it must be because of their peculiar essence or nature as men that they exhibit these traits and capabilities.

This tendency to explain the way of things through their "whats," their properties through their natures and essences, may lead to abuses and trivialities in the matter of knowledge. In fact, we are only too familiar with examples of this sort of thing. Why does opium tend to make men drowsy? Because of its soporific nature. Why do bodies exert a gravitational pull on one another? Because it is their nature to do so. Why do certain types of plover fly every year from Alaska to Hawaii? Because they are determined to do so by their very natures. Why are gases such that under certain conditions their pressure and volume vary inversely? Because it is of the nature of a gas to behave this way. And so on.

In other words, the notion of the dependence of traits and characteristics upon an essential nature may well serve the interests of laziness and triviality in matters of knowledge. Instead of trying to understand how in detail a given mode of behavior is determined by an essence, we merely say it is so determined and let it go at that. Or instead of investigating to see if external causes and influences may not be operating to produce certain characteristics in an object, we just sit back and say that surely they must be caused by the thing's nature.

Nevertheless, the fact that an instrument may be abused or misused by its users is not necessarily a reflection upon the instrument itself. It is the same with instruments of knowledge, and particularly with that instrument which we have called the predicable relationship of property or necessary accident. As we shall see later when we come to the chapter on argument, the uses of proof and demonstration and the advancement of knowledge through such demonstration simply cannot be understood save through a distinction between what is of the essence of a thing and what follows from it as a necessary accident. But of this, more later.[8] For the present, let us merely rest content with the common-sense recognition that the peculiar traits of a thing, the ways it behaves, and the ways it acts and reacts to stimuli—all these are somehow distinguishable from what the thing is just in itself and in its essence. In consequence, in our attempts to come to know what is true of a thing, we find that we have to distinguish between what is true of it essentially and what is true of it accidentally, albeit through a necessary accident.

EXERCISES

Identify the predicable (genus, differentia, species, property, or accident) to which the predicate in each of the following propositions belongs:

1. Automobiles are vehicles of transportation.
2. Acids turn litmus paper red.
3. Tired people are sometimes inefficient.
4. Mammals suckle their young.
5. Mammals have either hair or warm blood.
6. John is a man.
7. Houses are buildings.
8. Dinosaurs are extinct.
9. Human beings are naturally rational.
10. The party in power is usually reëlected in good times.
11. Dresses are worn by women and girls.
12. Music is a form of art.
13. Stalin was a Russian.
14. Human beings have a sense of humor.

[8] See below, pp. 226–232.

CHAPTER 9

PROPOSITIONS AND THE
DESIGNATION OF EXISTENTS

Summary of the Problem and Its Proposed Solution. In attempting to achieve a recognition of what things are in fact and in being, we proceed in terms of any one of five quite different sorts of "what." Thus, we may come to recognize what a thing is specifically, or what it is generically, or what it is as differentiated from others; or we may recognize what the thing is accidentally, and accidentally with respect either to a necessary or to a contingent accident. To put the same point a little differently, no matter what we wish to predicate of a given subject, that predicate (as expressive of what the subject is) will be related to its subject either as its species or as its genus or as its differentia or as its property or as a contingent accident of the subject. These are the five basic types of predicables or predicable relationships of predicates to subjects.

9-1 THE PROBLEM OF PROPOSITIONAL IDENTITY:
TAUTOLOGY OR CONTRADICTION?

Even with this much established, our old problem still remains—the very problem, indeed, which originally precipitated our discussion on the predicables. For how can we possibly say that S *is* P, when P necessarily has a different meaning from S? Indeed the foregoing doctrine of the predicables has accentuated the problem rather than solved it. For the doctrine merely serves to specify the precise ways in which the meaning of the predicate concept may differ from that of the subject. It may differ as the concept of a genus from the concept of that whose genus it is, or as the concept of a species from that of which it is the species, or as the concept of a differentia from the notion of what it differentiates, or as the concept of an accident from that of which it is the accident.

The problem is: granted that S and P thus differ in meaning, how can we possibly say that S is P? For to say that one thing is another seems to betoken some sort of relation of identity. Yet if the two concepts differ in meaning, to relate them by a relation of identity would seem to avoid such contradiction by eliminating these differences in meaning; we would seem to be left with nothing but the bare tautology S is S.[1]

We propose to meet this problem by maintaining both that P is related to S by a relation of identity, and also that P must differ in meaning from S in one or the other of the five ways. But how can we do so without falling afoul of the law of noncontradiction? This is possible only if one take into account not just what the S and P terms mean or *signify*, but also what they *designate*.[2] That is to say, although S and P have different meanings, they are nevertheless so used in a proposition as to designate one and the same thing or things.

Thus suppose one were to say, "The team played badly." Obviously, the concept "team" does not have the same meaning as that of "playing badly"; yet the very same thing that the concept "team" is here used to designate is also that which one designates as having played badly. Or suppose the proposition is "Some human beings are tubercular." Again, the meanings of the S and of the P terms are patently different. Yet the same individuals that one here designates by the concept "human being" one also designates by the concept "tubercular."

In other words, we solve our problem by continuing to insist that the relation of P to S is a relation of identity, but not an identity of meaning. Rather it is an identity in the sense that—to use our second example in illustration—the very same things that are designated by the subject term "human beings" are also designated by the predicate term "tubercular." And so also for any other S–P proposition.

How, you may ask, is this identity in *designatum* or designata—i.e., what is designated by the subject and the predicate terms—to be reconciled with the admitted diversity in *signata*—i.e., what is meant or signified by the subject term on the one hand and the predicate term on the other? The answer is that the nature of the predicable relationships themselves makes this clear, as soon

---

[1] Cf. above, pp. 116–118.

[2] The use of the words "designate" and "designation" as technical terms demands not merely explanation but perhaps even apology. For although they frequently occur in contemporary discussions of logic and semantics, we know of no instance where they are used in the particular sense that is given to them here. That sense is roughly the same as that of the technical term *suppositio*, as it is used, say, in a writer like John of St. Thomas. (Cf. John of St. Thomas, *Outlines of Formal Logic,* trans. by F. C. Wade, Marquette University Press, 1955, pp. 60 ff. For contemporary discussions, see Jacques Maritain, *Introduction to Logic,* Sheed and Ward, 1937, pp. 59–72; and Henry Veatch, *Intentional Logic,* Yale, 1952, pp. 193 ff.) For obvious reasons, one could not use the English word "supposition" to convey this meaning. Besides, what was needed was English words which could be conveniently paired in contrast with "signify" and "signification." Hence the terms "designate" and "designation." Nor do we feel that the technical meaning we are here bestowing on these latter words is either incompatible with or even alien to the meaning these words have in ordinary English.

For a contemporary effort to point up a somewhat similar, though by no means entirely similar, distinction, students might consider W. V. Quine's use of the words "meaning" and "reference" in his *From a Logical Point of View,* Harvard, 1953, *passim.*

as one reflects upon them a bit. Thus that same thing which has a certain specific nature will also have the generic and differentiating notes that go with that species. Or again, in the case of the accidental predicable relationships— e.g., "Some men are bald"—the same individuals that are here designated by the concept "men" are the very ones that are said to be afflicted with the accident of baldness. And so on.

9–2   DESIGNATION AND THE RELATION OF WHOLE AND PART

Apparently, then, save for mere tautologies, any affirmative proposition is obliged to honor a dual requirement: its subject and predicate terms must differ in meaning or signification but must have the same identical designation. As a further illustration of how this dual requirement operates, we may perhaps approach the whole matter from a somewhat different angle. Consider the following pairs of examples with a view to determining just what is wrong with the second member of each pair.

Some men are tubercular.
Some men are tuberculosis.

Stalin was a human being.
Stalin was human nature.

Human beings are animals.
Human beings are animality.

My pen is green.
My pen is greenness.

In each of these pairs of propositions the same situation repeats itself: in the first member of each pair the predicate is a so-called concrete term; in the second, an abstract term. Very well; why in the examples given is a concrete term required in the predicate? Why will not an abstract term do?

To answer this question, it will be necessary to remind outselves of a more or less common-sense difference between concrete and abstract terms. Briefly and figuratively, one might say that concrete terms are always double-barreled, whereas abstract terms are single-barreled. Thus the term "tubercular," for instance, signifies or conveys not just the notion of a certain disease, viz., tuberculosis, but in addition it connotes[3] or consignifies the notion of things or

---

[3] This use of the word "connote" differs alike from the modern use, as popularized by Mill, and from the more traditional use as it appears, for example, in the distinction between so-called absolute and connotative terms. For a discussion of all these different uses, see Veatch, *op. cit.*, p. 168 and note 8, pp. 413–414.

beings which have the disease. On the other hand, the abstract term "tuberculosis" signifies the disease alone and connotes nothing additional.

Or we might make the point in this way. Stalin, for instance, while he might have been said to *have* human nature, could hardly have been said to *be* human nature. The reason we could not say that Stalin was human nature is that he was so much more than that. He was dark-haired, inscrutable, ruthless, a reinterpreter of Marx, etc. But human nature as such does not entail any such characteristics. Being human certainly does not mean being dark-haired, to say nothing of being a reinterpreter of Marx. In other words, human nature is only a part of any individual human being. To be sure, it is the *essential* part, but still it is a part, simply because the individual human being is more than just the human essence itself. Accordingly, one cannot say that an individual human being is human nature. Rather one must say that he has human nature as a part of his total make-up.

In the light of these considerations, we might lay down the principle that in predication, one can never predicate a mere part of a whole but rather must always predicate a whole of a whole. That is to say, one cannot say that a whole simply is its part. It can only be itself, viz., that same whole. Indeed, to pass from logical wholes and parts to the sort of whole-part complexes one finds in the real world, the same principle is certainly borne out. A human being (i.e., a whole) never is just its head (a part); an automobile is not its wheel, nor a plant its flower. In other words, wholes must always be predicated of wholes, never parts of wholes.

This may be seen to explain why in the examples we cited the predicate terms needed to be concrete terms and could not be abstract. The reason is that a concrete term, while signifying a certain attribute or characteristic (i.e., a part), also connotes or consignifies the whole of which it is a part. Accordingly, in predicating a concrete term of the subject, one is properly predicating a whole of a whole.

But how, you will ask, does all this bear upon the twofold requirement which we mentioned for propositions, the requirement of diversity of signification and identity of designation? The answer is that in a proposition such as "My pen is green" the subject concept "pen" means or signifies something quite different from the concept "green." At the same time "pen," in addition to signifying "penness," i.e., the nature or character of being a pen, also consignifies or connotes a whole of which a nature or characteristic is a part. The same goes for the concrete concept "green." Accordingly, because each of these terms connotes a whole, it is possible to use them in a proposition in such a way that the whole connoted by "green" may be employed so as to designate exactly the same whole that is connoted by "pen." In other words, the very same thing or whole that is my pen is here taken to be identical with that thing or whole that is said to be green.

9–3   DESIGNATION AND PROPOSITIONAL CONTEXT[4]

Thus the supposed dilemma of either tautology or contradiction is solved by distinguishing between two kinds of identity: identity of signification and identity of designation. No genuine proposition is an identity of signification. Even in definitional propositions such as "A triangle is a three-sided plane figure" where the subject and the predicate both refer to the same nature or essence the meanings of the two concepts are not exactly the same, for the first intends that essence simply and in unanalyzed form while the second intends it through its complex structure. Only bare tautologies such as "A rose is a rose" are relations of identity of signification; and while one is free to call them "propositions" if one wishes, they do not seem to add anything to what the concept "rose" expresses by itself. But every affirmative proposition does involve an identity of designation, and every negative proposition functions precisely to deny such an identity. In addition to their significance, the two concepts in a proposition come to designate something, and to designate the same something.

To see more clearly what happens to a concept or term when it enters into a proposition, let us consider the concept "man." Taken just by itself it obviously signifies something, namely, human nature; or more accurately it signifies primarily this nature and secondarily the things which might possess this nature. In other words the concept "man," considered just in itself, has both comprehension and extension. Yet there is something which such a concept, considered alone, does not have. It does not have any actual reference to existence. From the concept alone we do not learn anything about the existence of what is signified.

It is different with the proposition. Indeed, the proposition's very function is to exhibit the concept's relevance to existence. Accordingly, no sooner do we form a proposition involving, for instance, the concept of "man" than we immediately think of that concept as applying to something which is in some sense or other real: "Man has the power of conceptual thought," "A man was seen entering the drug store," "Man is a universal concept." In each of these cases we think of something that exists in some fashion or other, and it is to this existent something that we apply the concept "man," together with everything that concept signifies. To be sure, this something may be quite different in the different propositions in which the concept "man" is employed. In the proposition "Man is a universal concept," for instance, the existent something to which the concept "man" is applied is different from what it is in a proposition such as "A man was seen entering the drug store." Yet however different these things may be to which the same concept is applied in different propositions, the important fact is that there is always something in some sense real which

[4] For a somewhat fuller treatment of designation see *ibid.*, pp. 193–213.

a concept is thought of as being applicable to as soon as it enters a proposition. Now this existent something to which a concept in a proposition is applied is what we have called its *designatum,* and this additional reference which a term takes on in a proposition is its *designation.* Accordingly we are now in a position to give a more concise definition of designation: *Designation is the reference of a term within a proposition to something somehow existent.* And it is the designations, not the significations—the designata, not the significata—of the subject and predicate which are identical in propositions.

We have just seen that a concept with one and the same signification (comprehension and extension) can have very different designations according as it is used in different propositions. What determines which existent or existents a given concept designates in a proposition? What determines the differences in the designata of one and the same concept, "man," in our three examples: "Man has the power of conceptual thought," "A man was seen entering the drug store," and "Man is a universal concept"? Since the concept "man" remains the same in all three cases, it must be the other elements in the propositions. And this is correct. The designation of any term is determined by the proposition of which it is a member, and, more specifically, *by the three main elements which constitute the proposition: that concept itself, the other concept (the subject or predicate), and the verb.* Thus the designation of any term is entirely a function of the total propositional context.

In our first example, "Man has the power of conceptual thought," the predicate term, "has the power of conceptual thought," is the differentia of and essential to the subject concept, "man." Hence the concept "man" is used in this proposition to designate all of the items in its extension, all possible men. In our second example, "A man was seen entering the drug store," the subject, the verb, and the predicate all converge to force the concept "man" to designate a particular, actual individual in the past. And in our third example, "Man is a universal concept," the predicate term requires that the subject, "man," be restricted in its designation to a being of reason, to human nature considered merely as abstracted from all its individual instances and held before the mind.

9–4   DESIGNATION AND THE VARIOUS MODES OF EXISTENCE

Thus the designation of terms is determined by the propositional context. But this is true only proximately, for the structure and function of the proposition itself, as a pure intention or formal sign, is determined by reality itself as the object of our propositional intentions. Hence in the last analysis the designation of terms is determined by the nature of reality. Now reality is extremely intricate, varied, and manifold; consequently our propositional intentions of it must likewise be of manifold kinds and varieties. More specifically, since the designation by terms in propositions is ultimately determined by the existence designated, there must clearly be, at least ideally or for complete knowledge, as many different kinds of designation as there are different existents and kinds of existence to be designated. A complete enumeration of all the kinds of designation is patently impossible, for it would require a complete knowledge of all the nooks and crannies of existence. But it is possible to list and briefly describe the main modes of existence and designation which are found, at least after analysis, in our common human experience. Let us consider some of the principal modes of existence and the corresponding types of designation, with our primary motive in so doing being to get a picture of the richness of the propositional instruments available to us.

Designation as Either Real or Mental. Compare the following propositions: "Man is a natural being," and "Centaurs are popular in Greek mythology." It takes but an instant's reflection to see that the term "man" in the first proposition designates something real, while the term "centaurs" in the second proposition designates a mere fiction, things which can only exist as an object of thought or imagination—beings of reason. Perhaps the most basic division we ordinarily make within the totality of being or "what there is" is, as we have seen,[5] the distinction between what is real, or at least was or can be real, and what is merely mental, what can never exist in the real world independently of someone's thoughts and feelings. Terms referring to real beings may be said to have real designation, while those referring to merely mental beings may be said to have mental designation.

Designation as Either Inclusive or Exclusive. Terms signifying natures which could exist in the real world may be used in propositions in such a way as either to include or to exclude real existence. Consider these two propositions containing the same subject concept: "Man is a rational animal," "Man is a universal concept." Now the concept "man" signifies a nature which is capable of existing in the real world. And in the first of these two propositions the verb and the predicate are such as to make the term "man" include precisely this kind of existence in its designation. But in the second proposition this is clearly not the case. There the predicate term, "universal concept," forces the subject term, "man," to exclude from its designation all of the really existing individuals which are a part of its extension. When a term whose extension includes real existents is used in a proposition to include those real existents in its reference, it may be said to have *inclusive* designation. But when such a term is used in a proposition to exclude from its propositional reference the real existents within its extension, it may be said to have *exclusive* designation.[6]

---

[5] Pp. 24–28.

[6] A term may also be forced to designate a mere word as in "Man is a three-letter word." This might be called verbal designation, but "man" is here actually a different term with a different meaning: "(the word) 'man'"; and such cases are therefore better considered as equivocations.

The reason for this possibility of one and the same concept's either designating or not designating the real things denoted by it is the fact, which we have already several times noted, that a nature or essence is able to exist not only in real individual things but also as abstracted from those individuals and held before the mind. When a given proposition focuses our attention only upon that abstracted essence, it thereby excludes reference to the real individuals possessing that essence; and the concept signifying that nature then has exclusive designation. But when a proposition focuses our minds on the individuals possessing that nature as well as upon that nature itself, it includes those individuals within its reference, and the relevant term is then said to have inclusive designation. Of course concepts such as "centaur," "proposition," and "argument," whose very significance is restricted to beings of reason, can never have inclusive designation in any proposition. And since they do not signify any real beings which could be excluded from their designation, we call their designation "mental" rather than "exclusive."

Inclusive Designation as Universal or Particular. Since a term with inclusive designation may designate any number of the items in its extension, and may designate them in various ways, there are accordingly several varieties of inclusive designation. In the proposition "All men are mortal," for example, the term "men" is used to designate all the items in its extension—all actual, possible, past, present, and future men. In such a case as this the term in question is said to have *universal* designation. But in a proposition like "Some men are bald" the term "men" designates some particular items in its extension and is said, accordingly, to have *particular* designation. True, it just could be the case that all men are bald; some men's being bald does not, as we shall see, rule out the possibility that all men are bald. Still, the proposition that some men are bald does not itself tell us whether or not all men are bald, so "men" here has only particular designation.

Universal Designation as General or Singular. Compare the proposition "All men are mortal" with the proposition "Socrates was mortal." Notice that "men" is a common or general name, referring to many individuals, while "Socrates" is a proper name referring to only one individual.[7] Yet in both cases the subject term refers to all of the items in its extension; "men" in the first proposition refers to all men, and "Socrates" in the second proposition refers to all of the only item which is present in its extension. A proper name, when it is truly proper or appropriate, signifies only one individual; hence, when used in propositions, it can designate only one individual. Yet it designates *all* of that

---

[7] Of course, there may be a number of individuals with the same proper name, but we can always further specify any such proper name so as to limit its application to only one individual—for example, "Socrates the Athenian philosopher who died in 399 B.C." The point is that when a proper name refers to more than one individual, it is no longer proper, but simply ambiguous.

one individual which it signifies. It designates the whole of its extension, and consequently it has universal designation. If you have difficulty in remembering that singular terms or proper names have universal designation, just remember to ask yourself: "Am I here talking about all or only some of this individual (e.g., Socrates)?"

Thus there are two kinds of universal designation: *general* or common universal designation, where the term in question is a general or common one and is used to refer to all of the items in its extension, and *singular* universal designation, where the term in question designates only a single individual, but nevertheless the entire extension of that term.

Nor are proper names the only kind of term having singular universal designation; the same is true of singular descriptions such as "*That tree* is deciduous." Here also the term in question designates only one individual, but that one individual constitutes the whole of the extension of the complex concept "that tree." That singular descriptions behave logically in the very same way as proper names can be easily seen from the fact that it is always possible to substitute one for the other. Thus instead of saying that "Socrates was mortal" we could say that "The philosopher who married Xantippe and who was Plato's primary inspiration was mortal." Or instead of saying, "George Washington chopped down a cherry tree," we may just as well say that "The boy who later became the first President of the United States chopped down a cherry tree." There are, as we shall see in more detail shortly, a number of words in the English language which we commonly use to indicate singular descriptions— words like "that," "those," "this," "these," "the," etc. And in all these cases the term thus modified has universal, singular designation.

The things designated by general universal terms are often only possibilities, as when we say that "All bodies not acted upon by external forces continue in a state of uniform motion or rest," for all actual bodies are acted upon by external forces. But the things designated by singular and particular terms seem usually (though not always) to be actual in the past or future if not in the present. Thus "Some trains have steam engines" refers to present actualities, and "Napoleon lost a war" refers to past ones.

General Universal Designation as Collective or Distributive.   Compare the proposition that "The men on the team numbered eleven" with the proposition that "The men on the team were tired." In the first case the predicate term, "eleven," applies not to each team member individually but only to all of them taken together as a collective whole. In the second case, however, the predicate term, "tired," applies to each of the men taken individually. In a case such as the first the term is said to have *collective* designation, for the individuals it designates are considered as one collection. In cases like the second the term is said to have *distributive* designation, for the individuals designated are considered as distributed into many. The collective or distributive *designation of* a term in a *proposition* should not, however, be confused with collective and distributive *terms* or concepts, which we discussed earlier,[8] for the examples in this paragraph show that a term which in itself is distributive (like "men") may be used in a proposition to designate either distributively or collectively. And even a term which in itself is collective (like "team") may be used in the plural to designate distributively, as when we say that "The teams enjoyed the game tremendously."

Particular Designation as Determinate or Indeterminate.   While terms having particular designation refer, as we have seen, only to some of the items in their extensions, this some may be either some *certain* one or ones or just some *one or another*. For instance, in the proposition that "A U.S. President was elected in 1952" we are talking about only some, not all, U.S. Presidents; yet we are talking about a certain determinate one—Dwight D. Eisenhower. In such a case the term in question ("U.S. President") has particular but determinate designation. By way of contrast, however, consider the proposition that "A U.S. President is required by the Constitution." Here it is clear that we are not talking about any one individual President; any President will do. In a case such as this, where we are not told which of the items in the extension the "some" refers to, the term in question has particular and *indeterminate* designation.

Other Types of Designation.   As we have said—though the point hardly needs to be labored—it would take at least the angel Gabriel to enumerate all the kinds of designation, for there would have to be as many as all the modes of existence and ways of intending existence. Yet we might mention at random a few other ways in which existence is commonly intended. One group of frequently used propositional or designational modes has to do with what we might call the relative power of existents—the degree to which they have a more or less firm toe-hold on being. Consider for example the following propositions:

1. Some triangles *are* equilateral.
2. Some triangles *are not* equilateral.
3. All triangles *must* have their internal angles equal to 180 degrees.
4. Triangles *need not* be equilateral.
5. Triangles *may* be equilateral.
6. Triangles *cannot* have their internal angles equal to 360 degrees.

Proposition 1 asserts simply that something happens actually to be the case. Proposition 2 asserts simply that something happens not to be the case in actual fact. Proposition 3 asserts that it is necessary that something be the case. Proposition 4 asserts that something is unnecessary, that its being so or not being so is contingent upon other factors. Proposition 5 asserts a certain situa-

[8] P. 63 above.

tion as being possible, and proposition 6, finally, asserts the impossibility of something. These degrees of being—actuality, nonactuality, necessity, contingency, possibility, and impossibility—are frequently called "the modes," and the branch of logic which has to do with propositions intending them is called "modal logic." Although this branch of logic is too complicated and subject to controversy to treat here, it is well to note these modes as a further indication of the richness of our logical tools and as material for future study.

Further, the existence of tenses (or of functionally equivalent forms in tenseless languages) indicates other variations in the mosaic of being and corresponding logical forms. To say that "The Americans fought for independence in 1776," for instance, is to talk about the past; and the terms in such propositions designate only those items in their extensions which existed in the past—and here only some of those. Likewise to say that "Americans are fighting a cold war" is to intend only present existents, and to affirm that "Americans will lead the world to universal peace" is to refer only to future existents. Thus the tense of the verb further specifies and restricts the designation of the terms to certain segments of their extensions.

While the kinds of designation are too numerous to list exhaustively, a chart of the main kinds may form a useful summary:

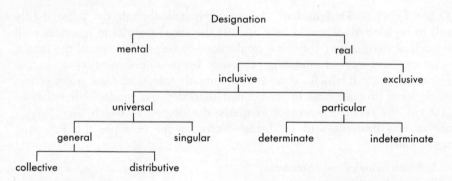

Ascent and Descent as Properties of Inclusive Nonsingular Designation. Having seen something of the richness of being and of our ways of designating it in propositions, let us turn to a very interesting property attaching to all the forms of inclusive designation save singular designation. This property is called *ascent* and *descent,* and will be important when we study inductive argument.

In inclusive designation the nature that is signified by the concept is thought of as existing not only as an object before the mind but also really in the things that possess that nature. Accordingly, given a concept with inclusive and general designation, we can either pass from that concept to the subordinate concepts and individuals which are included within its extension (descent) or pass from these individuals and subordinate concepts to the general concept that includes them (ascent). Thus descent and ascent are the propositional analogues of division and classification, respectively.

If we take the notion of "chair in this room," for instance, then from the proposition that "Every chair in this room is a straight chair" we can infer by a process of *descent* that "This chair is a straight one, this one is, this one is, this one is, etc." On the other hand, from a series of propositions enumerating every item in the extension of "chair in this room," we can by a process of *ascent* infer a universal proposition about "chairs in this room." If "This chair is a straight chair, and that one is straight, and that one is, etc.," then "Every chair in this room is a straight chair." Note that, since the individuals in the extension are indicated by concepts having singular designation ("this chair"), every *descent* is *from* a concept having general or particular designation *to* one having singular designation, and every *ascent* is *from* one having *singular* designation *to* one having general or particular designation. Or more briefly: every *descent* is *from* the general or particular, and every *ascent* is *to* the general or particular.

Since there are different kinds of nonsingular inclusive designation, more-over, there will correspondingly be different kinds of ascent and descent. In the case of terms whose designation in a given proposition is either *universal distributive* or *particular determinate,* the descent is always to a series of *propositions.* When the term from which the descent is made has *universal and distributive* designation, the propositions to which the descent is made are connected by "and." From the proposition that "Every atom of hydrogen has a positive and a negative charge of electricity," for example, we descend to the series of singular propositions that "This atom of hydrogen has a positive and a negative charge of electricity," *and* "This one does," *and* "This one . . . ," etc. But in cases where the term from which the descent is made has *particular and determinate* designation, the propositions to which the descent is made are connected by "or." For instance, from the proposition that "Some book from the library was lying on the dining-room table" we descend to the series of singular propositions that "It was this book from the library that was lying on the dining-room table" *or* "It was this book" *or* "It was this one," etc.

When the term from which the descent is made has either *universal and collective* or *particular and indeterminate* designation, however, the descent is always to a series of singular *terms* making up a *single* proposition, rather than to a series of propositions. In cases where the term from which the descent is made has *universal and collective* designation, the singular terms making up the single propositions are connected by "and." Thus from the proposition that "The men in the plane were five in all" we descend to the proposition that "This man in the plane *and* that one *and* that one, etc., were five in all"—*not* to the propositions that "This man in the plane was five in all" and "That man was five in all," etc. But when the term from which the descent is made has *particular and indeterminate* designation, the terms in the proposition to which the descent is made are connected by "or." From the proposition that "Some sort of conveyance is necessary for long-distance transportation" we descend to the proposition that "A train *or* a car *or* a ship *or* a plane, etc. (i.e., *some* one but without its making any difference *which* one), is necessary for long-distance transportation."

More briefly, descent from terms having *universal* designation is always to items connected with "and," while descent from terms having *particular* designation is always to items connected with "or." The chart will help give a clearer picture of all the various forms of ascent and descent:

ASCENT AND DESCENT

	Universal	Particular
	"and"	"or"
Propositions	distributive	determinate
Terms	collective	indeterminate

9–5 DESIGNATION AND TRUTH AND FALSITY

Since propositions contain two kinds of reference or intention—signification and designation—they may be false for one or the other or both of two reasons. Consider the proposition that "The Nazis invaded England." Here the existing state of affairs was quite different from what this proposition asserts it to have been, and the proposition is therefore false. Yet its terms still designate, for there certainly were Nazis and it is precisely these actual Nazis that the subject term designates. Hence the falsity of this proposition is due not to the failure on the part of the subject to designate something existing, but rather to the fact that what is here predicated of the subject simply does not pertain to the subject at all. Hence the falsity of this proposition is a predicational rather than a designational falsity.

By way of contrast consider the following propositions: "World War III was a catastrophe," "The 1929 stock market crash is the result of unregulated speculation," and "Napoleon will lose the battle of Waterloo." Clearly none of these propositions is true, for it is certainly not the case that World War III *was* a catastrophe, or that the 1929 stock market crash *is* the result of unregulated speculation, or that Napoleon *will* lose the battle of Waterloo. Yet in each of these three cases the predicate truly belongs to the subject: Napoleon *did* lose the battle of Waterloo; the 1929 stock market crash *was* the result of unregulated speculation; and, whether or not it ever will in fact be the case, World War III *would be* a catastrophe. Hence the falsity of these three propositions is not a *predicational* falsity.

What then is it that keeps these three propositions from being true? It is the simple fact that the subject terms, by their very natures, cannot possibly designate the kinds of existence which the copulas in these three propositions require them to designate. In the proposition that "World War III was a catastrophe" the copula requires the subject term to designate something existing in the past. But World War III, fortunately, has not yet come to be. Likewise in the second proposition the copula calls for a present existent while the subject signifies a past existent, and in the same fashion the copula in the third proposition demands a future existent while the subject refers to a past one. Hence the subject terms of all three propositions fail to designate. And this failure is the source of the falsity of each proposition. Consequently the falsity of these three propositions is a *designational* rather than a *predicational* falsity.

Failure in designation may also be caused by the very significance of the term itself, as when a term is self-contradictory like "circle-squarers." Consider, for example, the propositions that "All circle-squarers are non-mathematicians" and "Some non-mathematicians can square the circle." If the term "circle-squarers" is thought of as referring only to conceptual entities or beings of reason, these propositions could of course be true, for we can make our mental furniture behave as we wish even to the point of committing contradictions. Yet as these two propositions stand we would doubtless regard them as false because the term "circle-squarers" is now thought of as designating real, actual beings as well as merely conceptual ones, the term "real" being tacit in the original utterances: "All (real) circle-squarers are non-mathematicians." But this makes the subject term fail in designation because it is impossible for there to be any real, actual circle-squarers, and the propositions are therefore false. It is important to stress that such a term as this does have *significance*, for we know what we are talking about when we use it. And it therefore also has an *extension*, even if the extension covers only conceptual entities. But the point here is that terms with such merely conceptual significance cannot be made to designate real beings, and when such an attempt is made the result is a designationally false proposition.

It is also worthy of note that particular and singular terms seem more liable to fail in designation than general, universal ones. Compare, for example, the following three propositions:

1. Columbus' ship that sailed off the edge of the world was destroyed.
2. Some ships that sailed off the edge of the world were destroyed.
3. All ships that sail off the edge of the world are destroyed.

The first two propositions are obviously false, but we might well say that the third one is true. The reason for this is that the subject terms of the first two propositions do not designate anything, while the subject term of the third one does. The subject terms of the first two propositions imply that the world actually has an edge which ships could sail over, but since this is not the case these terms fail to designate anything. The subject of the third proposition, however, merely refers to a possible situation; and since it is true that the world could possibly—at least logically possibly—have an edge for ships to sail over, that term designates. The reason for this difference between general universal terms on the one hand and particular and singular terms on the other lies in a fact which we have already noted,[9] namely, that we usually use particular or singular terms to refer to the actual world about us and general universal terms to refer to the realm of possibilities. Thus we must be very careful not to think that a term lacks designation just because none of its referents are actual, for we would then rule out many important laws such as "All bodies not acted upon by external forces continue in a state of uniform motion or rest."

These considerations (as well as others) have led many logicians to lay it down as a general rule that particular and singular propositions *always* refer to the actual world and that universal propositions *never* do. But common usage does not seem to justify this rule for we frequently encounter universal propositions which clearly refer to actual existents—"All of the people in this room are U.S. citizens," for example—and also, though admittedly less frequently, particular propositions which refer to only possible situations—"Some Martians are males," for example. Yet it does remain true that the universal proposition is our usual tool for achieving the scope of the possible by abstracting from actualities, and that particular and singular propositions are our most frequent instruments for apprehending the actual. And for this reason the latter fail in designation more frequently than the former.

All of the propositions with non-designating terms which we have so far considered have been false, but this is not always the case; as a matter of fact, some of them seem clearly to be true. For example, we would almost certainly say it is true that "Socrates is not a Harvard professor" even though the present tense of the verb keeps the term "Socrates" from designating anything. And for that matter common usage sometimes seems to regard propositions with non-designating terms in even a third way, as neither true nor false. We might well pronounce "Some non-mathematicians can (really) square the circle" as clearly false, but what attitude would we take toward the proposition that "Jesus' wife was a Jew?" Well, we'd very likely say that such a statement was wrong or inappropriate rather than calling it false, because the trouble isn't so much with that proposition itself as with another proposition which it implicitly contains: "Jesus had a wife." *This* proposition is clearly false and so the proposition

[9] P. 134.

which contains it must of course also be false, though we hesitate to say so because it would probably be *true* that "Jesus' wife was a Jew" *if* he had a wife. Hence the falsity of a proposition whose lack of truth is due to a non-designating term pertains more properly to another proposition which it tacitly contains than to the whole proposition itself.

But if a proposition with a non-designating term may be either true or false (or "inappropriate"), how can we tell which it is? Unfortunately, there does not seem to be any absolute rule which is applicable here, and this question is the subject of considerable debate among logicians. Yet common usage seems to justify two rough generalizations: (1) When the proposition is *affirmative* we seem always to regard it as either false or "inappropriate," because it seems to be impossible to assert an affirmative proposition without tacitly asserting that the subject term refers to something somehow existent. Note here the affirmative examples we have just been using. (2) Some *negative* propositions we seem to regard as true and some as "inappropriate." Thus "Franklin Delano Roosevelt will not be the next U. S. President" seems true, but "Franklin Delano Roosevelt will not die" seems inappropriate rather than either strictly true or false. If he were to be alive in the future it would be false that "he will not die," but since he will not be it is, strictly speaking, true that he *will* not die. Whether a negative proposition is regarded as true or as "inappropriate" seems to depend on the extent to which the existence of referents of the non-designating term is necessary to the truth of the whole proposition. In "Franklin Delano Roosevelt will not be the next U.S. President," F.D.R.'s existence is not necessary to the truth of the proposition—on the contrary. But in "Franklin Delano Roosevelt will not die," his present or future existence is necessary for a situation in which he will in the future fail to die. Since "inappropriate" propositions are ultimately either true or false, however, we may revise our generalizations thus: *Among propositions with non-designating terms the affirmative ones seem always to be false and the negative ones to be sometimes true and sometimes false.*

Thus designation or existential reference as well as signification or essential reference is important in determining the truth of any proposition, and therefore, as we shall see,[10] important also in determining the relations among propositions and the validity of arguments.

Summary.   This completes our theoretical investigation of the nature and function of the proposition. That which is known through propositions is the existence or nonexistence or type of existence possessed by the essences apprehended in concepts. In order to accomplish its function of relating essences to existence, the proposition must have a dual intention: signification or essential intention and designation or existential intention. Just as the concept is a relation of identity between an essence in its abstracted state and that essence in

[10] Pp. 184–185, 202–205, and 316–319 below.

its individuated state, so also the proposition is a relation of identity, though here an identity of designata or intended existents rather than an identity of significata or intended essences. In all genuine propositions the two terms differ in their significance in the various ways indicated by the predicables, but in all affirmative propositions these different signified essences are intended as the same identical existent. The precise nature of the designational or existential intention of a proposition's terms is determined by the total propositional context. In some cases the propositional context keeps one of the terms from designating at all, even though the signified essences may in fact be linked; and this situation may cause the proposition to be false. The varieties of designation are as manifold as the ways of existing, but this extremely complex mosaic of existence and designation must of necessity be simplified in any practical ordering of our propositional tools. And to such a simplified working scheme of propositions we must now turn.

CHAPTER 10

A SIMPLIFIED SCHEME
OF PROPOSITIONS

A complete logic would include in its scheme of propositions as many different kinds of proposition as there are different kinds of designation. But this is
impossible in practice, we have seen, for since there would have to be as many
kinds of designation as there are kinds of existence, it would require omnis-
cience to list and omnipotence to handle all the various kinds of proposition.
At the same time, we must try to avoid the other extreme of oversimplification,
for then our scheme will not be sufficiently inclusive for fruitful application in
our human cognitive endeavors. Consequently a practical scheme of propositions should combine the greatest possible universality or richness with the
greatest possible simplicity. But since these two desiderata are to some extent
incompatible, our actual working scheme will have to be a compromise between
them. Let us now proceed first to present such a compromise, simplified working scheme of propositions and then to consider its scope and limitations.

10–1 THE QUANTITY AND QUALITY OF PROPOSITIONS

The Quantity of Propositions. In discussing the various kinds of designation
we saw that a term in a proposition may have either universal or particular
designation, and if universal either general or singular. By universal designation we meant that the term is so used in the proposition as to refer to all of
the items in its extension, and by particular designation that the term is so used
in the proposition as to refer to some of the items in its extension. This designation of either all or some of the items in the term's extension is called the
quantity of the term. Thus the quantity of a term with universal designation is
universal. In the proposition "All men are mortal," for instance, the quantity of
the term "men" is universal. A term with universal quantity is also said to be
distributed, for its comprehension is distributed over all of the items in its
extension. In like manner the quantity of a term with particular designation is
particular. In the proposition "Some men are white," for example, the quantity
of the term "men" is particular. A term with particular quantity is also said to
be *undistributed,* for its comprehension is not distributed over all the items in
its extension but rather over only some of them.

Now *the quantity of a proposition is determined by the quantity of its subject term.* Since the quantity of a term is either universal or particular, the quantity of a proposition is also either universal or particular:

1. A *universal proposition* is one whose subject has *universal* quantity or designation, i.e., one whose subject is *distributed.* For example:

   a. All natural things are temporal. (a universal general proposition)
   b. This man is temporal. (a universal singular proposition)

2. A *particular proposition* is one whose subject has *particular* quantity or designation, that is, one whose subject is *undistributed.* For example:

   Some natural things are organic.

The Quality of Propositions.   By the quality of a proposition is meant simply whether the proposition is affirmative or negative. An affirmative proposition is affirmative in quality, and a negative proposition is negative in quality. For instance, "All natural things are temporal" and "Some natural things are organic" are propositions whose quality is affirmative, and "No natural thing is eternal" and "Some natural things are not organic" are propositions whose quality is negative.

The Resulting A, E, I, and O Propositions.   Since there are two kinds of proposition when classified according to quantity (universal and particular) and also two kinds when classified according to quality (affirmative and negative), there will be four kinds of proposition in our simplified working scheme: universal affirmative, universal negative, particular affirmative, and particular negative. Traditionally these four kinds of proposition have been called, respectively, A, E, I, and O propositions, the symbolic letters coming from the two latin words, *AffIrmo* (I affirm) and *nEgO* (I negate). The complete[1] simplified working scheme of propositions is as follows:

A proposition: universal and affirmative ("All studies are painful.")
E proposition: universal and negative ("No studies are painful.")
I proposition: particular and affirmative ("Some studies are painful.")
O proposition: particular and negative ("Some studies are not painful.")

10–2   RULES FOR THE QUANTIFICATION OF TERMS

Since the quantity of any proposition is the same as the quantity of its subject term, the subjects of universal propositions are universal in quantity, i.e., distributed, and the subjects of particular propositions are particular in quantity, i.e., undistributed. But what about predicate terms? Their quantity or distribution is determined, not by the quantity, but by the quality of the

---

[1] Compound propositions of various kinds will be treated below, pp. 331–347, as forms of argument.

proposition. To see just how and why this is so, let us examine each of the four types of proposition separately.

First, negative propositions. In the E proposition, "No studies are painful," does the predicate term, "painful (things)," have universal or particular quantity; is it distributed or undistributed? Well, in negative propositions we separate the predicate from the subject. But do we separate the whole of the predicate, or only a part of it, from the subject? Are we excluding the whole class of painful things, or only a part of it, from the class of studies? *All* painful things, the whole class of painful things, you will say, for if we excluded only some painful things from the class of studies there would remain some other painful things which might in fact be studies, and this is not what we want to say when we say that "No studies are painful." In short, we are saying that "No studies are *any* painful things." Thus to separate or exclude the predicate from the subject is to exclude or separate the *whole* of the predicate from the subject. But then we are talking about the whole of the predicate, about *all* painful things; and the predicate is therefore distributed, or universal in quantity, in E propositions.

Such exclusion or separation and the consequent quantity of the terms can be made visually apparent by the use of a type of diagram known as "Euler circles,"[2] named after the eighteenth-century Swiss mathematician who originated them:

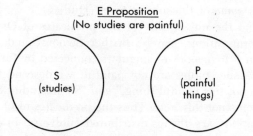

E Proposition
(No studies are painful)

S
(studies)

P
(painful
things)

Moreover, the fact that predicates of E propositions are distributed (universal in quantity) can be confirmed by a procedure which we have just learned, the procedure of *descent*.[3] We saw that if the descent is made to a series of singular propositions or terms which are connected by "and," then the designation of the pertinent term in the original proposition is universal. And this is the case with the predicates of E propositions: from the proposition that "No studies are painful" we descend to the series that "No study is this painful thing," *and* "No study is this painful thing," *and* "None this one," etc. Thus the predicate of an E proposition is universal or distributed.

[2] These and other similar diagrams are metaphorical rather than literal representations; and, while useful, they are dispensable in the study of logic. (See p. 160 below.)
[3] Pp. 136–138.

The same thing is true of particular negative propositions, of O propositions. For when we assert that "Some studies are not painful," for example, we are again separating the whole class of painful things from the subject—though in this case we are separating all painful things from only *some* studies. To negate the predicate of the subject is to exclude or separate the *whole* of the predicate from the subject. But then again, just as with the E proposition, we are talking about the whole of the predicate, about *all* painful things; and the predicate of every O proposition is therefore distributed (universal in quantity). Euler circles will make this character of O propositions visually obvious:

O Proposition
(Some studies are not painful)

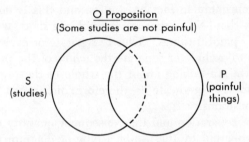

S
(studies)

P
(painful
things)

Notice here that the dotted line indicates the remainder of the subject class (studies) which we are *not* talking about in an O proposition, since we are there talking about only *some* of the subject term (studies).

Observe also that the universality of the predicates of O propositions, just like those of E propositions, can be further demonstrated by the fact that descent from them is to a series of singulars connected by "and." For from the proposition that "Some studies are not painful" we descend to the series that "Some studies are not this painful thing," *and* "Some studies are not this painful thing," *and* "Some not this," etc. Thus the predicates of O propositions, like those of E propositions, are always distributed (universal in quantity).

In view of these reflections, we may now state a general rule: *Negative propositions always have distributed (universal) predicates.*

But what about affirmative propositions? Let us first consider I propositions —affirmative particular propositions. In the proposition that "Some studies are painful," for instance, does the predicate term, "painful (things)," have universal or particular quantity; is it distributed or undistributed? Are we here talking about all painful things or about only some of them? Supposing that it is true that some studies (other than logic, of course) are painful, are we thereby asserting that some studies are *all* painful things, that no other things are painful besides these studies? Well, this could possibly be true (in the best, or nearly best, of all possible worlds), but we are certainly not *saying* that it is true when we say that "Some studies are painful." No, we are saying only that "Some studies are *some* painful things," and we are not committing ourselves one way or the other about the rest of the things in the world that are or may be painful, about the whole class of painful things. Hence the predicates of I propositions are particular in quantity or undistributed. Again, this fact can be made visually apparent through the use of Euler circles:

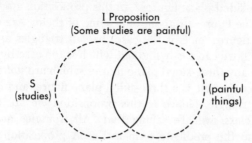

I Proposition
(Some studies are painful)

S
(studies)

P
(painful things)

Notice again that the dotted lines indicate the remainders of the two classes which we are not talking about in I propositions, since I propositions refer to only *some* of *each* of the two classes.

Furthermore, the process of descent can be used to confirm the undistributed or particular character of the predicates of I propositions, just as it was used to show the distributed character of the predicates of negative propositions. For if the singulars to which the descent is made must be connected with "or" rather than with "and," then, as we have seen, the designation of the pertinent term in the original proposition must be particular. And we see that this is the case with the predicates of I propositions: from the proposition that "Some studies are painful" we descend to the assertion that "Some studies are this painful thing, *or* this painful thing, *or* this one, etc."[4] Thus the predicates of I propositions are always undistributed or particular.

What about A propositions—affirmative universal propositions? In the proposition that "All studies are painful," for example, are we talking about all painful things or about only some of them? Again it is clear that we are referring in this proposition to only some painful things. We are clearly not saying that "All studies are *all* painful things," for there may well be—and cruel experience shows that there actually are—some painful things in the world which are not studies. No, we are again saying only that "All studies are *some* painful things"; we are taking no stand at all on the whole class of painful things. Consequently the predicate in this A proposition is undistributed or particular. The process of descent again furnishes us additional confirmation of this fact, for we must descend to a series connected by "or": "Every (or each) study is this painful thing *or* this painful thing *or* this one, etc."[5] That is, we are saying in this

---

[4] Note that the elements connected by "or" in this case must be terms rather than propositions, since the designation of "painful (things)" is indeterminate. See p. 137.

[5] See note 4.

proposition that "Every (or each) study is some painful thing or other." Hence the predicates of such A propositions as this one are undistributed or particular.

Unfortunately, however, the situation is a little more complicated, for not all A propositions have undistributed predicates. Consider the proposition that "All triangles are three-sided plane figures." In this proposition are we talking about all three-sided plane figures or about only some of them? Are all triangles only *some* three-sided figures, or is it the case that all triangles are *all* three-sided plane figures? Well, we can easily find out which is the case by asking ourselves whether there are any three-sided plane figures which are *not* triangles. Clearly there are not; every triangle is a three-sided plane figure, and every three-sided plane figure is a triangle. Hence in this proposition we are talking about all of the predicate class; we are saying that "All triangles are *all* three-sided plane figures." And the predicate term in this A proposition is therefore distributed or universal in quantity.

The universality of the predicates of some A propositions can also be confirmed by the process of descent, although here we must be careful that the descent occurs in the subject term as well as in the predicate term. It is indeed true that we cannot, from the proposition that "All triangles are three-sided plane figures," descend to the assertion that "All triangles are *this* three-sided plane figure and this one and this one, etc.," or even to the assertion that "All triangles are this three-sided plane figure, and all triangles are this one, and all this one, etc.," for the whole class of triangles cannot be any single thing. But if we make the descent in both terms at the same time, we can see that both are universal in quantity: "This triangle is this three-sided plane figure, and this triangle is this one, and this is this one, etc.," until we have exhausted the whole class of three-sided plane figures as well as the whole class of triangles.

Thus some A propositions have distributed or universal predicates. But *which* ones do? You may have noticed in the example we have just been considering that the predicate is the *definition* of the subject; "plane figure" is the genus and "three-sided" the differentia of the concept "triangle." And if you will recall from our study of definitions the fact that the first rule for a good or proper definition is that it be coextensive with, that is, neither broader nor narrower than, the definiendum, you will of course see at once why the predicate term ("three-sided plane figure") in the above proposition is distributed or universal in quantity. For if the subject is distributed—and it must be since this is an A proposition—then the predicate must also be distributed, for a definition must be coextensive with the subject defined. In short, the predicate of a "real definition"[6] or definitional proposition, that is, a predicate which is the definition of its subject, is always distributed or universal in quantity.

Furthermore, the predicate of an A proposition may be distributed even though it is not the definition of the subject, as in "John is the boy who is in

[6] See p. 81.

that room." But such cases are usually less troublesome than definitional predicates, since the former almost always contain some word which indicates that the predicate is distributed—"the" in this example—although the latter sometimes do too. So A propositions have distributed predicates when the latter are either definitions or definite descriptions.

Even this statement must be qualified. Let us continue with our same example: "All triangles are three-sided plane figures." But now let us suppose that the speaker of this proposition has never studied any geometry; let us suppose that after seeing quite a number of triangles he just happens to generalize his experience of the three-sided character of triangles without at all being aware of the fact that triangles are all of the three-sided plane figures there happen to be in the universe, that every three-sided plane figure is a triangle. Will such a person, when he utters the proposition that all triangles are three-sided plane figures, have the intention of giving a definition of "triangle"? Will he, in the proposition he is uttering, be speaking about all three-sided plane figures? Clearly not. *He* does not mean to give a definition; he does not intend to assert anything about all three-sided plane figures, even though what he says happens to be true of all of them. Hence the predicate term in his proposition designates only particular quantity; it is undistributed.

The important point to remember here is that every proposition is an *intention,* and that every intention is the intention *of some person.* Accordingly, two linguistic sentences which may seem to be exactly the same may signify two different propositional intentions. Since we are not yet very good at mind reading, it is frequently difficult or impossible to tell whether a given sentence, such as "All triangles are three-sided plane figures," signifies a definitional proposition or not. The best we can do is to try, if possible, to discover the speaker's (or writer's) propositional intention by further questioning, and to remember that *if* the sentence's propositional intention is a definitional one, then the predicate is distributed.

Thus the predicates of some A propositions are undistributed or particular, while the predicates of others are distributed or universal. Euler circles may help make this clear:

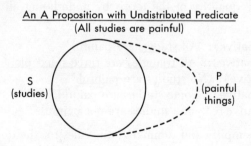

An A Proposition with Undistributed Predicate
(All studies are painful)

S
(studies)

P
(painful
things)

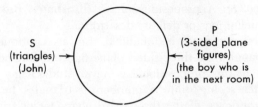

An A Proposition with Distributed Predicate
(All triangles are three-sided plane figures)
(John is the boy who is in the next room)

S
(triangles) →
(John)

P
(3-sided plane
figures)
← (the boy who is
in the next room)

However, to retain only one rule for all A propositions, it is possible to interpret any affirmative proposition with a distributed predicate as consisting of *two ordinary* A propositions, each with an undistributed predicate. Thus we may interpret the definitional sentence "All triangles are three-sided plane figures" as consisting of the two following propositions: "All triangles are three-sided plane figures" and "All three-sided plane figures are triangles," each of which is thought of as non-definitional and with an undistributed predicate. If we do this we can state one general rule which includes *all* A propositions and all I propositions as well: <u>*Affirmative propositions always have undistributed (particular) predicates.*</u> But such a decision is not of much help in practice, because we must then decide whether or not a given A sentence expresses two A propositions or only one, and this amounts to the same thing as deciding whether or not a given A proposition has a distributed predicate. Unfortunately, therefore, we cannot avoid the necessity of distinguishing between these two kinds of A propositions.

However, definitional propositions and ones whose predicates are definite descriptions constitute a minority of the A propositions in common usage. When in doubt it is always safer, at least in logic, to assume too little rather than too much. For these two reasons we shall *hereafter* <u>always interpret the predicates of A propositions as being undistributed except in those cases where we are very sure that they are distributed.</u>

We may now summarize our simplified working scheme of propositions, this time indicating the quantity of the terms by underlining all those which are distributed:

A (universal affirmative): "All <u>studies</u> are painful."
A (universal affirmative): "All <u>triangles</u> are <u>three-sided plane figures</u>."
E (universal negative): "No <u>studies</u> are <u>painful</u>."
I (particular affirmative): "Some studies are painful."
O (particular negative): "Some studies are not <u>painful</u>."

We may also now simplify and summarize the rules for the quantification (distribution) of terms (keeping in mind the exceptional case of distributed predicates of A propositions): *Universal propositions have distributed subjects, and negative propositions have distributed predicates.*

10–3 SCOPE AND LIMITATIONS OF THE SIMPLIFIED SCHEME

Having completed our examination of the structure of all the types of propositions[7] which will be used in the remainder of this book, we should now pause briefly to consider the scope and limitations of this simplified scheme. We noted earlier a point which is so obvious it hardly needs stress: that the complexity of reality makes it impossible in practice to work with all the different kinds of designation, and hence with all the different kinds of proposition, which are theoretically available to a knowing mind. What is needed, we saw, is a scheme which is as simple as possible and yet at the same time as rich and complete as possible. How does our fourfold scheme of A, E, I, and O propositions meet this need?

In the first place, it must again be noted that this scheme omits the modal forms of designation: necessity, contingency, possibility, and impossibility. This places a serious restriction upon the scope of our propositional scheme, but the sacrifice seems advisable in the beginning of the study of logic in view of the difficulties involved in modal logic. Even though we shall retain no distinct propositional forms for the modalities, however, we can still give them some consideration, for within our present scheme it is possible to interpret modal designations as being parts of the terms, the subject or the predicate. For example, we can interpret the proposition that "Every true science must be self-consistent" as saying that "Every true science is such that it must be self-consistent"; and we can interpret the proposition that "Men cannot live forever" as saying that "Men are mortal." True, our translations here do not mean exactly the same things as the originals, and, more specifically, they tend to confuse certain modes of existence with essences.[8] Still, as long as we are aware of this fact and keep in mind the necessity of later, more complete analyses of modal propositions, no damage is done.

In the second place, our simplified scheme of propositions ignores the verb tenses, the designation of past, present, and future time. Yet the temporal sense of the verb can be incorporated also to a certain extent in the terms, especially in the predicate. For instance we may interpret "Alexander the Great was a student of Aristotle" as "Alexander the Great is a man who was a student of Aristotle." Of course strictly speaking it is not true that Alexander

---

[7] All types of *simple* propositions. Compound propositions will be treated in Chap. 23 as forms of argument.

[8] See the discussion of the distinction between essence and existence on pp. 100–104. For a more general treatment of the tendency to essentialize existence see E. Gilson, *Being and Some Philosophers,* Pontifical Institute of Mediaeval Studies, 1949.

the Great *is* anything; rather he was. But again, so long as we do not forget the simplification we are making for the sake of convenience, we have not falsified the situation.

Next, since mental designation (e.g., "All concepts are universals") is determined solely by the comprehension of the very terms thus designating, we do not need any special propositional form for it. Exclusive designation (e.g., "Man is a universal concept") amounts in practice to equivocation, to the bestowal of a distinct meaning on the relevant term; and the intended meaning of the equivocal term (the term having exclusive designation) is usually[9] made clear by the other term in the same proposition. Thus the exclusive designation of the term "man" in "Man is a universal concept" is made sufficiently clear by the predicate term, "universal concept," so that no special propositional form is required for its recognition. The same thing is true, we believe, of the other types of designation listed on p. 136 above; the type of designation can usually be made sufficiently clear for most practical purposes by the elements in our four types of proposition.

Thus no serious damage seems to result from restricting the types of proposition to just the four for practical purposes, and the simplicity of this scheme will be amply justified, we believe, by the comparatively little intellectual baggage which we will need to carry with us during the rest of our journey in logic.

Degs Diagram the 14 spercizes on p. 125.

---

[9] There are exceptions, and we shall point them out when necessary.

CHAPTER 11

FROM LANGUAGE TO PROPOSITIONS

On Clarifying Assertions.　Since language is necessary for both the formulation and the communication of thoughts and knowledge,[1] we shall always find a linguistic entity wherever we find a proposition. Now language is notoriously slippery, as we have seen in the discussion of ambiguity, since it consists of artificial signs whose connections with their signata are as changeable and multifarious as human wills. Hence we are once again faced with the problem of identifying the formal signs conveyed by various artificial signs, but now at a different level: the level of propositions rather than concepts. Our present task is therefore parallel to our earlier one of identifying concepts through the detection and elimination of ambiguities in their verbal vehicles; it is the task of identifying and formulating the proposition conveyed by any given sentence.

In this process of identifying and formulating propositions we will ignore the noncognitive functions of language, since our task as logicians is to sharpen our cognitive instruments. Here it must again be carefully stressed and remembered that in isolating the proposition conveyed by a sentence we are by no means denying the other, noncognitive functions of that sentence—its emotive, directive, and other intentions. On the contrary, our procedure will consist simply in the deliberate abstraction from the sentence of just one of its various functions—the logical or cognitive—for a certain specific purpose. The same sentences might just as justifiably be regarded from a purely poetic, or propagandistic, or ceremonial point of view. Let us now turn to the task of clarifying our assertions through the isolation and formulation of the propositions contained in sentences, through the reduction of sentences to their logical form.

The Propositional Elements.　In extracting the cognitive meaning from any sentence so as to form a proposition, there are four elements which must be isolated and made clearly explicit: the subject, the predicate, the copula, and the quantifiers—the quantity or distribution of each of the two terms and the quantity of the proposition as a whole. We shall first formulate the proposition in linguistic form, retaining the particular significance of that proposition; and

[1] Pp. 20–22 above.

153

we shall finally express the proposition in a purely symbolic form, where the symbols abstract from the particular meaning of the proposition and present only its logical structure. Our paradigm will be:

Quantifier	Subject	Copula	Predicate
All	S̲	are	P
(No,		(am,	
Some)		am-not,	
		is,	
		is-not,	
		are-not)	

where the underlined terms are distributed or universal in quantity. Let us now turn to the procedure to be followed in this formulation of propositions from sentences.

11-1   THE PROCEDURE OF PROPOSITIONAL FORMULATION

There are of course other procedures which could be used just as well as the one we will present here, and it probably does not make much difference what procedure you use so long as it works for you and so long as you stick to it systematically. Without some definite procedure or other, however, you will probably find that you frequently make mistakes. The procedure presented below is one that has stood the test of time and has worked very well for many people. It cannot be overemphasized that the student should learn this, or some equivalent, procedure thoroughly and practice it frequently, for experience has shown that for most people the process of formulating propositions from language is one of the more difficult aspects of practical logic.

This procedure consists of four steps:

1. Isolate the subject and the predicate.
2. Identify the copula and its quality.
3. Identify the quantity of the proposition and the distribution of the terms.
4. Express the formulated proposition in symbols.

You will find that you can formulate many of the simpler propositions without consciously following these steps. But since many propositions are quite complicated, you should form the habit of always following these steps in this particular order (or some other equivalent procedure) in *all* of the propositions which you handle. Let us now carry out this procedure step by step and in detail, and illustrate it with examples.

11-1.1   Isolation of Subject and Predicate

Perhaps the easiest way to indicate visually the isolated subject and predicate is to enclose each in parentheses, and this is the procedure we shall follow. In the proposition that "All studies are painful," for example, this first step is carried out as follows:

All (studies) are (painful things.)

Notice that the word "things" (or some equivalent) which is tacit in the original sentence is made explicit in our first step. This is not always necessary, but it is sometimes very helpful.

Notice also that the words expressing a given term (the subject or the predicate) are sometimes physically separated in the original sentence, and that a consequent rearrangement of words may be necessary. Thus if we consider the sentence "He laughs best who laughs last," we see that the clause "who laughs last," though physically in the predicate position after the verb, actually modifies the word "he" and is therefore a part of the subject. *Who* laughs last? *He* laughs last. In such a case we would proceed as follows:

He laughs best who laughs last.

(He) (laughs best) (who laughs last.)
(He who laughs last) (laughs best.)

11-1.2   Identification of the Copula and Its Quality   *{ negative / affirmative*

There are (in English, of course) exactly six copulas: "am," "am-not," "is," "is-not," "are," and "are-not"—the affirmative and negative forms of the present indicative of the verb "to be." Sometimes the copula is already explicit in the original sentence, so that when we have isolated the subject and the predicate we have at the same time identified the copula and its quality. Thus in our first example as soon as we have

All (studies) are (painful things.)

we see at once that the copula is "are" and that the proposition is therefore affirmative in quality.

More often, however, as in our example about laughing, the copula is tacit in the original sentence, and it must therefore be made explicit by a separate step. This consists of inserting the appropriate copula between the subject and the predicate thus:

is
(He who laughs last) ∧ (laughs best.)

and then making the original verb into the verb of a relative clause in the predicate thus:

is one who
(He who laughs last) ∧ (∧ laughs best.)

or

(He who laughs last) is (one who laughs best.)

Some other examples may also help to clarify this second step:

I helped x.	(I) am (one who helped x.)
I didn't hurt x.	(I) am-not (one who hurt x.)
They will harm x.	(They) are (ones who will harm x.)
You won't tell x.	(You) are-not (one who will tell x.)
He works for x.	(He) is (one who works for x.)
She doesn't like x.	(She) is-not (one who likes x.)

Note in the above examples that the "not" is connected with the copula by a hyphen: "is-not," "are-not," "am-not." This is done to make clear the fact that it is the copula, and therefore the proposition as a whole, which is negative rather than the predicate. But notice also that in the above negative propositions the "not" could have been put with the predicate instead of with the copula without changing the meaning:

(She) is-not (one who likes x.)

equals

(She) is (not one who likes x.)

Although it does not really matter (for reasons we will see when we study the relations among propositions) whether the "not" is put with the copula or with the predicate, it is probably easier to put the "not" with the copula when the verb is negative and with the predicate when other parts of the predicate are negative. And observe finally that this procedure of inserting a copula and placing the verb in the predicate abstracts from the temporal designation of the verb, as was mentioned earlier,[2] though it retains its temporal significance in the predicate.

11–1.3   Identification of the Quantity of the Proposition and Its Terms

The next step is to discover the quantity of the proposition, that is, whether it is universal or particular, and to indicate that quantity by placing at the beginning of the sentence the appropriate quantifying expression. Sometimes this quantifying expression is already explicitly present in the original sentence, as in our first example:

All (studies) are (painful things.)

But often the quantifier is disguised or tacit and must be made clear and explicit. All quantifying expressions may be reduced to just three: "all" or "every" for A propositions, "no" for E propositions, and "some" for I and O propositions. What is the quantity of our second example, "He who laughs last is one who laughs best"? A little reflection here will show that the word "he"

[2] P. 151.

here means *anybody,* that "Anybody who laughs last is one who laughs best," and that the proposition is therefore universal. Even if you decided that the word "he" refers to a single individual, the proposition would still be universal since it would then be a singular proposition. Accordingly, since the proposition is universal and also affirmative, it is an A proposition and we indicate its quantity with the quantifier "every" or "all":

> Every (one who laughs last) is (one who laughs best.)

or

> All (who laugh last) are (ones who laugh best.)

When the proposition is a singular one, as for instance "Woodrow Wilson was our World War I President," the addition of the quantifier "all" is awkward and ungrammatical:

> All (of Woodrow Wilson) is (the man who was our World War I President.)

But it may help you to remember that singular propositions are universal in quantity.

In the proposition that "Virtue sometimes goes unrewarded," however, we see that the word "sometimes" indicates particular quantity so we formulate the proposition like this:

> Some (virtuous acts) are (things that go unrewarded.)

The English language has many different quantifying expressions—expressions which indicate all or some. Some of the more common of these are italicized in the following examples:

Universal Quantifiers

All men have to die.	All (men) are (mortal.)
Everyone may vote who is registered.	All (who are registered) are (ones who may vote.)
Any fool can do that.	All (fools) are (ones who can do that.)
They *always* make good grades.	All (of them) are (ones who make good grades.)
The general gave his orders.	All (the general) is (one who gave his orders.)
He *who* perseveres succeeds.	All (who persevere) are (ones who succeed.)
One who smiles makes friends.	All (who smile) are (ones who make friends.)
Whoever says that lies.	All (who say that) are (ones who lie.)
Whosoever is a friend in need is a friend indeed.	All (who are friends when one is in need) are (friends indeed.)

Universal Quantifiers

Whatever helps others is our duty.	All (things that help others) are (our duty.)
Whatsoever is true is virtuous.	All (things that are true) are (things that are virtuous.)
He can *never* say no.	All (he) is (one who can never say no.)

or

	None (of him) is (able to say no.)
No student studies all the time.	No (student) is (one who studies all the time.)
Nobody likes him.	No (person) is (one who likes him.)
None of these workmen loafs.	No (one of these workmen) is (a loafer.)

Particular Quantifiers

Some people laugh a lot.	Some (people) are (ones who laugh a lot.)
Several houses were destroyed.	Some (houses) are (things that were destroyed.)
People are *often* not very wise.	Some (people) are-not (ones who are very wise.)
Students *frequently* cram for exams.	Some (students) are (ones who cram for exams.)
The summers are *usually* hot.	Some (of the summers) are (hot.)
Sometimes people can laugh at themselves.	Some (people) are (able to laugh at themselves.)
Most industrious people succeed.	Some (industrious people) are (ones who succeed.)
A few women are good drivers.	Some (women) are (good drivers.)

But notice that in contrast to the expression "a few," which indicates an I proposition, the expression "few" indicates a particular but *negative*, or O, proposition.

Few women are good drivers.	Some (women) are-not (good drivers.)

"A few" has primarily an affirmative import, while "few" has primarily a negative import; we wish to deny something of certain things. When we say that "A few women are good drivers," we would not be consistent if we believed at the same time that "*No* women are good drivers." But when we say that "Few women are good drivers," we may very well believe that "No women at all are good drivers." To see more clearly that "few" does not have affirmative quality, note the proposition that "Few men are perfect." When we say this we hardly mean to assert that some men *are* perfect; on the contrary, we are saying that some men, perhaps even most men, and possibly even all men—though we refuse to commit ourselves on this point—are not perfect. The word "seldom" functions in exactly the same way as the word "few":

Men are *seldom* angels.   Some (men) are-not (angels.)

In short, "a few" always indicates an I proposition and "few" and "seldom" always indicate O propositions. And notice that the word "some" and its equivalents, while they do not *say* "all," are quite compatible with the truth of "all." Thus "some" means "at least one," that is, "one or more and possibly all."

The above quantifying expressions are certainly not all of the ones that we commonly use, and you should try to think of as many others as you can.

So much for identifying the quantity of the proposition as a whole. Once this is done, it is very easy to identify the distribution or quantity of the two terms, following the rule stated above on p. 151; and it is a good idea to make the distribution visually apparent by underlining or circling the distributed terms. Thus the distribution pattern of each of the four types of proposition might be indicated as follows:

A   All (who laugh last) are (ones who laugh best.)
E   No (student) is (one who studies all the time.)
I   Some (women) are (good drivers.)
O   Some (women) are-not (good drivers.)
A   Every (straight line) is (the shortest distance between two points.)
    (def.)

Or, if this definitional proposition is interpreted as two normal A propositions, then we have:

A   Every (straight line) is (the shortest distance between two points.)
A   Every (shortest distance between two points) is (a straight line.)

11–1.4   Symbolic Expression of the Formulated Proposition

The last step in our procedure for formulating propositions is to abstract not only from the noncognitive uses, but even from the particular cognitive content of the original sentence. This we do by symbolizing or diagraming the *type* of proposition, rather than the particular proposition, which is conveyed by the original sentence. And since there are just four types of proposition: A, E, I, and O (or five if we count the A proposition with a distributed predicate as a separate type), there will be exactly four different propositional symbolic expressions. Let us use, in the place of the copula, the lower-case letters a, e, i, and o to represent the type of proposition the original belongs to; let us use the letter "S" to symbolize the subject and the letter "P" to symbolize the predicate; and, finally, let us symbolize the distribution of these terms by underlining the distributed terms. Thus our four types of proposition are symbolized as follows:

A propositions: S̲aP
E propositions: S̲eP̲
I propositions: SiP
O propositions: SoP̲

Since we shall frequently want to translate back from the symbolic expression to the original proposition, however, we shall usually symbolize each of the two terms by some easily recognized initial letter, rather than by "S" and "P." Thus:

LaB—All (<u>who laugh last</u>) are (ones who laugh best.)
SeA—No (<u>student</u>) is (<u>one who studies all the time.</u>)
WiG—Some (women) are (good drivers.)
WoG—Some (women) are-not (<u>good drivers.</u>)
LaD—Every (<u>straight line</u>) is (<u>the shortest distance between two points.</u>)

In addition to using this type of symbolism, which might be said to represent quite literally the logical relationships in the proposition, we may also symbolize our formulated propositions by making a diagram of the relation between the classes designated by the two terms, a type of diagram originated by the English mathematician John Venn and known as a Venn diagram.[3] This diagrammatic representation of the relation between the two terms of the proposition is no more than a figurative or metaphorical representation of the actual logical relationships involved. Yet, as is so often the case with metaphors, they serve to illuminate these relationships in a way that would scarcely be possible if one were to consider them only literally and just in themselves. Now in a Venn diagram we represent the classes designated by the two terms with overlapping circles, and we represent the relation between these two classes by marking the appropriate sections of these circles. Thus the A proposition "All S is P" can be thought of as saying: "Every S is a P; there is nothing in the S class outside the P class." To indicate this on our diagram we simply cross out the part of S which lies outside of the P circle thus putting all of the S's inside the P circle:

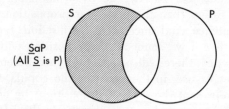

S   P

S̲aP
(All S̲ is P)

---

[3] Venn diagrams, like Euler circles, are quite useful but dispensable.

In like manner an E proposition ("No S is P") can be interpreted as saying that "There are no S's in the P class" and can accordingly be diagramed as follows:

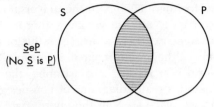

SeP
(No S is P)

I propositions ("Some S is P") say that there is at least one S in the P class, and we indicate that S with an "X" thus:

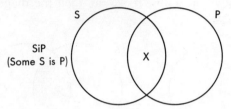

SiP
(Some S is P)

And O propositions ("Some S is-not P") say that there is at least one S *outside* the P class:

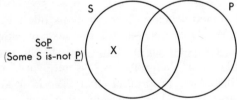

SoP
(Some S is-not P)

A propositions with distributed predicates, when they are interpreted as a single proposition, say that the two classes exactly coincide, that there are no S's outside P and no P's outside S, thus:

SaP (All S is [all] P)

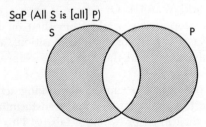

But if we choose to interpret them as consisting of two ordinary A propositions, then we will simply have two ordinary A proposition Venn diagrams exactly like the one above, one for SaP and one for PaS.

By now you may have been struck with the fact that there is a marked difference between the diagrams for the two universal propositions and those for the two particular ones, for there is no X in the universal diagrams to indicate that there are any S's or P's at all. But we know that in propositions with designating terms there are some existents, at least possible or conceptual ones, designated by these terms, although of course in propositions with non-designating terms like "World War III was a catastrophe" there are at least no S's. So aren't our above diagrams really diagrams of non-designating universal propositions, and shouldn't we place an X in the appropriate spot in order to diagram designating universal propositions like "All houses are buildings"?

We may do this if we wish, especially if we want to make it very clear that the proposition has designating terms. If we do, then the diagrams will look like this:

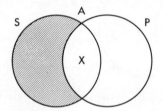 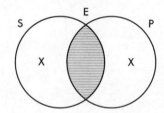

Yet within our present simplified scheme of propositions this addition of the X is really not necessary. We have decided for the sake of simplicity, you will remember, to shift the temporal sense of the verb to the predicate and always use a timeless copula: "am," "am-not," "is," "is-not," "are," or "are-not." Thus in our simplified scheme the proposition that "World War III was a catastrophe" becomes "World War III is something that was a catastrophe." In doing this we are assuming that there is an essence called "World War III" and that this essence is characterized by the essence "catastrophe in the past." But as soon as we have done this we see that the proposition is false *predication-ally*, because the predicate does not truly pertain to the subject, for pastness does not characterize World War III. Of course if such a catastrophe should occur in the future, this proposition would from then on be true instead of false; but this is also the case with the original proposition, "World War III was a catastrophe," which only shows that the former is, so far, a working equivalent of the latter.

In short, what we are doing in our simplified working scheme is translating temporal designation into temporal signification, transforming designational or existential falsity into predicational or essential falsity. This is not, as we have already seen, strictly true either to being itself or to our propositional instruments for grasping it; but the simplicity it introduces will, we believe, amply justify it in our working scheme, and no harm will be done so long as we remember that our predicational translation has lost something contained in the designational original. And when we have done this we can see that there are always members of both classes, always items in both circles of the Venn diagram, for the *extension*, as contrasted with the designation, of a concept always possesses at least *possible*, though sometimes not actual, members. Even in the case of propositions whose terms fail to designate because of the very meaning of the term instead of because of the demands of the verb, like "All circle-squarers are non-mathematicians" where the term "circle-squarers" is self-contradictory, the non-designating terms still have meaning and thus items in their extensions, even if they are only beings of reason.[4] Consequently there are always some S's and P's in our Venn diagrams, even if they are only possible or only mental ones. The only remaining question is just where in the diagram the S's and P's are. Now the shaded area rules out one of the portions of each circle, so the remaining portion is the only place where these items could be. Hence the X is already tacitly in that area, and it is therefore unnecessary, though harmless, to mark it down explicitly. So we shall continue to draw the diagrams of the universal propositions without using X's.

There is of course no limit to the number of different ways of symbolizing propositions; but one way may be better in one context and another better in another.

11–2   SOME SPECIALLY DIFFICULT LINGUISTIC EXPRESSIONS

Thus in logic the important thing to know about any given sentence is what *type* of proposition it conveys—whether an A, an E, an I, or an O. Often the type is quite obvious from the language. But there are a number of linguistic forms which are more difficult to interpret with respect to the type of proposition they express.

One of these is the expression "not all." On the face of it you might think that this indicates an E proposition, since "all" is a universal quantifier and "not" indicates a negative proposition. But consider the sentence, "Not all students are ambitious." Does this assert the E proposition that "No students are ambitious"? We hope not. No, a little thought will show that this sentence means to assert only that *some* students lack ambition without making any commitment as to *all* students. Hence this sentence expresses an O proposition: "Some students are-not ambitious." The same is true of the expression "all . . . are not" as for example in the sentence "All men are not fools": "Some men are-not fools." We shall soon see that the reason the expressions "not all," "not every," and "all . . . are not" indicate O propositions is that in these cases the "not" functions to contradict an A proposition and that the contradictory of an

[4] See the discussion on p. 139.

A proposition is an O.[5] But for the present it should be sufficient to reflect on the meaning of such sentences and to remember that these expressions always signify O propositions.

Another type of somewhat difficult linguistic expression is the *exceptive* sentence, so called because it contains as a key word "except," or some equivalent such as "but" or "save," and asserts an exception to some state of affairs. Exceptive sentences may be either affirmative or negative (negative ones are sometimes called "exclusive" sentences). How are we to interpret exceptive sentences?

Let us examine the sentence "Everyone except the Joneses had a good time." Careful thought will show that this sentence is really expressing two propositions: "Everyone other than the Joneses had a good time" and "The Joneses did not have a good time." The same thing is true if "save" or "but" or some other exceptive word is used instead of "except," and it is also true when the exceptive phrase appears in the predicate position: "Everyone had a good time but the Joneses." The same prevails, furthermore, in negative exceptive sentences such as "No one but the Joneses had a good time," this sentence expressing the two propositions "No one other than the Joneses had a good time" and "The Joneses had a good time." And again the same thing is true even if some other exceptive word is used, and even though the exceptive phrase appears in the predicate position, thus: "No one had a good time but the Joneses." In addition to the key words "but," "except," and "save," negative exceptive sentences have two other very common key words, "only" and "alone"; and they exactly equal "none but": "Only the Joneses had a good time" or "The Joneses alone had a good time."

Furthermore, the exceptive phrase may be a part of the predicate rather than the subject. Thus, for instance, the sentence that "His friends are all good students except in logic" is formulated as the two following propositions: "All of his friends are good students in subjects other than logic" and "None of his friends is a good logic student." And finally, exceptive sentences may also be *particular* rather than universal, though the latter seems to be more common. Thus "Some of his friends are good students except in logic" and "People are often fakers except when they're alone."

Such sentences which really express two propositions are called *exponible* sentences. Unfortunately, the situation is a little more complicated than we have so far indicated, for not all exceptive sentences are exponible, or at least not exponible in the same way as the above sentences. Consider the following: "Only men are admitted to Harvard College." This certainly says that "No *women* (or no non-men) are admitted to Harvard College." But does it also say, parallel to our earlier examples, that "*All men* are admitted to Harvard College"? On the contrary, it says something less than that; it says only that

[5] Pp. 174–177.

some men are admitted to Harvard College. Hence this sentence expresses, not two universal propositions, but rather one universal and one particular proposition: "No non-men are admitted to Harvard College" and "Some men are admitted to Harvard College." Notice here that the primary intention of this sentence is exceptive and therefore negative—to deny something of something; the affirmative function is definitely minor. Furthermore, as we shall shortly see in detail, the affirmative proposition here ("Some men are admitted to Harvard College") is actually already contained in and therefore deducible from the negative proposition ("No non-men are admitted to Harvard College"). Consequently it isn't even necessary to formulate the affirmative proposition separately, though it doesn't do any harm to do so.

Because of these complications, the best procedure to follow when confronted with an exceptive sentence is the following:

1. *Substitute "non-," "not," or "other than" for the exceptive word and then handle the sentence as you would a non-exceptive one.* (A bar *over* the letter symbol, e.g., H, conveniently indicates that it is negative.) For example:

Everyone but the heroes hated the war.
Everyone other than the heroes hated the war.

or

All non-heroes hated the war.

$$\overline{H} \qquad a \qquad W$$
All (non-heroes) are (ones who hated the war.) $\overline{H}aW$

2. *Then formulate any other proposition which may happen to be intended by the original sentence.* (This step is more difficult but less important than the first step.) In the above example the speaker probably intends to imply that

No heroes hated the war. $He\underline{W}$

but he may mean only that

Some heroes did not hate the war. $Ho\underline{W}$

These are certainly not all of the especially difficult linguistic expressions relevant to the formulation of propositions, and you will doubtless run into others. But we have here covered the most important and common ones, and constant vigilance and practice on your part will make you proficient in detecting and formulating the propositions expressed by language. The most important general rule to remember is to ask and re-ask yourself the question: *Exactly what does the speaker (or writer) intend to assert in this sentence?* In this task of propositional formulation there can be no adequate mechanical substitute for reflection.

11–3   SUMMARY EXERCISES

Having considered in some detail the procedure for formulating the **propo-**sitions expressed by language, let us now quickly review this **procedure as** a whole.

Example 1: "Turkeys often fail to enjoy Thanksgiving."

Step 1: *Isolate the terms:*
      (Turkeys) often (fail to enjoy Thanksgiving.)
Step 2: *Identify the copula and its quality:*
               are   things that
      (Turkeys) ∧ often (∧ fail to enjoy Thanksgiving.)
Step 3: *Indicate the quantity of the proposition and the distribution of the terms:*
      Some (turkeys) are ~~often~~ (things that fail to enjoy Thanksgiving.)
Step 4: *Express in symbols:*
$$T \qquad i \qquad\qquad \overline{F}$$
      Some (turkeys) are (things that fail to enjoy Thanksgiving.)

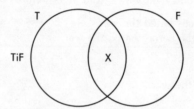

Example 2: "Few politicians can afford to be sincere."

Step 1: Few (politicians) (can afford to be sincere.)
                        are-not   ones who
Step 2: Some (politicians)   ∧ (∧   can afford to be sincere.)
Step 3: Some (politicians) are-not (<u>ones who can afford to be sincere.</u>)
             P   o   <u>A</u>
Step 4: Some (politicians) are-not (<u>ones who can afford to be sincere.</u>)

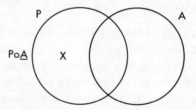

Example 3: "Only those may vote who have registered."
                exponible into two propositions:
      3A: "No one may vote who has not registered."

Step 1: No (one) (may vote) (who has not registered.)
          is one who
Step 2: No (one who has not registered) ∧ (∧ may vote.)
Step 3: No (<u>one who has not registered</u>) is (<u>one who may vote.</u>)
      $\bar{\text{R}}$ e   <u>V</u>
Step 4: No (<u>one who has not registered</u>) is (<u>one who may vote.</u>)

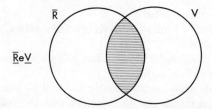

    3B: "All (or some of?) those who have registered may vote."

Step 1: All (those who have registered) (may vote.)
           are ones who
Step 2: All (those who have registered) ∧ (∧ may vote.)
Step 3: All (<u>those who have registered</u>) are (ones who may vote.)
      R   a   V
Step 4: All (<u>those who have registered</u>) are (ones who may vote.)

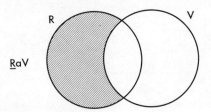

EXERCISES

Formulate the propositions conveyed by the following sentences, first in language and then in symbols, and make a Venn diagram of each.

1. Every year the ladies of Smithville conduct a tournament commemorating Martin's long service to the club.
2. The United National Association of Post Office Clerks will hold its forty-fourth convention in Cleveland.
3. Everybody went except those who had to work.
4. Students occasionally get good grades without working.
5. He works least who worries most.
6. Few of our citizens really appreciate the magnitude of the current arms expenditures.
7. Never have so many owed so much to so few.

8. The artist is seldom capable of looking at his own work objectively.
9. A strong international organization is the only way to lasting world peace.
10. Not all dictators are benevolent.
11. None of the regular members of the Yankee team and staff, save those with families or friends living in Philadelphia, wanted the Phillies to win the pennant.
12. The Navy, alone among all the services, desired the development of the new super aircraft carriers.
13. Successful people are often stuffy.
14. Only a few of New York's leading citizens are fully aware of the threat posed by the St. Lawrence seaway.
15. Anyone who believes that good will alone can bring about peace is a fool.
16. Dew frequently falls on clear nights.
17. Nobody but an imbecile would strike a match to see if he has any gas in his tank.
18. The coldest night of the month always coincides with the full moon.
19. The Wright brothers occasionally toyed with the idea of a helicopter.
20. U.S. citizens seldom experience any difficulty in entering Canada and Mexico.
21. The Republican party is the party founded by Abraham Lincoln.
22. War never solves anything.
23. All students are not guilty of the practice of memorizing without understanding.
24. The stadium is that type of building used for outdoor athletic events.
25. Seldom in the annals of modern medicine has a discovery had such far-reaching implications.
26. Only U.S. citizens over twenty-one years of age may vote.

CHAPTER 12

OPPOSITION OF PROPOSITIONS

Reformulating Assertions. It is a common experience that we try to make ourselves clear not only by trying to formulate our assertions very carefully and precisely but also by saying the same thing in other ways. Consider the following dialogue:

A: Only world government can give us lasting peace, I tell you!

B: Do you mean to stand there and deny the possibility of there being at least one other way to peace?

A: To *lasting* peace, I said. And that's exactly what I do mean!

B: What? Why that's the same thing as saying that no world government can ever fail to establish peace, and that's crazy! Why, look at the ancient world governments of Alexander the Great and Genghis Khan!

A: That's not what I said, and it doesn't follow from what I said! I said that *some* kind of world government, at least one kind, can establish lasting peace, and that no merely national government ever can!

Here speaker A first asserts a proposition, then rephrases it by denying an opposing proposition, and then again tries to make it clear by asserting two other propositions which agree with the first proposition and express it in a different way. This is a common and extremely useful practice, as we all know; and it involves the formulation and use of propositions which either agree or disagree with a given proposition. In order to be able to perform such transformations successfully and thus make our assertions entirely clear, we need to understand clearly and explicitly the various ways in which propositions may agree or disagree with each other.

Now the propositions whose agreement or disagreement is under consideration may have either the same or different terms; that is, they may have the same subjects and the same predicates (e.g., SaP and SeP) or they may have different subjects or predicates (e.g., SaP and P̄oS—i.e., non-PoS). Let us first consider the relations among propositions whose terms are the *same*.

There are exactly four different propositions having the same terms: A, E, I, and O—provided of course that A propositions with distributed predicates are treated as ordinary A propositions. These four propositions differ only with respect to their quality or quantity, but this means that they may also differ with respect to their truth and falsity, for they refer to different situations. If it is true that *all* men are fools, it cannot also be true that *no* men are fools. To introduce a technical term, the four types of proposition may differ in *truth-value.* By the truth-value of a given proposition is meant *whether that proposition is true, false, or undetermined in relation to another proposition.* Hence we shall consider that there are *three* truth-values: *true, false,* and *undetermined,* and they may be symbolized, respectively, by the letters T, F, and U. Strictly speaking, there are of course only two truth-values, true and false, and "undetermined" is rather the lack of determination of the truth-value of a proposition.[1] Yet this lack of determination is so important in considering the relations among propositions that it will be helpful to consider it as a distinct truth-value. Any proposition whose truth-value is undetermined in relation to another proposition is said to be *logically independent* of that other proposition.

12–1   THE SQUARE OF OPPOSITION

What are the relative truth-values of these four propositions, A, E, I, and O? Their truth-value relations may be exhibited visually through the use of what has traditionally been called *the square of opposition.* Since there are exactly four propositions, each one is indicated by one corner of the square, and the sides and diagonals of the square represent the relations among them.

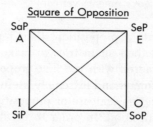

Let us now try to determine the relative truth-values of the four propositions and then enter them on the above square of opposition to complete it.

12–1.1   Implication

Let us start by assuming (perhaps contrary to fact) the truth of the A proposition that "All students are persistent." Now if this be so it is easy to see that the corresponding I proposition must also be true, that "*Some* students are

---

[1] Some modern logicians, however, have developed "multivalued" logics—systems of logic containing truth-values other than true and false.

persistent," for it is included in the original proposition. That this is so can also be seen by noticing that the Venn diagram of an A proposition tacitly includes the Venn diagram of an I proposition, thus:

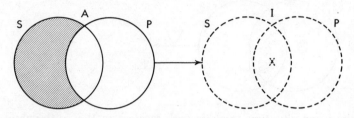

If the S's are not in the S$\overline{\text{P}}$ area—i.e., in the S non-P area—they have to be in the SP area, and this is what the I diagram says.[2]

Now let us assume that the E proposition, "No students are persistent," is true. If this be so then the corresponding O proposition must also be true, for if *no* students at all are persistent then it is obvious that *some* of them aren't. And this also can be made graphic with Venn diagrams:

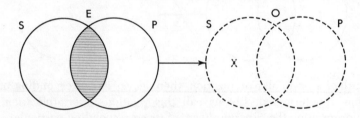

If the S's aren't in SP then they have to be in S$\overline{\text{P}}$.

Thus if the A is true the I is true, and if the E is true the O is true. In short, the truth of a universal proposition implies the truth of its corresponding particular proposition. Let us call this relation *subimplication*[3] and the particular proposition the *subimplicant* of its corresponding universal proposition. Thus I is the subimplicant of A, and O is the subimplicant of E.

Let us now begin, however, by assuming the truth of the I proposition, that "Some students are persistent." Does it follow that the corresponding A proposition is true, that *all* students are persistent? Unfortunately not. But neither does it follow that the A proposition is false, that it is not the case that all students are persistent. Rather, the truth or falsity of the A proposition in such a situation is simply unknown or undetermined. In short, *if I is true then*

---

[2] For situations in which the S term fails to designate, see the discussions on pp. 138–141 above and pp. 184–185 below.
[3] This relation is sometimes called *subalternation*.

A is undetermined. And this fact is visually clear on Venn diagrams, for the I diagram neither includes nor excludes the A diagram:

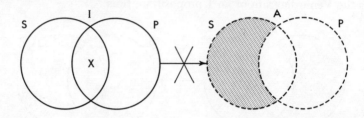

Exactly the same situation prevails with respect to the truth-value of E on the assumption of the truth of O: If it is true that "Some students are not persistent," then the E proposition that "No students are persistent" may be either true or false and hence is simply undetermined:

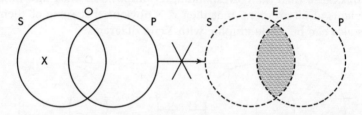

The truth of a particular proposition, then, leaves its corresponding universal proposition undetermined. Let us call this relation *superimplication,* and a universal proposition the *superimplicant* of its corresponding particular proposition. Thus I is the subimplicant of A, O the subimplicant of E, A the superimplicant of I, and E the superimplicant of O. And the truth of a superimplicant implies the truth of its subimplicant, but the truth of a subimplicant leaves the truth of its superimplicant undetermined. To summarize so far:

If the superimplicant is true then its subimplicant is true, but if the subimplicant is true the superimplicant is undetermined.

But now, instead of beginning with the assumption of the truth of one of these propositions, let us begin with the assumption of its falsity. Let us assume that the A proposition that "All students are persistent" is false. What then can we infer about the corresponding I proposition? Does it follow that *some* students are persistent, that the I is true? No, for it might very well be the case that *no* students are persistent. Well then, does it follow that the I proposition is false, that it is not the case that some students are persistent? Again no, for even if it is false that all students are persistent, it could be the case that some are. In short, the falsity of an A proposition leaves the I proposition undetermined in truth-value. And this fact is borne out by Venn diagrams:

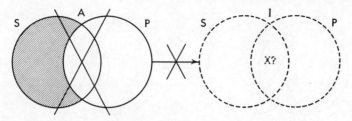

Even though we know from the falsity of A that the S$\bar{\text{P}}$ area is in fact not empty, we cannot know whether there is an X in the SP area.

And the same situation holds good for the other implicational relation, that of E to O. From the falsity of E—from the assumption that it is not the case that no students are persistent—we cannot tell whether or not some students are not persistent; it may or may not be so. Again, note the Venn diagrams:

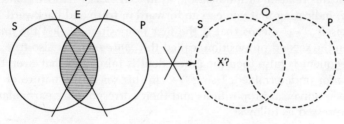

Although we know from the falsity of E that the SP area is not empty, we have no way of knowing whether or not there is an X in the S$\bar{\text{P}}$ area, and hence the truth of the O proposition is undetermined by the falsity of the E.

But what if we start from the falsity of the particular instead of the universal? What may we then infer about the corresponding universal? If it is false that "Some students are persistent," then it surely must be false to say that *all* of them are. Hence from the falsity of an I we can infer the falsity of the corresponding A:

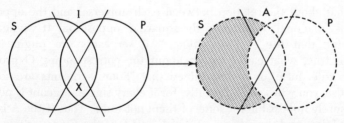

If in fact there is no X in the SP area, then it has to be in the S$\bar{\text{P}}$ area, which falsifies the A diagram. And the same is true with the other implicational relation. If it is false that "Some students are not persistent," it is obviously wrong to say that *none* of them are. Thus if O is false we know that E is false:

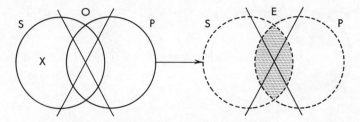

If there is actually no X in the S$\overline{\text{P}}$ area, then it has to be in the SP area, but this falsifies the E diagram, which claims that that area is empty.

To summarize again: *If the superimplicant is false its subimplicant is undetermined, and if the subimplicant is false its superimplicant is false.*

All this can be simply and conveniently generalized by using the symbol "→" to stand for this relation of implication, as in "SaP→SiP." Notice that the arrow is one-way, indicating that you can go forward in truth and backward in falsity. More precisely, "→" means that if the first proposition, called the *antecedent*, is true then the second proposition, called the *consequent*, is also true; and that if the consequent is false then the antecedent is false; and that everything else is unknown or undetermined. Using "→" in this sense, the nature of this relation between universal propositions and their corresponding particulars can be entirely expressed as follows:

SaP→SiP and SeP→SoP

or

A→I and E→O

or still more simply:

Superimplicant→ subimplicant

12–1.2   Contradiction

Now what about the relation between each universal and the opposite particular—the "diagonal" relation on the square of opposition? If we again begin by assuming that the A proposition, "All sergeants are pugnacious," for instance, is true, what can we infer about the corresponding O proposition? Will it be true, false, or undetermined that "Some sergeants are-not pugnacious"? False, you will say, and rightly, for if every single sergeant is pugnacious then it is surely impossible for some of them not to be. Thus if the A is true the O must be false. And the same is true of E and I: If the E proposition that "No sergeants are pugnacious" is true, the corresponding I proposition must be false, for it is certainly impossible to have both none of them and some of them pugnacious at the same time. And what if we begin by assuming the truth of the particular; what then about the opposite universal? If it is true that "Some sergeants are pugnacious" (I), it must be false that none of them are (E); and if it is true that "Some sergeants are-not pugnacious" (O), then it is surely false that all of them are (A). In short, the truth of any one of the four propositions implies the falsity of its diagonal proposition.

But what if we are told that one of these propositions is false, rather than true? Does this mean that its diagonal proposition must be true? If it is *false* that "All sergeants are pugnacious" (A), then it has to be *true* that at least some of them are not pugnacious (O); and if it is false that some of them are not pugnacious (O), it is surely true that all of them are (A). The same situation is true of the relation of E and I: If it is wrong to say that "No S's are P's" (E), then it must be right to say that some of them are (I); and if we are incorrect when we say that "Some S's are P's" (I), then we must surely be correct when we say that none of them are P's (E).

In short: *Propositions diagonally related on the square of opposition are always opposite in truth-value.* And this fact may be confirmed by a careful inspection of Venn diagrams:

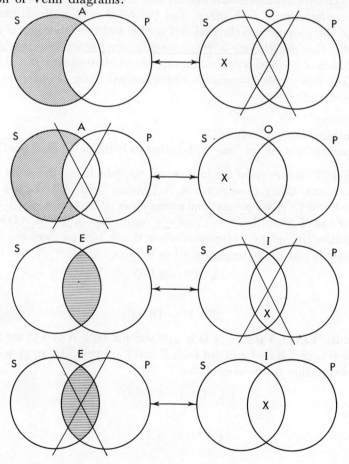

Here it is obvious that A and O must be exactly opposite in truth-value because the A diagram asserts that the $S\overline{P}$ area is empty while the O diagram directly contradicts that by asserting that that space is not empty but rather possesses at least one thing. Now the $S\overline{P}$ space must be either empty or not, and it can't be both. Hence one of the propositions must be true, and the other false. If, therefore, we are given either the truth or the falsity of either one of them, we can infer concerning the other that its truth-value is just the opposite. And the same thing goes for the relation between E and I: Since the E diagram states that the SP space is empty and the I diagram contradicts that state of affairs by placing something in that space, one and only one of them is true, for that space must be either empty or not, and it can't be both.

Since A and O, and E and I, directly contradict each other, as these diagrams make amply apparent, the relation existing between the propositions in each of these pairs is called *contradiction*; and propositions in this relation of contradiction are called *contradictories*. Thus A and O are contradictories, and E and I are contradictories, of each other. And the relation of contradiction means that one of the propositions thus related is true and the other one is false, or, more briefly, that *exactly one of two contradictory propositions is true.*

This relation of contradiction can be simply and conveniently stated by introducing three new symbols—symbols which we will have occasion to use frequently hereafter:

    "·" means "both . . . and."
    "−" means "not" or "is false."
    "∨" means "and/or" or "one or the other or both" or "at least one."

The symbol "∨" comes from the latin word *vel*, which has the same meaning "∨" receives here. Using these symbols, A·I means "both A and I are true," or just "both A and I"; A ∨ I means "one or the other or both of A and I are true," or "at least one of A and I is true"; and −A means "not A" or "A is false." With this symbolism the relation of contradiction which obtains between A and O and between E and I may be expressed as follows:

$$(A \lor O) \cdot -(A \cdot O)$$

and

$$(E \lor I) \cdot -(E \cdot I)$$

which reads: "Either A is true or O is true and not both A and O are true, and either E is true or I is true and not both E and I are true." Or to give a slightly different expression to the same thing:

$$(A \lor O) \cdot (-A \lor -O)$$

and

$$(E \lor I) \cdot (-E \lor -I)$$

which reads: "Either A is true or O is true and either A is false or O is false, and either E is true or I is true and either E is false or I is false." In order to express this relation of contradiction more briefly, however, let us introduce yet another symbol "$\underline{\vee}$" which will mean "one true and one false," or "one and only one true," or, finally, "exactly one true." Using this symbol the relation of contradiction may be stated thus:

$$(A \underline{\vee} O) \cdot (E \underline{\vee} I)$$

which reads: "Exactly one of A and O is true, and exactly one of E and I is true."

12–1.3 Contrariety

We have examined the relation between each universal and its particular and also the diagonal relation of contradiction. Now what about the relation between the two universal propositions?

If we assume the truth of the A proposition that "All scholars are pedagogues," then the corresponding E proposition, "No scholars are pedagogues," must be false, for it is impossible to have both all scholars and no scholars pedagogues at the same time. Likewise if the E proposition is true the A must be false. These conclusions may be confirmed by utilizing the relations of contradiction and implication: If A is true then O, its contradictory, must be false; and if O is false then E, its superimplicant, must also be false. Hence if A is true E is false. Likewise if E is true its contradictory, I, must be false; and if I is false its superimplicant, A, must also be false. Thus the truth of either universal requires the falsity of the other. Note that this is confirmed by Venn diagrams:

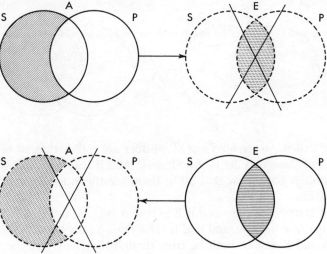

If all S's are inside P, it cannot also be true that the SP area is empty (which the E declares it to be); and if the SP area is empty, it cannot also be the case that it contains all the S's (as the A claims).

But what if we begin with the assumption of the *falsity* of one of these universal propositions? If it is false that "All scholars are pedagogues," is it thereby true that *no* scholars are pedagogues? Clearly not, for it might be the case that only some scholars are pedagogues. In like manner if we are given the falsity of the E proposition that "No scholars are pedagogues" we cannot thereby infer the truth of the corresponding A proposition that *all* scholars are pedagogues, for it might be that some of them are not. Once more we may use the relations of contradiction and implication to arrive at the same conclusion: If A is false then O is true (contradiction), and if O is true then E is undetermined (superimplication). Further, if E is false then I is true (contradiction), and if I is true then A is undetermined (superimplication). Thus the falsity of either universal leaves the other one undetermined. Again this conclusion is borne out by Venn diagrams:

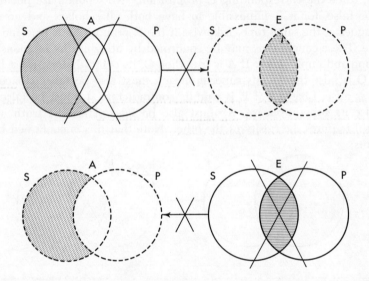

If it is false that there are no S's in S$\overline{P}$, it does not follow that *all* of the S's are there—some of them may be in the SP area. And if it is false that there are no S's in SP, it does not follow that *all* of them are there, for some of them may be in the S$\overline{P}$ area.

Thus if A is true E is false and if E is true A is false; but if A is false then E may be either true or false, and if E is false than A may be either true or false. In short: A and E cannot both be true, though they may both be false as for instance when, as seems likely, some students are persistent and some are not. This relation which obtains between A and E propositions is called *contrariety*, and A and E is each the *contrary* of the other. In its simplest terms contrariety means "*not both true*," or in other words "*at least one false*." This relation can be simply and conveniently stated by using the symbols we have just introduced:

$$-[(SaP) \cdot (SeP)] \quad \text{or} \quad -(A \cdot E)$$

which reads: "A and E are not both true." Or, since this is the same thing as saying that at least one of them is false, the relation of contrariety may also be expressed thus:

$$-(SaP) \vee -(SeP) \quad \text{or} \quad -A \vee -E$$

which reads: "Either A is false or E is false or both," or "A and/or E is false," or, finally, "at least one of A and E is false."

12–1.4 Subcontrariety

Let us now turn to the last remaining relation on the square of opposition, the relation between the two particular propositions, I and O. If it is true that "Some scalawags are paupers" (I), is it true, false, or undetermined that "Some scalawags are not paupers" (O)? Undetermined, for from the fact that at least some are paupers we cannot tell whether the others are paupers or not. In the same manner the truth of O leaves the corresponding I undetermined. This fact can also be seen by utilizing the other relations on the square of opposition. If I is true then E (its contradictory) is false, and if E is false then O (its subimplicant) is undetermined. Likewise if O is true then A (its contradictory) must be false, and if A is false than I (its subimplicant) is undetermined. Hence the truth of either I or O leaves the truth-value of the other undetermined.

If, however, we are given the falsity rather than the truth of one of these particular propositions, we can infer that the other one must be true. If it is not the case that even some scalawags are paupers, it necessarily follows that at least some of them are not. Likewise, if it is false that some of them are not, then at least some of them have to be paupers. The other relations on the square of opposition again confirm the same fact: If I is false E must be true, and if E is true then O has to be true. And if O is false A has to be true, and if A is true then I must be true. In short: *If either particular proposition is false the other one is true, but if either one is true the other one is undetermined.* Let us see this rule confirmed by Venn diagrams:

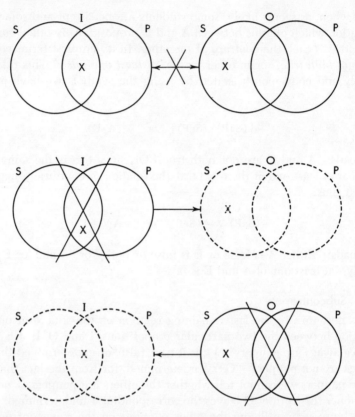

In the first pair of diagrams we see that the I and O diagrams do not include, but are consistent with, each other. Hence the truth of either implies nothing about the other. In the second pair we see that the falsity of I means that there are in fact no S's in the SP area, so it necessarily follows that they must be in the S$\overline{P}$ area, which is exactly what O says. And finally, in the third pair, we see that the falsity of O means that there are in fact no S's in the S$\overline{P}$ area, so the S's must therefore be in the SP area, which is what I declares.

This relation between the two particular propositions, I and O, is known as *subcontrariety*, and I and O are *subcontraries* of each other. Subcontrariety means that one or both of the subcontraries is true, or that both of them cannot be false. Notice how this relation differs from the relation of contrariety obtaining between A and E: A and E may both be false but they cannot both be true; I and O may both be true but they cannot both be false. Using the symbolism we have introduced, the relation of subcontrariety may be expressed thus:

$$I \lor O \quad \text{or} \quad -(-I \cdot -O)$$

which reads: "Either I is true or O is true or both," or "It is not the case both that I is false and that O is false."

Review. These relations obtaining among propositions having the same terms may be conveniently summarized by now filling in the details of the square of opposition with which we began this discussion:

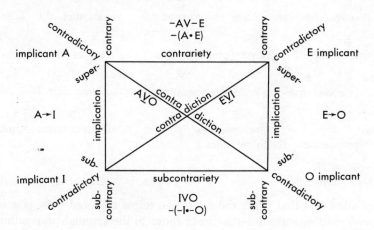

Once we understand these four relations (implication, contradiction, contrariety, and subcontrariety) which hold among propositions having the same terms, we need only know that some one of them is true or false in order to be able to determine the resulting truth-value of each of the others. Thus if O is false then A is true, I is true, and E is false; if E is true then O is true, A is false, and I is false; if A is false then O is true, and E and I are undetermined, etc. It is very important to proficiency in logic to practice this exercise and learn the square of opposition so that you can quickly give the truth-values of the three remaining propositions after being given the truth-value of the other one. Note, however, that the given proposition must be either true or false; if its truth-value is undetermined, if we do not know whether it is true or false, then we cannot tell anything about the truth-values of the remaining propositions.

In everyday life, however, propositions encountered which may be compared on the square of opposition will not be in symbolic form. Rather they will be expressed in ordinary language and must first be formulated as propositions and, for further convenience, in symbolic form before they can be thus compared. Consequently we must now combine our last two lessons; we must both formulate and compare on the square of opposition the propositions which we encounter. But remember that they can be compared on the square of opposition only if their terms are the same, only if they have the same subjects and the same predicates, thus differing only in quantity and/or quality. Let us carry through both procedures in the following example:

$$\underline{\text{E}} \qquad\qquad \text{a} \qquad\qquad \text{P}$$
(Election speeches) are always (propagandistic.)   assumed T (true)

$$\text{E} \qquad\qquad \text{o} \qquad\qquad \underline{\text{P}}$$
1. (Election speeches) are seldom (propagandistic.)   contradictory F (false)

$$\underline{\text{E}} \qquad\qquad \text{e} \qquad\qquad \underline{\text{P}}$$
2. (Election speeches) are never (propagandistic.)   contrary F

$$\qquad\quad \text{Some} \qquad \text{E} \qquad\qquad \text{i} \qquad\quad \text{P}$$
3. A few (election speeches) are (propagandistic.)   subimplicant T

$$\qquad\qquad\qquad\qquad\qquad \text{E}$$
Some   P   i   elec. speeches   different terms   unknown
4. Much (propaganda) is (to get votes.)

$$\underline{\text{H}} \quad \text{a} \quad \text{T}$$
5. (Horses) (have tails.)   different terms   unknown

Notice in number 4 that while the same two terms are used their positions as subject and predicate are different from those in the original proposition, and that number 4 can therefore not be compared with the original proposition on the square of opposition. There is, however, another way of determining the truth-value of such a proposition, and we shall learn that way as soon as we have considered some difficulties in the square of opposition.

12-2 DIFFICULTIES AND EXCEPTIONS IN THE SQUARE

The propositions we have used as examples in learning the square of opposition have all been general rather than singular ones; they have been subject-predicate propositions rather than existence propositions; and the designation of their terms has always been a real, inclusive designation. What happens, however, if we encounter a singular proposition, or an existence proposition, or a proposition whose terms have other than real and inclusive designation, or which lack designation altogether? Will the square of opposition hold good for these types of proposition as well? Let us see.

Let us consider the singular proposition "Socrates was a philosopher." If we want to oppose this proposition is doesn't sound right to say "None of Socrates was a philosopher" or "Some of Socrates was not a philosopher," or even that "Some of Socrates was a philosopher." Instead we would probably say simply that "Socrates was not a philosopher." And these two propositions truly do contradict each other: if the subject is simply Socrates, as such, then he must either have been a philosopher or not, and it is impossible that he be both a philosopher and not a philosopher. In short, whenever the subject of a singular proposition is considered simply, without qualification, then instead of having a square with four related propositions we have a *line* of opposition with only *two* propositions related by the single relation of contradiction, thus:

contradiction

affirmative ——————————————— negative

(Socrates was   (Socrates was

a philosopher.)   not a philosopher.)

However, it is always possible to quantify the subject of any singular proposition by considering its *temporal* extent. When we do this we have not just two propositions but four regular propositions: "Socrates was always a philosopher" (A), "Socrates was never a philosopher" (E), "Socrates was sometimes a philosopher" (I), and "Sometimes Socrates was not a philosopher" (O). These four propositions are related on the square of opposition in exactly the same way as the four forms of any ordinary proposition. Whether the singular subject is to be treated simply or as quantified in time seems to depend on whether the predicate is singular or general in its import. If, for example, it is Socrates' death which is in question, an event which can happen only once, we will have only two propositions related by contradiction on a line of opposition: "Socrates died in 399 B.C." or "Socrates did not die in 399 B.C." But if we are concerned with something that may happen a number of times, which is general in character, such as Socrates' relations with his wife, then we presumably have the usual four propositions related on the square of opposition: "Socrates was always nagged by Xantippe," "Socrates was never nagged by Xantippe," "Socrates was sometimes nagged by Xantippe," "Sometimes Socrates was not nagged by Xantippe." Which of these two interpretations is relevant in a particular case you will have to decide by reflection and experience.

Exactly the same situation holds good for existence propositions.[4] This is especially true where the existence proposition is also a singular proposition like "Zeus does not exist." When the singular subject is regarded simply, with no attention to its possible temporal extension, we have just two opposed propositions: "Zeus exists" and "Zeus does not exist." But if we are interested in the question of the temporal extent of this singular subject we again have four propositions and the square of opposition: "Zeus always exists," "Zeus never exists," "Zeus sometimes exists," and "Sometimes Zeus does not exist." The same is also true when the subject of the existence proposition is general. We may want to consider only whether "War exists" or "War does not exist," for example; but at other times we may be interested in the temporal question and have to consider four possibilities: "War always exists, "War never exists," "War sometimes exists," and "Sometimes war does not exist."

To summarize: *In singular and existence propositions the temporal extent*

---

[4] See the discussion of existence propositions on pp. 107–112.

of the subject may be either considered or ignored. When it is considered there will be four relevant propositions and the square of opposition, and when it is ignored there will be only two relevant propositions and only a line of opposition (contradiction).

Let us now consider how the square of opposition is affected by designational failures and changes. Let us suppose that you are an only child and that you are in the witness chair before a committee investigating communist subversion. Your examiner points an accusing finger at you and declares: "All of your brothers are communists!" You doubtless object strenuously to this accusation on the ground that you have no brothers and therefore certainly none that are communists. But in doing this are you committing yourself to the truth of the corresponding O proposition; are you saying in effect that "Some of my brothers are not communists"? Hardly, for that proposition would also be untrue and for the same reason—because you have no brothers. Thus, contrary to the square of opposition, the falsity of this A proposition does not imply the truth of its corresponding O proposition. Furthermore, the other two propositions on the square would also be untrue[5] rather than undetermined —that "Some of your brothers are communists" and that "None of your brothers are communists"—and again for the same reason, because you have no bothers.

In short, we have here a situation in which the relations on the square of opposition do not hold good because there are no members of the S class. How then would you logically oppose your accuser? There is only one thing that you could say: "It is false that all of my brothers are communists, and it is false simply because I have no brothers." In such a case, then, we have only two opposed propositions and only a line of contradiction instead of a square of opposition.

Of course your erstwhile accuser might playfully rejoin as follows: "But I mean your *imaginary* brothers. I know you don't have any real brothers, but I can imagine that you do and talk about those brothers, can't I?" "Of course you can," you might reply with considerable irritation, "but don't confuse them with the real brothers that I don't have! Furthermore, if you want to play that all of my imaginary brothers are communists, I can still contradict you by countering that some of my imaginary brothers are not communists!" Notice here that the falsity of *this* A proposition *does* imply the truth of the corresponding O proposition, and also leaves the corresponding E and I propositions undetermined just as the square of opposition prescribes. Thus the square holds for propositions whose terms have merely mental designation as well as

[5] The corresponding negative propositions might be called "inappropriate" rather than false, and in certain cases perhaps even true. See the discussions of propositions with non-designating terms on pp. 140 and 141. But this variability would still prevent the square of opposition from applying because the relations on the square require that the various truth-values be determined invariably.

for ones whose terms have real designation. But the designation must remain the same, either real or mental, for the square to apply. The falsity of "All of my *real* brothers are communists" does *not* imply the truth of "Some of my *imaginary* brothers are not communists." As a matter of fact, when this difference in designation is explicated the result is two obviously different terms, and of course propositions with different terms cannot be compared on the square of opposition. In short, the square applies when and only when the terms *designate,* and also have the *same kind* of designation.

In the case of certain propositions with non-designating terms, however, it almost looks as if the relations on the square of opposition would hold good. For example, if we start with the designationally false I proposition that "Some of the members of Plato's Academy are Harvard professors," the corresponding E proposition, "No members of Plato's Academy are Harvard professors," is true and the corresponding A proposition, "All of the members of Plato's Academy are Harvard professors," is false. So far the square of opposition holds good. But if it really does hold good then the corresponding O proposition, "Several members of Plato's Academy are not Harvard professors," must be true; yet this proposition in fact appears to be "inappropriate" or "queer" because it seems to involve the assertion that there now exist some members of Plato's Academy. And the same thing happens if we start with a negative proposition which is true in spite of a failure of designation on the part of one of its terms: "No members of Plato's Academy are Harvard professors." The corresponding I and A propositions are clearly false, but, again, the corresponding O is not true. Indeed, if it is true, as it seems to be,[6] that *all* affirmative propositions are untrue when they have non-designating terms, then we should expect the A and I propositions to be false anyhow. Once more, then, the square of opposition is inapplicable.

To summarize: *The square of opposition applies only to propositions whose terms designate, and have the same kind of designation.* Whenever there is a change or failure in designation the square of opposition simply does not apply, and the only relevant relation is a simple line of contradiction.

Having seen just when the square of opposition may be used and when it may not, let us turn to the question of the relations among propositions whose terms are different.

EXERCISES

1. Give the contradictory, the contrary (or subcontrary), and the implicant (sub- or super-) of each of the following propositions:
   a. Football is often a dangerous game.
   b. Never have the colleges been so crowded.

[6] See pp. 140–141 above.

    c. All is fair in love and war.

    d. Some countries do not require passports.

    e. No successful politician has his head in the clouds.

    f. Few statements are unbiased.

    g. People usually like to have friends.

    h. He is always irritable before he has his coffee.

2. "No one is truly happy who is a slave to his desires." Assuming that this is true, what is the truth-value of each of the following propositions? Assuming that this is *false*, what is the truth-value of each of the following propositions?

    a. Some people who are enslaved by their desires are truly happy.

    b. Everyone enslaved by his desires is truly happy.

    c. People enslaved by their desires are frequently not truly happy.

CHAPTER 13

CONVERTED AND OBVERTED
PROPOSITIONS

Relations Among Propositions Having Negated or Interchanged Terms.
We are now equipped to tell whether propositions agree or disagree with each
other when they have the same terms and differ only in quality and/or
quantity. But how can we compare propositions when their terms are different?
When one or both of the concepts utilized in one proposition are completely
different concepts from those utilized in another proposition (e.g., "Dema-
gogues always do more harm than good" and "Self-government is the way to
the greatest happiness"), the propositions can be compared only by finding
other propositions which share terms in common with these propositions. This
involves argument or inference, and we shall consider this type of comparison
when we come to the third logical tool, argument.

Frequently, however, two propositions will have the same basic concepts,
S and P, and will differ only in the subject or predicate position of these concepts, or in whether these concepts are positive or negative. Given the concepts
S and P, the following eight propositional combinations are possible: S–P, $\bar{S}$–P,
S–$\bar{P}$, $\bar{S}$–$\bar{P}$, P–S, $\bar{P}$–S, P–$\bar{S}$, $\bar{P}$–$\bar{S}$. Furthermore, each of these eight propositional
forms may be of the four different types—A, E, I, and O—thus forming thirty-
two different propositions utilizing the same basic concepts. Now how can we
compare propositions whose terms differ in these ways? Suppose, for example,
that Joe says, "Only those nations are free whose governments are in the hands
of the people," and that George says, "All nations are enslaved save those
whose governments are not in the hands of the people." Are they agreeing or
disagreeing with each other? There is a way of telling whether they are in
agreement or disagreement, and also of telling exactly why they are; and it is
to that topic that we shall now turn. But before we do, you might find it
instructive to try to decide now whether or not and why these two statements
agree so that you can compare your "before" answer with your answer "after"
you have studied the following logical procedures.

All that we need to know in order to be able to compare such propositions is
two simple operations for the transformation of propositions: *conversion* and

187

obversion. Conversion is concerned with propositions which differ with respect to the positions of their terms as subjects or predicates. Obversion is concerned with propositions which differ with respect to whether their terms are positive or negative. These two operations are independent of each other and may be learned and used in either order.

13–1   CONVERSION

The process called logical conversion consists basically in interchanging the subject and predicate of a given proposition while keeping it the same in quality—affirmative if affirmative and negative if negative. The resulting proposition is called the *converse* of the original, and the original is sometimes called the *convertend* in relation to its converse. Thus the converse of "Some agnostics go to church" (AiC) is simply "Some people who go to church are agnostics" (CiA).

There is, however, one other requirement, and a most important one, for valid conversion: *The quantity of a given term cannot be greater in the converse than in the convertend.* In other words: *A term which is undistributed in the original proposition cannot be distributed in the converse.* This is exactly parallel to the situation we discovered to pertain to superimplication on the square of opposition: Given the truth of a particular proposition (i.e., a proposition whose subject term is particular or undistributed), we can infer nothing concerning the truth or falsity of the corresponding universal proposition (i.e., the same proposition except with a universal or distributed subject). Both of these situations are simply particular instances of a very obvious general rule: *What is true of some of a class need not be true of all of that class.* We cannot turn "some" into "all"; unlike Rumpelstiltskin, logicians cannot spin straw into gold. Or to change the metaphor, "you can't make a silk purse out of a sow's ear." Or finally, as we all know, "you can't get something for nothing."

Of course it is perfectly possible to get nothing for something—or at least to get less from more. So it is perfectly valid with propositions to go from all to some, for what is true of all S's or P's must also be true of some of them; and indeed this is exactly what subimplication consists in, as we have seen. You *can* get straw from gold; you can buy sows' ears with silk purses—at least if the purses are not empty. Of course, no one wants to lose anything in the transaction if it can be helped. And so if we start with all it's best to try to keep all; if we have distributed terms in the convertend, we want to keep them distributed in the converse if possible.

In short, in valid conversion we can pass from all to all, from all to some, and from some to some, but never from some to all. In other words, a term which is distributed in the convertend may be either distributed or undistributed in the converse, but a term which is undistributed in the convertend must also be undistributed in the converse.

Thus the process of conversion involves two steps: (1) interchanging the two terms while keeping the quality constant and (2) checking the distribution to see that the quantity of each of the terms is exactly as great as it can be, but no greater. Let us now apply this process of conversion to each of the four types of proposition in order to discover their corresponding converses.

E and I Propositions: Simple Conversion. What is the converse of the proposition, "Saints never get potted"? Well, let us first interchange the two terms while keeping an E proposition, and then check the distribution of the resulting terms: "Nobody who gets potted is a saint." Since the convertend here is an E proposition (SeP) and since E propositions distribute both their terms, the converse will also be an E proposition with both its terms distributed. Thus SeP converts simply to PeS. In fact, these two propositions are entirely equivalent; they describe exactly the same situation, as is manifested by a Venn diagram:

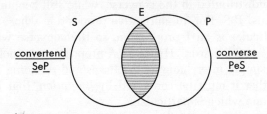

They both say that there is nothing which is both an S and a P.

Exactly the same situation is true of I propositions. To get the converse of "Some savants are parsimonious" we keep an I proposition but interchange the two terms: "Some parsimonious people are savants." Since both terms are undistributed in the convertend, they must also be undistributed in the converse, which they are since it is an I proposition. Thus SiP converts simply to PiS. Like the E proposition and its converse, the I proposition and its converse are entirely equivalent and describe exactly the same situation:

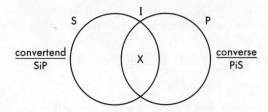

I prop

Both convertend and converse say that there is something which is both S and P.

Thus E and I propositions convert simply with no change in the distribution of their terms. The reason is simply that the subject of each of these propositions has the same distribution as the predicate: in the E both S and P are distributed, and in the I both are undistributed. Hence a reversal of their positions does not alter the distribution of their terms. But what about the other two types of proposition, where S and P are different in distribution?

A Propositions.   What is the converse of the A proposition that "All Spaniards are people" (SaP)? Our first step is to interchange the S and P while retaining the same type of proposition—here an A—thus: "All people are Spaniards" (PaS). But this is clearly absurd, for there are lots of people who aren't Spaniards. What is the trouble here? Our second step shows us: P in the converse is distributed (since it is there the subject of an A proposition) while in the convertend it is undistributed; and this violates the distribution rule, which says that you cannot go from some to all. Hence to get a valid converse we must make P undistributed in the converse, while still keeping the proposition affirmative, thus: P S. But an affirmative proposition whose subject is undistributed or particular is an I proposition, so the converse will have to be PiS: "Some people are Spaniards." Hence an A proposition cannot be converted *simply*, that is, by simply interchanging the terms and retaining the same type of proposition. Rather it must be converted by *limitation*, that is, by limiting the proposition to one which is particular.

That this must be so can be easily seen by remembering that an A proposition, "All S is P," "All Spaniards are people," really says that "All S is (*some*) P," that "All Spaniards are (*some*) people." Thus when we interchange the terms we must say that "*Some* P is . . . ," that "*Some* people are. . . ." True, given the original A proposition that "All S is P," that "All Spaniards are people," we would be justified by the distribution rule in saying in the converse that "Some P is (*all*) S," that "Some people are (*all*) Spaniards." And indeed we shall see later that we do in fact do this tacitly when we compare propositions with respect to their truth-values, either in the transformations which we are now studying or in the arguments that we shall study later on.[1] Still, we would not ordinarily say, "Some people are all Spaniards"; if we wanted to describe that fact we would probably say instead that "All Spaniards are people."

So the A proposition converts by limitation to an I proposition. Note the Venn diagrams:

---

[1] On this contrast between mere *transformations* of propositions and actual arguments or *demonstrations*, see below, Chap. 15.1.

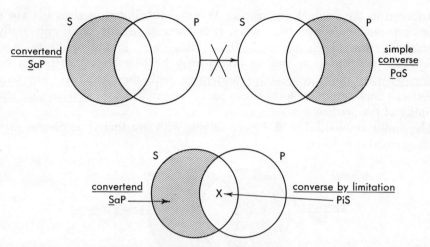

In the first diagram the emptiness of the S$\overline{\text{P}}$ area does not imply the emptiness of the $\overline{\text{S}}$P area. But in the second diagram the fact that there are no S's outside P does imply that the S's must coincide with some of the P's, that some P's are S's. Note, however, that a converse by limitation is not strictly equivalent to its convertend, that the situation described by PiS is not exactly the same as the one described by SaP. Rather the former is only a part of the latter situation, and in this respect conversion by limitation is strictly parallel to subimplication on the square of opposition.

Unfortunately, there is an exception to this rule that A propositions convert by limitation to I propositions, for we must again contend with our old non-conformist, the A proposition with a distributed predicate. What is the converse of the definitional proposition that "A square is an equilateral rectangle" (SaE)? Again we interchange the terms, retain an A proposition, and then check the distribution: "All equilateral rectangles are squares" (EaS). But this time our simple conversion has not violated the distribution rule, for although E (the subject of the converse) is distributed in the converse it is also distributed in the convertend as the predicate of a definitional proposition. Hence we need not limit our converse to an I proposition this time; rather the converse of our definitional proposition will be a simple converse and therefore an A proposition. Again this is apparent when we remember that a definitional proposition tacitly says that "All S is (all) P," that "All squares are (all) equilateral rectangles." Hence the simple converse really affirms exactly the same situation: "All P is (all) S"; "All equilateral rectangles are (all) squares."

Furthermore, A propositions may have distributed predicates and hence be simply convertible even when they are not definitions. Thus the proposition that "The Main Street bus is the one at the next corner" is simply convertible into "The bus at the next corner is the Main Street bus," since both terms are distributed in the original proposition. When a distributed predicate is not a definition—and sometimes even when it is—there is usually some universally quantifying word, such as "the," "that," "this," etc., in the predicate. And definitional predicates—as well as others—may be tested for distribution by seeing whether they are exactly coextensive with their subjects. But only experience and careful reflection can make us proficient in determining the quantity of the predicate.

The simple convertibility of A propositions with distributed predicates may be diagramed as follows:

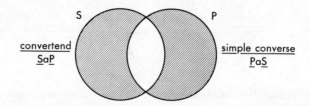

To summarize: _A propositions convert by limitation to I propositions except when they have distributed predicates, in which case they convert simply to A propositions:_ (SaP)→(PiS) but (SaP̱)→(P̱aS).

The Inconvertibility of O Propositions.   What, finally, is the converse of the O proposition, "Some sultans are not popular" (SoP̱)? Let us again follow our two-step procedure, first interchanging the two terms while retaining an O proposition and then checking the distribution: "Some popular people are not sultans" (PoS̱). But as soon as we do so we see that the distribution rule has been violated, for S is distributed in the converse but undistributed in the convertend. Well then, is there some way in which we can doctor this converse so as to make it a valid one? No, there is not, for the converse must be negative (since the converse is always the same in quality as its convertend), and we know that all negative propositions distribute their predicates. Hence there simply isn't any valid converse of an O proposition. _O propositions can never be converted._

You may confirm this fact of the inconvertibility of O propositions by noting that in the original proposition, "Some sultans are not popular," we are given information about only _some_ sultans; but since any kind of conversion of this original proposition requires the term "sultans" to become the predicate of a negative proposition and hence distributed, we are forced in the converse to make a statement about _all_ sultans, that "Some popular people are not (_any_) sultans," thus trying to go from some to all, which is impossible.

Nevertheless, despite the apparent reasonableness of this explanation, you may still remain unconvinced. Nor is there any doubt that a number of O propositions—perhaps even most of them—_seem_ at least to be convertible. For instance, if one says, "Some New Yorkers are not Republicans," does it not seem that one could also say, "Some Republicans are not New Yorkers"? Yet what about an inference such as the following: "Some human beings are not Republicans; therefore, some Republicans are not human beings"? What's wrong with this? To be sure, some of you might be inclined to say, "Nothing!" But this would perhaps be going rather far even for political partisanship.

No, the second inference is clearly invalid. But if the second inference is invalid, the first must be invalid also. For the form of the inference is exactly the same in both cases, SoP→PoS; and in both one goes from an undistributed S term in the convertend to a distributed S term in the converse.

Nevertheless, why is it that, although an inference from some human beings' not being Republicans to some Republicans' not being human is obviously invalid, there does not *seem* to be any fallacy in concluding that some Republicans are not New Yorkers from the fact that some New Yorkers are not Republicans? The answer is this: In the latter case, both propositions happen to be true: there are some New Yorkers who are not Republicans and also some Republicans who are not New Yorkers. But although both statements are true, the second is not true *merely on the basis of what is given* in the first proposition. It is true on other and additional grounds besides the bare information given in the previous statement. For as an analysis of the proposition shows, all that is given in the first statement is an undistributed S term, and from this alone one cannot draw a conclusion that pertains to every S. To be sure, the latter statement may well be true, but its truth does not follow simply from the information given in the first statement and from nothing else.

Once more, it is possible to figure this inconvertibility of an O proposition by means of a Venn diagram:

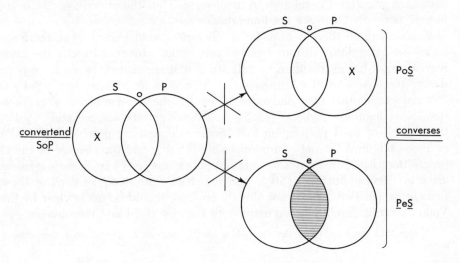

From the fact that there are some S's which are not P's, it follows neither that there are some P's which are not S's nor that there is nothing which is both P and S.

Thus logical conversion is the process of interchanging subject and predicate, retaining the same quality, and adjusting the distribution so that it is as great as possible but no greater than the distribution in the original proposition. The valid converses of each of the types of proposition are as follows:

Convertend	Converse
SaP	PiS
(SaP)	(PaS)
SeP	PeS
SiP	PiS
SoP	none

13–2   OBVERSION

So much for one of the two operations involved in comparing propositions whose terms are interchanged or negated, namely, conversion, which is concerned with the interchange of subject and predicate. Let us now turn to the other operation, obversion, which is concerned with propositions differing with respect to whether their terms are positive or negative.

Just as two minuses equal a plus in mathematics, so in logic two negatives make a positive; and this is the essence of obversion. *Logical obversion consists simply in negating both the copula and the predicate.* The resulting proposition is called the *obverse* of the original, and the original is sometimes called the *obvertend* in relation to its obverse. Thus the obverse of "Men are mortal" is simply "Men are not immortal."

That's about all there is to it, for in obversion, unlike conversion, there are luckily no exceptions: all four types of proposition obvert in exactly the same way. Using a bar over a term to indicate that it is negated, as we have been doing,[2] the obverse of the A proposition "All sailors are philanderers" (SaP) is "No sailors are other than philanderers" (SeP̄); the obverse of the E proposition "No salmon are pickerel" (SeP) is "All salmon are non-pickerel" (SaP̄); the obverse of the I proposition that "Some salesmen are purchasable" (SiP) is "Some salesmen are-not non-purchasable" (SoP̄); and the observe of the O proposition that "Some statesmen are-not politicians" (SoP) is "Some statesmen are other than politicians" (SiP̄). And the strict equivalence of each of these pairs of propositions, if it is not already obvious, should be made clear by the Venn diagrams. Each diagram maps both the obvertend and the obverse.

[2] Notice that the bar *before* the symbol, −(SaP), negates a *proposition* rather than a *term*.

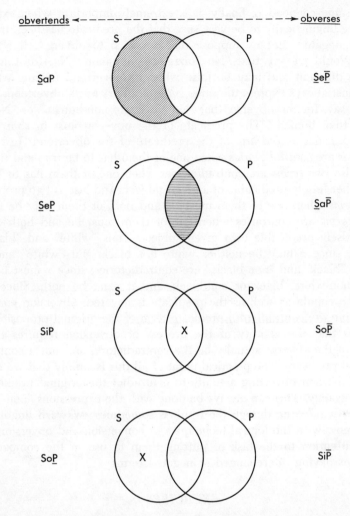

So obversion consists simply in negating both the copula and the predicate while keeping the subject term entirely unchanged, both in quality and in quantity. Hence the obverse of a universal proposition is always a universal, and the obverse of a particular proposition is always a particular. Note also that the practice which we have already introduced of connecting the "not" and the copula with a hyphen in O propositions ("Some S is-not P") is especially useful in obversion, for it helps us remember that it is the copula rather than the predicate which is negative. By the same token it is also helpful to use a hyphen to connect the predicate negative "non," where it is used, with the predicate thus: "Some S is non-P" or "Some S's are-not non-P's."

In this same connection, finally, it is extremely important when expressing the obverse linguistically to be very sure that the predicate has been truly and accurately negated. Let us suppose that we wish to obvert "All Nazis are human." Would we say that "No Nazis are inhuman"? No, for this means something different and may be false when its obvertend is true, while the obverse must always express the same state of affairs as its obvertend. Instead we would say, for the obverse, that "No Nazis are non-human" or "No Nazis are other than human." The predicate of the obverse must in short be the *contradictory*, not a *contrary*, of the predicate of the obvertend. Just as two propositions are *contradictories* when one of them has to be true and the other false, so also two *terms* are contradictories when one of them has to be truly and the other falsely predicable of a given subject. And just as two propositions are *contraries* when one of them must be and both of them may be false, so also two *terms* are contraries when one of them must be and both of them may be falsely predicable of a given subject. Thus "white" and "black" are contraries, since *x* may be neither white nor black. But "white" and "non-white," or "black" and "non-black," are contradictories, since *x* must be either white or non-white, black or non-black, and it can't be both. Since in the obverse the copula as well as the predicate is negated, obversion consists in *contradicting the contradictory* predicate term of the original proposition. But this means that the validity of the process of obversion requires that the predicate of the obverse actually be the contradictory, and not a contrary, of the original predicate. The practical point of all this is simply that we must be very careful when obverting actually to contradict the original predicate entirely and exactly. This can always be done with the expressions "non-," "not," and "other than," even though the result is sometimes awkward linguistically.

Armed now with the logical techniques of conversion and obversion, let us turn our attention to the task of putting them to use in the comparison of propositions having interchanged or negated terms.

EXERCISES

Give the *converse* and the *obverse* of each of the following propositions:
1. All foreign languages are strange.
2. Kangaroos are never safe among pickpockets.
3. A few fish can climb trees.
4. Few fish can climb trees.
5. George Washington was the boy who cut down his father's cherry tree.
6. Cats seldom dress for dinner.
7. Friends often disappear in times of trouble.
8. No scorpion fails to be poisonous.
9. Men are rational.
10. Man is the rational animal.

CHAPTER 14

PROPOSITIONS IN USE

14-1 DERIVATIVES OF CONVERSION AND OBVERSION

So far obversion and conversion may not seem to be very potent tools for the comparison of propositions, since each operation yields only one other proposition with equivalent truth-value. But this is only because these two operations have so far been considered separately. We need now only join them together to discover a much more powerful instrument.

Using conversion and obversion together, let us start with a single proposition, SeP for example, and see what we can get. First, converting this proposition gives us PeS. If we now again convert we only get back to our original proposition, SeP. But if instead of converting we this time obvert, we get a third and different proposition, Pa$\bar{S}$, which can in turn be obverted or converted. If we obvert Pa$\bar{S}$, we simply get back to its obvertend, PeS, which we already have; but if we now convert again we will get a fourth, different proposition, $\bar{S}$iP (note that the conversion is by limitation), and so on. In short, <u>by *alternating the two operations of conversion and obversion* we can get a series of propositions which are different from but the same in truth-value as the first one</u>. And since the first step in this series of alternating operations may be either conversion or obversion, we can get two series of propositions, one beginning with conversion and the other with obversion.

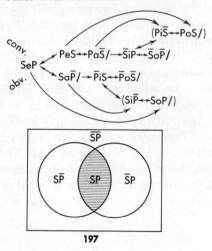

197

The diagram on p. 197 can show us just how many different propositions can be obtained from the single proposition SeP, by using conversion and obversion. Notice that what stops the series in each case is the presence of an O proposition which has to be converted. It is impossible to go any farther because, as we have seen, an O proposition has no valid converse and because obverting would merely duplicate the preceding proposition. To indicate this stoppage there is a stroke (/) in the above chart after each O proposition which needs to be converted. Notice also that the reason we get an O proposition in each case after starting with an E is that we arrive at an A proposition which must be converted by limitation to an I proposition.

Observe further in the above chart that each time we convert an A proposition by limitation we can start a second, minor series of derivatives, since the resulting I converse can itself be converted into another I proposition which is thus different from the original A convertend. However, as the chart shows, it is really not necessary to convert this I converse, for each of the resulting propositions on the minor lines is always a subimplicant of one of the other propositions and therefore derivable from it on the square of opposition. Thus $Pi\overline{S}$ is the subimplicant of $Pa\overline{S}$, PoS of PeS, $Si\overline{P}$ of $Sa\overline{P}$, and SoP of the original proposition, SeP.

We have so far said that this operation of "turning the obversion-conversion crank" produces propositions which are equivalent in truth-value to the original proposition. However, this it not quite true. If the original proposition is *true*, then it is the case that all of the derivatives will be true too. This is made apparent by the Venn diagram; if you look carefully you will see that all of the derivative propositions are mapped by the diagram of the original proposition. Notice that we have this time put the diagram in a box to indicate the things which are neither S nor P ($\overline{SP}$). However, if the original proposition is *false, then it is not necessarily the case that all of the derivatives are also false.* In particular, while the *universal* derivatives will also be false (if the original is false), the *particular* propositions *may be either true or false* and hence are *undetermined* in truth-value. To see that this is so, suppose that the original proposition (SeP) is "No salesmen are prosperous." We all know that this proposition is false—and some of you may in fact be counting on its falsity. Now the derivative proposition $\overline{S}iP$ will then be "Some non-salesmen are prosperous." Is this proposition false? Others of us may be hoping not, and we would probably all agree that our hope is amply justified by the facts. But if an obversion-conversion derivative always has the same truth-value as the original, this proposition would have to be false. The same situation is true of the derivative PoS, "Some prosperous people are not salesmen." This proposition also happens to be true even though the original proposition (SeP) is false. Notice how these facts crop up in Venn diagrams:

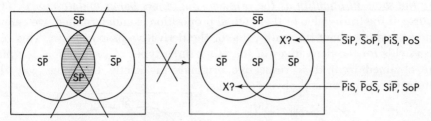

The fact that the SP area is not empty gives us no information at all concerning the occupation of the S͞P and S̄P areas.

Why is it that a particular proposition may be true even though it is logically derived from a universal proposition which is false? If you will but hark back to the square of opposition, you will quickly remember the answer: *the falsity of a superimplicant leaves its subimplicant undetermined in truth-value.* If it is false that no salesmen are prosperous it may be either true or false that some salesmen are not prosperous: from the fact that it is false that all salesmen are prosperous we cannot know whether or not some salesmen are prosperous. Now this rule of subimplication also applies in deriving propositions by obversion and conversion, and its precise point of application can be clearly seen in each of the major lines of our above chart of the derivatives of SeP. The falsity of the original proposition, SeP ("No salesmen are prosperous"), does indeed imply the falsity of all the universal derivatives through the last one, PaS̄ ("All prosperous people are non-salesmen"). But the falsity of PaS̄, "All prosperous people are non-salesmen," does not imply the falsity of its subimplicant, PiS̄, "Some prosperous people are non-salesmen." On the contrary, this subimplicant is simply undetermined in truth-value. And the same is true of the drop from universal to particular on the other major line of the above chart, and also of all of the other particular propositions there listed. Of course, these subimplicant derivatives *may* in *some* cases have the same truth-value as the false original; the point is that this is not always so and hence the truth-values of the subimplicant derivatives are undetermined *by the falsity of the original proposition.* It is for this reason that we have put a stroke (/) after each of the last universal derivatives—to show that after this point the falsity (though not the truth) of the original proposition leaves the derivative propositions undetermined in truth-value. And for the same reason the one-way subimplication arrow (→) is used between each A convertend and its I converse while a two-way arrow (↔) is used between all other pairs of propositions on our above chart to show that they are entirely equivalent.

Let us now generalize this situation concerning the truth-values of propositions derived by obversion and conversion: *If the original is true all the derivatives are true; but if the original is false only those derivatives are false which are the same in quantity as the original, the others being undetermined.* (Of course, if the truth-value of the original proposition is undetermined, we cannot know anything about the truth-value of the derivative propositions.) This rule also holds for the derivatives of the other three types of proposition, for they are obtained from their respective originals in exactly the same way, by alternate conversion and obversion, thus:

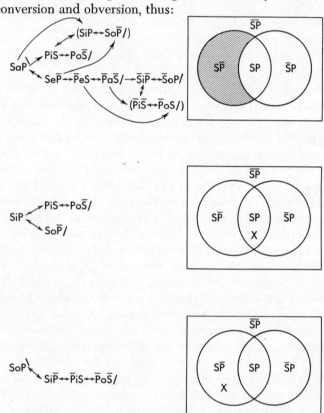

Thus the truth of SaP implies the truth of all its derivatives, the truth of SiP the truth of all its derivatives, the truth of SoP the truth of all its derivatives, the falsity of SiP the falsity of all its derivatives, and the falsity of SoP the falsity of all its derivatives. But the *falsity* of SaP implies the falsity of its *universal* derivatives; the particular derivatives are left undetermined by the falsity of SaP. And these facts are again indicated in the above charts by the strokes and arrows. The equivalence in truth-value of all the propositions which actually are equivalent can be checked by the above Venn diagrams, and to check on the fact that the falsity of an A proposition leaves its particular derivatives undetermined note the following diagrams:

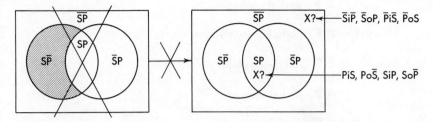

From the knowledge that the SP area is in fact not empty, we cannot infer anything concerning the habitation of the S̄P and SP̄ areas.

Now that we are acquainted with conversion and obversion and with all the derivatives it is possible to get by alternating these two operations, it might be interesting to know the names which logicians have given to these derivatives:[1]

partial contrapositives
full contrapositive
full inverse

SaP → PIS↔PoS̄/
SeP̄↔P̄eS↔P̄aS̄/→S̄iP̄↔S̄oP/ ←— partial inverse

full inverse
partial inverse
partial contrapositives

SeP ↗ PeS↔PaS̄/→S̄iP↔S̄oP̄/
SaP̄/→P̄iS̄↔P̄oS/ ←—full contrapositive

SiP ↗ PiS↔PoS̄/ ←— partial contrapositive
SoP̄/

SoP ↘ partial contrapositive
S̄iP̄↔P̄iS↔P̄oS/ ←—— full contrapositive

The first proposition on each line running from the original is, of course, either the converse or the obverse. The partial contrapositive, which is always either the obverted converse or the converted obverse of the original, is sometimes called simply (!) by those names. You will doubtless note from the abstract patterns exhibited above that <u>the contrapositive always interchanges the terms of the original and negates either one (if the partial contrapositive) or both (if the full contrapositive) of them, while the inverse always keeps the terms of the original in the same positions while negating either one (if the partial inverse) or both (if the full inverse) of them.</u> This is the pattern:

---

[1] There seems to be a logical mistake somewhere in this table of derivatives. Can you find it? We will point it out later.

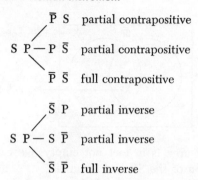

$\overline{\text{P}}$ S   partial contrapositive

S P — P $\overline{\text{S}}$ partial contrapositive

$\overline{\text{P}}$ $\overline{\text{S}}$ full contrapositive

$\overline{\text{S}}$ P   partial inverse

S P — S $\overline{\text{P}}$ partial inverse

$\overline{\text{S}}$ $\overline{\text{P}}$ full inverse

But the names of these derivatives of the obverse and converse are really not very important. What is important is that you know how to perform the operations of conversion and obversion quickly and accurately so as to obtain all of the possible valid derivatives of any given proposition.

We are now in possession of the tools needed to compare propositions which differ with respect to the position or quality of their terms. But before we try these tools out in practice, there is one last set of caveats which must be noted.

14–2   DIFFICULTIES AND EXCEPTIONS

If you will now go back to the charts of derivatives on pp. 200 and 201 above and study them carefully, you will see that we seem to have made a mistake somewhere, for there is a maverick in the A string. In those charts we did not plot the distribution of the terms, but if we do so now we will see that we have apparently violated the distribution rule:

$$\text{PiS} \leftrightarrow \text{Po}\overline{\text{S}}/$$
$$\underline{\text{S}}a\text{P}$$
$$\underline{\text{Se}\overline{\text{P}}} \leftrightarrow \underline{\overline{\text{P}}}e\underline{\text{S}} \leftrightarrow \underline{\overline{\text{P}}}a\overline{\text{S}}/ \rightarrow \overline{\text{S}}i\overline{\text{P}} \leftrightarrow \overline{\text{S}}o\text{P}/$$

We are given in the original proposition all of S but only some of P—that is, S is distributed and P undistributed. But in the last proposition on the second line, the partial inverse $\overline{\text{S}}o\text{P}$, P is distributed; we are saying something about all of P. Yet we have obtained $\overline{\text{S}}o\text{P}$ from $\underline{\text{S}}a\text{P}$ by a valid process, by alternately obverting and converting. If you examine the derivatives of the other three propositions you will see that this paradox occurs only in this one place. But one place is bad enough. How can we solve this paradox?

We can do so by remembering and reapplying something we learned in the chapter on definitions, namely, that for a term to be definable means that there is something else in the universe, at least as a possible being, which falls outside it and thus limits it. Thus we would hardly take the trouble to enlighten those know-it-all, supposedly educated cynics of the fact that "All black cats are unlucky" unless there were some things in the world besides black cats and unlucky things, unless there were some white and brown cats and some lucky things. But this is exactly what that maverick in the A string, the partial inverse of the A, asserts to be the case: $\overline{S}oP$—"there are some things which are neither S's nor P's," "there are some things which are neither black cats nor unlucky." Note how this is borne out by the Venn diagram:

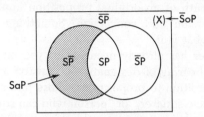

Of course, not all terms are definable. As we saw in Chap. 6–3, some are transcendental or analogical, extending over the full stretch of reality with nothing at all falling outside them to define them—terms like "being," "thing," "something," etc. But even here we would not use such terms in propositions unless we had in mind *some* kind of opposites for them—"nothing" or "non-being," for example. Of course, these opposites of transcendental terms are not real; they are only beings of reason. Yet they do have *that* status, and in that status they function as logical opposites for terms which can have no real opposites. Hence even in such a proposition as "Every being is something" we are assuming that there are logically some non-S's and non-P's which we refer to by terms like "nothing." So even in the case of such a proposition as this whose terms are transcendental, the partial inverse, $\overline{S}oP$, follows logically: "Some non-beings (as logical entities) are not anything."

Now when in the partial inverse we make explicit this contrast between the things that are S or P and the things that are neither S nor P, we are in fact separating the $\overline{S}P$ class from *the whole class* of things that are P. Hence P is there justifiably distributed. Such separation, and hence such distribution, of the P term is latent in the original SaP proposition; but since it is there not a part of the conscious intent of the proposition, the predicate of the original SaP proposition is rightly undistributed. There is really no contradiction at all, then; the partial inverse, $\overline{S}oP$, is validly derived from the original SaP proposition even though P is distributed in the former and undistributed in the latter simply because the intent of the original SaP proposition requires the possibility of distributing P consciously in another proposition.

But there is another paradox in our derivations by obversion and conversion. The proposition "No mathematicians can square the circle," for instance, is certainly true. Let us now convert it: "Nobody who can square the circle is a mathematician." Already something is beginning to look a little queer, but let us go ahead and obvert this converse: "Everybody who can square the circle is a non-mathematician." Something is really getting funny now, but let us go a step farther and convert this obverted converse: "Some non-mathematicians can square the circle." Now this proposition is blatantly false, you will rightly say: nobody can square the circle for it is impossible to do so. Yet we have obtained this partial contrapositive by valid processes of conversion and obversion from the original proposition, and nobody could doubt *its* truth. And we have said that the truth of an original proposition implies the truth of all its derivatives by obversion and conversion. Something is certainly rotten in Denmark, but just what is it?

Perhaps the answer has already occurred to you on the basis of what has been said about the bearing of designation on falsity[2] and about the relevance of the square of opposition to propositions whose terms do not designate anything.[3] The term "circle-squarer," or "person who can square the circle," cannot designate anything real, for it is impossible to square a circle. Of course, that term can be made to designate merely conceptual entities, as when we say that "Circle-squarers are all in your head." But in the proposition "No mathematicians can square the circle" it does not designate at all, because the term "mathematicians" is clearly intended to refer to real beings; and it therefore forces the term "circle-squarer" to refer to real beings too, which is impossible. Yet the proposition that "No mathematician can square the circle" is still true. Negative propositions, as we have seen, *may* be true even though their terms fail to designate. The terms of affirmative propositions, on the other hand, must designate in order for the proposition to be true. Hence the two affirmative propositions which we have just noted—"Everybody who can square the circle is a non-mathematician" and "Some non-mathematicians can square the circle" —are false. For that matter, as we have already suspected, the negative converse, "Nobody who can square the circle is a mathematician," is hardly one that we would ordinarily assert, though our attitude toward it might be not so much to call it false as simply not to use it because it seems "strange" or "inappropriate."

The point of all this is that the validity of derivation by obversion and conversion is based on the assumption that each term designates and retains the same designation in all its occurrences. If a term has merely conceptual designation in the original proposition, it must also have merely conceptual designation in each of the derivative propositions. Thus the partial inverse, "Some non-mathematicians can square the circle," does follow validly from "No mathematicians can square the circle" if the terms in both propositions are given only conceptual designation. But if the term "circle-squarer" is thought of as referring to real things, then it will entirely fail to designate and derivation by obversion and conversion will be invalid. In short, just as the terms of

2 Pp. 138–141.
3 Pp. 184–185.

propositions compared on the square of opposition must all designate and have the same kind of designation, so also *the terms of propositions compared by obversion and conversion must all designate and have the same kind of designation.* If there is a shift or failure in designation, then obversion-conversion derivation and comparison is simply not relevant.

14–3   DETERMINATION OF RELATIVE TRUTH-VALUES

With these difficulties and exceptions out of the way, let us arm ourselves with our tools of conversion and obversion and use them to compare the truth-values of propositions which differ with respect to the position or the quality of their terms. Since we are seldom in real life presented with propositions in the abstract, symbolic form in which we have been considering them, let us return to the world of concrete, actual sentences. As soon as we do this a comparison of their truth-values will require not only conversion and obversion but also the formulation of these sentences as logical propositions. Our procedure will involve three steps: (1) formulation of each of the sentences as a proposition, (2) manufacture of all the obversion-conversion derivatives of the proposition whose truth-value is known (*not* of the quaesitum propositions), and (3) comparison of each of the quaesitum propositions with the derivatives of the original proposition. Let us work one example out together:

Assumed		K a L	
true:	$\underline{K}a\underline{L}$	Every (one) (has a lonely heart) (who knows my anguish.)	
		$\bar{K}$ i L	
T	$\bar{K}i\underline{L}$	1. Many (who are unaware of my anguish) are (far from being lonely in heart.)	
		K e L	
U	KeL	2. None (who know my anguish) are (lonely in heart.)	
		$\bar{K}$ i L	
U	$\bar{K}iL$	3. Some (people who are ignorant of my anguish) (have lonely hearts.)	
		L o $\bar{K}$	
T	$Lo\bar{K}$	4. Few if any (lonely hearts) are (oblivious to my anguish.)	
		K e $\bar{L}$	
T	$Ke\underline{L}$	5. (People who can know my anguish) never (lack lonely hearts.)	

$$KaL \quad \to Li K \leftrightarrow \bar{L}o\bar{K}/$$
$$\hookrightarrow Ke\bar{L} \leftrightarrow \bar{L}eK \leftrightarrow \bar{L}a\bar{K}/ \to \bar{K}i\bar{L} \leftrightarrow \bar{K}oL/$$

Each proposition which appears in the list of derivatives is true since the original proposition is true, but any which fails to appear in the list of derivatives is, so far, unknown in truth-value.

14–4 THE LOGIC OF PROPOSITIONS IN APPLICATION

But this is true only so far. So far as comparison by conversion and obversion alone is concerned, propositions 2 and 3 above are undetermined in truth-value for they do not appear in the list of the derivatives of the original proposition. However, if we now combine comparison on the square of opposition with comparison by obversion and conversion, we can obtain further information about some quaesitum propositions. For example, we can tell that proposition 2 in the above problem is false since it is the contrary of the original proposition; we can also tell that proposition 3 is undetermined because it is the subcontrary of the partial inverse ($\overline{\mathrm{K}}$oL) of the original.

In brief, we want now to bring all of our techniques for the comparison of propositions to bear together. Any proposition which does not appear in the list of conversion-obversion derivatives of the original proposition may still *have the same two terms* as the original or one of its derivatives and differ from it only in quality or quantity. We can then compare the two propositions on the square of opposition. Occasionally, however, a quaesitum proposition will neither appear among the propositions in the derivation list nor have the same terms as one of those propositions so as to be comparable with it on the square of opposition. This will never happen when the original proposition is universal, for SaP and its derivatives contain all eight possible combinations of terms: S–P, $\overline{\mathrm{S}}$–P, S–$\overline{\mathrm{P}}$, $\overline{\mathrm{S}}$–$\overline{\mathrm{P}}$, P–S, $\overline{\mathrm{P}}$–S, P–$\overline{\mathrm{S}}$, and $\overline{\mathrm{P}}$–$\overline{\mathrm{S}}$; and so do SeP and its derivatives. But this will happen sometimes when the original proposition is particular, and when it does happen there is one final step that may be taken to determine the truth-value of that quaesitum proposition. This last step is to obtain the obversion-conversion derivatives of the *quaesitum* proposition in order to try to find a proposition having the same terms as the original proposition or one of its derivatives so that *these* two propositions can be compared on the square of opposition. This is usually possible, but sometimes even this last step fails to produce any basis of comparison. Hence quaesitum propositions examined by the last step may be either true, false, undetermined, or simply incomparable. Let us formulate this complete procedure for determining the truth-values of propositions utilizing the same basic concepts:

1. Formulate each proposition symbolically.[4]
2. Obtain the obversion-conversion derivatives from the original proposition.
3. Determine the truth-values of those quaesitum propositions which appear among the derivatives of the original proposition.
4. Determine the truth-values of those quaesitum propositions which can be compared with the original proposition or its derivatives on the square of opposition.

[4] See Chap. 11–1 for the complete procedure.

5. Try to determine the truth-value of any remaining quaesitum proposition by a comparison, on the square of opposition, of one of *its* derivatives with the original proposition or one of its derivatives.

These steps should always be followed in this order, because step 5 will usually be unnecessary and step 4 will often be unnecessary. Let us now work through a problem in which it is necessary to use all five steps:

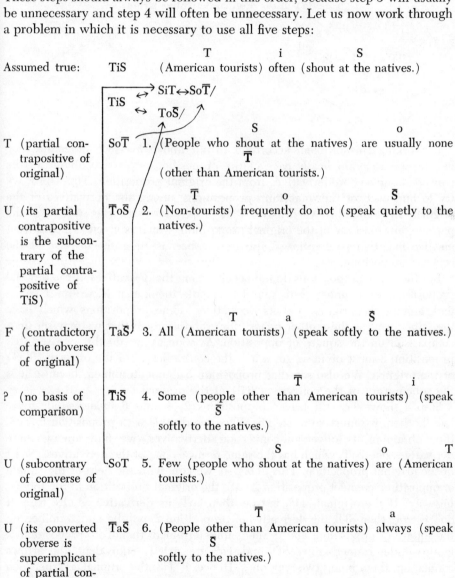

<table>
<tr><td></td><td></td><td align="center">T</td><td align="center">i</td><td align="center">S</td></tr>
<tr><td>Assumed true:</td><td>TiS</td><td colspan="3">(American tourists) often (shout at the natives.)</td></tr>
</table>

TiS ↔ SiT↔SoT̄/

TiS ↔ ToS̄/

<table>
<tr><td>T (partial con-
trapositive of
original)</td><td>SoT̄ 1.</td><td>S
(People who shout at the natives) are usually none
T̄
(other than American tourists.)</td></tr>
<tr><td>U (its partial
contrapositive
is the subcon-
trary of the
partial contra-
positive of
TiS)</td><td>ToS̄ 2.</td><td>T̄   o   S
(Non-tourists) frequently do not (speak quietly to the
natives.)</td></tr>
<tr><td>F (contradictory
of the obverse
of original)</td><td>TaS̄ 3.</td><td>T   a   S̄
All (American tourists) (speak softly to the natives.)</td></tr>
<tr><td>? (no basis of
comparison)</td><td>T̄iS̄ 4.</td><td>T̄   i
Some (people other than American tourists) (speak
S̄
softly to the natives.)</td></tr>
<tr><td>U (subcontrary
of converse of
original)</td><td>SoT 5.</td><td>S   o   T
Few (people who shout at the natives) are (American
tourists.)</td></tr>
<tr><td>U (its converted
obverse is
superimplicant
of partial con-
trapositive of
original)</td><td>T̄aS 6.</td><td>T̄   a
(People other than American tourists) always (speak
S
softly to the natives.)</td></tr>
</table>

T   o   S̄

T (obverse of   ToS̄   7. (American tourists) seldom (fail to shout at the natives.)
original)

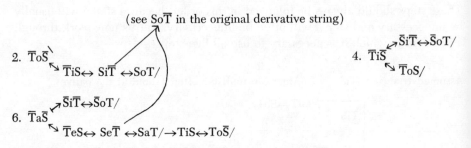

(see SoT̄ in the original derivative string)

2. ToS̄
   TiS↔ SiT̄ ↔SoT/

4. TiS̄
   SiT̄↔SoT/
   ToS/

6. TaS̄
   SiT̄↔SoT/
   TeS↔ SeT̄ ↔SaT/→TiS↔ToS̄/

In working this problem according to our above five-step procedure, we first formulate symbolically each of the propositions. Next we obtain all the conversion-obversion derivatives from the original proposition, TiS. Third, we try to find each of the quaesitum propositions among the derivatives of the original. In doing this we discover that proposition 1 is true since it is the partial contrapositive of the original proposition, which is given as being true; and we find that proposition 7 also is true because it is the obverse of the original proposition.

But the other propositions do not occur among the derivatives of the original proposition, so we must go to step 4 to handle them; that is, we must try to find, among the original and its derivatives, some propositions which have the same terms as these other quaesitum propositions so that we may set up a comparison on the square of opposition. As soon as we do this, we see that proposition 3 must be false, since it is the contradictory of the obverse (ToS̄) of the original. We also see that proposition 5 is undetermined, because it is the subcontrary of the converse (SiT) of the original.

Step 4, however, still leaves propositions 2, 4, and 6 unanswered; so to handle them we must go to step 5. When we do this with proposition 2, ToS̄, thus obtaining its obversion-conversion derivatives, we find among these derivatives one, SiT̄, which has the same terms as one of the derivatives (SoT̄) of the original proposition. This being so, we can, with the help of the square of opposition, connect proposition 2 with the original proposition in the following way: If the original, TiS, is true, then SoT̄, its derivative, is also true; if SoT̄ is true, then SiT̄, the derivative of proposition 2, will be undetermined on the square of opposition; and if SiT̄ is undetermined, then ToS̄, proposition 2, is also undetermined—since SiT̄ and ToS̄ are strictly equivalent, the arrows connecting them being two-way ones. Hence, if TiS, the original, is true, then ToS̄, proposition 2, is undetermined.

The same procedure tells us that proposition 6 also is undetermined. Following step 5 of our procedure to obtain the obversion-conversion derivatives of proposition 6, $\overline{T}a\overline{S}$, we find one, $Se\overline{T}$, which has the same terms as one of the derivatives ($So\overline{T}$) of the original proposition. This being so, we can connect proposition 6 with the original proposition as follows: If the original (TiS) is true, then $So\overline{T}$, its derivative, is also true; if $So\overline{T}$ is true, then $Se\overline{T}$, the derivative of proposition 6, is, by the square of opposition, undetermined; and if $Se\overline{T}$ is undetermined, then $\overline{T}a\overline{S}$, proposition 6, it also undetermined—since $Se\overline{T}$ and $\overline{T}a\overline{S}$ are strictly equivalent. Hence, if the original proposition, TiS, is true, then proposition 6, $\overline{T}a\overline{S}$, is undetermined.

In the case of proposition 4, however, when we apply step 5 to obtain its conversion-obversion derivatives, we find that none of them has the same terms as the original proposition or its derivatives. This means that we cannot connect proposition 4 with the original proposition via the square of opposition. Hence we must simply conclude that the original proposition leaves the truth-value of proposition 4 unknown.

Note in this problem that if the truth-value of the original proposition were false instead of true, the truth-values of the quaesitum propositions would not necessarily be simply reversed. If TiS were false then propositions 1 and 7 would indeed reverse from true to false, and proposition 3 from false to true. But propositions 2, 5, and 6, which are all undetermined when the original is true, would change to true, true, and false, respectively. (Try proving this for yourself.) And proposition 4 would still be unknown for there would still be no basis of comparison. Observe especially from the examples of propositions 2 and 6 that a proposition which is undetermined on the basis of the truth of the original proposition may turn out to be either true or false when the original is false. And notice finally that we can see at once, without using obversion-conversion or the square of opposition, that propositions 3 and 6 cannot be true, for they are universal and the truth of a particular proposition never implies the truth of a universal. However, when the original particular proposition is false, it is sometimes, but not always, the case that the universal quaesitum proposition is also false—as in proposition 6.

Summary of the Proposition.   Thus we conclude our examination of the second logical instrument, the instrument for intending the existence or "whether" of things, the proposition. While concepts are intentions only of essences, propositions relate those essences thus conceived to some kind of existence or nonexistence. We are sometimes concerned merely with whether or not a given essence exists, and in such cases our natural instrument is the existence proposition. More frequently, however, we are concerned with whether or not something is thus and so, with whether or not two essences coincide in existence; and in these cases our natural logical tool is the subject-predicate proposition. Such essences are certainly different in themselves, and hence the subject and predicate concepts which respectively signify them also differ in their significance. Yet this diversity of signification is, in the proposition, overcome by an identity of designation: the two different concepts designate or refer existentially to the same identical thing (in affirmative propositions). The types of designation or existential reference, which terms acquire only in propositions, and which are therefore functions not only of the significance of those terms themselves but also of the other elements in the proposition, are as numerous as the ways of existing. Hence the richness and variety of our logical and linguistic tools for apprehending existence necessarily transcends our cataloguing ability. Yet the main types of designation are fairly easy to see, and if we restrict ourselves to only two of these, quality and quantity, we get a simplified and readily workable scheme of four different kinds of proposition. When the sentences with which we are confronted in everyday life are formulated as belonging to one of these four types of proposition, we can readily and exactly determine their relative truth-values by two basic logical techniques: the square of opposition and conversion-obversion.

Yet we can do this only when we are told, or assume or take for granted, that one of these propositions is true or is false, for that proposition does not demonstrate its own truth-value. Thus our techniques for comparing and determining the relative truth-values of propositions still leave us in the dark as to their actual truth or falsity. How can we tell whether a proposition is really, in actual fact, true or false? Only by citing as evidence other propositions which show *that* and *why* a given proposition is true or false. But propositional techniques alone do not suffice to answer this question. In order to discover the actual truth or falsity of propositions, and the "why" or reason for their truth or falsity, we must now turn to the third logical instrument, the tool for apprehending the "why" of things: the technique of argument.

EXERCISES

1. From each of the following propositions derive all of the valid obversion-conversion derivatives (obverse, converse, contrapositives, and inverses), and express each of them both linguistically and symbolically:
   a. In my Father's house are many mansions.
   b. Silver always melts at 960.5° C.
   c. Nobody can travel faster than light.
   d. Spectators are seldom impartial.
   e. The victory is usually won by those who persevere.
   f. Every mathematical truth is hypothetically necessary.
   g. People who live in glass houses shouldn't throw stones.
   h. Most of the roads built under the new federal program will be limited-access highways.
   i. A concerto is that form of musical composition written for a solo instrument with an orchestral accompaniment.

j. Few if any scientists doubt that the moon will be reached within five years.

k. No party to the dispute objected to the waiver.

l. Hitler frequently had dreams of world conquest.

m. Many were the fond notes her merry voice did pour.

n. Everybody except a few bookworms groaned when the exam was passed out.

o. The statement issued by the school board was not incorrect in the opinion of the faculty.

p. Only a small minority felt that further action need be taken.

2. "Everybody will vote against the City Hall gang except the die-hard Republicans." Assuming that this is *true*, what is the truth-value of each of the following propositions? Assuming that this is *false*, what is the truth-value of each of the following propositions?

a. Anyone who won't vote against the City Hall gang is a die-hard Republican.

b. A few die-hard Republicans will fail to vote against the City Hall gang.

c. No one who votes against the City Hall gang is a die-hard Republican.

d. Those who will vote against the City Hall gang are frequently other than die-hard Republicans.

e. Several die-hard Republicans will vote against the City Hall gang.

f. Those who will fail to vote against the City Hall gang are never other than die-hard Republicans.

g. Few voters against the City Hall gang are other than die-hard Republicans.

h. Those who will vote against the City Hall gang are seldom die-hard Republicans.

i. Every single die-hard Republican will fail to vote against the City Hall gang.

j. Those who fail to vote against the City Hall gang are often die-hard Republicans.

3. "Every one of the Michigan delegates representing an urban or industrial area felt that the civil rights plank should be strengthened." Assuming that this is *true*, what is the truth-value of each of the following propositions? Assuming that this is *false*, what is the truth-value of each of the following propositions?

a. None of the Michigan delegates representing an urban or industrial area felt that the civil rights plank should be weakened.

b. Several opponents of strengthening the civil rights plank were Michigan delegates not representing urban or industrial areas.

c. All of those in favor of strengthening the civil rights plank were Michigan delegates representing urban or industrial areas.

d. All of the Michigan delegates representing urban or industrial areas were against any strengthening of the civil rights plank.

e. Few opponents of a strengthened civil rights plank were other than Michigan delegates representing urban or industrial areas.

f. Partisans of a strengthened civil rights plank were frequently Michigan delegates representing urban or industrial areas.

g. No delegates other than the Michigan ones representing urban or industrial areas were opposed to a strengthening of the civil rights plank.

h. All of those opposed to a strengthening of the civil rights plank were other than Michigan delegates representing urban or industrial areas.

    i. Delegates other than the Michigan ones who represent urban or industrial areas sometimes felt that the civil rights plank should be strengthened.

    j. No one except the Michigan delegates representing urban or industrial areas felt that the civil rights plank should be strengthened.

4. "Countries falling within the torrid zone are usually hot." Assuming that this proposition is *true*, what is the truth-value of each of the following propositions? Assuming that this proposition is *false*, what is the truth-value of each of the following propositions?

    a. Hot countries seldom fail to fall within the torrid zone.

    b. Hot countries always fall within the torrid zone.

    c. All countries which do not lie in the torrid zone are hot.

    d. Few countries falling within the torrid zone are cold.

    e. Hot countries never lie outside the torrid zone.

    f. All countries with cold or temperate climates are those which fall within the torrid zone.

    g. At least one country with a cold climate does not fall within the torrid zone.

    h. Countries lying outside the torrid zone frequently have moderate or cold climates.

    i. Several hot countries are situated in the torrid zone.

    j. No countries with other than hot climates fail to be situated in the torrid zone.

5. Are the following inferences valid or invalid, and why?

    a. Since what we are interested in is important, it follows that what we are not interested in is unimportant.

    b. Not all Democrats are Fair Dealers; consequently a number of anti-Fair Dealers are not against the Democrats.

    c. Since everyone that went to the dance had a good time, it necessarily follows that some of the people who did not have a good time did not go to the dance.

    d. Since none but the wise are truly good, all who fail to attain wisdom must be evil.

    e. As it is obviously false that all logicians are logical, it must be true that no logical persons are logicians.

    f. Everyone knows that it is false that Americans always vote against the party in power in bad times. Hence it has to be true that Americans never vote against the party in power in bad times.

    g. Everything which he attacked was worthy of being destroyed, so nothing worthy of destruction escaped him.

    h. As all good children go to heaven, no bad ones ever go there.

    i. Since what we revere is holy, it follows that few of the things that we do not revere are unholy.

    j. Not all people who are not discontented are unambitious; hence all contented people are ambitious.

    k. Since the seer is always solitary, no gregarious people are seers.

    l. Inasmuch as it is false that bad money always drives out good, it must be true that money that is not good seldom fails to drive out bad money.

PART III

ARGUMENT

CHAPTER 15

ARGUMENTS AND CAUSES

15–1 THE CONTRAST BETWEEN PROPOSITIONS AND ARGUMENTS

Almost everyone thinks logic has something to do with reasoning; and almost everyone thinks reasoning is an affair of arguing, proving, demonstrating, etc. Hence, most of us tend to suppose that being logical or having a logical mind involves simply a capacity for closeness of reasoning or cogency in demonstration. Nor is this commonplace altogether wrong. Yet it might be decidedly misleading if one were thereby led to believe that the whole concern of logic is simply with argument or demonstration.

Quite the contrary, as we have so often reiterated; logic is to be regarded as the human *organon* or instrument of knowledge and truth. Yet human knowledge or truth would seem to consist not in arguments and demonstrations so much as in propositions. For instance, we might be said to know *that* Caesar crossed the Rubicon, *that* the opposite angles formed by intersecting straight lines are equal, *that* silver melts at 960.5° C., *that* the human animal is morally responsible. Clearly, these are all propositions. Where, then, does proof or argument come into the picture?

Perhaps the question might be somewhat better posed in this way. In Part II in our discussion of propositions, we found that propositions were the instruments for intending what things are in fact. But clearly, if one apprehends the "whats" of things and so comes to know that things are and what is true about them, what more need one or can one know? Why should anyone imagine that besides concepts and propositions there must needs be such further instruments of knowledge as arguments?

Of course, the answer to these half-sophistic questions is easy. While it's true that propositions are our instrument for intending that or what things are —e.g., that S is P—still the human intellect can combine and separate subject and predicate concepts almost at will. Nor does the mere fact that a P concept has been predicated of an S mean that S is P really. For instance, one can very easily assert:

> Hey diddle diddle, the cat and the fiddle,
> The cow jumped over the moon.

But merely asserting it scarcely makes it true. Moreover, if one were seriously to insist that the cow did, or even that she did not, succeed in getting over this somewhat extraordinary hurdle, one would have to offer at least some sort of evidence in support of one's statement. Thus one might point out that the musculature of the cow is hardly sufficient to effect such a leap; or possibly that her respiratory system is not adequately equipped for flights through the stratosphere, etc., etc.

More seriously, though, we do find that there are scarcely any of our S-P propositions which do not require some sort of evidence in support of them. True, to assert that S is P is to intend or signify what S is. Yet how do we know that this is really what S is? What makes us suppose that the proposition which we have asserted is a true proposition? For instance, in our earlier cited propositions we simply stated that we know that Caesar crossed the Rubicon, that the opposite angles are equal, that silver melts at 960.5° C., and so forth. But how do we know these things? Why do we suppose them to be true? On what evidence do we make such assertions, etc.?

In short, questions of this sort we can quite legitimately raise with respect to almost any of the propositions that we formulate. Yet they are nothing but demands for proof or demonstration of these same propositions. Apparently, then, while it must be recognized that our knowledge strictly speaking is not contained in arguments, but rather in propositions, it is for the most part only through argument and demonstration that we are able to know our propositions are true.

Argument as Intending the "Whys" or Causes of Things.   Before we turn our attention to the sort of character and structure that an argument must have if it is to serve us as an instrument for the proof or demonstration of a proposition, let us follow that order of topics already laid down in our previous chapters and consider first of all what it is that an argument, considered precisely as an intention, intends, or what it is that comes to be known through the use of such an instrument of cognition as argument. In other words, following our customary procedure, we wish first to try to determine that which comes to be known through the use of argument, before we seek to determine that *through which* such a knowledge may be effected or brought about—viz., the instrument of argument as such.

Now so far as concepts and propositions are concerned, we have seen how one employs the former to intend the "whats" or essences of things and the latter to intend the "whether" or the existence of things. What, then, may arguments be supposed to intend? The answer is that just as concepts intend essences, and propositions the existence of essences, arguments intend causes— i.e., the "why" of things. Arguments or demonstrations, that is to say, are our means of answering the question "Why?" just as concepts and propositions are our means of dealing with "What?" and "Whether?"

But on what grounds do we assert that arguments are simply intentions of the "whys" and causes of things? The answer may be found through a somewhat more careful analysis of what we have just said about the nature of demonstration. Thus we suggested that what is proved in any demonstration is always a proposition. But an ordinary proposition is of the form S is P. Moreover, the P term must be related to the S, as we learned in our discussion of the predicables,[1] either as its genus, its differentia, its species, its property, or its accident. Accordingly, let us assume for the purposes of illustration that the proposition we are trying to prove, or give the "why" of, involves the predicable relationship of property: "Men are morally responsible," "The opposite angles of intersecting straight lines are equal," or "Silver melts at 960.5° C." Now what each of these propositions asserts is the fact of a certain attribute or accident inhering in a subject.[2] Consequently, when one asks why the proposition is true or on what grounds it is being asserted, one is really asking why that attribute inheres in that subject. But this is simply to ask for the cause of a certain kind of thing's having the characteristics or attributes that it does have.

Thus to ask why silver melts at 960.5° C. is to ask what there is about the nature of silver that causes or is responsible for this particular reaction. Or to take another example—accident—"Why did Caesar cross the Rubicon?" One might answer, "Because he wanted to seize control of the Roman state." Clearly the proposition introduced by "because" here intends to give the real cause of Caesar's action—in this case, his purpose or aim. Or suppose one were to ask— let us imagine in irritation over the cancellation of a ball game—"Why did it have to rain today?" The answer might be, "Because God willed it," or "Because the wind changed to the east." Each is obviously trying to give a real cause of a real fact or event.

More generally, may we not say that things in the real world are as they are because of various causal influences which originally brought them into being, or which, once they had been brought into being, operated upon them to change them and make them as they are right now? Moreover, if we are to understand things as they now are, do we have any alternative but to try to understand them in and through the causes that have made them that way? If we have a proposition asserting what a thing now is, and if we demand proof of that proposition, what we are really asking for are the causes or "whys" of that thing's being what it is. In other words, any argument advanced in proof of a proposition is really but an instrument for exhibiting the cause or causes responsible for the state of things which the proposition asserts to be the case.

[1] Cf. above, pp. 118–122.
[2] Cf. above, pp. 35–37.

15–2   CHANGE[3] AS THE ONTOLOGICAL SETTING OF CAUSATION

Our analysis of the logical instrument of argument seems to have brought us face to face with the metaphysical or ontological fact of causation. For if that which is intended in argument be the real causes of things as they are, we cannot very well understand the intentional function of argument without paying at least some attention to what causes are. Unhappily, though, anyone familiar with the history of philosophy knows that the notion of cause has proved so vexatious and so recalcitrant to understanding that the contemporary mood of philosophers in regard to the question would seem to alternate between despair and exhausted indifference.

Even so, it will perhaps be not too difficult to give a fairly plausible account of causation, based on our everyday human experience, even though the extension of that account to the somewhat more restricted and esoteric experience of the special scientists might occasion difficulties. In any case, we shall here content ourselves with merely trying to state in a crude and elementary sort of way what causation means to the human being qua human, and without worrying about what it might mean or not mean to the physicist qua physicist or the sociologist qua sociologist, etc.

Nor can we better begin perhaps than by simply focusing attention on that ubiquitous and inescapable fact of our human experience, viz., change. After all, there is nothing whatever in our world about us that has not come into being and that will not pass away; and even so long as it is or exists—at least if it is a substance—it will be subject to constant changes and alterations. Take human beings, for example: of no human being may it be said that he always has existed or that he always will exist;[4] instead, every being has come to be and some day will cease to be. Nor can any human being—even the most conservative—succeed in resisting change altogether; he at least has to breathe, his heart has to beat, he can't possibly stay in one spot all the time, his bodily metabolism has to keep functioning, and, last but not least, he cannot keep from growing older, however much he may succeed in not growing wiser.

Human beings are not the only beings that are subject to change; dogs and tadpoles, evergreens and fungi, protozoa and mammoths, massive rock formations and subatomic particles—all are caught up in this phenomenon of change and all are such that they themselves have come to be, just as in turn they one day will cease to be. Nor is it only things in the category of substance that come into being and pass away. It's the same with qualities: the colors of the rainbow, shadows on the rock, Einstein's knowledge of physics, one man's

[3] For an excellent discussion of change and the causes of change, see Wild, *Introduction to Realistic Philosophy*, Harper, 1948, Chaps. 13 and 14. Cf. also above, pp. 34–44.

[4] In the interests of simplicity, we are disregarding questions as to the immortality or eternity of the soul, or as to the resurrection of the body, etc.

health, another man's illness—each of these has manifested itself or come to be in time and one day will cease to be. And so with examples from any of the other categories—a woman's love, the relative location of two buildings, a man's girth, the hour of death; of not one of these things may it be said that it has existed from eternity to eternity.

Apparently, then, there is no "what" or essence—i.e., no definite determination of anything, be it substantial, quantitative, qualitative, relational, temporal, or what—that has not come to exist and that will not cease to exist.[5] Yet clearly, this being or existing of an essence is not self-explanatory; there must be some cause or reason why such a nature or kind of thing should have come to be, or why things should be the way they are. This perhaps is obvious. Nevertheless, the immediate question that presses upon us concerns the precise incidence of this thing which is called causation: Just how does a cause come into play so as to bring an essence into existence?

Matter and Form as Basic Principles in All Change. To answer this question, let us first note some of the fundamental and recurrent features that manifest themselves in all change. For one thing, if there is to be real change, as contrasted with, shall we say, a mere succession of events, there must be a something that changes, i.e., a something that undergoes the change or underlies the change. Otherwise one would be up against some such situation as the following: a certain state or condition of things (call it x) would prevail at time t_1; then at the next instant of time, t_2, a different state or condition would come to prevail (call it y). However, if there were nothing underlying this transition from one state to another, we should have to say that x was simply annihilated at the expiration of t_1, and that at the beginning of t_2 y was simply created *ex nihilo*.

Now such a situation, while it might be described as a succession of events, could hardly be called a change. Why not? Because there is nothing that changes, in the sense of a thing which is changed or which undergoes the change. Thus it is not the preceding event that could be said to undergo change. For so far from changing into something else or becoming different, it just ceases to be altogether. Nor is it the succeeding event that could be said to have undergone the change. For so far from its having been one thing and having then become another, it just suddenly came into being in the first place.

Further, we might even say that such a succession of events not only is not change but is not intelligible. For inevitably we understand change as a change *of* something, *by* something else, *into* something different. If there is nothing

---

[5] Once more we are oversimplifying. There are all sorts of questions as to whether essences, even though they do not exist necessarily but rather must come into being in the real world, do not have some sort of eternal and unchanging status in their own right and just in themselves. Cf. the Platonic theory of forms. Also there is the philosophical question of God's existence. The latter might be an example of an essence or "what" that does not come into existence or pass away and that does not change.

to be changed by another into something else, then our understanding feels frustrated and thwarted. For instance, in the case of a succession of events such as we have just described, how can the agent of the change bring the new event into being? For there is nothing for it to act upon. And how can it do anything, if there is nothing for it to act upon? It could not be said to act upon the preceding event, since that has ceased to be; and it could not act upon the succeeding event that is the effect, for the latter is what is brought into being as a result of the action; hence it could not be that which is itself acted upon. Does that mean, then, that there is just nothing for the cause to act upon? If so, how are we to understand the causal agency as actually working or operating to bring about a change, if there is nothing for it to work or operate upon?

If there is to be real change, then, and if it is to be intelligible, there must be something that changes, and it must be upon this something that the agent of the change acts in order to bring about the change. Moreover, this substrate of change, this internal principle of change as that upon which the cause acts and in which the change is wrought—this we may simply call matter[6] or the material principle of change. Nor is this principle of matter really any more than just a potentiality or ability or capacity to become different. Thus, as we say, the stone is now cool, but it is able to become warm; the man is now ill, but he is able to become healthy; the iron is now hard, but it is able to be melted, etc. In each of these cases we have to do with a being which is what it is but still is able to become other and different. Moreover, without this material element or element of potentiality in things, it would be simply impossible for these things to change. For if a thing is not *able* to change, then quite literally it cannot change. But an ability to change is simply a potentiality to become different, which potentiality is matter.

Besides this material element in change, there must also be another and corresponding element, viz., that of form. For in addition to being able to change, that which changes must necessarily change to something. That is to say, the change is always from having been something to being something. And it is just this element of determinateness and of discontinuity in change that is called form. The body that was hot becomes cool; it takes on a new formal determination: from having been hot, it has now become cool. Moreover, if there were no such determinate form which that which changes might be said to become or to change into, then quite literally it would not become anything or change into anything. There would be no change at all.

The Cause as Acting on the Matter.   Accordingly, all change would seem necessarily to involve these two elements: a material element which undergoes or submits to the change and a formal element which is precisely that which the

---

[6] Note that "matter," as it is here used as a philosophical principle to explain change, is a very different notion from "matter" as it is frequently used in the context of the physical sciences. Cf. Wild, *op. cit.*, pp. 286–291.

matter becomes, or which it is changed into, as a result of the process of change. By so conceiving change in terms of matter and form, we are at last in a position to answer our question as to the precise incidence of the cause in change. For what the cause does is to act upon the matter so as to produce the form. It brings the form to the matter. It operates upon the potency or capacity of the matter to become different and actually makes it different.

For instance, the stone which was once cool but was able to be warmed (material element) is actually made warm (formal element) by the sun (the cause). The body which was diseased (matter) is actually restored to health (form) by the healing art of the physician (cause). A gas (matter) when subjected to pressure (cause) shrinks in volume (form). The marble (matter) when worked by the sculptor (cause) takes on the form of the statue (form). And so on. In all of these cases the cause is simply the agent, or, as it is sometimes called, the efficient cause, which acts upon the material or potential element so as to effect a change, i.e., to realize or actualize a new and different form in the matter.

Moreover, if we call to mind our earlier doctrine of the categories,[7] we can see how it can be readily integrated into this account of change. For the categories may be regarded as so many different kinds of form or essence, and hence as so many different termini or formal elements in a process of change. Thus if it is a human being that comes into existence, it is a substantial form that is actualized in matter. On the other hand, if it is only a different quality or quantity that comes into being, it is then but an accidental form that is actualized in the material substrate. For instance, if a leaf turns from green to yellow, this is said to be a change in quality. Or if under pressure a gas decreases in volume, this is a change in quantity. Or if a molecule of hydrogen moves from one place to another, that is a change of place. And so on.

15–3   CAUSES AS INTENDED IN AND THROUGH ARGUMENT

With this integration of the categories into the general scheme of change, we may turn to a consideration of the relevance to logic of this whole account. For concepts, as we know, are intentions of "whats" or essences, and any essence comes under the heading of one or the other of the categories. Further, the predication of one concept of another in a proposition is a device whereby we are able to recognize whether a certain intended thing or entity is or is not thus and so, i.e., whether a characteristic falling under this, that, or the other category actually pertains to that thing or does not pertain to that thing in fact. Accordingly, when we move on into the context of argument, we find that the situation confronting us is something like this: A person asserts, say, that the

[7] Cf. above, pp. 34–38. For a more detailed account of the relevance of the categories to change, see Wild, *op. cit.*, Chap. 15.

volume of a certain gas that is under observation is diminishing. And one immediately asks "Why?" Clearly, the import of the question is: What is the cause that is operating to bring about this change of quantity in the material substrate of the gas? Similarly, a child seeing a peculiarly rough-looking character with a black eye might ask, "Daddy, why is his eye like that?" Nor is the child seeking for anything save the cause that is responsible for that particular form (the blackened condition of the eye) being present in that particular matter (the eye).

In other words, causes are the causes either of a substantial form's being actualized in its proper matter or of an accidental form's being in a substance. Moreover, a subject-predicate proposition being nothing but an instrument for intending the actual or possible existence of such a substantial form in its material substrate or of such an accidental form in its substance, we can understand how it comes about that an argument is always the demonstration of a proposition, and that the means of such demonstration must needs be through the recognition of a real cause of the existential situation that is intended or signified by the proposition.

Further, argument being thus ordered to the intention of causes, it naturally follows that any attempt to determine the different kinds of argument must have a regard for the different kinds of causes that may be intended in the arguments. Not only that, but inasmuch as there are different kinds of real situations requiring to be explained by different kinds of causes, any adequate account of arguments must take cognizance of these differences as well. Thus as regards the different kinds of causes, we have so far considered only the so-called efficient cause or agent. We shall see presently that there are other types of cause beside this one.

Likewise with respect to the various kinds of existential situation that are the objects of intention in the conclusions of arguments, it obviously is of some relevance to the type or kind of argument involved whether the predicable relationship of P to S in the conclusion to be proved be that of genus, differentia, species, property, or accident. For instance, is it the existence of an accident in a substance or the existence of the substance itself that we are trying to understand through its cause? For as we have already seen,[8] it is just such differences in the existential situation intended by propositions that determine the different predicable relationships in propositions. And as we shall see, differences of this sort have a direct bearing on the different kinds of argument that are used in the demonstration of the different kinds of conclusion.

15–3.1   Different Kinds of Causes as Determining Different Kinds of Argument

So far as demonstrations that proceed through the intention of efficient causes are concerned, we have no doubt said enough already. But efficient

[8] Cf. above, pp. 118–122.

causes are not the only kinds of causes. On the contrary, there is a sense in which we can quite legitimately speak of both the formal and the material elements in things as being causes as well—viz., as "formal" causes and "material" causes.

All this may seem strange, particularly in the light of our foregoing analysis of change. For the cause of change would seem to be precisely the efficient cause which brings the form to the matter or actualizes or realizes the form in the matter. How, then, is it possible to regard the form and the matter as themselves causes in turn? Besides, so far as common English usage is concerned, the word "cause" is usually used in the sense of efficient cause.

The peculiar role of form and matter as causes may perhaps be more readily understood if we think, not so much of the causes of change as such, but rather of the causes of that which comes to be as a result of change or is produced in the process of change—for instance, if we think not so much of the change that results in a given human being as of the product, the human being himself; or if we think not of the process of building a house but rather of the house that is built. In such cases, the import of the question "Why?" undergoes an unmistakable shift. We begin to concern ourselves with the question of why the man is as he is, or why the house is as it is, in contrast to the question of why the man is or why the house is, in the sense of what produced them or brought them into being. Or we might express the shift by saying that in the one case the question "Why?" is directed toward the *constitutive* causes of a thing's being; in the other case toward its *productive* causes.

Nor is there any doubt that these constitutive causes are the thing's very matter and form, i.e., the very elements that constitute it. The house, for instance, it what it is or is as it is, on the one hand, because of the materials—the wood, bricks, cement, concrete blocks, and what not—of which it is made; and on the other hand, because of its form, i.e., its design or plan as a result of which we say that those materials are in the form of a house, as contrasted with that of a bridge, a retaining wall, a factory, etc. Likewise, we might say that the material element in a human being is the body, and the form is the rational animating principle, the rational psyche, which makes the body to be the body of that kind of being rather than of some other.[9]

If we ask the question "Why?" in regard to a human being, then, we may well mean, "Why is a human being that way?" or "Why is he as he is?" And the answer must be in terms of the human being's formal and material constituents, which are the formal and material causes of a man's being the sort of being he is. For example, suppose we resurrect one of our earlier illustrations and ask, "Why is a human being morally responsible?" We might answer, "Because a human being is rational or intelligent." Here, clearly, man's

[9] This latter example is based on the traditional Aristotelian view of the composite nature of the human being. For a fuller account, see Wild, *op. cit.*, Chap. 17.

rationality or intelligence is not the efficient cause of moral responsibility, as if rationality somehow acted upon the material substrate in man to produce moral responsibility. On the contrary, the fact that man is responsible is due to man's being the kind of being he is, viz., a rational being. In other words, this is a case not of efficient causation but rather of formal causation.

For even clearer examples of formal causation we have only to turn to mathematics. Why is the sum of the angles of a triangle equal to two right angles? Ultimately, the cause or reason for this is simply the nature of the figure called "triangle." That is to say, triangles being what they are and having the peculiar formal determination that they do have, necessarily the sum of their angles will be equal to two right angles. But here obviously is no question of efficient or productive causation: the nature or form of triangularity does not make or produce or bring about the equality of the angles to two rights in the same way, say, in which a man makes or produces a table, or in which an increase in the pressure on a gas causes or produces a decrease in its volume. The case is rather one of formal causation, in which we recognize that a given thing or object has certain properties and characteristics simply in virtue of being the kind of thing that it is and not in virtue of any external, productive cause.[10]

Turning, then, to causation through the material cause, we find that it functions not unlike formal causation. That is to say, it is on the order of a constitutive rather than a productive cause. Thus to take our example of the house: a house is as it is not merely because of its form, i.e., its plan and structure, but also because of the materials of which it is built. If one asks why the house keeps out the cold as well, the answer might be, "Because of the insulating materials of which it was built." So also with a human being: it is obvious that he is as he is not merely because of his intelligence and rationality but also because of his physical make-up and constitution. Accordingly, certain questions of "Why?" in regard to human beings will have to be answered in terms of material causes.

In addition to efficient, formal, and material causes, there appears to be a fourth type of cause, viz., the final cause. For instance, suppose someone asks you, "Why are you studying logic?" Your first response might be "I don't know." But if your questioner were persistent and forced you to put a slightly greater strain on your intelligence, you might come up with the answer "Because it is a requirement." You would thus imply that you were but a helpless, passive recipient and that the university authorities were cruel and inhuman

[10] Of course, that there should be a triangle in the first place, it is necessary that an efficient cause shall have brought it into being—i.e., shall have realized or actualized the form of triangle in a particular matter. Nevertheless, no sooner is such a form thus brought into being than its various properties immediately follow from it by formal causation; and the formal determinations would still obtain even if there were no actual triangles at all.

efficient causes who were literally forcing this state or condition upon you, viz., that of being a student of logic.

So much for the realities of the situation. For purposes of illustration it might not hurt to consider the more ideal situation—it might even prove illuminating. Thus suppose when the aforementioned question were put to you, you were to answer, "Why am I taking logic? Why, because I want to." Now however unlikely it might be that this should ever be the true answer, one can readily see that if it should be the answer, a very different sort of cause would be involved. That is, your present happy or unhappy condition of being a student of logic would not be due simply and directly to what you are, i.e., to your form or your matter. Nor would it be due to a mere external efficient cause. Instead, it would be due to a certain purpose or objective that you had had in mind, a certain end in view: this would be the thing that caused you to enroll in a logic class and so become a student of logic.

For that matter, even supposing that it was not by your own choice but simply by requirement that you were in the class, still there would no doubt be some sort of final causation involved. Why did the university or college authorities pass such a requirement and so force you into your present miserable condition? They must have had some purpose or objective in mind. To be sure, to attribute any purpose or objective to university authorities might be even more gratuitous than to attribute such a thing to a student. Yet even as a condition contrary to fact it will do well enough for purposes of illustration.

The point is that if and whenever such things as ends, purposes, goals, aims, objectives, etc., function as causes, we have what is known as final (from *finis*, "end") causation. Final causation may perhaps be best understood by referring it more directly to the efficient cause. For just as the action of the efficient cause on the matter may be the reason *why* the form has come to be realized in the matter, so also the final cause is the reason *why* the efficient cause acts as it does so as to realize the form in the matter. Indeed, if one looks at final causes in this way, one can easily see how such causes in no sense need to be restricted to the domain of conscious purpose. True, all such purposes are final causes, but not all final causes are purposes. Thus as regards any efficient cause, we expect it to operate in a certain determinate way to produce a certain determinate result. But this is only to say that any efficient cause is determined to a certain end, not in the sense of a conscious purpose but rather in the sense of an appropriate terminus to its causal activity. The agencies of growth in living beings tend to produce regular and predictable effects. We don't expect a peach seed to grow into a five-story building, but into a peach tree (the end or final cause). Likewise, in inanimate nature the same principle is borne out. When you drive your car a long distance or put a sealed flask on a Bunsen burner, you do not expect the pressure in the tires, or in the flask, to decrease, but rather to increase.

15–3.2 Different Kinds of Conclusions as Determining Different Kinds of Argument[11]

The sense of the preceding paragraphs would seem to be that differences in the kinds of causes intended have some bearing on the differences in the kinds of argument through which these causes are intended. Nevertheless, we must be careful not to make too much of this point. For one thing it is frequently not possible, and more frequently not even necessary, to determine the precise sense of "why" that is involved in a given argument. It is frequently not possible simply because the events and happenings of the natural world may be opaque to our understanding, with the result that we cannot tell whether the intended cause be efficient, formal, final, or material cause. Besides, it is not always necessary for us to determine this, at least not for ordinary practical purposes. Thus I may know that the reason a given body floats is because its specific gravity is less than 1; yet I need scarcely trouble myself in such an instance with whether this "cause" be a formal, final, material, or efficient cause.

Moreover, as we shall have occasion to see in more detail later, there is a certain sense in which the form or structure of arguments remains the same despite differences in the kinds of causes intended by such arguments. Accordingly, if we are properly to see how arguments as such differ from one another we must consider not merely the differences in the causes that are the objects of intention but also differences in the kinds of conclusion that arguments are designed to demonstrate. Already we have remarked on how conclusions, being nothing but propositions, differ from one another according to the different types of predicable relationship involved in them—viz., generic, differentiating, specific, proper, and accidental relationships. In addition, we have seen how these different kinds of predicable relationship are used to intend the different kinds of real situations that are capable of becoming the objects of such propositional intention. Considering these different kinds of propositional intentions as so many different kinds of conclusion to be proved, we shall presently find that with respect to each of them one may properly inquire just what type of demonstrative argument is best adapted to the work in hand.

Consider first the case of a conclusion asserting a purely contingent accident: "That man is sitting down." If one asked "Why?" the answer—i.e., the demonstrative argument which would be required for an answer—would presumably have to be in terms of either efficient or final causes. Nor is the reason for this hard to understand. For necessarily, a purely contingent accident would be one which came to be in a given substance as a result of a process of change. And since final and efficient causes are the productive causes of change, it

[11] For a somewhat fuller discussion of the issues raised in this and the following section (15–3.3), see Veatch, *Intentional Logic,* Yale, 1952, pp. 286–300.

would be causes of this type that would provide the basis for the demonstration. For example, "Why is that man sitting down?" "Because he chose to do so"—final cause. Or "Why is that man sitting down?" "Because the court bailiff made him"—efficient cause.

On the other hand, suppose it be a necessary accident, or property, for which one is seeking the cause. For instance, why are human beings morally responsible for their actions? Or why does silver melt at 960.5° C.? Or why are triangles such that the sum of their angles is equal to two right angles? As our previous analysis has already shown, it is formal causation, rather than efficient causation, that is pertinent here. The reason is clear. Such necessary accidents are not present in their substances because of the action of any extrinsic agent upon the substance. These accidents follow from and are determined by the very nature of the substance itself, by its constitutive principle, in other words —in these instances by the formal constitutive principle.

Causes of Knowing and Causes of Being. But now let us look at conclusions in which the predicate expresses not an accident of the subject but its very essence. Let us consider species. "That is an angiosperm." "That is a gymnosperm." Suppose with respect to either of these two propositions the question "Why?" be asked. At once one can recognize that the question might give rise to a certain ambiguity. Commonly a question of this sort might be supposed to mean "Why?" in the sense of "Why do you say that?" or "How do you know that?" In other words, one person having asserted that a certain seed is an angiosperm, someone else might challenge him to produce his evidence for saying so. Nevertheless, the causes or reasons for our saying or _believing_ something to be as it is are not necessarily the same as the causes or reasons for its actually _being_ that way. For instance, I may know or believe that it is raining outside because the streets are wet. Yet the fact that the streets are wet, while it may well be the cause or reason of my belief, is certainly not the cause of the rain!

Accordingly, with reference to the propositions "That is an angiosperm" and "That is a gymnosperm," let us interpret the question "Why?" in the second sense rather than the first. Let us suppose that the question is designed to get at, not the mere causes of a person's _asserting_ these things, or _believing_ these things, but rather at causes of the thing's actually _being_ an angiosperm or _being_ a gymnosperm.

No sooner is the question so interpreted than one can recognize the sort of causal situation that is thereby envisaged. Thus as we have seen, it is not just accidents that come into being in the real world but substances as well. It is not merely substances that function as material substrates for the reception of accidental forms, but in addition pure matter, or prime matter as it has been sometimes called, is the substrate in which substantial forms are received. Moreover, change being the reception of a new form in matter, and the proper causes of change as such being efficient and final causes, it is clear that the causes or reasons we usually think of for a given substance's coming into being, or a given substantial form's being actualized in prime matter, tend to be efficient or final causes.

Making the transition, then, from the ontological domain to the logical, we may say that when the conclusion to be proved involves the predicable relationship of species, and when the "Why?" calls for a cause of being and not a mere cause of knowing, the relevant argument that demonstrates such a conclusion will naturally intend an efficient or final cause, not a formal or material cause.

The Problem of Definitional Predicates and Their Demonstration. Finally we come to propositions involving the predicable relationships of genus and of differentia, or definitional predicates as they are sometimes called. How may they be demonstrated? What sort of causes are to be appealed to to provide the "why" of such relationships? For instance, suppose that we consider the definition of triangle to be "a three-sided rectilinear figure." We might then form the proposition "A triangle is three-sided." But why is a triangle three-sided? What may be said to be the cause of this?

Unhappily, the question "Why?" this time poses curious difficulties. Think about it. Why is a triangle three-sided? What sort of cause could be operative here? Just how are you going to answer questions of this sort?

Note that we are not here asking for a "why" in the sense of "Why do you make such assertions?" but rather in the sense of "Why is that the case?"—not what is the cause of your *knowing* and asserting that a triangle is three-sided but what is the cause of a triangle's *being* three-sided. Such a cause, we suggest, simply is not to be found. The question "Why?" in this instance seeks to get at the cause or reason that a certain nature or essence (e.g., that of triangle) is itself, i.e., is the nature or essence that it is. But there just is no cause or reason for this.

True, there can be a cause or reason why a given *individual* should have come to have the nature or essence that it does have. Indeed, we have just seen how such a cause would have to be an efficient or final cause. So also there can be and must be an efficient or final cause to explain why a given individual thing of a certain nature or essence should have come to have a certain accident inhering in it. Yet it is quite a different thing to talk about a cause or reason why a given nature or essence itself is the nature or essence that it is. How could there be an external cause that would operate or act upon the very nature or essence of triangularity so as to make it three-sided? The thing is absurd.

Nor could there be a constitutive or intrinsic cause (i.e., formal or material cause) of such a thing either. To be sure, as we have seen, the properties that any given kind of thing has may be explained either by the formal or by the material principle that is constitutive of that kind of thing. For example, that a triangle should have the sum of its angles equal to two right angles is formally caused by the nature or essence of triangle. Nevertheless, though the essence may well be the formal cause of its own properties, it cannot very well be the formal cause of itself. Indeed, the properties of an essence are in a sense always distinguishable from the essence, usually as accidents from substance and hence as following from the substantial form. Yet clearly no essence is distinguishable from itself; nor could it possibly follow from itself. Hence there just is no way to demonstrate definitional predication through causes. The sort of thing that is intended through such predication doesn't have any causes, for the simple reason that nothing can be the cause of itself, nor can anything else be the cause of its being itself.

Unfortunately, though, if the argument of the preceding paragraphs be correct, the consequences would appear to be most embarrassing. There can be no demonstration of definitional predication—such was the thrust of the argument. But definitional predicates define the very "whats" of things themselves. They are our means of understanding the natures and essences of things. For example, "yellow," "human being," "triangle," "angiosperm," "silver," "greater than"—these are all concepts of essences or "whats." But if we want to understand these essences for what they are and not be content with merely naming them, we have to define them, i.e., recognize their genus and differentia in each case. Yet if the question be raised as to why "three-sided" is the differentia of triangle, or why "animal" is the genus of man, there is simply no answer—or at least that is what we seem to be arguing. There is no way, apparently, in which the truth of propositions containing definitional predicates can be made evident from the outside, or through other propositions, simply because there are no causes of a thing's just being itself, i.e., of its being what it is essentially. Instead, such propositions presumably have to be either self-evident or just not evident at all. That man is rational, that silver is an element, that a triangle is three-sided, that yellow is a color—these are truths which a person either sees or does not see. And if he doesn't see them, there is presumably nothing to be done about the matter.

But what could be more arbitrary? To think that any assertion as to the character of any "what" or essence is wholly indemonstrable and unsusceptible of any evidence or argument one way or another—this seems incredible. Yet if there be no cause of a "what" or essence being as it is, there would seem to be no possible way of proving that a given essence is the sort of thing it is.

15–3.3 Demonstration Through Effects

Demonstration Through Causes of Knowing Rather Than Causes of Being.
Fortunately, the situation is not quite as desperate as it might seem. Though there is no way of demonstrating definitional predication through causes,

demonstration through causes is not the only type or means of demonstration. On the contrary, we have already had occasion to remark on the distinction between the ground or reason for our *knowing* or asserting something to be so and the ground or reason for something's actually *being* so. But just what is the import of such a distinction?

We did give an example of the distinction. We said that one may know that it has been raining because the streets are wet; yet the streets' being wet is certainly in no wise a cause of its having rained. Very well, just what sort of demonstration can serve to provide a ground for our knowledge of a thing even though it be not a ground for the thing itself? It might seem that there could be no other ground or cause for knowing a thing to be so, save the very cause or ground for the thing's actually being so.

The answer is that although it is only possible for an effect to come to *be* through its cause, it is still quite possible for a cause to come to be *known* through its effect. And surely this is understandable enough, for in so far as an effect is the proper and characteristic work or product of a certain cause, it should be quite as easy to demonstrate or infer the cause from the effect as it is to demonstrate the effect from the cause. Hence although in the order of reality and the real world the process is always from cause to effect, in the order of knowing, the process may be either from cause to effect or from effect to cause.

Solution of the Problem of the Demonstration of Definitional Predicates. Returning to our problem in regard to definitional predicates, we may say that while propositions involving such predicates are wholly indemonstrable by any demonstration through cause, they may nevertheless be susceptible of a demonstration through their effects. For instance, one might say that we come to know that yellow is a color because it affects the eye in the way in which colors do. Or again, how do we know that man is an animal? Presumably it is because he performs the typical animal functions and behaves in the way animals do. But note: it is not human behavior that may here be said to cause man to be a human animal. Rather it is because man is the kind of animal he is that he behaves the way he does. In other words, the inference is from effect to cause, not from cause to effect. Consequently, the demonstration in such a case may not be said to give the cause or ground for man's *being* an animal or for yellow's *being* a color, but only the ground of our *assertion* that man is an animal or that yellow is a color.

Even in a somewhat more difficult case, such as that of triangles being three-sided, we may be said to come to know this by an inference from effects to cause. Put it to the test yourself. How did you come to know that it was of the essence of triangle to be three-sided? Surely, not through causes. For there are no causes of the three-sidedness of triangles. Such knowledge must have come about through observing the character of particular, individual triangles.

Indeed, the process of demonstration in this case is not unlike the process of abstraction in the case of concepts. But of this we shall have more to say later.[12] For the present, be it noted simply that the reason particular individual triangles have three sides is presumably because it pertains to the very nature of triangle to be three-sided. In other words, the former is but the effect or consequence of the latter. Hence to prove that it is of the essence of a triangle to be three-sided by an appeal to particular instances is simply to proceed by an argument from effect to cause.

So one is not after all forced to admit of an utter arbitrariness in one's assertion of definitional predicates—i.e., in one's assertion of what is of the very essence of a given "what" or essence. No, such assertions are susceptible of proof, and one can provide evidence in support of them. But such evidence and such demonstration must needs be in terms of effects rather than causes. And this, as we shall see, makes for a certain precariousness and weakness in all argumentation of this type.

However, for the present the upshot of these considerations, so far as the determination of the different types and varieties of argument is concerned, is simply this: No sooner does one attempt to determine the different types of demonstration with respect to the different types of conclusion that need to be proved than one is immediately struck by the fact that conclusions involving definitional predicates require a special and peculiar type of demonstration—viz., a demonstration through effects rather than through causes. Whereas species and accidents may be demonstrated through efficient causes, and properties through formal or material causes, genera and differentiae may not be demonstrated of their subjects through causes at all, but only through effects.

Nor is it the definitional predicates alone that are susceptible of demonstration through effects. On the contrary, we may come to know that a given individual belongs to a certain species because the effects of that specific nature are manifest in that individual's behavior. Likewise, the existence of certain properties or accidents in a given individual would presumably have certain effects so far as that individual was concerned. Hence it is quite conceivable that one might come to know of the existence of such properties or accidents in the first place by an inference from their manifest effects in the individuals concerned.

Consequently, we cannot rightly say that a demonstration through effects, as contrasted with causes, is adapted only to the proof of definitional predicates. It may be employed in the demonstration of any predicate. Nevertheless, whereas species, properties, and accidents are susceptible of demonstration through either causes or effects, the definitional predicates may be demonstrated only through effects and in no other way.

[12] See the discussion of induction in Chap. 16, especially pp. 241–243.

Summing up, then, we may say that a demonstration through effects differs from a demonstration through causes, in that the former provides only grounds for our *asserting* something to be so, whereas the latter exhibits the ground for its actually *being* thus and so. If we wish to continue to say, as we have said, that all argument or demonstration seeks to get at the "why," in contrast to propositions which intend the "whether" and concepts which intend the "what," we perhaps must qualify our assertion a bit in the light of what we have just seen to be true in regard to demonstration through effects. Thus the latter type of demonstration does not provide us with any reason why S is P in fact, but only with a reason why we may *assert* S to be P. On this account, it has sometimes been said that a demonstration through effects can never prove *why* something is so; it can do no more than demonstrate *that* it is so. The Scholastics, for instance, like to distinguish between a demonstration *propter quid* and a demonstration *quia*. Nevertheless, we see no reason to surrender our proposal that all demonstration or argument be regarded as a demonstration of the "why" provided that one recognize that in some cases it is only the "why" of an assertion whereas in others it is the "why" of the actual fact asserted.

The following outline may help to summarize and clarify this whole discussion:

Demonstration through causes of *being* ('through *causes*):

    Constitutive causes:

        Formal causes   Property
        Material causes   Species, accident

    Productive causes:

        Efficient causes   Accident
        Final causes   Accident

Demonstration through causes of *knowing* (through effects):

                Genus, differentia, species,
                 property, accident

EXERCISES

1. Which of the four kinds of causes is intended by each of the following arguments?
    a. He is going to night school so that he can get a better job. *FINAL* ~~FORM.~~
    b. Towels are absorbent because of their capillary structure. *EFFICIENT* ~~FORMAL~~
    c. I've just plugged the iron in so it will soon be hot. *FINAL,* FORMAL
    d. That building is extremely strong because it's made of steel-reinforced concrete. ~~MATERIAL~~ FORMAL

e. Women speak in a higher voice than men because of the structure of their vocal cords. ~~MATERIAL~~ *FORMAL*

f. This next ball will really sail because Mantle's at the plate. ~~FINAL~~ *EFFICIENT*

g. John's going to study hard so that he will pass the exam. *FINAL*

h. The nylon fibers make this rug longer wearing than any other kind. *MATERIAL*

i. April showers bring May flowers. *FINAL, EFFICIENT*

2. Are the following asserted reasons causes of being or causes of knowing? *C, K*

a. The Groundhog saw his shadow so we're in for six more weeks of winter.

b. Mr. X. Ecutive plays golf once a week, the paper reported, because he says it makes him forget the office. *C, B.*   *i cacon plays galf*

c. Those iron filings are making that funny pattern because there's a magnet underneath. *C, B.*

d. The engine's not even sputtering and we've got plenty of gas, so it must be electrical trouble. *C. K*

e. Ezekiel couldn't have studied because he flunked the exam cold. *C K*

f. Those are light streaks on your pictures so you must have opened the camera before rewinding the film. ~~C K C B~~ *C B*

g. We've got a full moon tonight; that's why the tide is so high. *C B*

h. No wonder you're using so much gas! That's the choke you've got pulled out to hang your purse on! *C B*

i. That statement has to be false because its contradictory is certainly true. *C B*

Knowing
cause to come to be known. thru its effects

Being
effect to come to be thru its cause

CHAPTER 16

MEDIATION AND IDENTITY
IN ARGUMENT

16–1 PROPOSITIONS AS EVIDENCING A CONCLUSION

At the outset of Part III we sought to press home a basic principle, viz., that all human knowledge, or at least all human knowledge of a scientific sort, is contained in propositions. Nor will it be amiss to reiterate this principle in the present context. For consider just by way of illustration a science such as chemistry. What is it anyway? By this question we do not mean to ask what chemistry is about, but rather what it is, considered precisely as a science. Obviously, as a science—i.e., as a *scientia* (from the Latin, *scire,* "to know")— chemistry is a body of knowledge. But a body of knowledge, we have said, is a body of propositions. And, in fact, are not the so-called truths of chemistry just so many true propositions? For example, truths such as *that* air is a mixture and not a compound, *that* iron under certain conditions will combine with oxygen but not with nitrogen, *that* under ideal conditions the pressure and volume of a gas will vary inversely—these are all recognizable as so many S–P propositions.[1]

Nevertheless, however obvious it may be that the science of chemistry consists in a body of propositions, it should be equally obvious that it does not consist in a wholly unordered and unrelated body of propositions. No, even if they be indisputably true propositions, more is required for a science than mere true propositions. In addition, as we say, the *evidence* for such true propositions must be adduced as well as the propositions themselves if one is to have genuine science.

Yet the interesting thing is that no sooner does one consider the evidence which is given in support of the truths of chemistry than one finds that this evidence consists of propositions also. Thus one maintains that air is a mixture and not a compound *because* air is never homogeneous. Or one states that iron will combine with oxygen *because* on repeated occasions it has been observed

[1] It would perhaps be more accurate to say that the first and second of these propositions just cited as examples are respectively a conjunctive and a concessive proposition (see below, pp. 333–335), rather than S–P propositions in the strict sense.

to do so. In each instance the "because" which presents the evidence for a given proposition is itself in the form of still another proposition. Moreover, if the proposition which one is seeking to provide evidence for is to be proved true, then the "because" by means of which one seeks to support it must also be a true proposition. Truth, in short, can be evidenced only through truth. Or, to express the same thing in a way that is more directly pertinent to logic, the truth of a proposition can be proved or demonstrated only through other true propositions.

Test this for yourself. Take any proposition you wish whose truth you want to prove or demonstrate. You cannot possibly do it save by citing other true propositions as evidence. And so it is with the science of chemistry or with any other body of knowledge whatever: what the science qua science consists of is nothing but a set of true propositions whose truth, in turn, is vouched for, so to speak, by still other true propositions.

This is not quite all there is to it. For it is not the case that a true proposition may be evidenced by just *any* true proposition. Thus it may be a true proposition that this is a dull book, and it may also be true that there are a great many Chinese on the face of the earth; but it is hardly conceivable that the truth of the latter should be cited as evidence of the truth of the former. No, for if one or more propositions are to be advanced as evidence of the truth of some other proposition, they must somehow or other have bearing upon it or be relevant to it. Accordingly, the immediate and proper concern of the logician in the doctrine of argument is with determining the various ways in which propositions may be brought to bear on other propositions so as to make their truth evident—i.e., so as to prove or demonstrate them.

Consider how this is to be tied up with what we have been saying throughout the whole of the preceding chapter. There we were concerned with showing that the object of intention in an argument is always a cause or a cause-effect situation. Now we say that the instrument through which the intention is brought about must needs be a certain arrangement or ordering of propositions so that certain of these propositions may be seen to have a bearing upon others, in such a way as to demonstrate these others and make them evident. But what precisely is the nature of this "bearing" which one proposition may be said to have on another? And what sort of ordering or arranging of propositions is required in order that certain propositions may be said to be demonstrative of others, and demonstrative in such wise as to effect an intention of a cause-effect situation?

What Such Evidencing Is Not.   Before we address ourselves to the task of stating what this bearing and ordering of propositions is, let us first make at least a passing suggestion as to what it is not. In earlier chapters[2] we became familiar with a certain technique for the *transformation* of propositions, and

[2] See above, Chaps. 12–14.

this technique clearly involved the bearing of certain propositions on others and the ordering and arranging of propositions with respect to each other. At the same time, the latter sort of bearing and ordering of propositions is definitely not the sort that is involved in *demonstration*.[3]

For instance, suppose one tries to argue that the existence of God can be proved, *because* the existence of any cause whose effects are clearly manifest may be proved from the existence of those effects. Obviously, what is involved is quite different from what would be involved if one were to say, " 'God's existence cannot be proved,' *because* 'God's existence is unprovable.' " In the former case the arrangement of propositions is with a view to demonstration; in the latter case it is with a view to mere transformation.

Again, how impressive would it be in geometry if one tried to prove that the sum of the angles of a triangle were equal to two right angles by merely adducing a proposition to the effect that nothing that is not equal to two right angles is ever the sum of the angles of a triangle? The point is that this would not be a case of proving or demonstrating a proposition at all, but merely a case of transforming a proposition into another having the same meaning as the first and differing from it only in form.

Apparently, then, for the demonstration, as contrasted with the transformation, of a proposition, one needs more than just another proposition of the same meaning or intention but differing only in form. One has to have a proposition or propositions which don't mean or intend to say the same thing as the proposition to be proved at all. Thus one might try to demonstrate that the sum of the angles of a triangle equals two rights on the ground that when two parallel lines are cut by a third line, both the alternate-interior angles and the exterior-interior angles are equal. But clearly, the second of these two propositions does not mean or say the same thing as the first. And in like manner the assertion that the existence of a cause whose effects are manifest may be proved from those effects certainly does not say the same thing as, nor is it a mere transformation of, "The existence of God can be proved."

What Such Evidencing Is.   Granted that the bearing which one proposition has on another in the case of demonstration is not the same sort of thing as it is in the case of transformation, what is it? To answer this question let us begin by sticking rather close to concrete illustrations. Let us consider a proposition from Euclidean geometry: The opposite vertical angles formed by intersecting straight lines are equal. Moreover, let us consider this proposition very simply, even simple-mindedly—i.e., without bothering our heads with the

---

[3] The distinction we are here seeking to draw between the *transformation* of propositions and the *demonstration* of propositions is to all intents and purposes the same as the traditional distinction between *immediate* and *mediate* inference, which one finds in most of the standard textbooks. The latter pair of terms has long been acknowledged to be misleading and unsatisfactory; hence our effort to replace them with terms which we hope may be somewhat more illuminating.

subtleties of modern mathematical theorists. We should all doubtless agree that the proposition is true.

But what is the evidence for its truth? How do we know it is true? Surely we must have come to know it at some time or other, since a knowledge of the truth of principles of geometry could hardly be supposed to have been innate in us. But if we came to know it or came to recognize it, there must have been something which served to make its truth evident to us. What could it have been?

To this the answer probably is that most of us originally learned the truth about the equality of opposite vertical angles from experience. How does a boy come to know that a straight line is the shortest distance between two points? Doubtless through experiences such as cutting across vacant lots rather than going all the way around on the sidewalk. And likewise with most of the other elementary truths of geometry.[4]

Specifically, as regards the particular geometrical proposition before us, the argument from experience by which it comes to be proved or demonstrated might be cast in the following form. We learn from experience that:

The opposite vertical angles in this
    case are equal,

        and

The opposite vertical angles in this
    case are equal,

        and

These also are equal.

We conclude, therefore, that any two opposite vertical angles are equal.

Clearly in this example we may see how the main features of argument which we have thus far remarked upon are in fact borne out. Thus what the argument is designed to prove is obviously a certain proposition which may be called the *conclusion*, viz., that the opposite vertical angles of intersecting straight lines are equal. Moreover, the evidence adduced in support of this conclusion likewise consists in a series of propositions which go by the name of premises. In this instance, the premises are simply a series of singular prop-

---

[4] It will no doubt seem to many that we are here treating geometrical truths as if they were no more or less than empirically established truths about the physical world. And so we are! Our excuse is that a careful distinction between mathematical truth and physical truth would only further complicate our already rather complicated exposition. Nor would it seem particularly to the point in a logic textbook. Perhaps we may be forgiven, then, if we continue to take full advantage of the illustrative value of simple truths in geometry without troubling to distinguish them from truths about the physical world in the more proper sense.

ositions to the effect that these angles are equal, and these likewise, and these, and these, etc. Finally, it is apparent that the propositions which here serve as premises have a certain bearing on the conclusion and are relevant to it. Nevertheless, as to the precise nature of this bearing we shall have more to say in the section immediately following.[5]

For the present let us attempt to illustrate further the general nature and character of argument by showing how this very same conclusion which we have just proved by one set of premises may also be proved by an entirely different set of premises—indeed, by an altogether different type of argument or demonstration. After all, we have only to think back upon those ancient days of wrath in our high-school geometry classes to realize that, although in the nature of the case it might be quite right and proper to prove the proposition about opposite vertical angles being equal by the method of demonstration we have just suggested, it would in no wise have been right and proper in the eyes of a stern and exacting geometry teacher. For to establish the equality of angles by the simple device of measuring them just isn't cricket—or better, isn't geometry.

Instead, one would have to proceed with one's demonstration in, say, some such fashion as this:

> The opposite vertical angles formed by intersecting
>   straight lines have the same supplementary angle
>   in common.
> But any two angles having the same supplementary angle
>   in common are equal.
> _____
> Therefore, the opposite vertical angles are equal.

Here again, in this example, we find exhibited all of those salient features of argument or proof we have thus far called attention to. Thus what is proved (viz., the conclusion) is a proposition, viz., that the opposite vertical angles are equal. Moreover, the way it is proved is by means of other propositions (premises) that are offered as evidence. And finally, the premises quite patently (though we may not as yet be able to explain just how) have a bearing on the conclusion.

Evidencing as Mediation.   Nevertheless, we cannot continue to evade this still outstanding problem as to just what this "bearing" of premises on the conclusion is. For it is only in so far as there is bearing of premised propositions upon a conclusion that the latter can be made evident through the former. Not only that, but in the section immediately preceding we were presented with two quite different ways or means of demonstrating one and the same proposition. Actually these two different ways are what we shall subsequently come to call by their technical names, *inductive* argument and *deductive* argument.

[5] See below, pp. 239–241.

But since the difference between induction and deduction can be understood only in terms of the different types or kinds of bearing which premises may have upon their conclusions, we must proceed at once to clarify this notion of the *bearing* of certain propositions on others.

Now the key to an understanding of bearing or evidencing is the notion of *mediation*. Or to put the same thing a little differently, any proposition that needs to be proved or demonstrated is one that is not immediately evident in itself; its truth can be made evident only mediately or through the mediation of something else. Consider once again, and this time a little more precisely, just what it is that gets proved or is made evident in an argument or demonstration. As we suggested earlier, it is necessarily a proposition. But a proposition, stating as it does what a thing is or what is true of it, must needs be composed of two and only two terms—S and P.[6] Accordingly, to determine whether S really is P or not, one must somehow mediate between these two terms so as to bring them together and show that a relation of identity holds between them—that S is P.

How can a mediation between two terms be effected? Well, one way—the inductive way—is by a simple appeal to observation. That is to say, we may come to recognize that S is P by observing it to be so in particular instances:

> This S is P,
> This S is P,
> This S is P,
> Etc.
> _____
> Therefore, any and every S is P.

In other words, it is our experience of S's being P in particular instances that serves to mediate between the two terms in the conclusion and so bring them together.

Thus it is through measuring the opposite vertical angles in particular instances of intersecting straight lines that the universal proposition about such angles being equal is made evident. Or again, one may convince oneself of the fact that silver melts at 960.5° C. by putting it to the test and observing that in each particular instance it is at this temperature that silver does in fact start to melt. Yes, even the conclusion that all logic textbooks are dull you may feel has literally been forced upon you by your own bitter individual experience with this one. In all these examples, in short, it is one's experience with individual instances that serves to mediate between, and so bring together, the two terms of a universal conclusion.

[6] Of course, there are other types of propositions besides subject-predicate propositions. Nevertheless, we suggest that all other types of propositions can best be understood as being really arguments—except for compound propositions in which the consequent is a mere transformation of the antecedent. On this, cf. below, pp. 333–347.

But now let us consider the very different sort of mediation that is involved when one undertakes to prove a conclusion deductively. This time it will not be one's experience with individual instances that serves to unite the subject and predicate concepts of the conclusion; rather it will be a third concept, different from the other two, yet connected with each of them in such a way as to effect a mediation between them. For instance, the opposite vertical angles may be said to be equal on the ground of their having the same supplementary angle. That is to say, it is the notion or concept of having a common supplementary angle that serves to bring together the S and the P terms of the conclusion.

And how does it do so? It does so in virtue of the fact that, on the one hand, any angles having a common supplementary angle are equal, and that, on the other hand, the opposite vertical angles formed by intersecting straight lines are precisely such as to have a common supplementary angle. In the former case the third or mediating concept (viz., that of angles having a common supplement) is recognized as being connected with the predicate of the conclusion (viz., the concept "equal"); and in the latter case this same third concept is recognized as being connected with the subject concept of the conclusion as well (viz., the concept of opposite vertical angles). These two concepts of the conclusion being seen to be thus connected with the same third concept, one thereby sees that they are also connected with each other.

And albeit the description in words of mediation via a third, or mediating, concept may sound verbose and awkward, the fact of such mediation is something so obvious and so familiar that we quite take it for granted. You can readily verify the thing for yourself by simply constructing examples of your own almost *ad libitum*. Thus you may ask, "Why do I dislike logic so intensely?" and answer, "Because of the dull textbook." Or "Why are human beings to be held morally responsible for their actions?" "Because of their rationality." Or "Why are towels able to dry hands?" "Because of their capillary structure." And so on.

In each case the proposition which was to be demonstrated, and which you put in the form of a question, was proved or demonstrated through a third or mediating concept. Thus:

Any rational or intelligent being is responsible for his actions.
Human beings are rational beings.
Human beings are responsible for their actions.

Any course in which the textbook is dull is one which I
    dislike intensely.
Logic is such a course.
Logic is a course which I dislike intensely.

Any substance with a capillary structure will readily
  absorb moisture.
Towels are of such substance.
Therefore, towels readily absorb moisture.

Each time, you see, your argument has the effect of mediating between the subject and predicate term of the conclusion by means of a common third, or, as it is usually called, a middle term.

16–2   THE DISTINCTION BETWEEN INDUCTIVE AND DEDUCTIVE MEDIATION

Having tried to make out our case that the so-called bearing which premises have upon a conclusion is to be understood precisely in terms of the mediation that is effected between the subject and predicate terms of the conclusion so as to bring about their union or identification in the proposition—having attempted this much, let us see if perhaps we can make a little clearer what the nature of the difference is between mediation in the case of inductive argument and that in the case of deductive argument. Already we have intimated that the difference seems to lie in the fact that in the one case the mediation is based on observation or experience, and in the other it is not.

Now clearly, in inductive argument it is this business of observation or experience that is supposed to make the conclusion evident. The truth of the conclusion is not itself a matter of direct experience; rather it is *from* experience, or in the light of experience, that it becomes evident. In this regard the passing from premises to conclusion in induction is analogous to the passing from sense experience to concepts in the case of abstraction. As we saw in our earlier discussion of concepts,[7] that which is conceived—the nature or essence which is the object of the concept in the strict sense—is not sensed just as such. Rather it is *from* what is apprehended in sensation that we come to apprehend intellectually the nature or essence (in and by means of an abstract concept). Correspondingly, then, we may say that the universal proposition forming the conclusion of an inductive argument is not seen to be true directly in experience; instead, it is from and in the light of what is directly seen to be true in particular instances that the universal conclusion is made evident.

But such is not the nature of mediation in the case of deductive argument at all. For there it is not in the light of experience that the conclusion is made evident, but rather in the light of the third or mediating concept. To recur to our earlier examples, and considering them just as such and in themselves, we find that *in the precise context of the given argument*[8] it is not in the light of

[7] Above, pp. 45–48.
[8] The necessity for this qualification is obvious. It may well be that a conclusion of a deductive argument is evident to us from experience. Even so, the deductive evidence is very different from the empirical evidence.

our experience that we come to see that human beings are morally responsible, but solely in the light of the concept of rationality. Or again, taking the argument precisely as given, it was not experience that made us see that towels are absorbent, but rather the mediating concept of capillary structure.

The point of the distinction that is here being made between induction and deduction might be said to be something like this: In the case of induction, as in that of abstraction, the cognitive process moves, so to speak, from the level of the sensible to that of the intelligible. In contrast, in deduction the process moves exclusively on the intelligible level. This is not to say, of course, that the premises which we employ in a deductive argument may not have been founded on experience and so established inductively. Indeed, there is no denying the fact that ultimately all our knowledge is derived from experience and based upon it. No, the only point is that in the actual process itself of any deductive argument the mediation is strictly and exclusively intellectual and in no wise experiential.

To use again our illustration about the opposite vertical angles, it may well be that it is from experience and inductively that a given individual has come to recognize that any angles having a common supplementary angle are equal. Also it may well be that it is from experience that one has come to recognize that the opposite vertical angles of intersecting straight lines have a common supplementary angle. Still, knowing this much, it is not then from experience that one concludes that the opposite vertical angles are equal. Quite the contrary. No further experience is then necessary for the conclusion; instead, it follows purely intellectually from the two premises. For the mediation that is here effected is purely and simply through a universal concept; and a universal concept, as we have seen, is the product of the intellect and not of the senses.

We may even go so far as to say that if one is certain one's premises are true, and if the structure of one's argument is correct, then one knows with certainty that one's conclusion is true not only in advance of all experience that might have bearing upon it but even in spite of all experience that might seem to have bearing. If, for instance, it should turn out that when we measure the opposite angles formed by intersecting straight lines they are found to be unequal, we should not question the conclusion of our deductive argument, provided we were certain of our premises. Instead, we should suppose that something must have been wrong with our measuring techniques, or that perhaps the intersecting straight lines were not true straight lines. But as for our conclusion that the opposite angles are equal, its truth having been certified intellectually, there is no way that it could be falsified by experience—provided always, of course, that we are certain of the premises of our deductive argument.

Note, however, that these provisos are not to be taken lightly. That is the very reason we inserted so many of them in the foregoing paragraph. For in actual fact, we human beings can doubtless never be so completely certain of our premises in a deductive argument that we can rely on the truth of the conclusion, not merely in disregard of, but even in a sense in defiance of, all experience. On the contrary, there is perhaps no deductive conclusion that is not susceptible of (and that does not even in a measure require) further verification and confirmation in experience—i.e., a supplementary demonstration through induction. Still, the point is that, however much a deductive conclusion may be subject to further demonstration through induction, considered just as such and in the context of the argument itself, the conclusion of a deductive demonstration is made evident not in the light of observation and experience but solely in the light of the mediating concept. Nor must this point ever be lost sight of if one hopes to appreciate the peculiar and characteristic instrumentality of the deductive argument.

True, in the concrete procedures of human cognition, induction and deduction may never be separated. One might even go so far as to say that there is no deductive argument where there is not also a corresponding inductive type of proof that is directly relevant and comes into play concurrently. And the same would hold also for an inductive argument with reference to the corresponding and relevant deductive demonstration. Yet even though inseparable, the two types of argument are quite distinct; and one cannot understand their concurrent functioning without understanding the distinct contribution of each.

To use a rather far-fetched analogy, one might say that it is rather like the situation which prevails in chemical compounds involving manganese. This latter element is extremely difficult to isolate completely in fact. But it still has its own character and makes its own distinctive contribution to the compounds of which it is a part. Nor could these compounds be properly understood unless one recognized the peculiar character of manganese for what it is in itself. So likewise with what we might term the purely intellectual evidencing that takes place in deduction, as contrasted with the evidencing through observation and experience that takes place in inductive demonstration.

In this account of the respective characters of deductive and inductive argument, we must be careful to bear in mind not only their utility as instruments of proof but also the fact that we human beings have no other instruments of proof. For as we have seen, if proof be always a proof of a proposition, and if a proposition be made up of an S and a P term, then proof is essentially a problem of mediation between two concepts. And how else is one to show that two concepts belong together unless it be either by an appeal to experience or by using a third or mediating concept? Try it yourself. Take any proposition you choose. Can you possibly show that its two terms belong together in any other way save one of these two?

16–3 IDENTITY AS THE STRUCTURAL FORM OF ARGUMENTS

Deductive Argument.   Having seen that causes come to be known through a process of logical mediation, and having also seen that such mediation may be effected either through the use of a middle or mediating concept (deduction) or through an appeal to particular cases or instances (induction), it remains for us to consider a little more precisely just what the logical forms or structures of mediation are. Already we know that the conclusion to be proved is a proposition and as such will involve a relation of identity (or nonidentity in the case of negatives). But not only the conclusion to be proved but also the evidence cited to prove it will take the form of propositions and hence of still further relations of identity (or its opposite, nonidentity). In short, the relation of identity promises to provide the key to an understanding of mediation in logical argument, just as it has formerly provided us with the key to an understanding of concepts and propositions.

And so it does. For instance, in the case of mediation through a middle term, i.e., in deductive mediation, one's concern is to demonstrate that a certain S is P. To do this, one attempts to find a mediating concept M. But in order that such a concept may really mediate, one must needs relate it on the one hand with the S concept and on the other with the P concept; in such wise S and P may then be related to each other. If one wishes to show—to revert to an earlier example—that human beings (S) are morally responsible for their actions (P), one might do so by appealing to the mediating concept of rationality or intelligence (M). One could then argue that human beings are rational beings (S is related to M) and that any rational being is morally responsible for his actions (P is related to M); hence human beings are responsible for their actions (S is related to P).

But note that this relating of two concepts to each other through the mediation of a common third concept involves nothing but relations of identity. Thus in the one premise P is identified with M and in the other M is identified with S, in order that in the conclusion P may be identified with S. This type of argument, in which a conclusion is proved through the mediation of a common third term, is called a syllogism; and the characteristic structure of a syllogism, we might say, is one of triple identity:

M is P
S is M
——————
S is P.

Inductive Argument.   Passing to induction and inductive mediation, it will be recalled[9] that in this type of inference we found that one proceeds from the sensible or the merely observed to the intelligible; or better, it is the observed

[9] See above, pp. 241–243.

particulars that provide the evidence for the universal principle; or, in terms of mediation, it is observation of particular cases that serves to mediate between the S and P terms of the conclusion to be proved. Thus why does one suppose that water boils at 100° C.? Because it has been observed to do so in particular instances.

This water boils at 100° C.,
And this does,
And this does,
And this does,
Etc.
___
All water boils at 100° C.

The Analogy Between Induction and Abstraction.   From this, then, we see that the form of an inductive inference involves a process from a number of singular propositions to a universal. But no sooner is the process of inductive inference so understood than it is seen to be strictly analogous to the process of abstraction. For just as abstraction in the area of concepts involves a passage from observed particulars to a universal concept,[10] so also induction in the area of argument involves a passage from singular propositions, that are, so to speak, mere reports of observations, to a universal proposition. In other words, just as in the former case the recognition of the "what" of a thing involves the abstraction of the nature or essence of the thing from all of the various extrinsic and individuating features that happen to pertain to it in the particular case, in the latter case the recognition of the "why" of a thing requires the inducing of that nature or essence which alone can make intelligible why the particular individual case should be as it is. For instance, we only know *what* this, that, and the other observed particulars are when we recognize them all as being instances of water. But we come to understand *why* this, that, and the other bit of water all boil at 100° C. only when we recognize that it pertains to the nature of water as such to boil at this temperature.

In the case of universal concepts, we saw that each of these may be said to be a relation of identity between an abstracted nature or essence and the individuals from which it is abstractable and to which it is applicable. Accordingly, induction being analogous to abstraction, we may say that the universal conclusion that is induced from the various singular propositions is related by a relation of identity to these singulars from which it has been induced and for which it provides the cause or ground.

Note that on this analysis induction, like abstraction, may be regarded as a two-way process. Abstraction involves both the separating of a "what" from the individuals of which it is the "what" and also the relating of this "what" back to these same individuals in a relation of identity.[11] In this way we are able,

___
[10] Above, pp. 47–48. Cf. also the operation of classification, above, pp. 70–75.
[11] See references given in note 10. Cf. also pp. 113–115.

through abstraction, both to recognize a "what" and also to recognize it as the "what" of certain individuals. But correspondingly in induction, the inducing of a universal principle from a number of singular propositions involves not only arriving at the principle but also reapplying that principle to the singulars. For instance, to become aware of the fact that water boils at 100° C., from observing this bit of water and that and the other to boil at this temperature, is at the same time to become aware of this principle as the ground and reason for water's behaving as it does in particular instances.

This two-way character of the inductive process is sometimes brought into clearer relief by actually contrasting a so-called inductive *ascent* with an inductive *descent*.[12] Ascent is exemplified by the inferring of the universal from the singulars:

> This water boils at 100° C.,
> This water boils at 100° C.,
> And so on.
> _____
> All water boils at 100° C.

On the other hand, descent is exemplified by the applying of the universal principle to (sc., identifying it with) the particular cases:

> Water boils at 100° C.
> _____
> Therefore, this water boils at
>   that temperature, as does this
>   and this and this, etc.

In any case, whether ascent and descent be considered as separable processes or as mere aspects of the one inductive process, they are strictly correlative with one another, and their correlation is founded on that relation of identity which is clearly involved in any inductive argument.

*induction — observation or experience
    level of sensible → intelligible*

deduction — intelligible level

[12] On the procedures of ascent and descent, cf. above, pp. 136–138.

CHAPTER 17[1]

ARGUMENT AND THE DILEMMA OF TAUTOLOGY OR NON SEQUITUR[2]

No sooner do we arrive at the conclusion that all argumentation, whether deductive or inductive, takes the form of a relation of identity than an obvious difficulty presents itself—a difficulty not unlike that which we encountered in our discussion of the proposition.[3] In the case of the proposition we found that to consider the relation of S to P simply as a relation of identity immediately suggests a dilemma: either the assertion that S is P is a mere tautology (S is S), or it is a contradiction (S is non-S).

Analogously, in the case of argument, if the form of the argument is a mere relation of identity, how can one be said to prove anything by the use of argument? That is, how can one pretend by means of argument to arrive at any new knowledge or new information? Will not one rather merely be repeating in the conclusion what has already been stated in the premises? Or, to take the other horn of the dilemma, if one supposes that by means of argument one really can prove something—i.e., can really demonstrate something that was not known or was not sure before—then presumably this can only be at the cost of violating the relation of identity, with the result that one's argument turns out to be a *non sequitur*. That is to say, in so far as one's argument leads to something new, to something not already contained in the premises, to that same extent it would seem that one has smuggled into the conclusion something for which there was no warrant in the premises.

---

[1] In this chapter and the one immediately following we undertake to consider and to answer certain difficulties in connection with both inductive and deductive arguments. These difficulties have been pressed with peculiar vigor ever since the days of the Scottish philosopher David Hume and have hence become almost commonplaces of modern philosophy. Nevertheless, since a consideration of difficulties and their refutation is not directly pertinent to the exposition of the doctrine of argument as such, the student will find that he can omit Chaps. 17 and 18 without serious loss of continuity.

[2] On what exactly is meant by a dilemma, see below, pp. 365–369.

[3] See above, sections 8-1 and 9-1.

17–1 THE SYLLOGISM AS EITHER A *PETITIO PRINCIPII* OR A *NON SEQUITUR*

This dilemma is not a mere tricky sophism that can be lightly dismissed as of no real moment. On the contrary, it is a dilemma which, in various forms, is taken seriously by nearly all modern logicians and philosophers of science, and which, we would suggest, in large measure accounts for that underlying skepticism so characteristic of contemporary accounts of the nature and methods of knowledge. Accordingly, it behooves us to subject this dilemma to the most thorough and elaborate, even if somewhat tedious and involved, scrutiny.

To begin with, let us consider just how the dilemma manifests itself in the case of deductive or syllogistic argument. To this end we perhaps need do no more than simply recapitulate the celebrated criticism of the syllogism which was revived and given its classic modern formulation by the famous nineteenth-century English logician John Stuart Mill.[4]

In sum, Mill's contention is that any deductive or syllogistic inference is a tautology precisely in the sense that it begs the question. And his argument is as simple as it is telling. He uses by way of illustration the rather threadbare textbook syllogism:

> All men are mortal.
> Socrates is a man.
> ∴Socrates is mortal.

Now, Mill asks, just how can these premises be taken to be, in any proper sense, evidence for the conclusion? How could one ever assert that all men were mortal unless one already knew about Socrates? And so long as one is in doubt about Socrates, or any other individual man for that matter, one could never assert the proposition "All men are mortal." Accordingly, the universal premise, so far from being evidence for the particular case mentioned in the conclusion, actually presupposes a knowledge of that particular case before it itself can be asserted. Clearly, then, the syllogism would seem to involve an obvious tautology or *petitio principii*.

On the other hand, to avoid the horn of the dilemma which would make of the syllogism a mere question-begging tautology, there would seem to be no alternative but to recognize the conclusion of the syllogism as a *non sequitur*—i.e., as just not following from the premises. Consider the matter in terms of symbols. One is seeking to prove that S is P, and one seeks to prove it by means of the mediating concept M. Yet unless *all* of M were P, the mere fact that S was M would not be sufficient to establish the fact that it was P. That is, unless

---

[4] See his *System of Logic*, Book II, Chap. III. For a convenient modern edition, see John Stuart Mill's *Philosophy of Scientific Method*, edited by Nagel, Hafner, 1950, pp. 120 ff.

all men were mortal, it simply would not follow that because Socrates was a man he was therefore mortal. Yet the minute one recognizes that all men, Socrates included, are mortal, it becomes the most useless tautology to go on to assert that Socrates is mortal.

Apparently, then, there is no escaping the horns of the dilemma: a syllogistic inference either begs the question or it just doesn't follow.

Nor must you think that you can simply shrug off Mill's criticisms as just so much idle theorizing which, while it might embarrass pedants who write logic texts, would have no pertinence whatever to an innocent and healthy-minded student who was obliged to read the texts. For just suppose that at this point in your reading you find you simply can't take any more, and you throw down your logic text in disgust, declaring to your astonished roommate, "I don't like logic." Your roommate wants to know why, and you reply, "Because logic is dull."

Surely, nothing could be more innocent and healthy-minded than this rejoinder. Yet ironically enough, for all its innocence and healthiness, your answer amounts to no more than an implied syllogism to which all of Mill's criticisms regarding tautology and *non sequitur* are strikingly pertinent. Why should the fact that a subject is dull explain your dislike of it? The truth is that it would not explain it at all, and the reason you give for your dislike would not even be a reason, unless it were also presupposed that every dull subject tends to evoke your dislike.

With this it becomes apparent that your seemingly quite sensible rejoinder to your roommate turns out to be a full-fledged syllogism:[5]

> Every dull subject is a subject I dislike.
> Logic is a dull subject.
> ─────────────────────────────
> ∴ Logic is a subject I dislike.

What then, would you say to a John Stuart Mill, should he be so rude as to suggest that you had simply begged the question you were trying to prove to your roommate? For one can easily imagine Mill saying, "How could you possibly suppose that every dull subject evokes your dislike unless you already knew about logic? But if you must already know your conclusion before you can assert your premise, then you can scarcely pretend to have proved your conclusion by means of that premise. Instead, you have merely begged the whole question."

Now even granting that your roommate is not a John Stuart Mill, and that he is quite willing to accept uncritically and at its face value your reason for disliking logic, still what would you say to the sort of objections that a Mill might make to your argument, or even that a roommate might make, should he have

[5] Thus in its original form your rejoinder was nothing but a so-called enthymeme or abbreviated syllogism, on which see below, pp. 322–325.

become infected with Mill's skepticism? For skepticism it is, and a skepticism about universals, since the source of this pesky dilemma would seem to lie precisely in that very element of universality which is so essential to all syllogistic mediation and in terms of which the relation of triple identity that constitutes the syllogistic structure is to be understood. Indeed, as we had occasion to note in the foregoing section, our knowledge that S is M just will not suffice for our concluding S is P unless we also know that *every* M must needs be P. And with this the dilemma immediately arises to plague us—and not just in the context of a logic course either, but right within the context of an innocent discussion with a roommate, provided of course that one have the wit and will to recognize and acknowledge it there.

17–2   INDUCTION AS EITHER A TAUTOLOGY OR A *NON SEQUITUR*

Nor is it just deductive or syllogistic inference that seems to be afflicted with the dilemma of tautology or *non sequitur*. No, for inductive inference appears to be just as badly off, if not worse. And once again we shall see that just as in the case of the syllogism, so also here, the difficulty stems from that very factor of universality which is so inseparable from the logical relation of identity, and which is therefore basic to both deductive and inductive mediation and demonstration.

Specifically, as we have already seen, the whole purpose of an inductive argument is to establish a universal conclusion from an observation of particular cases. Indeed, whereas a deductive argument has to start from a universal proposition as one of its premises, an inductive argument (at least in the case of inductive ascent)[6] does not start from a universal, but rather works toward universality in the conclusion. However, no sooner is induction so characterized than the dilemma of either tautology or *non sequitur* immediately presents itself.

Suppose that from an examination of the books in your bookcase you conclude that every one of them was published in the U.S.A. Just how would you establish this conclusion? Presumably, by taking up each book, turning to the title page, and observing that the place of publication was in each case in the U.S. Your induction would consist of a series of singular propositions followed by a universal conclusion:

This book was published in the U.S.
This book was published in the U.S.
This book was published in the U.S.
(And so on for every one of the books in the case)
∴ All the books in the bookcase were published in the U.S.

[6] See above, p. 246.

But surely it would be hard to find a more patent tautology than this. For what is the conclusion here but a mere restatement, in a kind of shorthand form, of what has already been said in the premises? Our very indication, in connection with the enumeration of the premises, that every book in the bookcase was actually examined and found to be published in the U.S., was tantamount to saying that the conclusion merely states over again what has already been stated in the premises.

On the other hand, if, in order to avoid falling into this manifest tautology, one conceives one's inductive argument somewhat differently, so that one does not suppose that in the premises every single item within the extension of the subject term of the conclusion has been investigated—if one chooses this alternative, then clearly one's inductive argument turns out to be a glaring *non sequitur*. For suppose that instead of examining all the books in your bookcase you examined only some of them. These you found to be published in the U.S. and then from this you concluded that all the books in your bookcase were published in the U.S. On what possible grounds would such a conclusion be warranted? How would the fact that some of your books—even, let us suppose, most of your books—were published in the U.S. justify your concluding that all of them were published in this country? After all, you have examined, and hence come to know about, only some of them. How, then, can you pretend to know about all of them? To do so is certainly to be guilty of a *non sequitur*.

17–3 THE IMPORT OF THESE CRITICISMS FOR MODERN SCIENCE

"But this is such a trivial example," you will say, "that of merely noting the publishers of the various books on a shelf! Why should it be supposed that a like dilemma would manifest itself in the case of the more important and significant inferences that emerge in the context of properly scientific knowledge?"

Even though the complaint of triviality be justified in the case of our particular example, this unhappily serves not a whit to mitigate the inescapability of the dilemma. The trouble is that any deductive or inductive inference, no matter how much it may be dignified by the prominent place it occupies in the context of genuinely scientific knowledge, is nevertheless wholly dependent upon the factor of universality. Thus in the case of the syllogism, it is only because the middle term is taken in its full universality that any sort of mediation between the two terms of the conclusion becomes possible at all. And likewise, in the case of induction, it is the universality of the conclusion that constitutes the whole point of the inference. But necessarily—or so it would seem—any such universality must be based either on an exhaustive enumeration of the items within the extension of the universal term—in which case the inference will be a mere tautology that begs the question—or on only a partial enumeration—in which case the inference will involve a *non sequitur.*

Nor need we content ourselves with simply asserting this dogmatically. One can actually see in the light of concrete examples just how this dilemma of tautology or *non sequitur* seems necessarily to manifest itself in the case of every inference, scientific ones no less than common, ordinary everyday ones.

17–3.1   The Problem of Induction or "Scientific Method"

Suppose we begin with some examples of inductive conclusions in the natural sciences. After all, it is popularly supposed, and with warrant, that the truly amazing flowering of modern Western science is in large measure due to a reliance upon observation and experiment, which, after all, is tantamount to a reliance upon induction. For example, consider such typical scientific laws as "Silver melts at 960.5° C.," "$v = gt$," "Rabbits are herbivorous," "Freely falling bodies accelerate at the rate of 32.2 ft./sec./sec." Clearly, all such laws are, considered with respect to their logical form, universal propositions. And how are such laws, in the form of universal propositions, established? Presumably, from experiments and observations upon particular falling bodies or particular rabbits or particular portions of silver. But what is this if not a clear case of *non sequitur?* From observing the behavior of a more or less limited number of falling bodies, for example, one attempts to draw a conclusion as to how all bodies must necessarily behave under such circumstances.

The fallacy here would seem to be as inescapable as it is obvious. For so far as falling bodies are concerned, no scientist would claim to have examined all falling bodies under all circumstances, and not just in the past and the present, but in the future as well. No, the thing is simply impossible. But if no one scientist, and not even all scientists together, has ever carried out such exhaustive observations of falling bodies, how can it possibly be asserted with any sort of adequate basis or justification that the acceleration of *any* freely falling body must necessarily be at the rate of 32.2 feet per second, every second?

Of course, one might make rejoinder to the effect that, even though our experience with falling bodies is by no means complete, still we have not as yet come across any that do not exhibit this rate of acceleration. And while we may someday find exceptions to the law of falling bodies and hence may have to revise the law, that still does not mean that we are not justified in accepting the law until such time as new evidence turns up that will compel us to alter or reject it.

This sounds sensible enough as a rejoinder. Nor is there any doubt that, no matter what a few would-be troublemakers among logicians may say to the contrary, every one of us, scientists and ordinary men alike, will, in our daily practice and behavior, go right on accepting various scientific laws, as well as countless common-sense rules of thumb, until they are shown to be inaccurate.

But this is not the point. The point is not whether in practice we shall continue to rely upon generalizations from experience; it is whether there is any rational or logical justification for our doing so.

After all, what could be more evident and obvious than that basic rule of inference which says that one cannot pass from an undistributed term in the premises to a distributed term in the conclusion?[7] That is to say, from mere knowledge of some of the items in the extension of a concept one cannot legitimately draw a conclusion about all of them. For instance, is it not conceivable that many a city-dweller may have been such a happy beneficiary of pure-food laws and efficient government inspections as never to have had the experience of opening a bad egg? Suppose, though, that he were to conclude from this that no egg was ever bad, or that there just was no such thing as a bad egg. Or again, supposing a freshman were to conclude from his limited but unforgettable experience of his first few classes at the university that every professor is an ass—would it be the moral injustice of his conclusion or simply the obvious logical fallacy that it involves that would be the more striking?

"Oh," you will say, "these examples are grossly unfair. For although they are examples of so-called inferences from 'some' to 'all,' they should never be confused with such inductive inferences as are performed in the sciences. In the case of the latter, a conclusion about 'all' is drawn only after very large numbers of cases have been observed or only after the conditions and circumstances of the observed cases have been varied considerably. In contrast, the above-cited conclusion in regard to eggs, to say nothing of the one in regard to professors, was based on utterly inadequate samples."

All of which is true enough. The only trouble is that it does not meet the issue. For in the case of scientific inductions, quite as much as in that of the more ordinary generalizations from experience, how does one know when one has observed "enough" cases, or how much variation is sufficient to provide a "fair" sample? Thus so far as falling bodies are concerned, there are infinite possible instances or occurrences of these. Very well, just how many must be observed before one can legitimately make a generalization in regard to all of them?

In the different sciences—physics, biology, psychology, economics, etc.—it is indeed pretty well agreed among the practitioners of the science just how much experiment and observation are necessary before warranted generalizations can be made in that particular area of investigation. And yet, however much agreement there may be among scientists with regard to such matters, the problem is whether this amounts to anything more than mere "agreement" —i.e., a mere arbitrary convention which scientists are conditioned to follow as a sort of rule of the game, but which has absolutely no basis or foundation in the nature of things.

[7] See below, pp. 306–307, and above, pp. 188–189.

Probability as a Possible Solution.   Confronted with this difficulty, according to which the entire edifice of modern science would appear to be erected
upon inductive inferences for which there seems to be not the slightest shred
of logical warrant, recent thinkers have cast about desperately for some expedient that will somehow save the situation.

One type of proposal that has been offered is that we fall back upon probability[8] as a means of justifying scientific conclusions. And what this proposal
amounts to is something like this: Of course, we shall be told, an inductive
inference from "some" to "all" will be fallacious if we suppose that a conclusion
in regard to all can be established with certainty on the basis of a mere examination of some. Indeed, the fallacy involved here can be made palpable in terms
of the familiar square of opposition.[9] For according to the rules of the square,
if we know that an I proposition is true (i.e., if we know that some S's are P's),
we cannot conclude from this that the corresponding A proposition is also
true (i.e., that all S's are P's). At the same time, we cannot conclude either
that the corresponding A proposition is false. Why not say, then, that although
from a knowledge of some we cannot conclude with certainty that all S's are P
we can at least suppose that there is some probability that all S's are P? What's
more, the probability of this conclusion will increase according as our evidence
in regard to the "some" increases both in variety and in extent.

Now quite apart from the seeming reasonableness of this proposal, it has the
further merit of being altogether consonant with the practice and outlook of
the sciences themselves. For is it not often suggested that the very hallmark
of modern scientific procedure is that the conclusions and laws which it establishes are never regarded as sacrosanct or inviolate, but as tentative only? In
this sense, there is no scientific law that the scientist will not regard as being
in principle the sort of thing that is altogether subject to being revised and
qualified, and perhaps even to being discarded altogether, as a result of further
investigation and experiment. But what does this amount to if not a habit on
the part of scientists themselves of regarding this law as being not certain, but
only probable?

   [8] Our use of the word "probability" calls for some explanation and perhaps even some
apology. Throughout this textbook we shall use the word only in the sense of the probability of the truth of universal propositions on the basis of particular instances. Nevertheless,
as is well known, the word is often used in a somewhat different sense, particularly in
connection with statistics and the so-called calculus of probability. In these latter contexts
one may speak of the probability of having a six turn up on a throw of a die, or the probability of an American's suffering a heart attack before he reaches the age of fifty. But
probability in this latter sense and the rival theories designed to explain probabilities of this
type (the so-called classical theory on the one hand and the frequency theory on the other)
—we simply cannot take time to go into these in a textbook of this limited scope. Suffice it
to say that such probability calculations and probability theories would seem to have no
direct bearing on the problems of induction and their solution.
   [9] Cf. above, pp. 171–172.

Unhappily this ingenious device of substituting probability for certainty as a means of avoiding the *non sequitur* involved in all inferences from "some" to "all" will not do the trick. For if we but consider a little more closely those relationships in the square of opposition[10] which were supposed to provide the basis for the probability considerations just outlined, we shall find that these relations serve to undermine the proposal quite as much as to sustain it. Thus it was argued that, although from the truth of an I proposition it could not be concluded with certainty that the corresponding A was also true, at the same time it could not be concluded that it was false either. Hence the way seemed open to regarding the A as probable, i.e., as a proposition that might well be true, in the light of the evidence adduced in the I proposition, but about which one could not be certain. Moreover, so far as it goes, this reasoning would seem to be unexceptionable. One might even flatly declare that the truth of the A is probable on the basis of the I.

The only trouble is that its falsity is equally probable! Granted that some S's being P's means that it is at least probable that all S's are P's, it is at the same time equally probable that some S's are not P's. For the truth of the O proposition, you will recall, is just as compatible with the truth of the I as the truth of the A is; if it is true that "Some cats are black," it may be true either that "All cats are black" or that "Some cats are not black." In short, a true I proposition bears the same relation to the O proposition as to the A, so that if we infer from the truth of I the probability of A, we may by the same token infer the probability of O. But O is the contradictory of A! So the truth of the proposition is probable on the basis of the I; but its falsity is equally probable. Accordingly, if on the basis of the present proposal the truth of a scientific conclusion turns out to be no more probable than its falsity,[11] it would hardly seem that the proposal had helped us much, so far as finding a warrant for the conclusions of science is concerned.

Verification of Hypotheses as a Possible Solution.   Very well. Since the expedient of substituting probability for certainty will not enable us to circumvent the embarrassing *non sequitur* that seems to be involved in inductive inference, let us look at another expedient that has upon occasion been proposed for getting around the difficulty. Why not regard inductive conclusions as really not conclusions at all in the strict sense, but only as possible hypotheses that have been suggested, but in no sense proved, by the evidence at hand? For instance, from considering the effects upon the economy that follow upon a debasing of the monetary system, an economist might set it up as a hypothesis that bad money drives out good. In other words, Gresham's law

[10] Above, pp. 179–181.

[11] It might be noted that while only a single contrary instance is required to establish the falsity of an inductive conclusion, its truth, it would seem, could be definitely established only if it were confirmed in all of its infinite possible instances.

would here be regarded as not so much an inductive conclusion drawn from heretofore observed cases, but rather as a mere hypothesis set up for the purpose of guiding future investigations and one which, far from having been proved, still remains to be verified or falsified through further observation and experience.

There is an obvious shortcoming in this proposal. For the proposal simply shifts the problem of the *non sequitur* from one domain to another. Thus the problem, instead of being one of how the universal law or generalization can originally be set up on the basis of an observation of a mere limited number of particular cases, now becomes one of how the universal law that has already been advanced merely as a hypothesis can ever be verified through a limited number of particular cases in the future. Indeed, the logical form or pattern into which any so-called verification of a hypothesis falls is the form of what we shall later call a "conditional syllogism."[12] In the case of Gresham's law, we might imagine that the verification of this law, considered as a hypothesis, would be on some such order as this:

> If bad money drives out good, then the proposed debasing of the Guatemalan coinage will soon force the genuine gold and silver coins out of circulation.
> The debasing of the Guatemalan coinage has, in fact, had just this effect.

> Therefore, the hypothesis is confirmed: bad money does drive out good.

Such an argument, however, is but an obvious case of what we shall later come to know as "the fallacy of affirming the consequent."[13] And pending our subsequent more detailed explanation, it is not hard to recognize the fallacious character of the argument merely on a common-sense basis. Consider the following:

> If a student is a genius, he will doubtless find many of his courses in college a waste of time.
> I find many of my courses in college a waste of time.

> Therefore, I must be a genius.

Now incredible as it may seem, there appears to be no getting around the fact that every enterprise of verifying a hypothesis in science, no matter how subtle and sophisticated it may be, is no more logically defensible than the rather silly argument just given.

Solution Through Definition. Now for another proposal. Why not, it is sometimes said—and many an ingenious student may have thought of this proposal himself—why not handle this whole business of induction simply in terms of definitions? Suppose we are bothered about the law of gravity. Having studied a little logic, we begin to wonder whether or not all physical bodies in

[12] See below, pp. 354–359, and section 25–1.
[13] See below, pp. 354–355.

our stellar universe are subject to the pull of gravitational forces. After all, no one physicist, and not even all physicists together, has examined every physical body to see if it is really subject to the law of gravity or not. Very well, in assuming that all bodies are thus subject to gravity are we not committing the familiar fallacy of going from some to all?

To which the answer might be that in this case the difficulty is purely gratuitous. For if *per impossibile* you should come across a physical body that did not obey the law of gravity, what would you do? Would you say that the law of gravity had been invalidated, or that you had actually found a physical body whose behavior was altogether exceptional in terms of the law? Of course not. You would say, "I must be dreaming!"

The point of this answer is that it is simply by definition that a physical body is the sort of thing that is subject to gravity. Hence if you come across something that apparently is not subject to gravitational forces, you recognize at once that it just couldn't be a physical body—it must be a dream or a hallucination or something of the sort. And the reason is perfectly clear, for if by definition a physical body is a thing subject to the force of gravity, then anything not subject to gravity just isn't a physical body. To suppose anything else would be quite as absurd as supposing that perhaps some day a person might either come across or devise a triangle with less than three sides!

Nor is this particular gambit—that of relying upon the very definition of the thing one is dealing with as a means of ruling out possible exceptions and deviations from the norm—unusual in the actual practice of scientists. To take a very trivial case, suppose that in an elementary course in chemistry you are given a routine laboratory assignment in connection with which you are told to melt some silver in order to show that its melting point was 960.5° C. And let us imagine that your experiment does not turn out right. (Curiously enough, even in laboratories this sort of thing does happen sometimes!) The silver, in other words, did not melt at the requisite temperature at all. What would you conclude? That the law to the effect that silver melts at 960.5° C. was wrong? Hardly. Instead, you would no doubt conclude that it was you who were wrong, and not the law, there having been some error presumably in the way in which you had gone about conducting the experiment. Moreover, the reason you would be so certain that the error was yours would be that it is presumed to be a part of the very definition of silver that its melting point is at that particular temperature. Hence the failure of the material you were working with to melt at 960.5° C. must mean that either there was some impurity in the silver or some other error crept into your procedure. For silver couldn't fail to melt at that temperature and still be silver—by definition!

It might be remarked in passing that this attempt at solving the problem of induction by appealing to definition certainly does obviate the *non sequitur* of proceeding from some to all. For if it is simply by definition that one knows that physical bodies are subject to gravitation, then not only does such knowledge not result from any inference from some to all, but in addition one can be absolutely certain that every physical body will gravitate, for the reason that one would not even call it a physical body if it didn't.

But alas, this very exhibition of the strength of this solution of induction by definition at the same time discloses its thorough weakness and arbitrariness. To see this clearly, we might change our example. Consider how on the basis of Ptolemaic astronomy the sun was thought to be a body which moved around the earth. Now it can hardly be denied that there was impressive empirical evidence in support of this conclusion, for think of the countless number of times and by how many countless numbers of men the sun has been observed to rise in the east in the morning, to traverse the heavens during the day, and finally to set in the west in the evening. Nevertheless, despite this impressive inductive evidence in its support, we are all familiar with how the Copernican heliocentric theory eventually displaced the Ptolemaic account of the sun's circular motion around the earth.

Suppose a Ptolemaic defender of geocentricism were to undertake to support his position by an appeal to definition. He might say that by definition the sun was a body which moved around the earth and not vice versa. And if one were to counter with all the empirical evidence that could be cited in support of the proposition that the sun does not move but is stationary, the die-hard Ptolemaic might reply: "Very well, even if I grant that that particular luminous body which we see daily in the heavens and which men have been wont to call the sun is actually stationary and is not in motion, that still does not prove that the sun is stationary. For by definition the sun can only be a body which moves around the earth. Hence if that body which men have been accustomed to call the sun can be shown to be stationary, that only means that it can't be the sun; we shall just have to call it by some other name."

Does our example seem far-fetched? Perhaps. Yet it serves to point up the precise weakness of any attempt to solve the problem of induction by means of definition. For although words may, of course, be defined in any way we choose, and although on the basis of our arbitrary definitions we may either consent or refuse to let a certain word be applied to certain things, still men's proper scientific concern is not with how words are to be used but rather with what real things are. By resorting to definitions we might assure ourselves that the word "body" would never be rightly applied to something that was not subject to gravitation, or that the word "sun" would never properly be applied to anything that does not move around the earth. But so what? Our real concern is to know whether the things we are accustomed to call "physical bodies" really are subject to gravitation or not—no matter which names we choose to call them in the future. And so also as regards the sun: whether we name it "sun" or not makes no difference; what we want to know is whether that large luminous orb in the sky does in fact move around the earth or whether the earth moves around it.[14]

The Pragmatic Solution.   "But," you may say, in utter disgust by now, "what difference does it make whether inductive procedures in science are logically defensible or not? At least they are pragmatically defensible, they 'work,' they 'pay dividends,' they enable us to find our way around in the world and to achieve a control of the forces of nature the like of which mankind has never known before. Why, then, worry about whether the inductive, empirical methods of the sciences can pass muster in the eyes of the logicians or not? Why not just say 'Pfui!' to logic?"

No doubt the long-suffering reader will welcome this forthright proposal as if it were a breath of fresh air amid an almost unalleviated stuffiness. Yet as is so often the case with what seems most fresh, it soon proves to be no match for the eventual triumph of what is most stale. In this case the vigorous expedient of simply justifying induction pragmatically turns out to be little more than a feeble begging of the question all over again. For in effect, what our pragmatically minded critic is saying is something like this: Our entire experience up to now has shown that inductive procedures are practically reliable, however much they may be theoretically or logically indefensible; why not then simply consider that they will continue to be reliable in the future, and quite without benefit of any logical justification? But note the form which this argument takes:

> In our experience up to now S (viz., inductive procedures) has been found to be P (viz., reliable); or in other words, Some S is P.
> Therefore, we may conclude that S will necessarily continue to be P in the future; or in other words, All S is P.

Thus, lo and behold, the attempted pragmatic justification of induction itself presupposes the legitimacy of the very passage from some to all, which is precisely what it was professing to justify! In short, while all this may sound very stale, it unhappily has the embarrassing feature of apparently being quite unanswerable.

Sticking-to-the-Facts as a Possible Solution.   There is still another expedient that might occur to many as a possible way of saving the situation, and it is an expedient which scientists of an older generation were somewhat wont to employ, albeit it is not the sort of thing scientists would be quite so inclined to

---

[14] It might be noted that this attempt to solve the problem of induction serves to recall our earlier distinction (above, pp. 81–83) between mere verbal or nominal definitions on the one hand and what we have called conceptual and real definitions on the other. Thus he who would solve the problem of induction merely by appealing to definitions is in fact appealing only to definitions of words—e.g., of the word "sun"—whereas what is required is a definition not of a word but of the real thing the word is supposed to signify—e.g., the sun itself.

say nowadays. Why could not one simply take the position that what science does, or at least should do, is always to stick strictly to the observed facts, never allowing itself to venture out beyond the actual data and empirical evidence that are before it? Would not this obviate the necessity of ever having to go from some to all or of risking any such thing as a so-called "inductive leap"?

The answer is "Yes." Such a program, if carried out, would certainly avoid anything in the nature of a *non sequitur* from some to all. But alas, having thus barred the door to a *non sequitur,* one would in effect be merely opening the window to the most trivial sort of tautology. Consider a simple proposition from botany: "All angiospermous plants are either monocotyledons or dicotyledons." If this proposition is to be interpreted as having no extension beyond actually observed cases, perhaps it should be reworded so as to read more accurately: "All the plants thus far observed among the angiosperms have been found to be monocotyledons or dicotyledons." Similarly, a chemist really should not, in all strictness, say simply, "Silver melts at 960.5° C." No, for if his generalization is restricted only to observed cases, he should rather say, "All the silver that we have thus far experimented with has been found to melt at 960.5° C." But now compare these rephrased and restricted scientific statements with a rather different sort of statement made in a somewhat different context. Suppose that in reading the morning paper you should happen to notice that the first line on the front page began with the word "the," as did also the second and third and fourth lines as well. You might then remark, "Every line that I have read thus far begins with the word 'the.'" Certainly nothing could be truer than this, but also nothing could be more trivial and insignificant. And note: in making this generalization, you would not have gone beyond the observed cases; in this respect your "conclusion," if you could call it such, would not involve any fallacy of *non sequitur.* At the same time, it would be an utterly insignificant tautology as well, and for precisely the reason that it does no more than merely register the sum of your observations so far.

But correspondingly, if scientific generalizations are to be restricted exclusively to instances thus far observed, all scientific laws will thereby be turned into tautologies of no greater significance than "Every line that I have read thus far begins with the word 'the.'" And, what is even more serious, if scientific laws are to be thus restricted to observed cases, then no such law can ever be used as a basis for scientific prediction. Thus if your presumably scientifically grounded conviction that all bodies gravitate must be interpreted to mean no more than that all bodies thus far observed gravitate, you have absolutely no grounds for preferring to walk out the door of a third-floor classroom rather than out of the window. After all, your scientific knowledge of the effect of gravitation on physical bodies would be strictly confined to cases that have already occurred and been observed. However, your exit from the classroom at the end of the next hour is something that has not yet occurred and hence has not yet been observed, and so does not fall within the scope of the law of gravitation, assuming the latter to have been cribbed, cabined, and confined within the area of hitherto observed cases.

Clearly, any interpretation of scientific laws which would make them incapable of providing a basis for future predictions cannot be tolerated. For a science without predictions would no doubt strike us as being no science at all. Accordingly, to attempt to defend the legitimacy of scientific inductions by restricting them wholly to hitherto observed cases is to throw the baby out with the bath.

Or to express the same conclusion in another way, we might say that all scientific conclusions, if they are to be significant and not wholly trivial, must needs be genuine inferences from what has been observed; they cannot be mere tautologous registers of what has been observed and no more. But this would only appear to render the task of making an honest woman of science quite impossible: she is placed forever in the compromising position of having to make those illicit inductive inferences from some to all!

17–3.2   The Problem of Deduction or Scientific Prediction

Unfortunately, the prolonged and no doubt rather tedious discussion which we have just worked through for the purpose of showing the acute embarrassment which all modern science finds itself in as a result of the seeming indefensibility of its basic inductive procedures may have caused us to lose sight of the fact that modern science is in no less embarrassing a predicament on account of its deductive procedures than it is on account of its inductive ones. This oversight is likely to be all the more serious because there is a rather widespread popular misconception that the natural sciences, being rooted and grounded as they are in experience and observation, are therefore able to dispense with all a priori speculations and flights of pure reason such as have traditionally been associated with deduction. In fact, it is not unusual to hear not only sophomores but college undergraduates generally confidently tossing off invidious comparisons between the a priori deductive methods of philosophers of former ages and the up-to-date empirical methods of modern science.

It takes only a little reflection to realize that such a reading of intellectual history is over-simple to say the least, and that so far as modern science is concerned it is no less dependent on deduction than it is on induction. For one thing, as we have already intimated in the section immediately preceding,[15] there just wouldn't be any such thing as science, in the modern sense of the word, without prediction, but prediction is always and inescapably syllogistic in character.

This last somewhat downright assertion will presumably be met with a certain skepticism. To be sure, it may be admitted that some such thing as

[15] See above, pp. 260–261.

prediction is essential to science; otherwise science would be no different from history. Thus a flat statement of a historical fact—e.g., "No government of the present French Republic has so far been able to continue in office for more than two years"—does not as such involve a potential forecast as to the duration of future French governments. By way of contrast, consider a statement that quite patently pertains rather to political science than to history in the strict sense: "On the basis of the present French consitution, no government can ever be very stable or hope to remain in office for any long duration." Now clearly, however inaccurate and however loose and imprecise one may consider this latter statement to be, it nevertheless is implicitly predictive by its very nature: it purports to state not simply what the character of French governments has been in the past but what it must inevitably be on the basis of the present constitution, and hence by implication what it will be, quite as much as what it has been and is.

Why do we say that all scientific predictions are necessarily syllogistic, when considered from the point of view of this logical form or character? Well, to exploit once more the example we have just cited, we might exhibit the logical form of the relevant predictive forecast in this way:

> No French government, on the basis of the present constitution, can very well remain long in office.
> The new French government which is in process of being formed by M. ———— will still operate within the framework of the present constitution.
> ∴ The new French government will hardly be able to remain long in office.

Nor is it hard to understand why all scientific predictions must be syllogistic in this way. For what is a prediction but a forecast, on the basis of a universal principle, of what certain particular events or happenings that fall within the extension of that universal principle will be like? And what is a syllogism save just such a subsumption of particular cases under a general rule or universal principle, functioning as a major premise in the argument?[16]

Indeed, it is in connection with this use of the syllogism for purposes of prediction that one can best understand the peculiar way in which mathematics has come to be employed in modern science and has proved to be of such extraordinary utility. For when scientific predictions are based upon precise mathematical calculations, what the scientist is really doing is employing his mathematical computations as a major premise in a syllogism. The specific materials or natural forces that he is dealing with are then treated as particular cases or instances that exemplify or embody the more general mathematical structures and relationships. Accordingly, on the basis of this application of the general to the particular the scientist then predicts that the precise numer-

---

[16] More specifically, the particular type of syllogistic argument here envisaged would be a syllogism in Figure I, on which see below, p. 303.

ical relationships that hold with respect to the pure mathematical forms and structures will also pertain to the more particular materials or forces that embody these forms and structures.

To use a very naïve but also comparatively unequivocal illustration, suppose that we are attempting to predict nothing more elaborate and complicated than that two apples times two more apples will be four apples. The syllogistic form of argument that underlies and is implicit in this prediction, even though it be practically never necessary to take the trouble to make it explicit, would presumably be something like this:

> Any two things, no matter what they may be, if taken twice, will yield four things.
> Two apples taken twice would thus be an instance of two things taken twice.
> Hence, two apples taken twice will necessarily be four apples.

Now what we are suggesting is that every use and employment of mathematics in natural science, for purposes of accurate prediction, no matter how subtle and complicated it may be, must involve just such a simple, basic syllogistic form as is exemplified in our seemingly trivial example predicting that two apples times two more will equal four apples. But alas, no sooner do we suggest this than all of those telling criticisms of the use of the syllogism in inference will now be seen to apply to, and hence presumably to invalidate, the entire enterprise of scientific prediction. For the syllogism, as Mill said, simply begs the question. Making the application to the present instance, how can we legitimately predict that two apples taken together with two more will make four apples? For our prediction is dependent upon the truth of the more general principle that any two things taken twice will make four things. Yet how could one possibly know that such would be the case with any two things whatever, if one did not first know that such would be the case with any two apples? So we have a *petitio principii*, and presumably not merely in the case of the trivial prediction that twice two apples will make four apples but also in the case of any scientific prediction, no matter what it may be.

Nor is it merely as an instrument of prediction that the syllogism is important in science: in addition and of even greater importance is the role of the syllogism as an instrument of explanation. For as we shall try to show in more detail later,[17] there is a certain sense in which induction—even supposing it can be shown to be valid—is never capable of doing more than showing *that* something is so; it is never capable of providing an explanation of *why* it is so. In consequence, with respect to nearly all the empirical generalizations of the sciences it is always possible to ask why things should be or behave the way they have been observed to do. That bodies tend to fall when released is

[17] Below, pp. 282–283.

obvious from experience; but why do they? That silver melts at a certain temperature is established on the basis of observation; but why should it behave this way rather than some other? That towels are absorbent we know from experience; but why are they, and what is the explanation of this fact?

Now how may the "why" questions of scientific laws be answered? Presumably, the only way is through the use of a middle term. Why are towels absorbent? Because of their capillary structure. Why are the opposite vertical angles formed by intersecting straight lines equal? Because they have the same supplementary angle in common. Why are horses herbivorous? Because of the restrictive adaptation of their digestive organs. Clearly, each of these "explanations" is syllogistic in character:

> Every substance whose surface has a capillary structure is absorbent.
> Towels are substances with such a surface.
> ∴ Towels are absorbent.

> Any angles that have the same supplementary angle in common are equal.
> The opposite vertical angles formed by intersecting straight lines are such angles.
> ∴ The opposite vertical angles are equal.

> Any organism whose digestive organs are exclusively adapted to the digestion of plant food is herbivorous.
> Horses are organisms whose digestive organs are so adapted.
> ∴ Horses are herbivorous.

But in view of the criticisms of the syllogism which we have already considered, what is the explanatory value of these syllogistic structures which, as we have seen, commend themselves so naturally as instruments of explanation and which in fact are constantly employed in the sciences for just such purposes of explanation? When examined in the light of what Mill says about the syllogism, it begins to appear as if such deductive arguments, far from providing explanations of the propositions that require to be explained, actually presuppose an understanding of such propositions before the supposedly explanatory arguments can themselves even be formulated.

To scrutinize a bit more closely just one of our above-mentioned examples, how does one know that organisms having a certain kind of digestive apparatus are herbivorous? Presumably, one knows this simply from having observed that organisms (*horses among them*) having that sort of digestive apparatus are in fact herbivorous. But then the universal truth that all organisms of a certain kind are herbivorous, far from being able to explain why horses should be this way, actually appears to be no more than a summary statement or register of the fact that horses are indeed herbivorous, as are a number of other animals of similar kind. And this explains absolutely nothing. It's as if we were to try to explain why this particular blade of grass is green by merely stating that all the other blades of grass on the lawn are green too.

Indeed, this is why many, if not most, contemporary logicians and philosophers, reflecting upon the apparently inescapably tautologous character of all deductive demonstration, have come to the conclusion that all deduction by its very nature is simply incapable either of explaining anything or in any genuine sense of disclosing or demonstrating the nature of anything whatever. Instead, it can no more than simply "unpack" or spin out what has already been more or less arbitrarily wadded together and rolled up within one's cognition beforehand.

Yet if the syllogism be thus sterile and effete, the whole scientific enterprise of prediction and explanation is thereby equally condemned to sterility and failure.

CHAPTER 18

UNIVERSALITY AND THE ESCAPE
FROM THE DILEMMA

It must seem as if we have just been sweating out a prolonged and stifling steam bath of skepticism, and so we have. It is high time to start to clear the air. The results of the preceding pages are nothing short of fantastic; if they could be accepted at face value, the whole edifice of modern science, resting as it does upon an elaborate structure of interlocking inductive and deductive inferences, would have to be written off as utterly baseless. There must be something wrong somewhere.

What is even more serious and more fantastic, if the arguments of the preceding chapter are sound, then not only will the whole edifice of our science come tumbling down, but the much more important edifice of our everyday world and our common-sense knowledge of it will also collapse. And this would be bad indeed. In this day of veneration for science we sometimes forget how far more important to us than all of our scientific knowledge put together is our knowledge of our own everyday world. For one can be a human being, even a very wise and intelligent one, without knowing much about physics or chemistry or biology. But one cannot even be human without having some insight into the day-by-day world of men and things, of human happenings and nonhuman events. And even this day-by-day world emerges for us and begins to take on form only in consequence of the most intricate set of inductive and deductive inferences. For that matter, the very arguments that we used throughout the preceding chapter to show the complete inadequacy and indefensibility of both induction and deduction were themselves a complex tissue of inductions and deductions.

18–1 NOMINALISM AS THE SOURCE OF THE DILEMMA

Moreover, unless we be much mistaken, the source of the trouble lies precisely in that attitude of nominalism which we have already had occasion to describe in another connection.[1] In our initial account of both deductive inference and inductive inference we were at pains to point out that universality

---

[1] See above, pp. 50–52.

was somehow the nerve of both types of inference. It was precisely through the universality of the middle term that a so-called syllogistic mediation was able to be effected. Likewise with induction, the whole point of the procedure was that it was supposed to carry us from a manifold of particulars to a universal somehow present or implicit in them all. Little wonder, then, that a right understanding of universality would seem to be the key to a right understanding of all inference, whether deductive or inductive. And this is just where the relevance of nominalism begins to be apparent. For the peculiar thrust of nominalism is its insistence that universals are mere arbitrary groupings or sums of particulars, there being no like nature or character in the particulars themselves that might be said to answer to the one concept which we have of them all, and which could serve to justify our classification of them all under a common heading.

Nominalism and Mill's Criticisms of the Syllogism.   At first sight, it might seem rather incredible that so innocent appearing a doctrine should be the source of such a devastating skepticism in regard to both induction and deduction. Yet suppose we briefly reëxamine Mill's criticism of the syllogism in the light of nominalism. Mill's contention, it will be remembered,[2] was that when one tries to prove that Socrates is mortal on the ground that he is a man and that all men are mortal one inevitably begs the question, for the reason that one could not forcibly assert that all men are mortal (the major premise) unless one already knew about Socrates (the conclusion).

Certainly, nothing would seem to be more unanswerable than this, but is it really so? Indeed, when looked at in a little different light, we wonder if the whole difficulty here may not begin to appear largely gratuitous. We even wonder if Mill himself could have taken it too seriously. For consider something that we are all quite familiar with—say, apples. Is there anyone who would—apart from the artificial posing that sometimes goes with philosophizing —deny that he knew what an apple was? To be sure, he might not be able to give a precise definition of what an apple is; likewise, he probably would not claim to be able to recognize always and with absolute infallibility whether a given thing that somebody might happen to hand him actually was an apple or not. Yet he would unhesitatingly say that he knew what an apple was. We venture to suggest that even Mill would have said as much too. Note that what is involved here is the rather simple fact that all of us do have a universal concept of apple, even though no one of us would ever claim that either he or anyone else had ever examined all the apples that there are in the world, past, present, and future. One is reminded of the rather celebrated Aristotelian dictum[3] to the effect that one can know the universal without necessarily knowing all the particulars that fall under it.

[2] See above, pp. 248–250.
[3] Cf. *Analytica Posteriora*, 71a, 26 ff.

To take just a little different example, suppose that one were to ask a chemist what the boiling point of water is. He would doubtless say that it was 100° C. (making allowances for deviations due to atmospheric pressure or other differences). Yet surely our chemist would never for a moment consider that his statement somehow presupposes that every conceivable bit and parcel of water had been examined and had been found to boil at 100° C. What he does presuppose, though he may never express it in so many words, is Aristotle's principle that of course it is possible to know the universal without necessarily knowing all the particulars that come under it.

We might even go farther and say that unless we could presuppose the truth of Aristotle's dictum, i.e., unless we could somehow know the universal without having to know all the particulars in its extension, we could never understand anything; we could not even talk or say anything, since all human thought and speech involve the use of universal concepts, which we simply do in fact have in our minds, but which we certainly do not come by as a result of any prior familiarity with every possible particular instance of such universals. Nevertheless, it is this very principle which Mill, perhaps unconsciously, is calling into question in his criticism of the syllogism; it is as if he were saying that one cannot possibly know the universal without knowing every particular, and thus that one cannot even know what an apple is without first knowing every individual apple, or that one cannot know something about human beings generally (e.g., that they are mortal) without first knowing about every human being individually.

Nor is it hard to see that it must be his nominalistic presuppositions that are responsible for Mill's tendency to call into question a principle which one cannot very well call into question and at the same time consistently continue to think and talk at all. For as we have seen, the thrust of nominalism is to deny that there is any sort of like nature or essence present in a set of particulars by apprehending which we then know what all the relevant particulars are essentially. But to deny such a nature or essence is to commit oneself to regarding each individual as absolutely distinct and different from every other and as having nothing in common with any other. Little wonder that on such a basis one could not possibly claim to know the universal without first knowing all the particulars that come under it. On the contrary, in this context the universal actually amounts to no more than an arbitrary sum or grouping of particulars which could only be consequent upon an exhaustive enumeration of these same particulars.

On the other hand, no sooner does one remove these nominalistic presuppositions and acknowledge that there are natures and essences which different individuals may be said to have and share in, and in respect to which they may be said to be like one another, and in terms of which one can understand the "what" of all of them indifferently—no sooner does one accept this than Aristotle's principle once more becomes significant: one can know the universal without necessarily knowing all the individuals that come under it. Not only that, but the very rehabilitation of the Aristotelian dictum serves to take the starch right out of Mill's criticism of the syllogism. The syllogism does not have to be regarded any longer as a mere empty tautology or *petitio principii*. Quite the contrary; if one can know the universal without knowing about all the particulars that are subsumed under it, then one can perfectly well know that all men are mortal without necessarily knowing about Socrates. Or put more generally, one can know that every M is P without necessarily having to have any prior knowledge either that S is M or that it is P. Likewise, our earlier difficulties as to how one could legitimately use universals for purposes of scientific prediction and scientific explanation also disappear the minute the syllogism is recognized as capable of being something more than a mere question-begging argument.

Nominalism and the Criticisms of Induction. Nor is induction such a very different case either. Once more nominalism is the fly in the ointment. Thus, to begin with, one can readily see that the entire problem of induction is really but an inverted form of the problem that bothered Mill in connection with the syllogism. For as Mill envisaged this latter problem, it was simply a matter of how, from a supposed knowledge of "all," one could draw a conclusion in regard to "some" without begging the question. And the reason Mill[4] thought such an inference was bound to be question-begging was that he tacitly assumed one could never arrive at a knowledge of "all" without first going through an exhaustive enumeration of every item within the extension of the "all," which prior enumeration, of course, would perforce have already included the "some" as a part of itself, thereby causing the whole question to be begged. But note that this assumption of Mill's is itself nothing but an evocation, in turn, of the problem of induction. Or better, the assumption does not simply evoke the problem of induction; it implicitly denies that it ever can be solved. For the problem of induction, as we have seen, is how one may legitimately infer something about "all" from a mere knowledge of "some." Apparently, however, in the light of his assumption regarding the syllogism, Mill would have to deny that one ever can bring off an inductive inference legitimately. Quite the contrary; what that assumption implies is that the only way one can legitimately arrive at a knowledge of "all" is through an exhaustive enumeration of all.

In short, the shaft which Mill aimed at the syllogism must needs be equally fatal to induction as well. Hence happily and inversely, it should prove to be no less harmless with respect to induction than we have seen it actually turn

[4] It should be remarked, perhaps, that we are interpreting Mill here, not reporting his actual words and statements.

out to be with respect to the syllogism. The only venom which Mill's arrow has can readily be traced to the nominalistic presuppositions of the doctrine. For we have only to remind ourselves once more of the Aristotelian principle that it is possible to know the universal without necessarily knowing all the particulars that fall under it. At once it becomes apparent that this principle not only serves to rehabilitate the syllogism but is itself, so to speak, a standing refutation of the whole problem of induction. For if it be possible to know the universal in this way, it is possible to achieve a knowledge that pertains to all, even though one's investigations have necessarily not gone beyond some.

There would seem to be no reason to doubt this Aristotelian principle, so far as it pertains to inductive inferences, unless it be on grounds of nominalism. For if each individual is so wholly distinct and different from every other as to have nothing in common with any other, then clearly one will have no reason whatever to suppose that what is true of one will be true of another; and naturally, on such a basis any inference from "some" to "all" would be a blatant *non sequitur*. On the other hand, if there are real natures and essences present in individuals, such that whatever pertains to the nature of one will necessarily pertain to any other of a like nature or essence, then the inference from "some" to "all" will no longer give the appearance of being so utterly unwarranted. We might even say that on this basis inductive inference really ceases to be a passage from "some" to "all" in the nominalistic sense altogether; rather it is an inference from observed cases to a nature or essence, i.e., to the actual "what" or "why" that is present in these particular instances and that determines them to be as they are. And clearly, once one recognizes something as pertaining to the nature or essence of the individuals observed, one thereby recognizes that the same thing will pertain to all other individuals of a like nature or essence. For instance, as soon as one becomes aware through experiment that it pertains to the nature of silver to melt at a certain temperature, one immediately sees that any and all silver must needs melt at that temperature. Nor would there seem to be any trace of a *non sequitur* in such an inference.

The Import of Nominalism for the Predicables. Before quitting this topic of nominalism and its import with respect to the validity and reliability of deductive and inductive inference, we might well consider this import in still another connection. Thus far we have discussed deductive and inductive arguments in complete abstraction from the various types of predicable relationships[5] that may hold between the terms of the propositions making up such arguments. Let us look at some of the implications of nominalism so far as these relationships are concerned.

We might begin by contrasting two rather different types of syllogistic argu-

[5] See above, pp. 118–122.

ment. And to this end suppose we adapt to the syllogistic form one of our earlier examples of an inductive argument:

Every book in my bookcase was published in the U.S.
The red book on the second shelf is a book in my bookcase.

∴ The red book on the second shelf was published in the U.S.

Now over against this example, let us see Mill's example of a syllogistic argument:

All men are mortal.
Socrates is a man.

∴ Socrates is mortal.

Applying the analysis worked out in preceding sections, cannot one see that there is an obvious difference between these two arguments? In the latter case, the major premise may be regarded as involving no mere enumeration of individual human beings but rather as expressing what pertains to the very nature or essence of men as such. In the former case, the statement that the books in one's own bookcase are all published in the U.S. certainly does not purport to be an assertion of what pertains to the very nature or essence of "book in my bookcase." On the contrary, one readily recognizes that there is nothing about the fact of being a book in a certain bookcase that necessitates its being published in the U.S. Rather, it just happens to be the case that all those books were published in the U.S. Consequently, in this instance the major premise does involve an actual enumeration and examination of every individual item in the extension of the subject term.

But what is this distinction between these two different types of major premise but a distinction between propositions involving different predicable relationships? Thus in the one case—that of the proposition about the books in the bookcase—the predicable relationship is that of a mere contingent accident. In the other case the relationship is an essential one. (Specifically it is that of a property or necessary accident, but any of the essential predicable relationships would have done just as well for purposes of illustration.)

Moreover, the interesting thing to note is that in the case of the first syllogism cited above—that in which the major premise involves a mere accidental predicable relationship—Mill's criticism becomes entirely relevant. For the predicable relation in the major premise being a mere accidental one, the assertion about all the books does involve an enumeration of every one. But if for the assertion of the universal major premise a prior knowledge of every individual subsumed under it is required, then any syllogism based on such a premise will inevitably beg the question. That is to say, if one cannot profess to know that all the books in one's bookcase were published in the U.S. without first knowing about the red book on the second shelf, then any attempt to prove something about the latter by means of one's knowledge of the former will be a clear case of a *petitio principii*.

Now the upshot of all this is that unless the universal premise of one's syllogism involves a necessary or essential predicable relationship, Mill's criticism becomes immediately pertinent. Indeed, it was precisely because Mill's nominalism led him to suppose that the only possible predicable relationship was the purely accidental one that he supposed his criticism to hold of all syllogistic arguments, whereas as a matter of fact it holds only of those purely trivial syllogisms[6] in which the predicable relationship involved in the universal premise is that of a mere contingent accident rather than of anything necessary or pertaining to the essence of the subject.

Similar considerations would apply, *mutatis mutandis,* in the case of induction quite as much as in that of deduction. For in terms of predicable relationships, all of the nominalistic criticisms of induction seem to presuppose that the only sort of universal proposition one ever attempts to prove by means of inductive argument is that involving a mere accidental predicable relationship. For instance, if one seeks to prove that all the books in one's bookcase were published in the U.S., and if one has actually examined only some of the books in the bookcase, then obviously one's argument will be a clear *non sequitur,* an attempted inference from "some" to "all."

On the other hand, the minute one recognizes that, save in the most trivial cases, the sort of proposition one attempts to demonstrate in an inductive argument involves a necessary predicable relationship—e.g., that it pertains to the very essence of silver to melt at 960.5° C.—the minute one conceives of induction in this way, it at once becomes apparent that the standard criticisms of induction all proceed from a nominalistic bias.

18–2   UNIVERSALITY REAPPLIED; NOMINALISM REPUDIATED

Despite this prolonged and relentless exposé of nominalism, have we really succeeded in scotching it? Granted that we are somewhat clearer as to the nature and the frequency of the nominalistic presuppositions that underlie the usual criticisms of both deduction and induction, have we actually succeeded in disposing of the specific nominalistic objections—particularly the objections to induction? Indeed, supposing we have shown that the reason nominalists have such an easy time in discrediting induction is that they do not recognize any real natures and essences in things and hence do not admit of any propositions involving more than mere accidental predicable relationships, would not the nominalist have a ready answer to all this? Would he not say that this is

[6] Such syllogisms may be said to be trivial in the same sense in which a proposition of the form S is S may be said to be a trivial proposition. Cf. above, pp. 116–117.

simply the point at issue—whether there are such things as natures and essences? For why should one suppose that there are? And how could one possibly come to know them, if there are any?

We could easily imagine a nominalist making some such rejoinder as this:

"I am quite willing to concede that if one can recognize anything like a real nature or essence, and can consequently formulate propositions involving an essential predicable relationship of predicate to subject, then, truly, the usual criticism of induction as passing from 'some' to 'all' may be adjudged irrelevant and unfair. Yet what reason does one have for supposing there are such things as real natures and essences?

"In fact, is the inference from observed particulars to the nature or essence that is supposed to be present in all these particulars any less questionable than the inference from 'some' to 'all'? Is not the whole history of science littered with discarded 'essences' which scientists and philosophers from time to time have thought they had succeeded in inducing from an observation of the facts, but which later turned out to be just so many bogus entities? Ancient astronomers, for instance, thought that it pertained to the very nature of the sun to move around the earth. Aristotle thought it of the essence of light bodies to tend toward the periphery of the universe. And so on, for any number of other comparable examples.

"Nor must one suppose that the reason these inductive inferences were invalid is that they were based on insufficient observation. Just think of the number of times men have seen the sun rise in the morning and set in the evening, or have observed flames to dart upward and smoke to rise slowly in the sky. Certainly, it would be hard to find any scientific generalizations that could be said to rest on a more impressive array of empirical evidence. Yet they are nonetheless mistaken for all that—at least so contemporary scientists tell us. Accordingly, what is the advantage of an inference from observed particulars to an essence over an inference from 'some' to 'all'? It may be admitted that the latter always involves a *non sequitur;* a knowledge of what is true of 'some' is never sufficient to teach us what is true of 'all.' But is an inference to a supposed essence in any better case? For when is it that the empirical evidence really becomes sufficient to warrant this conclusion? Presumably, there is just as much insufficiency in the one case as in the other."

When challenged in this way by the nominalist, we admit that inductive inferences by the very nature of the case are precarious and subject to error, but on a realistic basis they may be seen to be at least in principle warranted, whereas on a nominalistic basis they have no possible warrant.

To begin with, why not recognize that knowledge is a difficult and painstaking process for human beings, fraught with repeated mistakes and false starts? And particularly is the inductive search for the "whats" and the "whys" of things subject to error. Hence one ought never to claim more than mere probability and tentativeness for one's inductive conclusions. Yet the mere fact that many mistakes have been made and will continue to be made in our search for the essences of things does not mean that the whole enterprise is baseless and unwarranted. On the contrary, although physicists today would no longer hold that it is of the essence of light bodies to tend upward, they would hardly say that our knowledge of physical bodies had not progressed since Aristotle's time. They would probably insist that we actually know a great deal more about such bodies than Aristotle did—i.e., more about what pertains to their nature and what does not. Not only that, but the modern physicist, even in his very demonstration of Aristotle's errors, would certainly take pains to point out what there was about the nature of light bodies that would cause them, when subject to the pressure of air, to move away from the earth rather than toward it. That is to say, the modern scientist, if he stops to reflect upon his procedures at all, will not imagine that his view of the nature of physical bodies has been substituted for Aristotle's quite arbitrarily and without there having been any transition from the one to the other. He will recognize that Aristotle had a real insight into the nature of things but that, even so, it was an insight that was imperfect and subject to revision and improvement in the light of subsequent evidence and findings.

And what if the nominalist objects to such a defense on the ground that if we can make appeal to tentativeness and probability he can too? Just as we profess to claim no more than a groping and approximate knowledge of the natures and essences of things, so the nominalist might say that he too claims no more than the same kind of knowledge for his propositions about "all," conceived purely nominalistically. Moreover, just as we have insisted that an inaccurate and misleading knowledge of essences is replaced by an ever more accurate and adequate knowledge of these essences, the nominalist might retort that his mistaken and erroneous propositions about "all" of this or that or the other come to be replaced by ever more correct and reliable propositions about "all" of these same things.

However plausible and justifiable this sort of rejoinder might seem to be, on closer scrutiny it turns out to be a line of defense that is not properly available. For as we have seen, an inference from "some" to "all" is *in principle* unjustifiable. That is to say, if every individual is assumed to have nothing in common with any other, and if it is denied that there is any common nature or essence in virtue of which we are able to recognize that what will be true of one will also be true of all other individuals of the same kind—if one starts out from these nominalistic presuppositions, there is no ground whatever for holding to an "all" conclusion even tentatively or for accepting it as even probable.

On the other hand, there is nothing that is *in principle* unwarranted and unjustified about our passing from an awareness of sensory particulars to the intelligible nature or essence that constitutes their very "what" and makes them to be what they are and as they are. So far from being unwarranted, this passage from the sensible to the intelligible is simply what the higher processes of knowledge or scientific cognition consist in. Indeed, from the outset of our investigations, we have seen how our human knowledge involves just such a process of abstraction, of passing from the particular to the universal, from the sensory to the intelligible, from the individual to the essence or the "what," and back again in the process of reidentification. Accordingly, what we are now considering in regard to induction and deduction is but the application in the domain of argument of what we have all along found to be characteristic of human knowledge as a whole—a movement from particular to universal and back again.[7]

18–3 DIFFERING STANDARDS FOR INDUCTION AND DEDUCTION

But you may still have qualms. For it may perhaps have occurred to you that in these most recent attempts of ours to justify the tentative and merely probable character of all inductive inference, we have apparently gone directly counter to those several earlier arguments[8] which we adduced in order to show that anything like an appeal to probability would not save induction after all —indeed, that all such devices as having recourse to the verification of hypotheses, or relying upon a pragmatic justification, or trying to solve scientific questions by definition, were quite in vain.

Surely, though, our earlier conclusions in regard to these devices must somehow have been misplaced. For such devices could not be entirely in vain. On the contrary, if the considerations presented in the immediately preceding pages have shown anything, it is that, induction being in principle justified, all these specific procedures—verification of hypotheses, using the pragmatic test, appealing to definitions, etc.—are thereby rendered legitimate as particular means for insuring the probability of inductive conclusions. Very well, then, may we not resolve the whole issue simply in this way? Those earlier arguments of ours are to be interpreted as showing no more than that the various specific means which men employ in order to render inductive conclusions more probable cannot themselves be used to justify induction in principle. On the other hand, once induction is justified independently and on other grounds—as in our arguments against nominalism—then there is every reason to suppose that hypotheses are subject to legitimate processes of verification, that inferences from observed particulars to a universal principle are at least probable, that there is at least a pragmatic justification for accepting a universal principle until specific evidence is found to the contrary, etc.

[7] Cf. above, pp. 113–116.
[8] Above, pp. 254–255.

Even so, there still seems to be a difficulty here. For was it not clearly shown in our earlier discussion that any attempt at verifying a hypothesis necessarily involves one in the fallacy of affirming the consequent, or that for every universal conclusion that can be shown to be probable on the evidence at hand it is possible to show that its contradictory opposite is equally probable, and so on, and so on? Consequently, even if induction has now been shown to be in principle justifiable, that still would not seem to obviate the patent fact that specific types of inductive argument do fall afoul of obvious fallacies.

To all of which we reply that the whole trouble here arises from a certain uncritical tendency that all of us are inclined to fall into of supposing that inductive arguments, once formulated, must then be judged by exactly the same standards of validity and cogency as deductive arguments. Yet any such assumption is at once unfortunate and unfair. For while in a sense induction and deduction are related to each other as a road going up a mountain is related to the same road going down the mountain, still, considered precisely as logical devices, inductive arguments and deductive arguments perform quite distinct and different functions. Or stated a little differently, the inductive process of going from observed particulars to the natures or essences present in them and common to them is a type of cognitive operation that is not reducible to or replaceable by any deductive operation or process whatever.

Thus one might recall the graphic and picturesque way in which Aristotle describes the process of induction. "It is," he says, "like a rout in battle stopped by first one man making a stand and then another, until the original formation has been restored. . . . When one of a number of logically indiscriminable particulars has made a stand, the earliest universal is present in the soul: for though the act of sense perception is of the particular, its content is universal —is man, for example, not the man Callias. A fresh stand is made among the rudimentary universals, and the process does not cease until the indivisible concepts, the true universals are established: e.g., such and such a species of animal is a step towards the genus animal, which by the same process is a step towards a further generalization."[9]

Now exploiting this figure of Aristotle's, we may say that, just as in military operations the tactics that are requisite for the re-forming of a broken and shattered line of troops are quite different from the tactics that govern the use of such a line once it has been re-formed, so also in the context of logical inference the rules that govern the inductive establishment of a universal principle in the first place will certainly be different from the rules that govern its further employment once it has been established.

For example, consider once again that earlier argument, based on the relations in the square of opposition, which we used in order to show that any

[9] *Analytica Posteriora,* 100a, 11–100b 4.

inference from an I proposition to an A must be such that its conclusion can be no more probable than its contradictory opposite. Looked at anew in the light of our present considerations, this argument can now be seen to be quite beside the point. For in fact, the two cases of an inference from an I to an A in the context of the square and of a similar-appearing inference in the case of induction are really not comparable. So far as the square of opposition is concerned, one has to do only with the transformation of propositions—i.e., with merely expressing the same truth or saying the same thing over again in a different way. In contrast, in induction one is actually trying to establish a new truth, to prove or demonstrate a conclusion in the light of evidence.

If a person makes the statement, "Some silver melts at 960.5° C.," one is certainly not expressing the same truth all over again, only in a different form, if one goes on to add, "All silver melts at 960.5° C." On the other hand, if as a result of observing some silver to melt at 960.5° C. one concludes that this is a property pertaining to the very nature of silver and that therefore all silver melts at that temperature, this would be a genuine inference from evidence to a new truth, not a mere transforming of the propositional formulation of the same truth. Here we can see the reason that an inference from an I to an A proposition in the context of the square of opposition is not allowable, whereas an inference from a number of singular propositions to a universal in a genuine inductive inference may be not merely allowable but even indispensable to the growth of science and knowledge generally.

Similar considerations would apply with respect to the criticisms directed against those other specific types of inductive demonstration. Once again, it would seem that the criticisms derive their force entirely from the uncritical assumption that induction must meet exactly the same standards of cogency as deduction. For example, why was it argued that all attempts at verifying a hypothesis are necessarily fallacious? The reason, it will be remembered, was that as soon as such a procedure of verification is analyzed after the pattern of the conditional syllogism and is judged by its standards, it is seen to invariably commit the fallacy of affirming the consequent. Yet is not the point here rather different from what one might at first suppose? To be sure, it is not only illuminating but even necessary that arguments in verification of hypotheses be considered as having the same logical form as a conditional syllogism. But the consequence of this is not that any and all such arguments in verification of hypotheses commit the fallacy of affirming the consequent, but rather that this fallacy simply isn't applicable when the hypothetical argument is directed at establishing an inductive conclusion in contrast to a deductive one.[10]

To illustrate the same point by a little different example, it might be remarked that Aristotle once undertook to show how an ordinary inductive

[10] See Chaps. 25 and 26.

inference from observed particulars to a universal principle could readily be cast in the form of a regular categorical syllogism in Figure III. Such an argument appears to commit the fallacy of illicit minor.[11] To be sure, Aristotle's particular example may strike us as quaint and outmoded, but the principle involved is perfectly clear.

> Man, the horse, the mule are long-lived.
> Man, the horse, the mule are bileless.
> ------
> Therefore, all bileless animals are long-lived.[12]

May we conclude from this example that any inductive inference from particulars to a universal is invalid? No, the conclusion would rather seem to be that whenever an inductive argument is thus cast in syllogistic form the regular rules of syllogistic cogency just aren't applicable for purposes of induction.

Following out the same line of considerations, one can show how there is even some warrant for that seemingly very feeble attempt to justify inductive procedures simply on the basis of a definition of terms. To be sure, mere arbitrary and nominal definitions are of no help in this connection. And in this sense the earlier criticism still stands, according to which it was pointed out that one could certainly not prove that silver melts at 960.5° C. merely by appealing to the fact that silver has come to be conventionally defined in terms of such a melting point. On the other hand, if on the basis of considerable inductive evidence one has come to the conclusion that there is something about the nature of silver that determines it to melt at that temperature, then while one's conclusion may certainly be mistaken and is at best only probable, this very probability that one has here got hold of something necessarily connected with the essence of silver is sufficient to account for and to justify a tendency to rule out seemingly contrary instances as illusions. In such a context, there would even be ground for saying that the contrary instances just couldn't be instances of silver "by definition." Even if subsequently it were to be shown that silver does not necessarily melt at that temperature and that the law was mistaken, that still would not mean that formerly one was not warranted, on the basis of the inductive evidence then at hand, in ruling out apparently contrary instances on the basis of the definition of silver.

And with this, we hope that enough has been said by way of rehabilitating and showing the entire legitimacy of the probable inferences that are characteristic of induction. That the prevalent skepticism in regard to them should ever have arisen is due, as we have seen, primarily to the nominalistic presuppositions that are so marked a feature of contemporary thought. In addition, these nominalistic doubts have been more than reinforced by a certain

---

[11] See below, pp. 303 and 306.

[12] *Analytica Priora*, 68b, 10; quoted from Ralph Eaton, *General Logic*, Scribner's, 1931, p. 487.

uncritical tendency to apply to induction the same criteria and standards of cogency that are properly applicable only to deductive inferences. Nevertheless, no sooner does one recognize that all these difficulties in regard to induction are due entirely to our habits of viewing induction in a false light than the difficulties themselves happily begin to appear gratuitous and unnecessary. It may be hoped that at long last we can have done with them!

CHAPTER 19

INDUCTION AND DEDUCTION AS
MUTUALLY SUPPLEMENTARY

19-1 WHY AND HOW THEY SUPPLEMENT EACH OTHER

Now that we have disposed of some of the principal doubts and difficulties connected with deduction and induction, let us return to a further consideration of the actual use and functioning of our deductive and inductive instruments in the business of acquiring knowledge. In the somewhat lengthy accounts which one must give of the nature and character of each of these tools, to say nothing of the tedious refutation of objections that one has to engage in, it would not be surprising if we had more or less lost from view the way in which these tools actually work in the concrete. Specifically, we may fail to recognize how the two processes of deduction and induction tend to supplement each other when it comes to providing evidence for the propositions in which our knowledge and understanding of things is contained.

The Primacy of Experience and Hence of Abstraction and Induction. At the outset, be it noted that a fundamental presupposition of our whole examination of human logical tools and instruments is that all of our knowledge is derived from experience and observation. There is no such thing as a pure a priori knowledge which is simply innate in our minds and stands in no need of being made evident to us in and through our experience of the world in which we find ourselves. On the contrary, there is nothing that we recognize as being so save in so far as we recognize it as being so in fact. Moreover, we only recognize it as being so in fact from having observed it to be so in fact. Direct experience, then, is necessarily the basis of all knowledge, and abstraction and induction are necessarily the first steps or the first operations in all knowledge, deduction being somehow secondary and supplementary.

We must tread carefully here, so as not to fall into misunderstanding. For one thing, to say that experience provides the ultimate evidence for all our knowledge, and that in consequence knowledge arises in the first place by abstraction and induction from experience, must not be interpreted as meaning that the abstract concepts and the inductive generalizations which we thus arrive at through experience are mere summaries of the particular items in that experience. Thus the universal concept "man" does not represent a mere sum or collection of the individual men whom we have observed. Nor is the generalization "Silver melts at 960.5° C." a mere shorthand for the fact that each time the experiment has been tried thus far it has turned out that way. No, for on such an interpretation abstraction and induction would be turned into tautologies, which, as we have seen, would seriously distort their proper function and character.[1]

The true purpose of both abstraction and induction is to lead from a sensory awareness of particulars to an intellectual apprehension of the stable natures or essences in those particulars. At the same time—and this is the contrary error—intellectual apprehension of essences, which is made possible through the instrument of the concept and of inductive argument, is not to be thought of as an apprehension, though conditioned by a preliminary sensory experience, of something wholly beyond and above the ordinary objects of the senses.

No, one may frankly acknowledge that what is apprehended by the senses and what is apprehended by the intellect are, materially at least, one and the same thing. Both faculties, that is to say, have the same material object;[2] both open out on the same world. And while it is the senses which may properly be said to present this real world to us, it is only the intellect which is capable of understanding it and recognizing the various items in it for what they are.[3] We might even borrow one of Toynbee's metaphors and say that the process of knowing involves a veritable "withdrawal and return": for while in abstraction and induction we do extract and draw something out of the manifold data of sense—and in this sense withdraw ourselves from these data—we do so precisely for the purpose of returning to the data in order to comprehend and understand them and know them for what they are. That is why the universal and abstract concept "man" is but a relation of identity to, and hence predicable of, each of the individuals from which it has been or could be abstracted. In other words, a universal concept is both derivative from and also interpretive of the particulars from which it has been abstracted and to which it is applicable.

And so, *mutatis mutandis,* with induction. For as we have already seen,[4] the explanatory process of inductive descent is strictly correlative with the derivative process of inductive ascent.

The Role of Deduction: It Discloses the "Why."   Where and how does deduction fit into this picture? Already we have suggested that, unlike abstraction and induction, deduction is not a process that carries us from the sensible to the intelligible; instead, it moves wholly on the intelligible plane.[5] However,

[1] This is simply the argument of the entire preceding chapter.
[2] On the precise meaning of this expression, see above, Chap. 3, p. 47, note 1.
[3] Cf. the earlier figure borrowed from Professor Gilson, above, p. 106.
[4] Above, p. 246.
[5] Above, pp. 241–243.

if such is the character of deduction, one may well ask, "But what, then, is its use, and why is it necessary?" To which we reply, "Deduction is a necessary supplement to induction." Still, the question is, How does it supplement it, and why is it so necessary?

Perhaps it will be remembered that in the course of one of our earlier discussions[6] we had occasion to remark that whereas induction is capable of merely showing *that* something is so, it is only through deduction that we can ever hope to explain *why* something is so. To revert to our rather shopworn example, it is quite possible to show by means of an inductive generalization that the opposite vertical angles formed by intersecting straight lines are equal. But the strictly empirical evidence in support of this conclusion—viz., that these opposite vertical angles, when measured, are found to be equal, and these are, and these are, and these, etc.—in no wise indicates why this should be the case. And the same principle would seem to be exemplified in the case of any other inductive generalization one might mention—that damp air tends to cause iron to rust, that water boils at 100° C., that hydrogen has an atomic weight of 1.008, that bad money drives out good, etc.

Moreover, just as we have only to scrutinize inductive argument in order to see that by its very nature it is incapable of showing why anything is so, so likewise we have but to consider the structure of syllogistic argument in order to see that for its part it is precisely adapted to the purpose of getting at the "why." For as we have already had occasion to illustrate earlier,[7] one has but to ask the question "Why?" with respect to any proposition he is seeking to demonstrate and he will recognize at once that it can be answered only by advancing a concept which can serve as a middle term in a syllogism.

Why is it that the opposite vertical angles are equal? Because they have the same supplementary angle in common, and any two angles having the same supplement are equal. Why are towels absorbent? Because of their capillary structure, anything with such a structure being by nature absorbent. Why is that country's foreign policy considered to be such a failure? Because it has served to alienate all of the country's allies, and any foreign policy that does this must be pronounced a failure. And so on and on, for it would be possible to produce examples *ad infinitum*.

Clearly, then, deduction supplements induction precisely in the sense that having established *that* something is so by means of induction, we naturally seek to know *why* it should be so, and such demonstration can be brought about only by deduction.[8] And not only is this confirmed by our own common

---

[6] Above, pp. 263–264.

[7] Above, pp. 240–241.

[8] This statement might seem to be inconsistent with our main theme that argument, whether deductive or inductive, is designed to disclose the "why," just as the proposition and the concept are instruments designed to disclose the "whether" and the "what." How,

everyday experience, where we observe, say, that our car starts badly in cold weather, and then want to find out why; or where we notice that corn will grow well at the far end of the garden but not at the near end, and naturally we are curious to know why; or where we discover that advertising our particular products through one medium brings in much larger sales than doing so through another, and again we seek to find the reason. But also in the whole history of science, this same tendency to supplement induction by deduction, to follow up a discovery that something is so with an explanation of why it should be that way, is confirmed again and again.

The Necessity That Each Supplement the Other. From the foregoing considerations there should begin to emerge a rather clear picture of the mutual supplementation of induction by deduction and of deduction by induction. Thus that induction needs to be supplemented by deduction is obvious from the fact that induction can never acquaint us with more than the fact that something is so. For an explanation as to why it is so the instrument of deduction is required.

On the other hand, that deduction needs to be supplemented by induction is obvious on a number of counts. In the first place, since all knowledge must ultimately be derived from experience, clearly the abstractive and inductive procedures which carry us from the sensible to the intelligible must precede the purely deductive procedures which move exclusively on the intelligible plane.

But there is even more telling evidence of the fact that a syllogistic or deductive demonstration can never, so to speak, stand alone but must always presuppose a prior induction. And that is that no syllogism can ever prove its own premises. It can only prove its conclusion on the basis of the premises or, better, on the assumption of the premises. Thus assuming it to be true that opposite vertical angles have a common supplement, and also that any angles having a common supplement are equal, it will also be true that the opposite vertical angles are equal. But likewise, assuming it to be true that anyone who ever chopped down a cherry tree is utterly disreputable and that George Washington once chopped down a cherry tree, it will also be true that George Washington is utterly disreputable.

In other words, all that the structure and rules of the syllogism guarantee

---

then, can we now apparently turn around and say that inductive argument does not disclose *why* a thing is so but only *the fact that* it is so?

This inconsistency is more apparent than real and is traceable to a certain ambiguity in our terminology. For it will be remembered that in one of our earlier discussions of the nature of inductive demonstration (see above, pp. 227–232) we sought to make clear that inductive argument, while it could provide a ground or a "why" for our *believing* or affirming that S is P, could not make evident why S should *be* P. Thus in the former more general sense of "why," induction is certainly capable of disclosing the "why," but in the latter more specific sense it is not.

is that the conclusion follows validly and correctly from the premises. That the conclusion is not merely valid but true cannot be guaranteed by a syllogism just as such. No, to be assured of the truth as well as of the validity of a conclusion, one must needs ascertain on other grounds (i.e., on other grounds than those provided by the syllogism itself) that the premises of one's syllogism are true.

But how is one to be sure of the truth of the premises of a given syllogism? After all, if the syllogism is to serve as an instrument of knowledge, it will not suffice to demonstrate one's conclusions as merely following validly from the premises; one must also be able to demonstrate their truth. And this, as we have seen, requires that one's premises be true. Again, how is one to make certain of the truth of the premises?

Well, one way, of course, is to construct further syllogisms to prove the truth of the premises of the first syllogism. Thus if one of the original premises says that any angles having the same supplementary angle are equal, one might prove this by arguing that any angle plus its supplement equals 180°, and that consequently any angles having the same supplement would be equal, on the principle that when equals are subtracted from equals the results are equal. Likewise, one might construct another syllogism to prove the second premise, viz., that the opposite vertical angles have the same supplement.

But clearly, such a procedure of demonstrating the truth of the premises of a syllogism by means of still other syllogisms will in the long run get nowhere unless it be supplemented by some other procedure of demonstration. For by the very nature of the case every syllogism has two unproved premises. If, then, one undertakes to prove each of the premises of an original syllogism by other syllogisms, each of these syllogisms, in turn, will have two more unproved premises. And so on *ad infinitum*. In short, to rely exclusively upon the syllogism as the means of providing premises for syllogistic inference would seem not only to get nowhere but to get nowhere fast!

Without question, therefore, deduction and the syllogism are in no wise self-sufficient as instruments of demonstration. They require supplementation by some other means or devices for proving or evidencing propositions. Nor can that other means be anything but induction. We saw how in order to prove that the opposite vertical angles are equal one might use as a major premise in one's syllogism the proposition that any angles having the same supplement are equal. To prove this, in turn, one might construct another syllogism one of the premises of which would be "If equals be taken from equals, the results are equal." What, then, about this premise? Would it not seem that rather than try to construct another syllogism in proof of this, one might consider such a principle to be simply evident on the basis of human experience—i.e., on an inductive basis?

Such, then, we may suppose, is the way deduction is supplemented by induction: ultimately it is through induction and only through induction that true premises may be supplied for deduction.

19–2 IS THIS A VICIOUS CIRCLE?

Unhappily, the foregoing account of the necessity of supplementing induction by deduction and deduction by induction may, by its seeming tight rigidity, threaten us with a most embarrassing consequence. For if every conclusion that is inductively established calls for a supplementary deductive demonstration showing why it is so, and if every deductive demonstration ultimately presupposes a prior induction as the source of its premises, do we not therewith have the makings of a thoroughly vicious circle?

Self-Evident Propositions. Fortunately, this threatened circle will be found not to materialize the minute one considers the various kinds of conclusion that may be made evident through induction. For some of these conclusions are of such a nature as not to require a supplementary deductive demonstration.

Specifically, the kind of inductive conclusion that is so distinguished is that in which there is a definitional predicable relationship between the subject and predicate of the conclusion. Already we have had much to say about such propositions and about how they cannot very well be demonstrated by any external evidence of the sort provided by a third or mediating term.[9] Thus how is one to prove or demonstrate that man is rational (the predicable relationship of differentia to species) or that man is animal (the predicable relationship of genus to species)? One can, of course, give inductive evidence of such definitional predicable relationships. But as for a deductive demonstration, there just is no sort of mediating term that could explain why a given nature or essence is the kind of nature or essence it is. Rather, either it is self-evident that a thing is the kind of thing it is, or it is not evident at all.

Let us consider a few more examples. With respect to the proposition "Silver melts at 960.5° C." one can quite meaningfully and legitimately ask, "Why?" That is, one can demand a deductive demonstration that will explain what there is about the nature of silver that causes it to melt at that temperature. In contrast, one could never properly demand to know what there was about the nature of a thing that causes it to be the kind of thing it is—i.e., to have the nature that it does have.

Or again: "A whole is greater than any one of its parts." If someone asks, "Why should this be?" would not one have to answer, "But that is just what a whole is. It is that way by definition.[10] That's what we mean by a whole." One

---

[9] See above, pp. 228–232.

[10] This expression should not be misunderstood: it does not mean that a whole is that way by our own arbitrary and purely conventional definition; rather it is that way by a real definition, i.e., by the very nature of the case in reality. Cf. above, pp. 80–83.

cannot, strictly speaking, explain why it should be that way—i.e., why it should be the kind of thing it is.

Or consider the so-called law of noncontradiction that is basic to both logic and metaphysics. As pertinent to logic, it might be formulated as the basic rule of the square of opposition: contradictory propositions cannot both be true. As a fundamental law of being, one might express the principle thus: a thing cannot both be and not be at one and the same time and in one and the same respect; or a thing cannot both have a certain characteristic and not have it at one and the same time and in one and the same respect. Now how would one go about demonstrating the principle of noncontradiction, in the sense of explaining why things should be that way? Obviously, such a thing is impossible. Try to do it yourself. Try to explain just why a thing cannot both be and not be at one and the same time. You can't do it, because that's simply what one means by a thing's being or existing: you mean that it is or exists and hence is not nonexistent.

So much for examples of so-called self-evident principles or propositions.[11] To say that they are self-evident means simply that they are evident in and through themselves: there is no third concept other than and outside the subject and predicate concepts of the propositions which can mediate between them and so explain why that predicate pertains to that subject. At the same time, the fact that such propositions are self-evident in this sense does not mean they have not been made evident through experience—i.e., inductively. For just as we learn what human nature is through experience, so also we learn from experience a fundamental law of being like the law of noncontradiction. In neither case may we be said to have an innate or a priori knowledge of such principles; rather they become evident to us through a process of induction.

We can see, then, that not all inductive conclusions require a further deductive demonstration showing why they are so. Propositions with definitional predicates, or predicates which are transcendental and ubiquitous, and thus applicable to all things, are such that we recognize why they are so, simply in virtue of the nature and meaning of the terms themselves and without any mediation through a middle term. But with this our threatened vicious circle is broken. For although *most* inductively established conclusions require a supplementary deductive demonstration, not all of them do. And those which do not are of such a nature as to be able to serve as ultimate premises for deductive demonstrations of the "whys" of things.

---

[11] Be it noted in this connection that for a principle to be self-evident does not necessarily mean that it is obvious or readily apparent or immediately evident *to us*. On the contrary, it means that the principle is evident in *itself*; but for us to recognize the self-evidence of a principle may be difficult and require no little experience as well as concentration. For a fuller discussion of this distinction between a principle's being *objectively evident* in itself and its being *subjectively evident* to us, cf. Veatch, *Intentional Logic*, Yale, 1952, pp. 296–297.

19–3   EXPLANATION BY HYPOTHESIS IN MODERN SCIENCE

19–3.1   Induction in a Secondary Role?

Does this account of the ultimacy of inductive demonstration in certain con-texts of human cognition and of the mutual supplementation of induction and deduction in all other contexts really square with the facts? Does it present a true picture of what actually happens in the procedures of the natural sciences? Without a doubt, most contemporary philosophers of science would say "No." And curiously enough, they would say "No" precisely because of our insistence upon the primacy and ultimacy of induction. We say "curiously enough" be-cause in the popular mind at least the primacy and ultimacy of empirical evi-dence and hence of inductive evidence is held to be the very cornerstone of modern scientific method.

However, in recent years reflection upon the nature of scientific procedures, particularly in physics, has led to a seeming repudiation of the principle of the primacy of induction in science. Thus Professor Margenau, the distinguished American physicist, flatly declares: "The physical scientist . . . tries to avoid induction, and he inclines to look upon fields yielding only to inductive analysis as unconquered territory rather than his proper domain. . . ． The exact sciences are, after all, deductive in their major phases." [12]

An even more significant observation perhaps is that of the eminent English historian Herbert Butterfield. Discussing the origins of modern science, he remarks:

Now, if we are seeking to understand this birth of modern science, we must not imagine that everything is explained by the resort to an experimental mode of pro-cedure, or even that experiments were any great novelty.[13]

In fact, we shall find that in both celestial and terrestrial physics—which hold the strategic place in the whole movement—change is brought about, not by new observa-tions or additional evidence in the first instance, but by transpositions that were taking place inside the minds of the scientists themselves. In this connection it is not irrelevant to note that of all forms of mental activity the most difficult to induce, even in the minds of the young who may be presumed not to have lost their flexibility, is the art of handling the same bundle of data as before, but placing them in a new sys-tem of relations with one another by giving them a different framework, all of which virtually means putting on a different kind of thinking-cap for the moment.[14]

Actually, we suggest that this type of interpretation of scientific method, which would thus relegate induction to a markedly secondary role, is prompted mainly by two considerations. In the first place, it is noted, as we have noted

[12] Henry Margenau, *The Nature of Physical Reality,* McGraw-Hill, 1950, p. 249.
[13] *The Origins of Modern Science,* G. Bell, 1950, p. 68.
[14] *Ibid.,* p. 1.

too, that the ordinary inductive conclusion merely establishes that something is so. But anything like adequate understanding requires an explanation of why it is so. For instance, Margenau remarks in connection with the problems of explanation in the field of thermodynamics:

In thermodynamics proper, observables are connected by what are sometimes called *empirical* relations, with the term empirical understood in a very limited and specific way. The "laws of motion" in this science are primitive equations combining the observables themselves. In a certain sense, the laws do not say "why" bodies behave thermodynamically as they do. While this connotes no defect of the methods of thermodynamics as a science, it nevertheless raises a question as to the possibility of other modes of explanation, of theories that "go behind" the phenomenological structure of thermodynamics and its minimal assumptions.[15]

And in similar vein Mr. Campbell asserts:

Indeed many laws in science are termed "empirical" and regarded with a certain amount of suspicion; if we inquire we find that an empirical law is simply one of which no theoretical explanation is known. In the science of physics at least, it would almost be more accurate to say that we believe our laws because they are consequences of our theories than to say that we believe our theories because they predict and explain true laws![16]

Apparently the modern physicist, not content with mere empirical or inductive generalizations, seeks to go behind the observable phenomena and to develop theories and hypotheses from which empirically established propositions may be deduced and in terms of which they may be explained. Such an enterprise, however, at once raises the problem which we have already discussed: where are premises to be found for deductive explanations and demonstrations? Now, by our account the only sorts of proposition that in the final analysis could properly perform this role would be self-evident propositions— propositions which, though they are inductively arrived at, are nevertheless found to be evident simply in and through themselves.

However, the physicist would say that he just doesn't find any self-evident propositions. Not only that, but—and this is the second consideration which we think is relevant to the depreciation of induction in modern science—he would also say that the explanatory theories and hypotheses which he (the physicist) does develop in order to explain the actual phenomena in physics are not inductive generalizations at all. Indeed, far from being based on experience or observation, they appear to be pure intellectual constructs, conjured up wholly a priori and often as products of the mathematical imagination. For instance, consider Newton's first law of motion: a body will continue indefinitely in motion or at rest unless acted upon by external forces. Obviously, this proposi-

[15] *Op. cit.*, p. 268.
[16] Norman Campbell, *What Is Science?* Dover Publications, 1952, p. 71.

tion cannot be established by the same sort of inductive argument as that used to show that silver melts at 960.5° C. In the latter case, one observes over and over again that silver does melt at this temperature. But in the former case, no one has ever observed even once—to say nothing of over and over again—a physical body continuing in motion to infinity.

A better example might be taken from Campbell. He is discussing the so-called Dynamical Theory of Gases, by which all sorts of specific laws in regard to gases may be explained—e.g., Boyle's law, Gay-Lussac's law, etc.

According to this theory, a gas consists of an immense number of very small particles, called molecules, flying about in all directions, colliding with each other and with the wall of the containing vessel; the speed of the flight of these molecules increases with the temperature; their impacts on the walls of the vessel tend to force the wall outwards and represent the pressure on them; and by their motion, heat is conveyed from one part of the gas to another in the manner called *conduction*.[17]

Campbell then makes this comment in regard to the evidence in support of the theory:

Molecules are not things which we can see or feel; they are not, like the ordinary material bodies to which the laws of dynamics are known to apply, objects discernible to direct perception. We only know that they exist by inference; what we actually observe are gases, varying in temperature and pressure; and it is only by these variations that we are led to suspect the existence of the molecules. . . . If somebody denied the existence of molecules, how could we prove him wrong? We cannot show him the molecules; we can only show him the gases and expound the theory.[18]

Apparently, the major explanatory theories and hypotheses of science do not rest on inductive or empirical evidence at all. Indeed, we suggest that right here is the source of so many of those extraordinary-sounding pronouncements which one often hears scientists make nowadays. For instance, no less a figure than Einstein has characterized modern theories of physics as "free inventions of the human mind." "The natural philosophers of [former] days," he remarks, "were . . . most of them possessed with the idea that fundamental concepts and postulates of physics were not in the logical sense free inventions of the human mind but could be deduced[19] from experience by 'abstraction'—that is to say by logical means."[20] In contrast, the physicists of today have come to recognize that the "axiomatic basis of theoretical physics cannot be extracted from experience but must be freely invented."[21] Thus "it seems that the human mind has first to construct forms independently before we can find them in things. Kepler's marvelous achievement is a particularly fine example of the

17 *Op. cit.*, pp. 81–82.
18 *Op. cit.*, pp. 85–86.
19 As we are using terms, the better word here would be "induced."
20 *Essays in Science*, Philosophical Library, 1934, p. 16.
21 *Ibid.*, p. 17.

truth that knowledge cannot spring from experience alone but only from the comparison of the inventions of the intellect with observed fact."[22]

If one ventures to ask how it happens that theories which are completely a priori and "free inventions of the mind" nevertheless turn out to be applicable to experience, Einstein would appear simply to throw up his hands at the question and reply that this is simply "a mystery that we shall never understand."[23] It is "what Leibniz describes so happily as a preestablished harmony."[24]

As a matter of fact, one might cite another quotation in the same vein, this time from Campbell:

But why do they (i.e. scientific laws) predict? We return once again to the question which we cannot avoid. The final answer that I must give is that I do not know, that nobody knows, and that probably nobody will ever know. The position is simply this. We examine our past experience, and order it in a way that appears to us most simple and satisfactory; we arrange it in a manner that is dictated by nothing but our desire that the world may be intelligible. And yet we find that, in general, we do do not have to alter the arrangement when new experience has to be included. We arrange matters to our liking, and nature is so kind as to recognize our arrangement, and to conform to it![25]

19–3.2 A Broadened Account of Induction

There is no doubt that this statement of the nature of explanatory theories and hypotheses in science is quite at variance with our account of the necessary supplementation of all deductive explanation by induction. Not only that, but currently fashionable accounts of scientific explanation by hypothesis are of further embarrassment because of their unmistakably nominalistic and skeptical import. For if there is no basis in fact for our explanatory notions and theories, then our use in science of universal concepts and propositions as explanatory hypotheses will have no justification other than the pretended pragmatic one of their workability; and even their workability will have to be written off as an utterly inexplicable mystery.

Clearly, something must be done to obviate these consequences. Yet the task is not easy, simply because so-called explanation by hypothesis is an indispensable instrument in modern science. Besides, it must be frankly admitted that the explanatory hypotheses which scientists actually employ are certainly not of the character of self-evident principles. Nor does it seem likely that we shall very soon acquire such insight into the natures and essences of things

---

[22] *Ibid.*, p. 27.
[23] Quoted from an article by A. P. Ushenko, "Einstein's Influence on Contemporary Philosophy," in *Albert Einstein: Philosopher-Scientist*, edited by Paul Arthur Schilpp, Library of Living Philosophers, 1949, p. 636.
[24] *Ibid.*
[25] *Op. cit.*, p. 71.

in the natural world that we shall be able to erect our sciences on a foundation of self-evident truths rather than on mere hypotheses.

How, then, is it possible to regard scientific hypotheses and theories as anything but arbitrary constructs or inventions of the mind, with all the nominalistic and skeptical consequences which this entails? Yet there may be another alternative after all. For is it true that scientific hypotheses and theories are such arbitrary inventions as they are often represented as being? Surely there would seem to be some sort of empirical support or warrant for them. True, they may not be inductively warranted after the manner of self-evident principles. Also, since by their very nature they are supposed to "go behind" the phenomena they are designed to explain, there may not be the direct inductive evidence in support of them that there is, say, for an ordinary empirical generalization like "Silver melts at 960.5° C." But this is not to say that there is no empirical or inductive evidence for them at all. Indeed, we suggest that the concept of induction be broadened and expanded so as to take account of precisely this phenomenon of explanation by hypothesis.

To this end, however, we must first examine a little more closely what is involved in this strange mode of demonstration which we have termed explanation by hypothesis. For the interesting thing about it is that it is a complex type of proof involving both induction and deduction. It involves induction in that the law or generalization which is supposed to require "explanation" is presumed to have already been established by induction. At the same time, it involves deduction in that the explanation of the law consists simply in the deduction of the law from the hypothesis. The difficulty is that the explanatory hypothesis itself, which is the source of the explanation, would seem to be established neither inductively nor deductively; nor can it be considered to be in any sense self-evident.

But let us take an illustration[26]—a particular scientific theory that has tended to become an almost classic example of explanation by hypothesis. That is the famous Copernican hypothesis in astronomy. As is well known, what Copernicus did was to insist upon a heliocentric account of the movements of the heavenly bodies to replace the traditional geocentric accounts as elaborated by the Ptolemaic astronomers.

Suppose we flatly put the question: How did Copernicus arrive at his famous proposition that the sun, instead of revolving around the earth, was actually stationary, and that the earth, as well as the other planets, revolved around it? Did this become evident to him through an inductive or a deductive argument,

26 The remainder of this section is reproduced almost verbatim from Veatch, *op. cit.*, pp. 325–331. It perhaps should be remarked also that the account here given of explanation by hypothesis is not to be found either in Aristotle or in any of the classical logicians of the realistic tradition. At the same time, we are confident that the theory here developed is a legitimate extension of these classical realistic doctrines for the purpose of meeting a rather new situation.

or did he take it as self-evident? The answer, of course, is that none of these alternatives explains the source of the evidence. Rather we must recognize that, Copernicus' proposition being in the nature of a hypothesis, it was not so much something for which he had evidence as something he offered in evidence, or better in explanation, of something else.

As regards empirical evidence—i.e., the sort of evidence that would warrant an inductive generalization—there was clearly nothing of the sort in support of Copernicus' proposition. No one—neither Copernicus nor anyone else—had ever *observed* the sun to be stationary or the earth to be moving around it. Instead, all that astronomers had actually observed were the different *positions,* relative to the earth, of the various planets at different times. Moreover, these planets had been observed to appear in these various positions quite regularly and at definitely stated intervals. In other words, from what had been observed, the only inductive generalizations that one could formulate were of this sort: "There is something about the nature of planet x (whether Mars or Venus or Saturn or what not) that causes it to appear at position p_1 at time t_1, p_2 at t_2, p_3 at t_3, etc."

Nevertheless, it was impossible to determine simply from observation *what* there was about the nature of x that was causing this behavior. Indeed, here was but a case of that inescapable weakness of all induction which we have already had occasion to note: induction may be able to supply evidence *that* something is so, but never evidence as to *why* it is so. What was called for was some sort of deductive demonstration that would explain *why* the planets appeared where they did when they did.

This is precisely what the Copernican hypothesis did: it provided the sort of premise that was required for a demonstration of why the planets appeared where and when they did. In fact, any explanatory hypothesis that is employed in the sciences is supposed to do just this: to provide such principles or premises as will make evident why certain natural phenomena occur as they do.

The next question is this: Granted that a hypothesis by its very nature must be such as to provide evidence as to why certain things are as they are, what is the evidence for the hypothesis itself? As regards the Copernican hypothesis, we have already seen that the evidence in its support is not empirical. Likewise, considered just in itself, the proposition that the sun is stationary and the earth revolving is not self-evident; nor can it be said that this principle was itself deduced from some prior principle. What, then, is the warrant for accepting the hypothesis? The answer is that its warrant consists merely in the fact that through it one can supply deductive evidence of why certain natural phenomena occur as they do.

But what sort of warrant is this? After all, what we have here called the "warrant" for a thing means simply the evidence for it, yet any mediating evidence must be either deductive or inductive; but for a hypothesis such as we have been considering there would appear to be neither deductive nor inductive evidence. Could it be, then, that in scientific knowledge the need for deductive demonstrations is so great that we must simply accept such demonstrations on faith, even though there be no evidence in support of their premises?

Such a conclusion seems so incredible that before accepting it we would perhaps do well to take an altogether different example of explanation by hypothesis to see whether the same situation would prevail there as prevailed in the case of the Copernican hypothesis. This time we shall consider Darwin's hypothesis of natural selection and the particular account of it that has been given by Julian Huxley. Huxley has conveniently undertaken not only to describe Darwin's explanation by hypothesis but also to analyze it with a view to discriminating those elements in it which are properly inductive in character from those which are properly deductive. This is how he puts it:

In the *Origin and Descent of Man,* Darwin adopted a type of reasoning that is somewhat rare in science—an intimate combination of the inductive and the deductive. Almost at the outset he develops the great deductive principle of Natural Selection. Granted that animals and plants vary, and that some at least of the variation is inherited; granted also that all animals and plants produce more offspring than can survive, and that therefore a constant struggle for existence must occur; then it follows that throughout organic nature there must be operative the agency which he christened Natural Selection, by which more of the variations that were better suited to the conditions of life will on the average survive, and that some of this improvement will be transmitted to subsequent generations.

This principle would then account for the fact that organisms are in general beautifully adapted to their surroundings and their way of life; when conditions are constant and organization cannot be further improved, it will keep animals and plants true to their well-adapted type; when conditions change, or when improvement in organization is still possible, it will lead to change in the organisms; this change will be slight and gradual, but if continued over the enormous spaces of geological time, it will be able to produce any degree of alteration; thus not only the slight differences between related species and genera can be accounted for by natural means, but also the long-continued trends revealed by geological history, and the whole evolution of the higher groups of organisms from simple primitive forms.

This is the deductive principle of natural selection, later supplemented by the subsidiary principle of sexual selection, which Darwin supposed to operate by giving advantage to males in the struggle for mates, instead of to all members of the species in the struggle for existence. These two principles together Darwin considered would account for all organic evolution and its results, including detailed adaptation, the facts of geographical distribution, the change of type during geological time, the existence of rudimentary organs, the recapitulation of past racial history during the development of the individual, and the special displays and display-characters of male animals.

His inductive treatment falls under two heads. The first is the establishment of the bases for his deduction—the facts that animals and plants do vary, that variation is in part inherited, and that there is over-production of offspring and a struggle for existence with consequent survival of the fittest. This he naturally places before the chapters in which he develops the general theory of natural selection.

The second part of his inductive treatment consists in collecting examples of what may be expected to occur as a result of natural (and sexual) selection—specialized adaptation, long-continued improvement and general organization, courtship-displays, the divergent evolution of animals and plants when geographically isolated, and so forth. These he at one and the same time explains as a result of selection, and adduces as a proof of the existence and power of selection, thus combining inductive and deductive reasoning in a single argument.[27]

From this account of the Darwinian hypothesis it is easy to see how closely the structure of the argument in this case parallels the structure of the argument in the case of the Copernican hypothesis. For one thing there is the hypothesis itself, that of natural selection. Huxley terms this "the great deductive principle" (i.e., a principle which can serve as a premise for a deductive demonstration of why) and it parallels the heliocentric proposition of Copernicus.

For another thing, there are those several propositions which have all been arrived at through inductive argument, but which still require a deductive demonstration showing *why* they are so. In the case of the Darwinian theory, such a proposition would be the one stating that organisms are in general beautifully adapted to their surroundings and way of life. In the case of the Copernican hypothesis, such propositions would be those stating that such and such planets appear at such and such places at such and such times.

Moreover, starting from these inductively established propositions as facts that still require explanation, both the Darwinian and the Copernican theories involve deductive demonstrations of these facts from the respective hypotheses that have been proposed; and finally both theories would involve further inductions in verification of such other consequences as might be deduced from the proposed hypotheses.

So much for the parallel structure of the two explanations by hypothesis. There is also a parallel problem: that of the evidence for the hypothesis itself. After all, the inductive evidence in support of the fact of adaptation is hardly to be thought of as evidence in support of the hypothesis designed to explain the fact. Likewise, the deductive argument from the hypothesis could hardly be regarded as supplying evidence of the hypothesis, simply because no deductive argument is ever a proof of its own premises.

However, the problem is not insoluble, nor is it necessary to conclude that an explanatory hypothesis is something for which we have no evidence and

[27] *The Living Thoughts of Darwin,* edited by Julian Huxley, Longmans, Green, 1939, pp. 13–15.

which accordingly must be accepted merely on faith. On the contrary, the evidence for such a hypothesis, we suggest, is inductive, and yet the induction is of a somewhat different sort from what we have encountered thus far.

As a matter of fact, if one chooses to consider it very broadly and loosely, there are many senses in which the term "induction" might be used, although all the senses have a certain analogy. Most commonly and properly "induction" is used of that process by which from experience we establish that S is P. Somewhat less commonly and more broadly, one might even call abstraction a kind of induction. Thus whereas in the former case one proceeded by induction from singular empirical propositions to a universal proposition, so also in abstraction one proceeds from particular sense data to a universal concept.

Stretching the term still farther, we may suggest a third type of induction— this time an inductive process which serves to establish not a concept or a proposition but a whole causal or syllogistic argument.

The more one reflects upon it, the more it would seem to be an induction of just this sort that is involved in the setting up of an explanatory hypothesis. After all, in explanation by hypothesis one is not really concerned to prove the truth of the hypothesis *considered just as a single proposition.* On the contrary, of the simple proposition *standing alone*—whether it be the proposition that the earth moves round the sun, or the proposition that a principle of natural selection is operative in nature, or what—there is no direct empirical evidence whatever, and of course no deductive evidence either. Rather the evidence is of the *whole causal complex* involved in the explanation of adaptation by natural selection or of the movements of the planets with reference to the central position of the sun, etc.

Besides, the fact that there is an induction of this third type explains why, as was suggested earlier, the only apparent warrant for our accepting a given hypothesis would seem to be its fruitfulness as a premise for deductive explanation. Strictly speaking, of course, this is no warrant at all, since no deductive argument is ever a proof of its own premises. On the other hand, the minute we recognize that what we are seeking to find a warrant for is not just the hypothesis all by itself but rather the hypothesis together with the explanatory deduction founded upon it, then it becomes clear what the nature of the evidence is in such a case and what that evidence is an evidence of.

For example, in the instance of the Darwinian hypothesis, no one has ever observed natural selection actually occurring, any more than anyone in Copernicus' time had ever observed the earth actually passing around the sun. In this sense there is no empirical evidence of the hypothesis considered just in itself. But from *what* is observed—i.e., from the occurrence of variations, the inheritance of variations, the overproduction of offspring, the struggle for existence, etc.—from all these observable happenings one can *infer* that some such thing as natural selection is causing the adaptation of organisms to their environments.

This inference is precisely of the sort which we have chosen to call an induction of the third type. That it is not an induction which leads simply to an apprehension of essences is obvious. That it is not an induction which leads merely to a recognition that two objects are in reality connected is likewise obvious. It is an induction which leads to a recognition of a causal order underlying and making intelligible the connections between the various objects of knowledge.

Why do we call this third type of induction "induction," if it is thus different from the other two? The answer is that like every type of induction this third type involves a passage from the sensible to the intelligible. Just as a universal concept is to the sense data from which it has been abstracted, so also is a universal proposition to the sensory evidence from which it has been inferred; and so, too, is an explanation by hypothesis to the observable phenomena from which it has been derived.

Moreover, all of these analogous inductive procedures are clearly distinguishable from a procedure of strict deductive demonstration, for whereas the former are all analogous in that they involve a passage from the sensible to the intelligible, the latter moves entirely on the intelligible plane.

To be sure, this must not be taken to imply that induction of the third type does not involve deduction as one of its component elements. For that matter, it involves induction of the ordinary type as one of its elements too. This was what was meant when it was suggested earlier that explanation by hypothesis involves both induction and deduction. The initial impetus to the setting up of an explanatory hypothesis must necessarily come from the fact that one has concluded through an inductive inference *that* two objects are connected; and one wants an explanation of *why* they are connected. Once the hypothesis has been set up, one then proceeds purely deductively to demonstrate the same conclusion that had originally been established by induction, the only difference being that what was before only a demonstration of *the fact that* has now become a demonstration of *why*.

Since the deductive demonstration in such a case proceeds merely from a hypothesis and not from self-evident principles, the real problem in explanation by hypothesis is the problem of the evidence for the explanation as a whole, i.e., for the hypothesis *together with* the deductive demonstration based upon it. What we are suggesting is that the inference which leads to an awareness of this whole inductive-deductive complex, i.e., the whole underlying causal order, is really an inductive inference, an inference from the observable to the intelligible. Accordingly, it is in this sense that basically and fundamentally explanation by hypothesis must be regarded as an inductive rather than a deductive procedure.

Such an extension of the notion of induction may seem in the final analysis both far-fetched and unwarranted. Yet it may at least serve the purpose of showing how hypotheses can perfectly well be regarded as being in a sense inductions from experience and hence intentions of experience. More specifically, indeed, they would seem to be instruments for coming to know the causal order and structure of what is given in experience. So regarded, hypotheses would not then appear to be what so many contemporary logicians seem to think they are, viz., wholly arbitrary fabrications of a sort of free-wheeling mathematical intellect, whose pertinence to the given data cannot be explained but must be accepted as a veritable mystery of a preëstablished harmony.

Summary of the Nature and Function of Argument. Thus we conclude our theoretical examination of the nature, function, and principal types of argument. While concepts give us the "whats" and propositions the "whethers," arguments present us with the "whys" or causes of things, either the causes of the things' being what they are or else the causes of our knowing that these things are as they are. Within the context of logic this means that in argument we adduce certain propositions, called premises, as evidence for another proposition, called a conclusion, the common or middle term of the premises bridging the gap between the subject and predicate of the conclusion. This middle term which mediates between S and P in the conclusion must always be a universal, but it may be apprehended either abstractly in a concept or concretely in immediate experience. In the former case we have deductive argument; in the latter case inductive argument. Inductive and deductive argument are mutually supplementary, deduction explaining the reason for the truth of propositions (which may or may not be established inductively) and induction establishing the truth of the premises which are used in deductive explanation. In some cases, however, the deductive premises can be established neither inductively nor deductively; and in these cases (when the proposition is not immediately evident) we must have recourse to an induction of a different type, hypothesis, which abstracts from the data of experience a whole causal order rather than merely a single essence or a combination of essences in a single proposition. With this general theoretical background we are now in a position to begin a detailed study of the various forms of argument.

EXERCISES

1. Are the following arguments deductive or inductive?
   a. The Republicans are going to win the November election, Mr. Gallup reported. Of those interviewed who were not undecided 59 percent said they plan to vote Republican.
   b. Everybody will agree that swimming is the most healthful sport, for it exercises more muscles of one's body than any other sport and this is of course more healthful.

    c. Platypuses are viviparous and all vivaparous animals are mammals. Ergo, platypuses are mammals.

    d. The Yankees have the odds on the pennant again this year, for they've won it more than any other club.

    e. It's going to rain. Listen to the thunder! Every time I've heard it thunder like that it rained.

    f. It's going to rain. Listen to the thunder! Every time it thunders like that it rains.

    g. Airplanes defy the law of gravity for anything that goes up defies the law of gravity.

    h. Mankind will always progress onward and upward, for we are today far more advanced than we were 2000 years ago.

    i. Porpoises are fish for anything that swims in the water is a fish and porpoises certainly do that.

2. Are any of the following propositions immediately evident (self-evident)?

    a. All black cats are black.

    b. All black cats are unlucky.

    c. All blackberries are black.

    d. All black berries are black.

    e. Every body gravitates.

    f. All men are rational.

CHAPTER 20

STRUCTURE AND RULES
OF THE SYLLOGISM

"Now, if reality is change and nothing but change, and consciousness is change and nothing but change, consciousness is reality and all reality is of the same sort as consciousness."[1]

Is this argument valid or invalid? "Well," you might say, "I certainly don't believe that it's true that reality and consciousness are nothing but change." But that's not the question here. The writer is not saying that reality and consciousness are actually nothing but change—though he may believe this to be so. He is saying that *if* they are nothing but change then it is true that "consciousness is reality and all reality is of the same sort as consciousness." In short, the writer is asserting that the conclusion follows validly from the premises, that if the premises are true the conclusion must be true. And this is the meaning of *validity:* an argument is *valid* exactly when the conclusion *would* have to be true *if* the premises were true. This being so, is the above argument valid or not? Well, you might say that it seems o.k., or that, on the contrary, there seems to be something fishy about it, though you can't say exactly what it is. But we want to know more than that; we want to know definitely whether or not it is valid, and also exactly why it is valid or invalid. There are exact logical procedures for answering these questions, and it is to those that we must now turn.

20–1 FROM LANGUAGE TO SYLLOGISMS

On Clarifying Arguments.   Before we can apply our logical techniques for the determination of the validity or invalidity of such arguments as the above, we must first make those arguments perfectly clear by formulating them in exact logical terms, just as we had to formulate propositions logically before we could test their relative truth-values. Logical formulation is necessary, again, because of two facts. First, words, sentences, and paragraphs are artificial, material signs, and their significance varies more or less from person to person and from time to time thus creating the possibility of ambiguity in any par-

[1] C. E. M. Joad, *Guide to Philosophy,* Random House, 1935, p. 547.

ticular linguistic utterance. The logical formulation of an argument has for one of its tasks the elimination of ambiguity so as to produce a perfectly clear, unequivocal argument. Second, language has, as we have seen, various non-logical functions such as the emotive, the ceremonial, and the directive which must be temporarily disregarded by logicians in order to focus exclusively upon the logical or cognitive function. Hence the logical formulation of arguments has as its second purpose the abstraction from all the noncognitive functions of the language under consideration. Our procedure for the logical formulation of arguments is strictly parallel to that for the logical formulation of propositions.

The Syllogistic Elements. As we have seen, a syllogism (from the Greek words *logos,* "thought" or "reason," and *syn,* "together") consists in the relating of two terms on the basis of their common relation to a third term. The basic operative principle here is that things related to the same thing are thereby related to each other. In order to effect such relation, a syllogism consists of exactly three propositions containing exactly three terms, each term occurring twice, thus:

$$M - P$$
$$S - M$$
$$\overline{S - P}$$

The proposition whose truth is being established is called the *conclusion,* and it is ordinarily placed last. The other two propositions, which are offered as evidence for the conclusion, are called the *premises.* The predicate of the conclusion is known as the *major term,* and it is often symbolized as "P." The subject of the conclusion is called the *minor term,* and it is frequently symbolized as "S." The premise which contains the major term is known as the *major premise,* and the premise which contains the minor term is known as the *minor premise.* In formulating syllogisms logically, the major premise is conventionally placed first. The third term, which occurs in both premises and which effects the mediation between the major and minor terms, is called the *middle term,* and it is usually symbolized as "M." Let us now turn to the procedure for formulating syllogisms.

The Procedure of Syllogistic Formulation. Since a syllogism contains three propositions, the procedure for the formulation of a syllogism involves our earlier procedure for the formulation of propositions. And since propositions contain terms, that procedure also involves our techniques for the identification of concepts by the elimination of ambiguity in words. The procedure here given for formulating syllogisms is of course nothing but one attempt to codify the practice which we all follow more or less consciously—for we all have frequent occasion to straighten out arguments. While there are doubtless better statements of this straightening-out procedure than the one given here, it must once again be emphasized that you should pick some procedure, stick to it

systematically, and practice it frequently, for without any systematic procedure at all you will discover that you are much more likely to make mistakes.
As was noted in connection with propositional formulation, here again experience has shown that this process of extracting logical structures from language
is for most people one of the more difficult aspects of practical logic. Hence it
is very important that you practice this process frequently on many different
examples until you attain proficiency in logical formulation. Our procedure for
the formulation of syllogisms will be the following:

1. Identify and formulate the conclusion.
2. Identify and formulate each of the two premises.
3. Arrange the three propositions as follows: major premise first, minor premise
   second, and conclusion last.

To get a clear picture of this procedure in action, let us first take a very simple
example:

> Since no sergeants are malleable and all privates are malleable, it follows that
> no sergeants are privates.

We first identify the conclusion. What is it the speaker wants to prove? That
"No sergeants are privates." That this is the conclusion is clearly shown by the
key words "it follows that." Having identified the conclusion, we now simply
formulate it logically and symbolically as we have learned to formulate any
proposition:

$$S \quad e \quad P$$
SeP   No (sergeants) are (privates.)

Our second step is to identify and formulate each of the premises. Since in a
syllogism any proposition which is not the conclusion must be a premise, the
two remaining propositions in the above syllogism must of course be premises.
Moreover, the fact that they are premises is also indicated by the key word
"since," for this word shows that what immediately follows it is offered in
evidence for some conclusion. And having now identified the two premises we
formulate them as usual:

$$S \quad e \quad M$$
SeM   No (sergeants) are (malleable.)

$$P \quad a \quad M$$
PaM   All (privates) are (malleable.)

Our last step consists in arranging these three propositions so that the major
premise is first, the minor second, and the conclusion last, thus:

$$PaM$$
$$\underline{SeM}$$
$$SeP$$

Or, in language: "All privates are malleable, and No sergeants are malleable; hence, No sergeants are privates."

It is usually fairly easy to tell intuitively which proposition is the conclusion and which ones are the premises, but it helps to note various conclusion- and premise-indicating words which are frequently used. Some of the more common conclusion indicators in the English language are: "hence," "therefore," "consequently," "it follows that," "so," "so that," "then," and "thus." And some of the more common premise indicators are: "because," "since," "as," "if," "for," "on account of," and "inasmuch as." In some cases an argument will contain both a conclusion- and a premise-indicating word, but more frequently it will contain just one of these, either a conclusion or a premise indicator but not both, the status of the other element being clear by process of elimination. And occasionally an argument will not contain either one, the conclusion and the premises being indicated by the punctuation or inflection as, for example, in the following: "The radical is not always unselfish; your mere malcontent, for example, is often a selfish being, and every malcontent is, of course, a radical." In the last analysis there can be no mechanical substitute for intuition and reflection in identifying the conclusion and premises, for what is required is a grasp of the intention of the speaker or writer.

Let us finally apply this procedure for the formulation of syllogisms to a slightly more difficult case, such as the one given at the beginning of this chapter. Whenever we encounter arguments in written form we can conveniently formulate them right where they stand, like this:

$$
\begin{array}{cccccc}
 & & \text{R} & \text{a} & \text{C} & \text{Re}\bar{\text{C}} & \text{T} \\
\text{Te}\bar{\text{C}} & \text{RaC} & \multicolumn{5}{l}{\text{Now if (reality) is (change) and no(thing but change,) and (conscious-}} \\
 & & & \text{a} & \text{C} & \text{Te}\bar{\text{C}} & \text{T} \quad \text{a} \\
\text{Re}\bar{\text{C}} & \text{TaC} & \multicolumn{5}{l}{\text{ness) is (change) and no(thing but change,) (consciousness) is}} \\
 & & \text{R} & & \text{R} \; \text{a} & \text{T} \\
\text{RaT} & \text{TaR} & \multicolumn{5}{l}{\text{(reality) and all (reality) is (of the same sort as consciousness.)}}
\end{array}
$$

Notice that this argument actually consists of two syllogisms, for each proposition is expressed in two different ways. The second formulation of each premise is the obverse of that premise, and the second formulation of the conclusion is the simple converse of the conclusion. Notice also that the symbol "T" ("thought") is used for the term "consciousness" in order to avoid confusion, since the symbol "C" is already used for the term "change."

20–2   MOODS AND FIGURES OF SYLLOGISMS – *Variables*

As soon as we have formulated our syllogism symbolically we see that there are only two variables in its structure: the type of proposition which occurs in each of the three places (whether an A, an E, an I, or an O) and the position of the middle term. These two variables determine the number of different syllogistic structures—though, as we shall see, not all of them are valid.

The propositional type pattern of a syllogism is known as its *mood*. For example:

MaP		PeM		MaP	
SaM	Mood AAA	SiM	Mood EIO	MiS	Mood AII
SaP		SoP		SiP	

To read the mood of a syllogism simply read the three propositional types in the conventional order: major premise, minor premise, and conclusion. Since there are three propositions in a syllogism and each of them may be any one of the four types of proposition, there are sixty-four possible syllogistic moods, though again they are not all valid.

The position of the middle term determines the *figure* of a syllogism. Since the middle term must occur once in each of the two premises in order to have a syllogism at all, and since each of the two premises has two possible positions for the middle term, there are four possible middle term patterns or figures. They are conventionally identified as follows:

Figure I	M — P S — M S — P	Figure III	M — P M — S S — P
Figure II	P — M S — M S — M P	Figure IV	P — M M — S S — P

If you will notice the direction taken by the change in middle term pattern, you may be able to remember the figures more easily. If we now multiply the number of possible moods by the number of figures, we see that there are 256 possible syllogistic forms, although, again, most of these are invalid.

20–3   SYLLOGISTIC AXIOMS AND FALLACIES

As soon as we have formulated a given syllogism and determined its structure, we are ready to test its validity. But in order to do this we must know which syllogistic structures are valid and which are not, and in order to know *this* we must possess some sort of evaluation technique. There are a number of techniques for determining the validity of syllogisms; of these we shall here utilize two.

The first and perhaps most basic evaluation technique is the axiomatic one. It consists simply in recognizing a number of rules or axioms which must be obeyed by valid syllogisms and then seeing whether a particular syllogism conforms to them. If the syllogism under consideration violates one or more of the axioms it is invalid; if it does not violate any of them it is valid. These rules are here regarded as axioms in the sense that while it may be possible to demonstrate them on the basis of other assumptions it is not necessary to do so, for their truth can be grasped intuitively. The number of axioms or basic rules varies somewhat from one logician to another, but some of these rules are unnecessary since any syllogism which violates one of them also violates one of the other rules. The minimum number of necessary rules we shall use is conveniently the same as the number of fingers on your hand. Axiom 1 concerns the *number* of terms, axioms 2 and 3 the *quantity* or *distribution* of the terms, and axioms 4 and 5 the *quality* of the propositions.

Axiom 1: There must be exactly three unambiguous terms. This first rule might be considered merely a part of the definition of any syllogism, valid or invalid. But the presence, usually hidden and due to an ambiguity, of more than three terms is so common in purportive syllogisms that it seems helpful to consider it as a rule of validity. Consider the following argument: "Since a mark is a visible sign and the German monetary unit is a mark, the German monetary unit is a visible sign." Each of these propositions is true, yet the conclusion does not follow from the premises. Why? Because the middle term, "mark," is ambiguous and hence really two terms instead of one, thus giving the syllogism four terms instead of three. The minor term ("German monetary unit") is identified with one of these concepts while the major term ("visible sign") is identified with the other one. Hence there is no real mediation between the two concepts in the conclusion, and no basis for inferring the conclusion from the premises. This double middle term and consequent lack of mediation can be manifested diagrammatically thus:

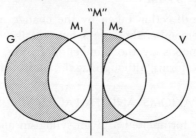

Since G and V are related to different meanings of the supposed middle term, they are actually related to two different terms. Hence there is no bridge or mediation between them, and consequently no valid inference. It is possible, of course, for this first axiom to be violated blatantly by a syllogism which has four, or even more, obviously different terms. But such argumentation is usually so fallacious that it carries no plausibility and hence is seldom encountered. But arguments whose middle terms carefully conceal ambiguities are plausible and therefore fairly frequent.

Some syllogisms which apparently contain more than three terms may, however, be translated into syllogisms containing only three terms by obverting one or more of the propositions. Consider the following syllogism: "All of his friends are unpleasant, because they are all stingy and no stingy people are pleasant." This syllogism has four terms as it stands; but if we obvert the last proposition we get "All stingy people are unpleasant," thus eliminating the extra term and leaving the syllogism with exactly three terms.

Syllogisms which violate this first axiom are said to commit *the fallacy of four (or more) terms*, or, when the presence of the fourth term is due to an ambiguity in the middle term, *the fallacy of ambiguous middle*.

Axiom 2: <u>*The middle term must be distributed (universal) at least once.*</u>
Consider the following argument: "All men are monkeys, because all men are animals and all monkeys are animals." This syllogism is obviously invalid, but exactly why is it invalid? As soon as it is formulated, we see that the middle term, "animals," is undistributed or particular in both its occurrences:

$$\underline{\begin{array}{l} \text{MaA} \\ \text{Men a A} \end{array}}$$
$$\text{Men a M}$$

Since this so, the animals referred to in each of the premises are only part, and not all, of the animals that there are. And since *this* is so, then the parts of the class "animal" designated in the two premises may be (and of course actually are) two *different* parts. But this amounts to having two different middle terms—"animal–1 and "animal–2"—so this syllogism could be considered as violating axiom 1 and therefore committing the fallacy of four terms. Diagrams may help make this clear:

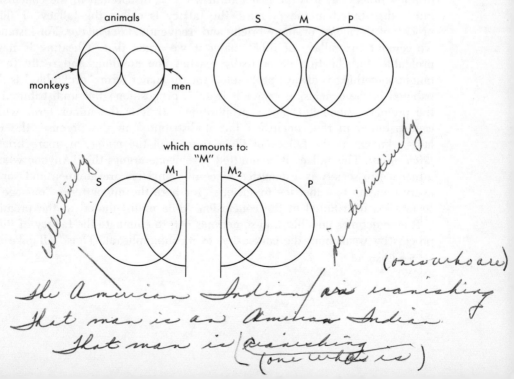

which amounts to:
"M"

the American Indian are vanishing
that man is an American Indian.
that man is vanishing
(one who is)
(ones who are)

Unless either the major or minor term is related to the *whole* of the middle term, there is no way of knowing whether they are really related to the same thing and hence really related to each other, for if each is related only to a part of the middle term these parts may always be different ones and thus in effect two different terms. We have already seen that universality is the heart and core of reasoning and that without it arguments become either mere tautologies or else blatant *non sequiturs*,[2] and the present axiom is additional proof of that fact. Hence the basis of mediation, the middle term, must always be taken in its full universality in at least one of its occurrences. It may be distributed or universal in both of its occurrences or in only one of them, but on no account may it be distributed in neither of them.

A syllogism which violates axiom 2 is said to commit *the fallacy of undistributed middle*. If you will now look back at the argument with which we began this chapter, you will see that it is twice guilty of this fallacy of undistributed middle for it consists of two syllogisms and in neither of them is the middle term distributed.

Axiom 3:   If a term is distributed in the conclusion, it must also be distributed in the premise. We have already met this rule in other forms when we saw, in studying the relations among propositions, that we cannot pass from a particular to a universal proposition on the square of opposition nor obtain by obversion or conversion a proposition with a term greater in universality or distribution than the same term in the original proposition. And in any event the truth of the rule should be sufficiently obvious: you cannot get "all" from merely "some"; you can't make a silk purse out of a sow's ear.

Any syllogism which violates this third axiom is said to commit *the fallacy of illicit process*. If it is the major term which is distributed in the conclusion but undistributed in the premise, the fallacy is called the fallacy of illicit process of the *major*, or, more briefly and frequently, *illicit major*. For instance, we commit the fallacy of illicit major if we argue that "Cheating is never profitable, for cheating never really teaches you anything and really to be taught something is always profitable," for the major term, "profitable," is distributed in the conclusion (since it is an E proposition) but undistributed in the premise (since it is an A proposition). If it is the minor term which is distributed in the conclusion but undistributed in the premise, the fallacy is known as the fallacy of illicit process of the *minor*, or, more briefly, *illicit minor.* This fallacy is committed if someone argues that "Anyone who is a menace to society is a gangster, since all gangsters are gunmen and surely every gunman is a menace to society," for here the minor term, "menace to society," is distributed in the conclusion while undistributed in the premise.

It is sometimes possible, and sometimes not, to eliminate the fallacy of illicit process by weakening the conclusion to its subimplicant. Thus "All pike are

[2] See Chap. 18.

meaty, all meaty things are succulent, hence all succulent things are pike," a syllogism guilty of illicit minor, may be made valid by weakening the conclusion to its subimplicant proposition, "*Some* succulent things are pike." But note that the resulting conclusion is not equivalent to the original one.

Axiom 4: At least one premise must be affirmative. Consider the following argument: "Boosters are always constructive, for boosters are never over-critical, and over-critical people are never constructive." This argument commits *the fallacy of two negative premises*. But exactly why is this a fallacy? Examine the following diagram:

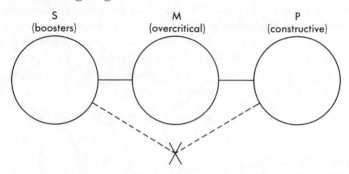

S
(boosters)
M
(overcritical)
P
(constructive)

Negative propositions always separate their terms from each other, and by separating S from M and also P from M, we are left with no basis for relating S and P. Since the middle term is linked with neither of the other terms, it cannot serve to link them to each other. In Chapters 12–14 on the relations among propositions we saw that we can infer nothing about a second proposition unless we have definite information about the truth or falsity of the first one. The present situation is parallel; unless we have knowledge of a positive relation between M and either S or P we cannot conclude anything about the relation of S and P. And both rules are but particular instances of the more general truth that knowledge comes only from knowledge, not from ignorance.

In some cases a syllogism guilty of the fallacy of two negative premises may be corrected by obverting one or both of the premises so as to make them affirmative. Thus in the example just given we may obvert the minor premise to "Boosters are always other than over-critical," thus making this premise affirmative. But notice that we now have four terms—"over-critical" and "other than over-critical." Following the procedure mentioned in connection with axiom 1, we may also try to eliminate this fourth term by obverting. This could be attempted with either premise, but since we have just succeeded in curing the minor premise let us try it with the major. In order to get the term "over-critical" into the predicate position where we can by obversion identify it with the term "other than over-critical" in the minor premise, we must first convert the major: "Constructive people are never over-critical"→"All constructive people are other than over-critical." This done we have avoided the fallacy of four terms as well as the fallacy of two negative premises. Yet we don't seem really to have cured the syllogism, for notice that after all this work our syllogism now commits the fallacy of undistributed middle. And you will see that any other attempt to doctor it will only produce some other disease. In other cases, however, the obversion of one of the premises so as to make it affirmative will yield a valid syllogism. Thus the argument that "Elephants never sneeze because they never use pepper and no one on a pepper-free diet ever sneezes" has two negative premises, but if we obvert the minor premise we get the following valid syllogism: "No one on a pepper-free diet ever sneezes. All elephants are on a pepper-free diet, hence elephants never sneeze." And observe also that our obversion of the minor premise has cured this syllogism not only of two negative premises but also of having four terms.

   Axiom 5: <u>*If a premise is negative the conclusion must be negative, and vice versa.*</u> Inspect the following diagrams:

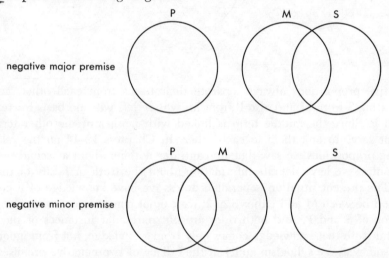

If either premise is negative, then either S or P must be separated from M. And if either S or P is separated from M, the only ground of mediation, then that term must also be separated from the other term. In short, since M is the only way of relating S and P, the separation of either S or P from M (a negative premise) must mean their separation from each other (a negative conclusion). Furthermore, the same diagrams show us that the separation of S from P requires that one or the other of these terms be separated from M—that is, that a negative conclusion requires a negative premise.

   To argue that "All stalwarts are patriots, because no stalwarts are martyrs and all martyrs are patriots," for instance, is to commit *the fallacy of affirmative conclusion with a negative premise*—and the same is true of the first example considered above under axiom 4. The correlative *fallacy of negative conclusion* with affirmative premises is committed by the syllogism that "No stalwarts are patriots, since all stalwarts are martyrs and all martyrs are patriots." (Notice that this second syllogism also commits the fallacy of illicit major.) Here again, as with axioms 1 and 4, it is possible to eliminate the offending proposition by altering its quality through obversion; but as before the resulting syllogism may commit some other fallacy.

These five rules or axioms are sufficient for the determination of the validity of any syllogism. There are also three other rules with their corresponding fallacies which are frequently referred to by logicians, although they are extra and needless intellectual baggage since any syllogism which violates any of them will also violate one or more of the five axioms. The three corollary rules are as follows:

Corollary 1:   At least one of the premises must be universal. The corresponding fallacy is known as *the fallacy of two particular premises.* To see that this rule is unnecessary, we have only to prove it on the basis of the five axioms. A convenient way of doing this is to use the indirect method of proof, or *reductio ad absurdum,* a method especially useful in proving relatively basic or fundamental propositions. We know from the square of opposition that the contradictory of a false proposition must be true. Hence to prove the truth of any proposition we need only prove that its contradictory is false by showing that it contradicts either itself or some proposition known to be true.

Using this method to demonstrate corollary 1, we begin by assuming that it is false, or, what is the same thing, that its contradictory—that *both* premises are *particular*—is true. Now if this be so then one of these premises must be an I (for at least one must be affirmative—axiom 4) and the other must be an O to distribute M (axiom 2). And the conclusion must be negative (axiom 5) and therefore distribute P. Thus P, as well as M, must be distributed in the premise (axiom 3). But this is impossible because there is only one distributing position in the premises—the predicate of O. Hence either axiom 2 or axiom 3 is violated; that is, we have either undistributed middle or illicit major. Consequently any syllogism with both premises particular is invalid; at least one of the premises of every valid syllogism must be universal, and corollary 1 is established.

Corollary 2:   If a premise is particular the conclusion must be particular. The corresponding fallacy is known as *the fallacy of universal conclusion with a particular premise.* The truth of this corollary may be seen immediately and intuitively, for getting a universal conclusion from a particular premise amounts to getting "all" from "some." However, this corollary may also be demonstrated indirectly as follows: Assume a universal conclusion with at least one particular premise. If the conclusion is an E proposition then S and P, as well as M, must be distributed in the premises (axiom 3). But this is impossible since one of the

310 Logic as a Human Instrument

premises must be affirmative (axiom 4), and with one of them particular there are only two distributing positions. Hence the conclusion must be an A proposition. And this means that the minor premise must also be an A to avoid illicit minor (axiom 3), since both premises must be affirmative (axiom 5) and I has no distributing position. But then the major premise must be an I proposition (since both premises must be affirmative and one is assumed to be particular). This, however, leaves M undistributed in both occurrences, and we have the fallacy of undistributed middle. Consequently we cannot have a universal conclusion with a particular premise, and corollary 2 is established.

However, we may validly have a particular conclusion with both premises universal—for we can get some from all. The syllogistic moods AAI and AEO are examples of these so-called "weakened" and "strengthened" syllogisms. A syllogism is said to be *weakened* when the conclusion is weaker than (the subimplicant of) one that might be obtained from the same premises. AAI and EAO in Figure I are examples of valid weakened syllogisms. And a syllogism is said to be *strengthened* when one of the premises is stronger than (the superimplicant of) one that might be used to get the same conclusion. AAI and EAO in Figure III are examples of strengthened syllogisms.

Corollary 3: Any syllogism with a particular major premise and a negative minor premise is invalid. The corresponding fallacy is known as *the fallacy of particular major with negative minor*. This corollary can be established indirectly by the same sort of procedure used to establish corollaries 1 and 2. The student should demonstrate corollary 3 for himself, in order to familiarize himself with the axioms and also to gain practice in indirect proof.

These three corollaries may be useful if you seem to remember them easily, but since they are unnecessary it is probably not worth while spending much time in memorizing them. The same is true of certain special rules for each of the four figures, but these are included among the exercises at the end of this chapter for the student's information and as practice in using the axioms and indirect argument.

EXERCISES

Using the indirect method of argument described and exemplified on pp. 309–310, prove the following special rules for the four figures of the syllogism.

1. Figure I:
   (1) The minor premise must be affirmative.
   (2) The major premise must be universal.
2. Figure II:
   (1) One premise must be negative.
   (2) The major premise must be universal.
3. Figure III:
   (1) The minor premise must be affirmative.
   (2) The conclusion must be particular.

4. Figure IV:*
   (1) If the major premise is affirmative, the minor must be universal.
   (2) If either premise is negative, the major must be universal.
   (3) If the minor premise is affirmative, the conclusion must be particular.

(*Note that the contradictory of a conditional proposition, "If p then q," is "p and not q," *not* "If p then not q." See pp. 335–337 below.)

CHAPTER 21

SYLLOGISMS IN USE

Once we have logically formulated our syllogisms and are in possession of the five axioms, we are ready to test the validity of these syllogisms. Let us first see which syllogistic forms are valid and then proceed to the evaluation of particular linguistic arguments.

21–1 DETERMINATION OF VALID SYLLOGISTIC FORMS

We have seen that there are 256 possible syllogistic structures, since there are four different types of proposition (A, E, I, and O) possible for the major premise, four for the minor, four for the conclusion, and four different figures; and since $4^4 = 256$. Most of these possible forms are invalid, and we can proceed most easily to tell which are valid and which are not by considering only the premises without regard to either the conclusion or the figure. Since there are four possible major and four possible minor premises, there are sixteen possible combinations of premises:

AA	EA	IA	OA
AE	~~EE~~ Ax. 4	~~IE~~ Cor. 3	~~OE~~ Ax. 4
AI	EI	~~II~~ Cor. 1	~~OI~~ Cor. 1
AO	~~EO~~ Ax. 4	~~IO~~ Cor. 1	~~OO~~ Ax. 4 & Cor. 1

Of these sixteen possible sets of premises, eight are invalid with any conclusion and in any figure because they violate the axioms and/or corollaries indicated. The remaining eight sets of premises are valid with some conclusion or other and some figure or other. Since there are four possible conclusions and four possible figures for each of the eight sets of premises, we have reduced our number of possibly valid syllogistic forms to 128.

But this number is still far greater than the number of valid forms. If we were to evaluate all of the 128 possibly valid forms by our axioms, or with the aid of the special rules for each of the four figures (listed among the exercises at the end of Chapter 20), we would come out with the following twenty-four valid syllogistic forms, six in each of the four figures:

Figure

I	II	III	IV
AAA ⟩	AEE ⟩	AAI° ⟩	AEE ⟩
AAI°⟨	AEO°⟨	AII	AEO°⟨
AII	AOO	EAO° ⟩	EAO° ⟩
EAE ⟩	EAE ⟩	EIO ⟩	EIO ⟨
EAO°⟨	EAO°⟨	IAI ⟨	AAI° ⟩
EIO	EIO	OAO ⟨	IAI ⟨

The forms marked "°" are weakened or strengthened moods. Each of the weakened moods is immediately derivable from the superimplicant mood which points to it by an arrow. And each of the strengthened moods immediately implies the subimplicant mood to which it points by an arrow. Thus nine of the twenty-four forms are immediately related on the square of opposition to others of them and in this sense are not independent forms. Hence we might say that we have fifteen valid syllogistic forms plus the square of opposition with which to obtain nine others. Yet these weakened and strengthened moods can be counted as distinct forms, making twenty-four valid forms in all.

These considerations are more esthetic than practical in value, however, since we do not really need to know which syllogistic forms are valid in order to test the validity of concrete linguistic syllogisms. All we need to know is the axioms and how to formulate the syllogisms logically. Let us now apply this knowledge to the evaluation of particular syllogisms.

21–2 TESTING SYLLOGISMS BY THE AXIOMS

Our procedure consists simply of two steps: (1) formulate the syllogism symbolically (this step of course consists in turn of the steps listed on p. 301 and (2) test the resulting symbolic structure by the axioms (the corollaries may be used or not, as you please). These rules and their corresponding fallacies are:

Rules	Fallacies
Axiom 1: Exactly three unambiguous terms.	Ambiguous middle, or four (or more) terms.
Axiom 2: Middle term distributed at least once.	Undistributed middle.
Axiom 3: Terms distributed in the conclusion must be distributed in the premise.	Illicit major, or illicit minor.
Axiom 4: At least one premise affirmative.	Two negative premises.
Axiom 5: A negative premise requires a negative conclusion, and vice versa.	Affirmative conclusion with negative premise, and vice versa.

Rules	Fallacies
Corollary 1: At least one premise universal.	Two particular premises.
Corollary 2: A particular premise requires a particular conclusion.	Universal conclusion with a particular premise.
Corollary 3: No conclusion from a particular major and negative minor.	Particular major with negative minor.

Any syllogism which violates one or more of these axioms (or corollaries) is thereby invalid, and any which conforms to all of the axioms (and corollaries) is thereby valid. Let us carry out this evaluation procedure in a concrete case.

A student once advanced the following argument in a philosophy paper: "Characteristic of space and time is that they are both finite. If mind is outside space and time, finitude cannot be attributed to it. Mind, therefore, must be infinite and eternal." Is this argument valid? Let us apply our techniques and see.

$$
\begin{array}{ll}
\text{S}\overline{\text{T}}\text{aF} \quad \text{S}\overline{\text{T}}\text{aF} \\
\underline{\text{MeST}\leftrightarrow\text{Ma}\overline{\text{ST}}} \\
\underline{\text{MeF}\leftrightarrow\text{FeM}} \\
\text{MeF}\leftrightarrow\text{Ma}\overline{\text{F}}
\end{array}
$$

	ST		a	F
Characteristic of (space and time) is that they are both (finite.)				
	M	a	ST	F e
If (mind) is (outside space and time,) (finitude) cannot be attributed to (it.)				
	M	M	a	F̄
(Mind,) therefore, must be (infinite) and eternal.				

Invalid; fallacy of illicit major (violation of axiom 3)

Notice that the conclusion is asserted in two equivalent ways. Notice also that the syllogism as it is presented has four terms ("space and time" and "outside space and time"), or even five terms ("finite" and "infinite"), and that since each of these terms is so obviously the contradictory of one of the others we have reduced it to the other by obverting the proposition in which it occurs so as to produce a syllogism with exactly three terms. Observe finally that the term "eternal" in the conclusion is here ignored because it does not occur in the premises; if we wished to evaluate the proposition that "mind is eternal" as a conclusion of this argument, we would have to explicate another syllogism from this one in which there occurred the premise (here tacit) that "whatever is infinite is eternal."

21–3   TESTING SYLLOGISMS BY VENN DIAGRAMS[1]

The Venn diagrams which we used in the chapters on propositions and their interrelations can also be used, in a slightly modified form, to provide a simple graphic test of the validity of syllogisms, once they have been formulated logically. Since a syllogism contains three terms instead of just two, our syllogistic Venn diagram must consist of three circles, interrelated, as before, to

[1] Since Venn diagrams are metaphorical rather than literal representations of syllogisms, the Venn diagram test is less basic than the axiomatic one.

indicate the possible relations among the three terms. The principle governing the Venn diagram test is extremely simple. Since a valid syllogism is one in which the conclusion necessarily and inevitably follows from the premises, a diagram or map of the premises of a valid syllogism will therefore include the diagram or map of the conclusion. And since an invalid syllogism is one in which the conclusion does not necessarily or invariably follow from the premises, a diagram of the premises of an invalid syllogism will not include the diagram of the conclusion (though it may not exclude it either). Hence to test a syllogism by Venn diagrams we simply plot the two premises on the three-circle diagram and then see if the diagram of the conclusion appears there. If it does the syllogism is valid; if it does not the syllogism is invalid.

Let us first illustrate this test with easy examples. We know (from p. 313 and by the axioms) that the syllogism AAA in Figure I is valid. Let us use the Venn diagram test on it:

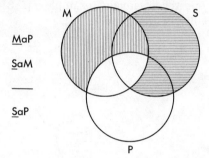

Since MaP means that all of the M's are in P, that there are no M's which are not in P, we plot it by crossing out the $M\overline{P}$ area. In the same fashion we plot SaM by crossing out the $S\overline{M}$ area. Having done this we see the map of the conclusion appear in the diagram: since the $S\overline{P}$ area is automatically crossed out, the conclusion, SaP, follows validly from the premises.

When a syllogism contains a particular premise it is helpful to *plot the universal premise first*. The reason for this can be seen by testing the syllogism

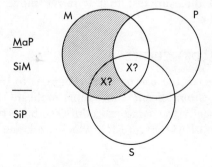

AII, Figure I, which we also know to be valid by the axioms and from the list on p. 313. (See the diagram on p. 315.)

If we try to map the particular premise first, we discover the X may go in either of two possible areas, SMP̄ or SMP; and so we don't know from that proposition alone which of these two areas to put the X in. As soon as we plot the universal premise, however, we see that the SMP̄ area is empty and that the X must therefore belong in the other one of the two areas. If we had plotted the universal premise first, it would have been clear immediately that there was only one place for the X to go; hence it is useful always to plot the universal premise first. Having plotted our two premises, we find that we can read the diagram of the conclusion, SiP, for it says that there is at least one thing which is both S and P and our inspection of the diagram shows us just such an X. Hence the syllogism is valid.

Invalid syllogisms show up on Venn diagrams just as well as valid ones, as is borne out by testing our recent invalid example (p. 314) which argued for the infinity and eternality of the mind:

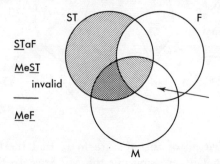

If the conclusion, MeF, followed validly from the premises, its diagram, the emptiness of the MF area, would appear as soon as the premises were plotted. But since it does not, since part of the MF area is not empty, the syllogism is invalid. Notice, however, that the Venn diagram test does not show that the reason this syllogism is invalid is that it commits the fallacy of illicit major. It is a defect of the Venn diagram test that it never shows which particular fallacy has been committed.

21–4 DESIGNATIONAL DIFFICULTIES

One final caution concerns the use of Venn diagrams to test weakened and strengthened (that is, subimplicant and superimplicant) syllogisms. For example, if we follow exactly the same procedure we have been using to test the strengthened syllogism EAO, Figure III, which we know by the axioms to be valid,

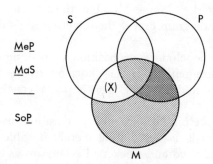

MeP

MaS

———

SoP

it would seem as though the conclusion does not appear and that the syllogism is therefore invalid, for the conclusion, SoP, says that there is at least one thing which is an S and not a P but no such X appears on the diagram. This difficulty is only apparent, however, for if the term "M" designates, then there must be some M's somewhere; and if, as the two premises say, they are not in the other three areas, they must be in the SMP̄ area—as is shown by the X in parentheses. But this plots the conclusion, SoP, so the syllogism is valid.

However, if M does not designate in either occurrence, if there are no M's at all, this syllogism is invalid since then the S's may or may not be P's:

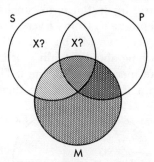

But if S also is a non-designating term, if there are no S's either, then the syllogism is valid *provided that S be taken in a non-designating sense:*

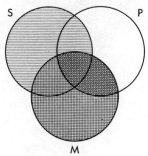

Here it follows validly that "Some S's (but there aren't any) are-not P's," since it's true from this diagram that if there were any S's they would have to be other than P.

Thus it is invalid to conclude a proposition with designating terms if the middle term fails to designate in either of its occurrences, though premises with a non-designating middle term may imply a conclusion with a *non-designating* term.

Some logicians, interpreting all particular propositions as designating actual existents and all universals as designating merely possible ones or else none at all,[2] reject the strengthened and weakened syllogisms as invalid unless there is explicitly added as a premise an existence proposition asserting the actual existence of members of the relevant universal class or classes. But this procedure does not seem justified since everyday usage indicates that merely possible designation and designational failure are not peculiarities of universal propositions alone.[3] But it is true, as we have just seen, that any syllogism is invalid which shifts from non-designation to designation, and it is also true that any syllogism is invalid which shifts from merely possible to actual designation, for these two situations consist in saying more in the conclusion than we are given in the premises, and we know that this is always invalid.

Furthermore, this is true with respect to the major and minor terms as well as the middle term. If we try, for instance, to conclude that "There are some (actual) Martians which reproduce" from "Every (possible) Martian is alive and all living things reproduce," we will be guilty of an invalid inference, for we will be concluding something about actually existing Martians when we are only given information about merely possible ones. This situation can be made apparent in a Venn diagram if we restrict the diagram to actual existents:

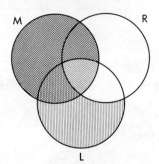

The conclusion, "Some (actual) M's are R's," does not appear: there is no actual X, and can be none, which is both an M and an R because there are no

[2] See p. 140.
[3] See p. 140.

actual M's. Notice, however, that the shift in designation, when explicated, amounts to the presence of four terms ("possible Martians" and "actual Martians"), and this of course violates one of the axioms anyway. Exactly the same situation is true when the shift is from non-designation to designation. It is invalid, for instance, to argue that "The North American colonies declared their independence, for they will be subject to oppression and all colonies subject to oppression have declared their independence," for the term "North American colonies" designates in the conclusion but fails to do so in the premise (because of the future tense). But note again that this shift in designation may be interpreted as the fallacy of four terms: "colonies which *will be* subject to oppression" and "colonies which *have been* subject to oppression."

To summarize: *It is invalid to designate more in the conclusion than is designated in the premises.*

Summary of the Syllogism. The syllogism is a form of deductive argument which consists of three propositions and three terms, each term occurring twice. The predicate of the conclusion is the major term, the subject of the conclusion is the minor term, and the third term, which occurs in each of the premises, is the middle term. The premise which contains the major term is the major premise, and the one containing the minor term is the minor premise. The mood of a syllogism is its propositional type structure in the conventional order of major premise, minor premise, and conclusion—e.g., the mood AAA. The figure of a syllogism is the positional pattern of the middle term: Figure I is M–P S–M; Figure II, P–M S–M; Figure III, M–P M–S; and Figure IV, P–M M–S. In order to evaluate a syllogism we first formulate it logically, using the procedure for the logical formulation of propositions plus the detection of the conclusion and premises, and then test it by some technique such as the axiomatic or Venn diagram techniques. For example, to evaluate an argument such as the following one presented by a student in a philosophy paper, we proceed as follows:

The idea of human nature is involved in developing an ethical theory in a
$$H^1$$

H^1aU manner that can be shown by a sort of syllogism. That is, (the ultimate
　　　　　　　　　　a　　　　　　　U　　　　　　　　　　　E

EaU nature of man) is (universal,) but (an acceptable ethical theory) would
　　　　　　　　　　a　　　　　　　U　　　　　　　　E　　　　　　　　a

EaH^2 also have to be (universal;) therefore, (an ethical theory) would have (to
　　　　　　　　　　H^2

take human nature into account.)

Invalid; undistributed middle and four terms

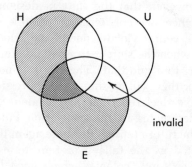

Notice that the Venn diagram technique cannot be used to detect the fallacy of more than three terms (or the *nature* of any other fallacy), and that its use in the above example requires the neglect of the fourth term—although we shall see later that a four-term Venn diagram is possible and can sometimes be useful.

In everyday life, however, the syllogism is often met in various disguised forms. Some of these are almost immediately recognizable as syllogisms, but others are more complicated and disguised. Armed with our knowledge of syllogistic structure and our techniques for testing syllogisms, let us now turn to these variations on the syllogism.

EXERCISES

Formulate and test, using the axioms and/or Venn diagrams, each of the following syllogisms:

1. "Substance is indivisible and God, being one, is likewise indivisible. So God is in all things and all things are in God." (student essay)
2. At least some syllogisms are valid, for some arguments involving four terms are valid and all arguments that involve four terms are syllogisms.
3. "All hopeless people are pessimists, for we know that all pessimists are miserable and that all hopeless people are also miserable.
4. No gasoline stations are exempt from the chain-store tax, and hence no gas stations are profitable, since all stores exempt from the chain-store tax are profitable.
5. No hard-working people are farmers, because all wealthy people are hard-working and no farmers are wealthy.
6. All doctrines of relativity are man-made, for they are printed in books, and everything printed in a book is a human creation.
7. Some psychologists are religious, since some scientists are religious and all psychologists are scientists.
8. Successful bluffing and the passing of examinations both require a cool head, so the latter may be regarded as an example of the former.

9. Agreeable companions do not ask questions or make criticisms. Hence animals are agreeable companions, for they do neither.

10. Rational beings are accountable for their actions; brutes, not being rational, are therefore exempt from responsibility.

11. He eats least who is least hungry. He is least hungry who eats most. Hence, he who eats most eats least.

12. Unchaperoned parties are avoided by nice girls; Spring Day parties will, however, be chaperoned. Consequently, nice girls will not avoid them.

13. Effeminate students are never athletes, for all athletes are men of repute among the students, and no men of repute among the students are effeminate.

14. Everybody knows that all campaign speeches are interpretations of a political platform. Therefore some propaganda speeches are campaign speeches, since interpretations of political platforms are often propagandistic.

15. All the good die young. But you aren't good, so you're safe.

16. Not all metaphysicians are dogmatists, because some metaphysicians love the truth, and clearly no lover of truth is a dogmatist.

17. "A body is that which has three dimensions. But the sacred scripture attributes three dimensions to God, for it says in *Job* XI, 8: 'he is higher than heaven . . . , deeper than Hell . . . . longer than the earth and broader than the sea.' Therefore God is a body." (Thos. Aquinas, *Summ. Theol.*, Q. 3, Art. 1, Obj. 1)

18. "In connection with my syllogism I find implicit in Sartre's article: (The Communist Party is the party of the working class. I am for the working class. Hence I accept the politics of the Communist Party.) I must add that another, more essential syllogism, is involved of which the first proposition is 'The Communist Party is the party of the left***'" (from an article in the *New York Times* Sunday Magazine)

19. "This Good would not exist in human history. Nor could it be thought, since thought is the substance of human history." (student essay)

20. The belief of the natives of Borneo that only he is brave who has taken the head of an enemy is a false belief. Hence, since none of your enemies has lost his head through your endeavors, you are a brave man.

21. "Universal love does not generate discontent, therefore religion, which is the embodiment and institutionalization of this principle, would not generate discontent." (student essay)

22. Since some statesmen are politicians and most politicians are dishonest, it must be true that at least some statesmen are dishonest.

23. Only skilled workers know how to operate a linotype machine, but a sizable proportion of the *New York Times* staff does not know how to do so. Therefore it stands to reason that at least a few of the *New York Times* staff members are not skilled workers.

24. All metals, it is true, are conductors of electricity. But then the atmosphere is not a metal and therefore cannot be a conductor of electricity.

CHAPTER 22

SYLLOGISTIC VARIATIONS:
ENTHYMEMES AND SORITES

22-1 THE ENTHYMEME

Perhaps the most frequent syllogistic variation met in everyday life consists in the suppression of one of the propositions of a syllogism. "Blessed are the merciful, for they shall obtain mercy" may not initially appear to be a syllogism, since only two propositions have been expressed. Yet it takes but little reflection to see that there is actually a third proposition tacitly present here: "Blessed are the merciful, for they shall obtain mercy (and all who obtain mercy are blessed)." Such truncated syllogisms are known as *enthymemes* (from the Greek words *en*, "in," and *thymos*, "mind" or "spirit").[1]

The discovery and formulation of an enthymeme's suppressed proposition is usually simple, because we know that in every syllogism there are exactly three terms (at least apparently) and that each term occurs twice. Hence to find the missing proposition we need only form a proposition which contains those two terms each of which has so far occurred only once. In addition, the proposition thus formed should be one which will make a valid syllogism, though this is not always possible. Thus in our above example, "Blessed (B) are the merciful (M), for they (M) shall obtain mercy (O)," the tacit proposition must combine the terms B and O—since they have so far occurred only once—in such a way as to make the syllogism valid, if possible. Since the conclusion is an A proposition the tacit proposition must also be an A, and since O, the middle term, is so far undistributed, it must be the subject of this A proposition. We see that our explicated enthymeme looks like the diagram on p. 323. Notice that parentheses are used to indicate that the proposition so enclosed

[1] Aristotle, the originator of the term, seems to have employed it in a somewhat different sense. See the *Analytica Posteriora*, 71a, 8–10. Nevertheless, the use of the term "enthymeme" to signify an abridged syllogism goes back to the very earliest commentators on Aristotle. For an excellent brief discussion of the meaning of the term and its history, see H. W. B. Joseph, *An Introduction to Logic*, Oxford, 1916, p. 350, n. 1.

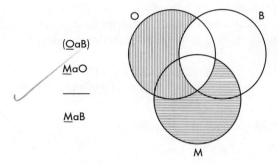

is tacit, and observe also that the conclusion, "Blessed are the merciful," means "All merciful people are blessed."

Sometimes it is impossible to supply any tacit proposition which will make the enthymeme into a valid syllogism. Consider the following enthymeme: "All high-type citizens are liberals, because all liberals are interested in the welfare of their country." The term "liberals" (L) has occurred twice, but the terms "high-type citizens" (H) and "interested in the welfare of their country" (I) have so far occurred only once. Hence the tacit proposition must combine these two terms, H and I. And since the conclusion is affirmative and universal, this tacit proposition must also be an A proposition. But which of the two terms is the subject and which the predicate? Let us try both possibilities in order to make a valid syllogism if possible:

	LaI		LaI	
Invalid;				Invalid;
undistributed	(HaI)	(IaH)		illicit
middle	———	———		minor
	HaL		HaL	

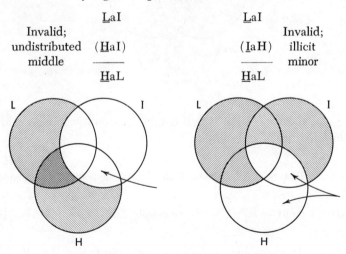

As soon as we have done this, we see that it is impossible to supply a tacit proposition which will make this particular enthymeme valid.

The enthymematic proposition may be any one of the three in the syllogism. When it is the major premise which is tacit, the argument is called a *first order* enthymeme. The following is an example from a student's essay:

$$\text{T}^1 \qquad \text{a} \qquad \text{B} \qquad\qquad \text{T}^2 \quad \text{a} \qquad\qquad \text{R}$$
(ḆaR)   (Whatever we think) (must be,) so that (thinking) is therefore (reality.)

Ṯ¹aB   B   a   R

T²aR   [Since (that which must be) is (reality.)]

Invalid; four terms

When it is the minor premise which is implicit, the enthymeme is said to be of the *second order,* like the following:

$$\text{P} \quad \text{a} \qquad \text{V} \qquad\qquad\qquad\qquad \text{H}$$
H̱aV   Every(one) (desires virtue,) because (whoever desires happiness)

(P̱aH)   a   V   P   a   H

P̱aV   (desires virtue.) [and all (people) (desire happiness.)]

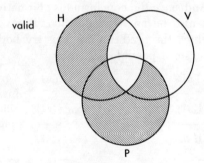

valid

And when it is the conclusion which is tacit, the enthymeme is said to be of the *third order.* Here is an example:[2]

$$\qquad\qquad\qquad\qquad\qquad\qquad\text{I} \qquad\qquad\qquad\qquad\text{a} \quad \text{H}$$
I̱aH   I̱aH   PARRIS: All (innocent and Christian people) are (happy for the

$$\qquad\qquad\qquad\qquad\qquad\qquad\text{T} \qquad\qquad \text{a} \qquad\qquad \bar{\text{H}}$$
ṮeH̱↔TaH̄   court in Salem!) (These people) are (gloomy for it.) [and hence

$$\qquad\qquad\qquad\qquad\qquad\text{T} \qquad\qquad \text{e} \qquad\qquad\qquad \text{I}$$
(ṮeI̱)   (these people) are not (innocent and Christian.)]

² Arthur Miller, *The Crucible,* Viking, 1953, p. 94.

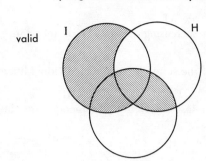

valid

Notice in this example that the minor premise must be obverted in order to avoid having four terms. Third-order enthymemes, where the listener or reader is left to draw his own conclusion, constitute a form of innuendo and are rhetorically very effective, for after all Parris, in this speech, does not actually *say* that "These people are not innocent and Christian"!

Thus the enthymeme does not constitute an independent form of argument, but the frequency of its use makes its understanding very important and, in addition, the search for the tacit premise is excellent intellectual training. In a broader sense of the term most arguments are enthymemes, because almost all arguments entail unexpressed premises or assumptions. And in this broader sense the habit of searching for the tacit assumptions which are the silent determinants of one's thoughts takes on an extremely important aspect; it should be consciously cultivated in all of one's endeavors and certainly throughout the whole of one's study of logic. But let us now turn to another more specific case of the search for tacit propositions in another variation of the syllogism: the sorites.

22–2   THE SORITES

We have seen that the enthymeme is a syllogism with a suppressed proposition. If we put two or more enthymemes together to form one argument, we have a *sorites* (from the Greek word for "chain"). Thus a sorites is an argument consisting of two or more syllogisms each one of which has a suppressed proposition.

Consider the following argument: "Liberals believe in increasing the power of the state. Whoever believes in increasing the power of the state is against individual liberty. And whoever is against individual liberty is a fascist. Hence all liberals are fascists." In order to formulate the missing propositions so as to complete the syllogisms contained in this sorites and thus to evaluate the argument as a whole, let us follow our usual procedure:

    L   a   I

(Liberals) (believe in increasing the power of the state.) (Whoever believes in

    I   a   A   A

increasing the power of the state) is (against individual liberty.) (Whoever is against

                 a   F   L   a   F

individual liberty) is (a fascist.) Hence all (liberals) are (fascists.)

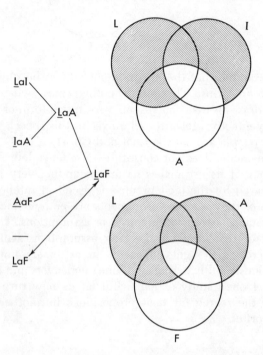

After formulating the four explicit propositions we take any two premises which have a common term and draw from them a conclusion containing the other two terms combined in such a way as to make, if possible, a valid syllogism. Thus LaI and IaA yield LaA. We then continue the same procedure for the other premises, counting the conclusion which we have just drawn as a premise for the final conclusion. Thus the two remaining premises, LaA and AaF, have a term in common and should therefore yield a conclusion combining the other two terms: LaF. We now have two syllogisms—IaA, LaI, hence LaA; and AaF, LaA, hence LaF—and we see by the axioms and by Venn diagrams that they are both valid. And since their final conclusion, LaF, is the same as the conclusion of the original argument, that argument is therefore valid.

If a sorites consists of just two syllogisms so that it has only four terms in all, it is possible to construct a four-term Venn diagram to test it without bothering to analyze it into two distinct syllogisms by explicating the hidden propositions. Thus a four-term Venn diagram for the above sorites would look like this:

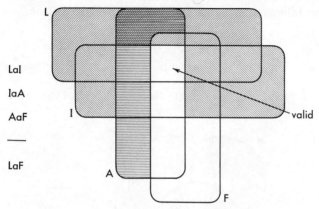

The procedure for plotting the premises is the same as for a three-term diagram: to plot LaI we cross out all of the L area that is outside the I area; to plot IaA we cross out all of the I area that falls outside the A area; and to plot AaF we cross out all of the A region which is outside the F region. When we have done this we see that the diagram of the conclusion, LaF, has automatically appeared, for all of the L region outside of the F area is crossed out. The sorites is therefore valid.[3]

Thus a sorites is a chain of two or more syllogisms in which the conclusion of each one save the last is both tacit and also a premise in the next syllogism. There are two types of sorites according as the first premise contains the subject or the predicate of the final conclusion. A sorites whose first premise contains the subject of the conclusion is known as an *Aristotelian* sorites. It is always of the form: A is B, B is C, C is D, D is E, therefore A is E—where the subject of the conclusion is the subject of the first expressed premise and the predicate of the conclusion is the predicate of the last expressed premise. The Aristotelian sorites is also called the *progressive* sorites because the terms are expressed in a progressive order. Our recent argument about liberals and fascists is an example of an Aristotelian or progressive sorites.

A sorites whose first expressed premise contains the *predicate* of the conclu-

---

[3] A four-term diagram may be used to test and exhibit an ordinary syllogism which commits the fallacy of four terms; if you will try it on the four-term enthymeme analyzed on p. 324 you will see that this is so. In this case, however, there is little point in using the four-term diagram because in order to use it on a regular syllogism you must have already decided that it has four terms, and if you know this you already know that the syllogism is invalid.

sion is called a *Goclenian* (after Goclenius, 1547–1628) or *regressive* sorites, and it is always of the form: A is B, C is A, D is C, E is D, therefore E is B— where the predicate of the conclusion is the predicate of the first expressed premise and the subject of the conclusion is the subject of the last expressed premise. The following is an example of an invalid Goclenian or regressive sorites:

<table>
<tr><td>B</td><td>a</td><td>I</td><td></td><td>F</td><td>a</td><td>B</td><td></td><td></td><td>H</td></tr>
</table>

All (bigots) are (intolerant.) All (fanatics) are (bigots.) Every (one who hates the

<table>
<tr><td></td><td>a</td><td></td><td>F</td><td></td><td>S</td><td>e</td><td>H</td><td></td><td>S</td><td>e</td></tr>
</table>

truth) is (a fanatic.) No (scientist) (hates the truth.) So no (scientist) is

I

(intolerant.)

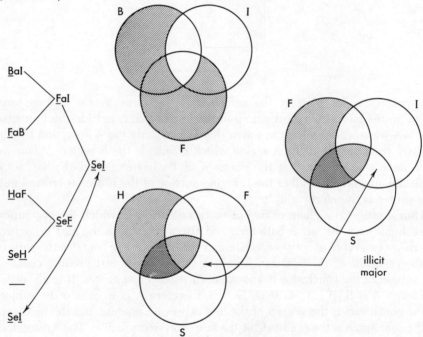

The construction of a single Venn diagram for this argument—a diagram showing all the interrelations of five, or even more, terms—is too complicated and illegible to be worth while, though you might like to prove this to yourself. In this particular case there is a short cut which can be used to show that this sorites is invalid without going through any of the above procedures: since the term "I" is distributed in the conclusion but undistributed in the premise, the sorites as a whole must be fallacious (with the fallacy of illicit major) no matter what the character of the component syllogisms.

Since sorites are simply chains of syllogisms, our techniques for evaluating syllogisms are also sufficient for sorites. However, there are also special or corollary rules for each of the two types of sorites:

Corollaries for the Aristotelian (Progressive) Sorites:

1. Only the *last* premise may be *negative.*
2. Only the *first* premise may be *particular.*

Corollaries for the Goclenian (Regressive) Sorites:

1. Only the *first* premise may be *negative.*
2. Only the *last* premise may be *particular.*

You can easily prove these corollaries for yourself by using the same procedure which we used to prove the syllogistic corollaries on pp. 309–310.

EXERCISES

1. Supply the missing proposition, formulate, and test each of the following enthymemes, naming any fallacies that are committed:
   a. All treaty violations are dangerous to peace, for all things dangerous to peace are potential causes of war.
   b. "Blessed are the peace-makers, for they shall be called children of God."
   c. Those documents can't be genuine, or they would have been referred to by the author's contemporaries.
   d. "The nominalists have always been ecclesiastical reformers, as their views were incompatible with the church of Rome." (student essay)
   e. No fellow travelers are communists, for all fellow travelers are liberals.
   f. Anyone who's absent a lot will surely fail the course, and you've now been absent ten times.

2. Supply the missing propositions, formulate, and test each of the following sorites, naming any fallacies that are committed:
   a. It can be rigorously demonstrated that no socialists are under thirty-five years of age. Thus, no socialists are real Americans; all real Americans are native-born citizens; all native-born citizens are eligible for the presidency; and none eligible for the presidency are under thirty-five years of age.
   b. Sales taxes are a form of robbery; the taxes on cars are sales taxes; and all additions to the price of cars are taxes. Therefore, all additions to the price of cars are a form of robbery.
   c. "Moral law is categorical and universal; that is, independent of anything. Moral law is good and this is a self-evident proposition. Now you say, 'Why must moral law be categorical?' It is quite clear that good exists independent of man. Thus we have established that good is independent of experience in that it is not dependent on man or anything in the material universe. Thus the moral law is not dependent on situations created by man in his material universe. It is immutable. Being categorical, it follows that the immutable moral law cannot be altered by time or space and hence is immortal.

   "It is generally admitted that that which is true is immutable, inalterable, and since the inalterable and immutable have already been proved to be moral, it follows that that which is true is the moral law. From this it follows that that which is not the moral law is not true. Above we demonstrated that the mutable is not moral law. Combining the proposition just mentioned with the the one of this paragraph, namely that that which is not moral is not true, we find that that which is mutable is not true, hence the mutable law is not true law but false law." (student essay)

d. Animals are organisms; vertebrates are animals; mammals are vertebrates; possums are mammals; Pogo is a possum; hence, Pogo is an organism.

e. All flying saucers have ailerons. Anything with ailerons can turn on its longitudinal axis. Anything that can turn on its longitudinal axis possesses esthetic value. Cockroaches never possess esthetic value. Hence you'll never find a cockroach that's also a flying saucer.

CHAPTER 23

COMPOUND PROPOSITIONS
AS SYLLOGISMS

The propositions with which we have dealt so far have been composed merely of terms in a certain relation to each other—e.g., "Trees are plants," "Birds are animals." We must now see that such simple propositions may themselves be combined to produce compound propositions: "Trees are plants and birds are animals." Compound propositions are very common in ordinary thought, speech, and writing. They may be of various degrees of complexity since a compound proposition may in turn become an element in a still more complex proposition, such as "If trees are plants and birds are animals, then trees and birds belong to different biological families." Not only are compound propositions of various degrees of complexity; they are also of various types, since there are different ways of connecting the component propositions—by "and," by "if . . . then," by "since," by "or," etc. Now all these various kinds of compound propositions may either themselves be arguments or else enter into and determine specific kinds of arguments. In this chapter we shall consider compound propositions *as* arguments, and in Chapter 24 we shall consider them *in* arguments.

23–1 THE MAIN TYPES OF COMPOUND PROPOSITIONS

23–1.1 A Scheme for Classifying Compound Propositions

Compound propositions may usefully be classified according to two different principles: the mode of intention and the reality intended. When classified according to the *mode of intention,* compound propositions are either *categorical* or *hypothetical.* A categorical proposition, such as "There are black clouds in the east and it's going to rain," asserts something to be a fact unconditionally, or, as we say, "categorically." Notice that all simple propositions are categorical. A hypothetical proposition such as "If the black clouds are in the east, then it's going to rain" asserts something conditionally, as being dependent upon something else, as being true on the basis of a certain hypothesis. Thus we use categorical propositions when we feel that we are unconditionally sure of our assertions, and we use hypothetical propositions when we are willing to assert the truth of something only on the condition of something else's being true.

When classified according to the nature of *the reality intended,* compound propositions are either *conjunctive* or *implicative.* A conjunctive proposition, like "Roses are red and voilets are blue," intends the mere coexistence of two or more things or facts without finding any causal connection in this togetherness. It just happens to be the case both that violets are blue and that roses are red, but the color of one is not asserted to be the cause or effect of the color of the other. If we should say, however, that "Roses and violets have green leaves because of the chlorophyll they contain," we would be using an implicative proposition, for we would be asserting that there is some causal connection between the realities signified by the two component propositions, between the greenness of the leaves and the chlorophyll they contain. Thus we use conjunctive propositions when the realities which we wish to formulate or communicate merely happen accidentally to coexist, and we use implicative propositions when those realities are causally connected with each other. All the arguments we have studied are, or at least purport to be, implicative compounds; and if the propositions forming any one of these arguments should be joined together into one proposition, that compound proposition would be an implicative one. Conjunctive propositions are never arguments as they stand, but they may sometimes be expanded into arguments where the two component propositions belong to the same syllogism (in case they have a common term) or to different syllogisms if other connecting propositions can be found.

Observe that these two ways of classifying compound propositions overlap:

MODE OF INTENTION

		categorical	hypothetical
REALITY	conjunctive		
INTENDED	implicative		

Thus a given compound proposition may be categorical and conjunctive, categorical and implicative, hypothetical and conjunctive, or hypothetical and implicative.[1] Each of the components of a conjunctive proposition is called a *conjunct.* In implicative propositions the causal component or premise is known as the *antecedent* and the effect component or conclusion the *conse-*

[1] These terms are sometimes used in other senses, and the meanings here intended are sometimes expressed in other terms.

quent. Let us now use this classificatory scheme to get a better understanding of the most common types of compound proposition.

23–1.2   Types of Compound Proposition

A compound proposition whose component propositions are connected by "and" or some equivalent such as "also," "furthermore," "in addition," etc., is called a *conjunctive* proposition. Thus "It is raining and I'm hungry" is a conjunctive proposition. Using our symbol "·" for "and" and the letters "p," "q," "r," etc., to stand for the component propositions, a conjunctive proposition may be represented symbolically as: p·q. Conjunctive propositions are obviously conjunctive on our above scheme, and it is perhaps just as obvious that they are also categorical rather than hypothetical. Thus the truth of a conjunctive proposition requires the truth of each of its conjuncts: "It is raining and I'm hungry" is true when and only when "It is raining" is true and "I'm hungry" is true. These true conditions can be demonstrated schematically by what is called a *truth-table,* a table which exhibits all of the possible combinations of truth and falsity of the component propositions and the corresponding truth-values of the whole compound proposition. Thus the truth-table for a conjunctive proposition is:

$$p \cdot q$$

TTT
FFT
TFF
FFF

The truth-values for the whole proposition, in these four different situations, appear under the "and"; and this truth-table shows that an "and" or conjunctive proposition is true exactly when all of its conjuncts are true. This is the case also even if, as sometimes happens, the proposition contains more than two conjuncts.

A compound proposition whose component propositions are connected by "because," "since," "therefore," "consequently," or some equivalent is called a *causal* proposition. "Since it's late I'm hungry" is an example of a causal proposition. Causal propositions are clearly implicative, since they assert that two things are causally connected. They are also categorical, since they assert unconditionally that these causally related things truly exist. In fact, causal propositions are usually simply the syllogisms—or enthymemes or sorites—with which we are already familiar. The only difference is that in a syllogism, enthymeme, or sorites the component propositions are separated, while in the corresponding causal proposition the component propositions are combined into one single compound proposition. If the causal proposition consists of three propositions with two terms each of which occurs twice, like "Since birds have backbones and everything with a backbone is an animal, then birds are animals," it corresponds to an explicit syllogism. If it consists of less or more than three propositions or does not contain a term which occurs twice—e.g., "Birds are animals because they have backbones"—it corresponds to an enthymeme or sorites, and you will have to do some premise searching.

Yet not all causal propositions are syllogistic arguments, for in some of them the antecedent is related to the consequent by obversion or conversion or by relations on the square of opposition, and in others the antecedent is inductive, rather than deductive, evidence for the consequent. "Since all birds have feathers, anything without feathers is other than a bird" is an example of the former; "Since the water in this flask, and in this one, and in this one freezes at 100° C., all water freezes at 100° C." is an example of the latter. The former we have already studied;[2] the latter we have already examined in one connection and will later examine in another.[3] In many cases, however, the cause asserted may be either inductive or deductive evidence for the asserted effect, depending on the nature of the other, tacit premise. Thus "The plane should encounter icing conditions because it's going through a cold front," a causal proposition, is an inductive argument if the tacit premise is something like "Planes going through cold fronts in the past have usually encountered icing conditions." But if the tacit premise is "All planes that go through cold fronts encounter icing conditions," then the cause asserted is deductive evidence for the effect, and the causal proposition is expansible into a regular syllogism.

Since a causal proposition is both categorical and implicative, it must meet two requirements in order to be true: (1) Both the antecedent and the consequent must be true (since it is categorical), and (2) there must truly be an implicative connection between antecedent and consequent (since it is implicative). We are familiar with the symbol "→," which represents an implicative connection, as the relation of a superimplicant to its subimplicant (A→I and E→O). Let us now introduce the symbol "⊢" to represent the fact that the proposition it precedes is being asserted categorically: thus "⊢p" means "p is categorically true." Using these symbols we can conveniently represent the truth conditions of causal propositions on a truth-table:

$$\vdash p \rightarrow \vdash q$$

T	T	T	T
F	T	T	F
T	F	T	F
F	F	T	F
T	T	F	F Impossible
F	T	F	F
T	F	F	F
F	F	F	F

[2] See Chap. 14.
[3] Pp. 241–246 above and Chaps. 25 and 26 below.

Notice that this truth-table must have eight rows of truth situations because the truth-value of the whole causal proposition is determined by the truth-values of three, rather than two, components: the antecedent, the consequent, and the implicative connection between them. Since there are two possible truth-values, truth and falsity, for each component, the number of rows in a truth-table with x components will be 2^x. A simple way of insuring that all possible truth situations have been listed is to alternate T and F singly under the first component, doubly under the next, quadruply under the next, etc. Observe also that one of the situations in the above truth-table is not only false but impossible, for it asserts the existence of the implicative connection which makes the truth of the antecedent guarantee the truth of the consequent and yet asserts at the same time that the antecedent is true while the consequent is false.

A compound proposition whose components are connected by "although," "still," "nevertheless," "but," "even though," "in spite of," etc., is called a *concessive* proposition. Consider the following example: "She still loves him even though he's always cruel to her." This proposition is certainly categorical, but is it conjunctive or implicative? Here the situation is a little more complicated. The man's cruelty certainly seems to have some bearing on the woman's love, yet the former is not given as the cause of the latter, nor should we expect it to be—unless we are masochists or suspect the woman of masochism. What we should expect, on the contrary, is that the man's cruelty would be the cause of the woman's *not* loving him. Thus instead of uttering the above proposition we would expect the speaker to say: "Since he's always cruel to her, she no longer loves him." But what we get instead is a denial of this causal proposition and its consequence.

In short, *a concessive proposition is the denial of a corresponding tacit implicative proposition.* The concessive proposition affirms the antecedent or "cause" and yet denies the consequent or "effect" in that presupposed tacit implicative proposition. Thus the analytic paradigm of a concessive proposition is: "Although p (in 'Since p then q'), not q." So every concessive proposition presupposes an implicative compound, but as the denial of that compound it is not itself an implicative compound. On the contrary, it is itself a conjunctive proposition—a conjunctive proposition one of whose conjuncts is the denial of the consequent in a presupposed tacit implicative proposition. Hence concessive words like "although," "even though," "but," etc., function like the conjunctive word "and," *except* that the former also deny tacit implicative compounds. So the truth-table for a concessive proposition is the same as the one for a conjunctive proposition, except that it may also sometimes be useful to explicate and make a truth-table for the tacit implicative proposition which it presupposes.

A *conditional* (sometimes called "hypothetical") proposition is one whose constituent propositions are connected by "if . . . (then)" or some equivalent. The following is a conditional proposition: "If you jump out of a twentieth-story window, (then) you will be killed." Conditional propositions are clearly *hypothetical,* since neither the antecedent nor the consequent is categorically asserted to be a fact. The speaker of the above example is *not* saying that you actually are jumping out of a twentieth-story window or that you actually will be killed; he is only saying that *if* the one *should* happen then the other *would* also happen. And it is also pretty obvious that this conditional proposition is *implicative* rather than conjunctive, for there is clearly a causal connection between jumping out of a twentieth-story window and being killed.

Thus conditional propositions are just like causal ones except that they do not categorically assert the existence of their components. Compare for instance the following two propositions: "*Since* he jumped out of a twentieth-story window, he *was* killed." "*If* he *should* jump out of a twentieth-story window, he *would* be killed." Both propositions assert—and assert categorically—the existence of a causal connection between two events. Hence a causal connection must actually exist before either proposition can be true. The causal proposition also asserts categorically the truth of its antecedent and consequent, and its truth therefore requires, as we have just seen, the truth of these two components as well as the truth of the causal connection between them. The conditional proposition, on the contrary, does not assert the truth of its antecedent and consequent, for it is merely hypothetical; and it may therefore be true even though both of its components are false. The only truth claim made by a conditional proposition is the truth of the implicative connection, and this implicative connection means only that *if* the antecedent *were* true then the consequent *would necessarily have* to be true. Hence a conditional proposition is true in all cases except when the implicative connection is nonexistent, or when the antecedent is true and the consequent is false. These truth conditions for conditional propositions may be exhibited in a truth-table:

$p \rightarrow q$	
T T T	T
F T T	T
T F T	F
F F T	F
T T F	F Impossible
F T F	T
T F F	F
F F F	F

Whenever we have $\rightarrow$ false or else the antecedent true with the consequent false, or both, the whole conditional proposition is false. Notice again that one of the truth situations is impossible, for that situation asserts the existence of the implicative connection and yet at the same time asserts that p is true and q is false—a contradiction, for the meaning of the implicative relation is precisely that if the antecedent were true the consequent would have to be true too.

Thus conditional propositions are hypothetical and implicative. Unfortunately, however, this statement must be qualified, for what about a conditional proposition such as "If Jack's a football star, then I'm a monkey's uncle"? Though this proposition is certainly hypothetical, it doesn't seem to be implicative, for it would be pretty far-fetched to assert any causal connection, however remote and intricate, between Jack's athletic prowess and the speaker's biological status. Must we therefore conclude that some conditional propositions are conjunctive rather than implicative?

Well, it certainly seems reasonable to conclude that there is no causal connection between the *being* referred to in the antecedent and the *being* referred to in the consequent of the above proposition—that there is, in other words, no assertion of any *ontologically* implicative situation. Yet a closer inspection of this proposition will show that it nevertheless still asserts an implicative situation. Exactly what does the speaker of this proposition have in mind? It is obvious that he does not believe that Jack actually is a football star, and also that he's pretty well convinced that anything that would make him believe that Jack *is* a football star would also make him believe some incredible situation such as one of his sibling's having given birth to an ape. Now this analysis indicates that there is after all an implicative connection between the components of this proposition, for what the speaker means to assert is that his *belief* in the antecedent would be the cause, directly or indirectly, of his *belief* in the consequent. Thus the implicative connection in this conditional proposition is a cognitive one rather than an ontological or real one. Though the situation intended by the antecedent is not the cause of the situation envisaged in the consequent, the belief in the antecedent would be a ground for believing in the consequent. We have already acquainted ourselves with the distinction between causes of being and causes of knowing,[4] and we may now see that *ontologically* implicative propositions are examples of intentions of causes of *being* while *cognitively* implicative propositions are examples of intentions of causes of *knowing*.

May we therefore conclude that *all* conditional propositions are implicative in intention, either ontologically or cognitively? Well, it is always possible to fabricate conditional propositions which have no implicative intention of any kind and are therefore purely conjunctive, like "If rain is dry then pencils contain graphite," since words are only artificial signs and can be made to mean whatever we want them to. But it seems pretty clear that the bona-fide conditional propositions which are used in normal discourse are all implicative

[4] Pp. 227–228.

in intention, most of them ontologically and the rest of them cognitively, even though the precise causally connecting links may be hard to find in certain cases. If a conditional proposition, "if p then q," were purely conjunctive, it would merely say that "it happens accidentally to be the case that you will never have p without also having q," and its truth-table would then not contain any column for the possible truth-values of the implicative connection:

$$
\begin{array}{c}
p \to q \\
\hline
\text{T T T} \\
\text{F T T} \\
\text{T F F} \\
\text{F T F}
\end{array}
$$

Since a conditional proposition whose intention is only conjunctive says only that "it just so happens that whenever p occurs q also occurs," the truth of the whole compound proposition is a function merely of the truth-values of its component propositions, and so it will be false *only* when the antecedent is true and the consequent is false. While we have seen that implicative conditionals also must satisfy this condition, they must meet as a second requirement the truth of the implicative connection. However, this shorter truth-table may also be conveniently used for implicative conditionals if we wish to abstract from the question of the existence or nonexistence of the implicative connection.

We have already seen that causal propositions are compressions of either syllogisms or inductive arguments or, less frequently, relations of propositions by obversion-conversion or on the square of opposition.[5] Since conditional propositions (as implicative) are the hypothetical equivalents of causal propositions, it is easy to see that the same is true of conditional propositions. "Since he jumped out of a twentieth-story window, he was killed," a causal proposition, is a first-order enthymeme which is tacitly the following syllogism:

                    H a   J   H a   K
(JaK)   Since (he) (jumped out of a twentieth-story window,) (he) (was killed.)

HaJ   J   a
─────   [for every (one who jumped out of a twentieth-story window) (was
HaK
              K
          killed.)]

The same is clearly true of the corresponding conditional proposition, "If he jumps out of a twentieth-story window he will be killed," *except* that this proposition, being hypothetical, does not assert the truth of either of the explicit propositions.

[5] Pp. 333–334.

```
          H  a                          J                    H  a      K
(JaK)     If (he) (jumps out of a twentieth-story window,) (he) (will be killed.)

?HaJ                                    J ·                             a
─────     [for every (one who jumps out of a twentieth-story window) (will be
?HaK
              K
          killed.)]
```

The tacit major premise may be either categorical or hypothetical, since this does not affect the implicative connection; but the implicative connection must of course be asserted categorically. And when the antecedent of a conditional proposition is inductive, rather than deductive, evidence for the consequent, the proposition may be translated into an equivalent inductive argument or, by adding the appropriate major premise, into an ordinary syllogism, just like the last example.

When conditional or causal propositions do not have a recurrent term in the antecedent and consequent, however, they are not so easily handled, for then they are compressions of sorites rather than of enthymemes, and it often takes considerable energy and ingenuity to ferret out the tacit propositions. Consider, for instance, the following conditional proposition: "If baffled people are dangerous, then anxious people are never faithful." Unlike the example we have just been considering, the component propositions in this example do not share a common term; they have among them four terms instead of only three. Hence this conditional proposition is an abbreviation of a sorites rather than of a single syllogism. With some ingenuity we can formulate the missing propositions—which may or may not be the propositions the speaker actually had in mind—and thus expand this proposition into the following series of syllogisms:

```
?BaC      All baffled people are careless.        hypothetical
(AaB)     (All anxious people are baffled.)
──────
(?AaC)    (All anxious people are careless.        hypothetical)

(DaE)     (All dangerous people are evasive.)
(CaD)     (All careless people are dangerous.)
──────
(CaE)     (All careless people are evasive.)

(CaE)     (All careless people are evasive.)
(?AaC)    (All anxious people are careless.        hypothetical)
──────
(?AaE)    (All anxious people are evasive.         hypothetical)

(EeF)     (No evasive people are faithful.)
(?AaE)    (All anxious people are evasive.         hypothetical)
──────
?AeF      No anxious people are faithful.          hypothetical
```

Since the antecedent of the original conditional proposition is asserted only hypothetically, all of the conclusions derived from it must also be hypothetical. But if the original proposition had been a causal rather than a conditional one, all of the propositions in the corresponding sorites would have been categorical.

While many implicative propositions correspond to sorites rather than to enthymemes, there is unfortunately no other way to test the truth of such a proposition when it occurs *alone*. However, as we shall soon see, when a conditional proposition is implicatively linked with other propositions, there is, fortunately, a much quicker and easier way to evaluate the inference.

An *alternative* (sometimes called "disjunctive") proposition is one whose components are combined by "or" or "either . . . or," and the components are called *alternants*. "Either you study hard or you don't pass the exam" is an example of an alternative proposition. Is this type of proposition categorical or hypothetical? At first glance it might appear to be categorical, but a little reflection will show that neither alternant is being asserted as true and that alternative propositions are therefore hypothetical. The speaker is not asserting that you study hard, nor is he asserting that you don't pass the exam. He is only saying that one or the other of these situations must be true, that if either one of them is false then the other one has to be true.

Is he also saying that *only one* of the alternants is true—that if either one is true the other one must be false? Apparently not in our above example, for it is certainly possible for both alternants to be true. It just might be the case, unfortunately, that you study hard and still don't pass the exam. But in other alternative propositions it is clear that the speaker or writer intends to assert that only one of the alternants is true. "John's in either the living room or the kitchen" is a case in point, since he couldn't be in both places at once.

Thus we must recognize two kinds of alternative propositions. Those which include the possibility that both alternants are true are called *inclusive* alternative propositions. In these propositions "or" means "and/or" or "one or the other or both." We have already become familiar with this meaning of "or" as the relation which obtains between subcontraries on the square of opposition,[6] and we have symbolized it with "V." Alternative propositions which exclude the possibility that both alternants are true are called *exclusive* alternative propositions. In these propositions "or" means "exactly one true" or "one or the other but not both." And this meaning of "or" we have discussed before as the relation holding between contradictories on the square of opposition,[7] and we have symbolized it as "V̠." To decide whether a given alternative proposition is inclusive or exclusive, simply ask yourself whether both of the alternants could be true—or better, whether the user of the proposition *intends* that both of them could be true. If the answer is "Yes," the "or" is inclusive; if "No," then

[6] Chap. 12–1.4.
[7] Chap. 12–1.2.

exclusive. When in doubt as to which meaning is intended, it is safer to interpret it as inclusive, since this assumes less.

Thus alternative propositions are hypothetical. They assert not the truth of the alternants but only the truth that the alternants are connected in such a way that if one is false the other must be true—and also, in the case of the exclusive alternative proposition, that if one of them is true the other has to be false. This shows us that they are also implicative rather than conjunctive, for they are directly equivalent to conditional propositions. Since any inclusive alternative proposition says that if either one of the two alternants is false then the other one must be true, it is equivalent to two conditional propositions. And since any exclusive alternative proposition says that if either one of the alternants is false then the other one must be true, and also that if either one is true the other one must be false, it is equivalent to two *conjoined pairs* of conditional propositions. Using the symbol "−" as the negation of any proposition, we can conveniently exhibit these equivalences on truth-tables:

```
(−p → q)                    (p∨q)                      (−q → p)
F  T  T | T                 TTT | T                    F  T  T | T
T  T  T | T                 FTT | T                    F  T  F | T
F  F  T | F                 TFT | F                    F  F  T | F
T  F  T | F                 FFT | F                    F  F  F | F
F  T  F | T                 TTF | T                    T  T  T | T
T  T  F | F  Impossible     FTF | F  Impossible        T  T  F | F  Impossible
F  F  F | F                 TFF | F                    T  F  T | F
T  F  F | F                 FFF | F                    T  F  F | F
```

```
  [(−p → q) · (p → −q)]           (p∨q)              [(−q → p) · (q → −p)]
 T | F  T T  F T T F | F Imp.    TTT | F Imp.      T | F  T T  F T T F | F Imp.
 T | T  T T  T F T F | T         FTT | T           T | F  T F  T T T T | T
 F | F  F T  F T F F | F         TFT | F           F | F  F T  F T F F | F
 F | T  F T  F F F F | F         FFT | F           F | F  F F  F T F T | F
 T | F  T F  T T T T | T         TTF | T           T | T  T T  T F T F | T
.F | T  T F  F F T T | T         FTF | F Imp. Imp. F | T  T F  F F T T | T
 F | F  F F  F T F T | F         TFF | F           F | T  F T  F F F F | F
 F | T  F F  F F F T | F         FFF | F           F | T  F F  F F F T | F
```

Notice that the truth-value of a negated proposition is always the opposite of that same proposition affirmed. Since p∨q means that there exists an implicative connection such that p and q cannot both be false, p∨q is true in exactly those situations where this implicative connection truly exists and one or both of the alternants are true. And since p∨q means that there exists an implicative connection such that exactly one of p and q is true, p∨q is true in those situations where this implicative connection truly exists and exactly one of the alternants is true. Observe also that since "and" is not implicative it needs no special truth column, and that the truth column under it is therefore the truth column for the whole conjunctive proposition (whose conjuncts are conditional propositions). Understanding these things, we can see that the equivalence of these sets of propositions is demonstrated by the fact that their major truth columns are the same. Since the inclusive alternative proposition is equivalent to only two conditional propositions while the exclusive is equivalent to two *pairs* of them, the former is often called a *weak* and the latter a *strong* alternative proposition. Notice finally that since p⊻q is equivalent to two conjoined pairs of conditional propositions, its truth column includes *two* impossible situations—one for each of the conditionals in each of the equivalent pairs.

Since alternative propositions are equivalent to conditional ones, it would seem that many of the former, as well as many of the latter, must be equivalent to enthymemes or enthymematic sorites, the rest of them being equivalent to inductive arguments or else to immediate relations among propositions. This is true, but it is not possible to convert alternative propositions directly into syllogisms as is the case with conditional and causal propositions. Thus if we take the proposition "Either you study hard or you don't pass the exam" and make the first alternant into the minor premise and the second into the conclusion of a syllogism, the tacit major premise would have to be "Nobody who studies hard passes the exam":

$$\begin{array}{lll} & \text{S} \qquad\qquad\quad \text{e} \qquad\qquad \text{P} \\ (\underline{\text{S}}e\underline{\text{P}}) & [\text{No}(\text{body who studies hard}) \ (\text{passes the exam.})] \end{array}$$

$$\begin{array}{lll} & \text{Y} \quad\ \text{a} \quad\ \text{S} \\ \underline{\underline{\text{Y}}aS} & (\text{You}) \ (\text{study hard.}) \end{array}$$

$$\begin{array}{lll} & \text{Y} \qquad \text{e} \qquad\ \text{P} \\ \underline{\text{Y}}e\underline{\text{P}} & (\text{You}) \ \text{don't} \ (\text{pass the exam.}) \end{array}$$

This syllogism is valid—because we have made it so with the tacit major premise we have supplied; but just for that reason there seems to be something radically wrong with it. For we would not expect the speaker of the original alternative proposition to mean that nobody who studies hard passes the exam, nor would we expect him to mean that studying hard will result in failure. On the contrary, he means to say that failure will follow from *not* studying hard, and this is true because everybody who passes must study hard. The reason for the difficulty is simply that a syllogism, like a conditional proposition, says that the truth of the consequent follows from the *truth* of the antecedent, while an alternative proposition says that the truth of the "consequent" follows from the *falsity* of the "antecedent." Hence in order to translate an alternative proposition into an equivalent syllogism it is first necessary to change it into one of its equivalent conditional propositions, thus:

$$
\left.\begin{array}{c}
(\text{YaS}) \\
\text{V} \\
(\text{YeP})
\end{array}\right\}
\rightarrow
\left.\begin{array}{c}
-(\text{YaS}) \\
(\text{YeP})
\end{array}\right\}
$$

(P̱aS)	(All who pass the exam study hard.)
?Ye̱S̱	?You do not study hard.
?Ye̱P̱	?You do not pass the exam.

or

$$
\left.\begin{array}{c}
(\text{YaS}) \\
\text{V} \\
(\text{YeP})
\end{array}\right\}
\rightarrow
\left.\begin{array}{c}
-(\text{YeP}) \\
(\text{YaS})
\end{array}\right\}
$$

(P̱aS)	(All who pass the exam study hard.)
?Y̱aP	?You pass the exam.
?Y̱aS	?You study hard.

Notice that the contradictory of YaS is here an E proposition (YeS) because the former is a singular proposition (*You . . .*) and there is only one opposed proposition to a singular. Of course we may, as we have seen,[8] quantify the subject, "you," temporally: "Sometimes you do not study hard" (YoS). But then we would also have to quantify that same term in the conclusion (YoP), and so we would still have a valid syllogism. But such quantification is unnecessary here, for the expression "*the* exam" makes it clear that the speaker is referring to only one part of "your" life, though to *all* of that one part.

Since an *exclusive* alternative proposition is equivalent to two pairs of conditional propositions, it will be equivalent to two pairs of syllogisms (or sorites or inductive arguments) rather than to just two arguments. You can easily demonstrate this for yourself by following the same procedure as for an inclusive alternative and by adding the other two equivalent conditional propositions.

Just as the implicative connection in conditional propositions is sometimes a cognitive rather than an ontological one, so also is this the case with alternative propositions. "Either he's not what he's cracked up to be or I'm the King of Siam!" may also be expressed as "If he's what he's cracked up to be then I'm the King of Siam!" and in both cases the speaker is asserting a causal connection among his ideas. In the case of the alternative proposition he is saying that anything that would cause him to *disbelieve* in the first situation would also (directly or indirectly) cause him to *believe* in the second one. In the case of the equivalent conditional proposition he is saying that anything which would make him *believe* in the first proposition would also make him believe in the second. Of course since we can make words mean what we want them to, it is always possible to construct alternative propositions in which no implicative situation is intended at all, but we don't do this in normal speech and thought. If we did have such a conjunctive alternative proposition, our truth-table would not record the truth possibilities of the connection, and the alternative proposition would be true when the appropriate alternants were true regard-

[8] Pp. 182–184.

less of the existence or nonexistence of an implicative connection between them:

p ∨ q	p V̱ q
T T T	T F T
F T T	F T T
T T F	T T F
F F F	F F F

As with conditional propositions so also with alternative ones, these shorter truth-tables can be conveniently used for implicative propositions whenever it is unnecessary to concern ourselves with the question of the existence or non-existence of an implicative connection.

Alternative propositions may also contain more than two alternants: "Either her father or her brother or her boy friend will take her to the ball game." Such propositions are handled exactly like those with only two alternants. If the "or" is inclusive, the proposition is true whenever one or more of the alternants are true; if it is exclusive it is true whenever exactly one of the alternants is true. The only difference is that the truth-table under a proposition having more than two alternants needs a truth column under only *one* of the "or's":

p ∨ q ∨ r	
T	TTT
F	TTT
T	FTT
F	FTT
T	TTF
F	TTF
T	FTF
F	FFF

A proposition of the form "not both p and q" $[-(p \cdot q)]$ is called a *disjunctive* proposition, and the component propositions are known as *disjuncts*. "It won't be both cloudy and cold tonight" $[-(cl \cdot co)]$ is an example of a disjunctive proposition. It is immediately evident that disjunctive propositions are hypothetical rather than categorical, because neither disjunct is being asserted as true—nor as false. All that is being asserted is that they are not both true. You will remember that this is the relation we encountered between contrary propositions (A and E).

However, the disjunctive proposition is unlike the other hypothetical propositions (conditional and alternative) in being sometimes conjunctive and sometimes implicative, and it is frequently difficult to tell whether a given disjunctive proposition is the one or the other. The hallmark of the implicative proposition is the intention of a necessary connection, and this necessary connection, especially in disjunctive propositions, is often signalized by the use of some modal word such as "cannot" or "impossible." Thus "You can't be selfish and still have friends" is a disjunctive proposition which is implicative, for the word "can't" makes it clear that the speaker feels there is a necessary connection between selfishness and lack of friends. On the other hand, "Podunk and Hickville didn't both lose last Friday" is merely conjunctive since the user seems to be asserting that this situation is merely a matter of fact. There may, of course, be some underlying reason; the two teams may have played each other, for example. But the user doesn't seem to have any such implicative connection in mind.

Other disjunctive propositions, in which no modal word occurs, are more difficult to interpret. For instance, is the proposition that "It won't be both cloudy and cold tonight" implicative or conjunctive in intention? One could adduce as an underlying connection that the presence of clouds at night retards the radiation of the heat from the earth; on the other hand, it is sometimes very cold even when it's cloudy. And in any case the speaker may not be aware of either of these facts. Whenever we have any reasonable doubt that a given disjunctive proposition has an implicative intention it is safer to interpret it as being merely conjunctive, since in that way we are assuming less.

Just as alternative propositions have conditional equivalents, so also every disjunctive proposition has two equivalent conditional propositions and one equivalent alternative proposition. This can be seen by examining the meaning of disjunction. "$-(p \cdot q)$" means that both of the components cannot be true, or that at least one of them is false. Another way of saying this is to say that one or the other or both are false $(-p \lor -q)$, an alternative proposition. And another way is to say that if either of the disjuncts is true the other one is false: $(p \to -q)$ and $(q \to -p)$, two conditional propositions. One important thing to remember, however, is that these propositions are equivalent only when they are alike in intention, that is, only when they are both implicative in intention or both conjunctive in intention. In order to formalize this important distinction we will use the symbol "N" (for necessity) to indicate that a disjunctive proposition has an implicative intention. Thus $N-(p \cdot q)$ is an implicative disjunctive proposition while $-(p \cdot q)$ is a conjunctive disjunctive proposition.

The above equivalences are borne out by the following truth-tables:

$[N - (p \cdot q)]$		←——→ $(-p \lor -q)$		←——→ $(p \to -q)$		←——→ $(q \to -p)$	
T F TTT	F Imp.	F TF	F Imp.	T T F	F Imp.	T T F	F Imp.
F F TTT	F	F FF	F	T F F	F	T F F	F
T T FFT	T	T TF	T	F T F	T	T T T	T
F T FFT	F	T FF	F	F F F	F	T F T	F
T T TFF	T	F TT	T	T T T	T	F T F	T
F T TFF	F	F FT	F	T F T	F	F F F	F
T T FFF	T	T TT	T	F T T	T	F T T	T
F T FFF	F	T FT	F	F F T	F	F F T	F

[−(p · q)] ←————→	(−p∨−q) ←——→	(p → −q) ←————→	(q → −p)
F TTT	F F F	T F F	T F F
T FFT	T T F	F T F	T T T
T TFF	F T T	T T T	F T F
T F·F F	T T T	F T T	F T T

If you try giving *different* truth columns to the various implicative connections in the first set of truth-tables, you will see that those four propositions are equivalent only when the truth-values of their implicative intentions are the same. As with conditional and alternative propositions so also with disjunctive ones, it is more convenient to use the shorter truth-tables even for implicative disjunctive propositions whenever the question of the truth or falsity of the implication is unimportant to the task at hand.

One useful rule that may be induced from the above equivalences is this: To transform an alternative proposition into an equivalent disjunctive proposition or vice versa we need only change the propositional connective and then negate both components and the whole proposition: (p∨q)↔ −(−p· −q) or (p·q)↔ −(−p∨−q), a relation known as De Morgan's law.

Since every implicative disjunctive proposition is equivalent to a conditional and an alternative proposition, it is also equivalent to a syllogism or set of syllogisms (or to an inductive argument or an immediate relation of propositions). Like the alternative connection, however, the disjunctive connection is only tacitly sequential (passing from the truth of one of the disjuncts to the falsity of the other) and thus also must first be translated into one of its conditional equivalents before being translated into a syllogism:

		(SeF)	(No selfish people have friends.)
−{(YaS) · (YaF)}	(YaS) → −(YaF)	?YaS	?You are selfish.
		?YeF	?You do not have friends.

or

		(FeS)	(No one who has friends is selfish.)
−{(YaS) · (YaF)}	(YaF) → −(YaS)	?YaF	?You have friends.
		?YeS	?You are not selfish.

If, however, the disjuncts do not contain a common term, then the equivalent conditional propositions will be translatable only into sorites, like the one on p. 339.

Like alternative propositions, disjunctive propositions may contain more than two disjuncts: "It's impossible for Fred to be at home, at school, and at work all at the same time" [−(h·s·w)]. But these are handled exactly like two component disjunctive propositions, except that it is not necessary to have a truth column under more than one of the "ands":

$$-(h \cdot s \cdot w)$$

F	TTT	T
T	FFT	T
T	TFF	T
T	FFF	T
T	TFT	F
T	FFT	F
T	TFF	F
T	FFF	F

This discussion of the various kinds of compound proposition may be summarized by using our original classificatory scheme:

MODE OF INTENTION

		categorical	hypothetical
REALITY	conjunctive	conjunctive concessive	disjunctive
INTENDED	implicative	causal	conditional alternative disjunctive

23–2 RELATIONS AMONG COMPOUND PROPOSITIONS

We have seen that every conditional proposition has an equivalent alternative, disjunctive, and another conditional proposition. We have also seen that conjunctive, causal, and concessive propositions, being categorical, can never be equivalent to these hypothetical propositions. Such a categorical proposition may be the precise truth-value opposite (the contradictory) of one of these hypothetical propositions, or it may be opposed to it in only some of its truth-value situations; but its truth-value can never be exactly the same. Finally, we have also learned a technique for the comparison of compound propositions with respect to their truth-values—namely, the truth-table. Equipped with all these tools, we are now able to solve problems involving compound propositions.

Let us suppose that a discussion has arisen concerning the advantages and disadvantages of compulsory health insurance. Seven people are present and they make the following statements:

A: If compulsory health insurance is enacted, the average standard of health will rise.

B: Compulsory health insurance is in force, and still the average standard of health won't rise.

C: If the average standard of health doesn't rise, compulsory health insurance isn't enacted.

D: Either compulsory health insurance is not enacted or the average standard of health will rise.

E: If compulsory health insurance is not enacted, the average standard of health will not rise.

F: Since the average standard of health will not rise, compulsory health insurance will not be enacted.

G: It's impossible to have compulsory health insurance enacted and yet not have a rise in the average standard of health.

Are these people agreeing or disagreeing with each other? How can we tell for sure?

Well, we may of course simply try to intuit the meanings of the various assertions, or we may memorize all the equivalent forms of all the various types of propositions. But the first method is extremely fallible, especially with more complicated assertions, and the second is quite cumbersome as well as fallible. Or, since we know that implicative compound propositions are equivalent to syllogistic arguments, we may translate each such compound into its corresponding syllogism or set of syllogisms and then proceed to test the validity of those syllogisms. But this method can sometimes be quite complicated (note the example on p. 339), and besides it will not work for conjunctive propositions because they are not translatable into syllogisms. An easier and less fallible way of deciding such questions is by using truth-tables.

To use the truth-table test for such problems as the above, we must first formulate each of the propositions symbolically. Our procedure here is strictly analogous to the formulation of simple propositions and syllogisms. The difference is that in assertions and arguments involving compound propositions it is whole propositions (and their negations) which recur rather than simply terms. Hence we do not need to analyze the various propositions into their component terms; we need only analyze them into their component propositions, using one symbol for each component proposition. And instead of the connective being some form of the verb "to be," it will be $\rightarrow$, $\lor$, $\underline{\lor}$, $\cdot$, or $-(\cdot)$. Thus the seven above propositions about compulsory health insurance may be formulated as follows:

A: $c \rightarrow r$ C: $-r \rightarrow -c$ E: $-c \rightarrow -r$ G: $-(c \cdot -r)$
B: $c \cdot -r$ D. $-c \lor r$ F: $\vdash -r \rightarrow \vdash -c$

Notice that in F's proposition both components are asserted ($\vdash$), since it is a causal proposition.

The formulation of compound propositions is usually an easier task than the formulation of simple ones, but there are a few special expressions which need to be understood. The word "if" clearly indicates that what follows it is the antecedent of a conditional proposition, but what about the expression "only if"? Does "The President's in the White House only if he's in Washington" mean "If the President's in Washington, then he's in the White House"? No, for he might be in some other part of the city. Rather what is meant is that "If the President's in the White House, then he's in Washington." Thus the expression "only if" indicates that the proposition which follows it is a *necessary* condition, but not necessarily a *sufficient* condition, for the other component proposition. Hence the proposition which follows "only if" must be the consequent rather than the antecedent of a conditional proposition. In brief, "only if" is the exact equivalent of "then."

The expression "if and only if" simply combines the functions of "if" and "only if" so that the proposition which follows it will be both the antecedent of one conditional proposition and the consequent of another. Thus "We'll have six more weeks of winter if and only if the Groundhog sees his shadow" yields two propositions: "If the Groundhog sees his shadow we'll have six more weeks of winter" (s→w) and "If we'll have six more weeks of winter then the Groundhog sees his shadow" (w→s). By using the symbol "↔," which we have already used to express the relation between equivalent propositions, we may express "if and only if" propositions more briefly: s↔w.

How is the word "unless" to be interpreted? Consider the proposition "I won't help you unless you help me." This clearly means "If you don't help me, then I won't help you" (−y → −i). Thus "unless" may always be interpreted as "if not." However, since −y → −i is equivalent to the alternative proposition y∨−i, "You help me or I won't help you," the word "unless" may also always be interpreted as "or." There are, of course, other somewhat difficult expressions which need to be interpreted in the formulation of compound propositions, but these are the ones which most frequently cause trouble.

Having formulated the propositions symbolically, we need only construct a truth-table to compare them. But should we use the longer truth-table, which indicates the truth situations for the implicative connections, or is the shorter one sufficient? We may of course use the longer one, though then the truth-table under any conjunctive proposition will have to be repeated so as to make that truth-table the same length as those under the implicative propositions— since conjunctive propositions intend no implicative connection under which a special truth column could be put. Moreover, if it were the actual truth or falsity of the above propositions which we were interested in, we would be compelled to use the longer truth-table, since some of these propositions might be false because of the nonexistence of their intended implicative connections. However, it is not the actual truth or falsity of these propositions which we are interested in, but rather their *agreement* or *disagreement*. We do not now want to know whether they are in fact true or false; we want to know whether the others *would* be true (or false) *if* any one of them *were* true (or false). In other words, since our present question is: "What effect would the truth or falsity of one of these propositions have on the truth or falsity of the others?" the particular reason for the falsity of any proposition is unimportant. Consequently we may here abstract from the question of the existence of the asserted implicative connections and use the shorter truth-table, thus saving time and effort.

Using the shorter truth-table, then, let us assume that speaker A's proposition is true. Each of the other propositions must either agree or disagree with A's, or, more precisely, each of the other propositions will then be either true, false, or undetermined. And the truth-table will tell us exactly which of these three situations is the case. If a quaesitum proposition's truth column is *exactly the same* as that of the proposition whose truth-value is given (A's), then it will be the *same* in truth-value as that original proposition—true if the original is true and false if the original is false. If a quaesitum proposition's truth column is *exactly opposite* to that of the original proposition, then its truth-value will be the *opposite* of that of the original—false if the original is true and true if the original is false. And if a quaesitum proposition's truth column is *partly the same and partly different* in relation to that of the original proposition, then its truth-value will be *undetermined*—since we do not know which of the truth situations may actually be the case. With all these preliminaries finally aside, let us now compare the above propositions on a truthtable:

Assumed

T	F	T	T	U	U			T
A	B	C	D	E	F			G
c → r	c · −r	−r → −c	−cVr	−c → −r	⊢ −r →	⊢ −c		−(c · −r)
TTT	TFF	F T F	F TT	F T F	F	F	F	T TFF
FTT	FFF	F T T	T TT	T F F	F	F	T	T FFF
TFF	TTT	T F F	F FF	F T T	T	F	F	F TTT
FTF	FFT	T T T	T TF	T T T	T	T	T	T FFT

Thus we see that speakers C, D, and G agree with speaker A, while speakers B, E, and F disagree with him—E's and F's assertions being undetermined and B's being false when A's assertion is true. If A's assertion had been assumed false instead of true, then C's, D's, and G's would have been false and B's true.

The only prerequisite for comparison of compound propositions is that they contain the same component propositions (or their negations), just as the only prerequisite for comparison of simple propositions by obversion and conversion is that they have the same component *terms* (or their negations). Let us carry out this truth-table comparison of compound propositions in one more example:

F   −dVp   Assuming that it is false that (^{−d}"The Democrats will not win in '64) ^Vunless (a third world war will be ^ppostponed"), state the truth-value (T, F, or U) of each of the following propositions:

F   d → p   1. (The Democrats will ^dwin in '64) [→]only if (a third world war will be ^ppostponed.)

U   ⊢ p → ⊢ d   2. ^{⊢ p}Since (a third world war will be postponed,) [→](the Democrats ^{⊢ d}will win in '64.)

T   d · −p   3. (The Democrats will win in '64)^d and (a third world war will ^{−p}not be postponed.)

U   −d → −p   4. If (the Democrats do not win in '64,)^{−d} [→](a third world war will ^{−p}not be postponed.)

F   −p → −d   5. If (a third world war is not postponed,)^{−p} then [→](the Democrats will ^{−d}not win in '64.)

F   −(−p · d)   6. It's crazy to believe that[−] (a third world war will not be ^{−p}postponed) while at the same time affirming that (the Democrats ^dwill win in '64.)

U   d V −p   7. Either (the Democrats will win in '64)^d or ^V(a third world war will ^{−p}not be postponed,) but not both.

F	F	U	T	U	F	F	U
given	1	2	3	4	5	6	7
−dVp	d → p	⊢ p → ⊢ d	d · −p	−d → −p	−p → −d	−(−p · d)	d V −p
T TT	F T T	T F F	F F F	T F F	F T T	T F F F	F F F
F TT	T T T	T T T	T F F	F T F	F T F	T F F T	T T F
T TF	F T F	F F F	F F T	T T T	T T T	T T F F	F T T
F FF	T F F	F F T	T T T	F T T	T F F	F T T T	T F T

Proposition 7 could also have been formulated as a conjunction of an inclusive alternative and a disjunctive proposition, $(d \lor -p) \cdot -(d \cdot -p)$; but its formulation as an exclusive alternative proposition is simpler. Note that if the original proposition had been given as true, then propositions 1, 5, and 6 would have been true and proposition 3 would have been false.

In this way compound propositions can be interrelated and compared. Yet a compound proposition is sometimes not merely a summation of an argument but itself one constituent in an argument. Let us now turn to a study of these arguments which involve compound propositions.

EXERCISES

1. Below is a list of compound propositions. (1) Formulate each both linguistically and symbolically. (2) Form an equivalent proposition belonging to each of the other types of compound proposition, checking your procedure with truth-tables. (3) Construct the categorical syllogism (or sorites) equivalent to the given proposition.
   a. It's going to be a cold winter since the caterpillars have long fur.
   b. You do what I say or else you're fired!
   c. It was possible to give the Egyptians control and still have the Suez Canal efficiently run.
   d. Midwestern will win all its games this year if Katterwhooski doesn't sustain any injuries and the playing field is relatively dry.
   e. I'll pass this exam easy unless the prof springs something funny.
   f. Even though he's currently in a slump, Mantle will still beat Ruth's record.
   g. The colleges and universities will be able to meet the educational needs of the sixties only if there is a sizable increase in teachers' salaries.
   h. The murderer has to be either the butler or the lawyer and it clearly couldn't be both.
   i. If the present split in the Democratic party over the civil rights issue continues, then we may expect to see the Negro vote return to the Republican party.
   j. You can't do that and get away with it!
   k. Either Hitler's really dead or else he's pulled off the biggest hoax in history.
   l. Although he knew he couldn't pass, he kept on studying.
   m. There will be an effective international organization if and only if nuclear weapons reach a strength sufficient to destroy whole nations.
   n. Inasmuch as purchasing power has now exceeded productive power, there will be a continuing inflation.
   o. Either Plato or the Cynics or the Cyrenaics represent the historical Socrates.
   p. If it is indeed impossible for farm prices to return to their previous high and still eliminate all government subsidies, then we can look forward to a period of semi-socialization of agriculture.
   q. If you believe that, you're a bigger fool than I thought!
   r. The president will die in office unless he takes it easier.

s. If the indicated development of American opera comes to fruition, then either the myth of the arts as effeminate will at last have been destroyed or else American society will become increasingly stratified.

t. Public education will surpass private in excellence provided that taxes remain high.

u. The Mexican standard of living can certainly approximate that of America if a feasible way is discovered of irrigating the large northern areas.

v. The climate will become increasingly warm and air-conditioning will be installed almost universally.

w. We may look forward to the complete elimination of all virus-induced diseases provided only that the private foundations continue their support of medical research.

x. The secretary of state is in Washington at the moment, or else he's in Cairo.

y. An immediate transfusion was necessary because of the severe bleeding.

z. If the Ford Foundation's capital were now divided equally among the inhabitants of the U.S., every person would receive about $15.

2. "If Ivy's line lasts three quarters, Midwestern will not score once." If this proposition is *true,* what is the truth-value (T, F, or U) of each of the following propositions? If it is *false,* what is the truth-value of each of the following propositions?

a. It is not possible both for Ivy's line to last three quarters and for Midwestern to score once.

b. If Midwestern does not score once, Ivy's line will last three quarters.

c. Ivy's line will not last three quarters or Midwestern will not score once.

d. If Midwestern scores once, Ivy's line will not last three quarters.

e. If Ivy's line does not last three quarters, Midwestern will score once.

f. Ivy's line will last three quarters and Midwestern will score once.

3. "The students will show an increased sense of responsibility provided that the Honor System amendment is passed." If this proposition is *true,* what is the truth-value of each of the following propositions? If it is *false?*

a. The students will show an increased sense of responsibility unless the Honor System amendment is not passed.

b. The students will not show an increased sense of responsibility and the Honor System amendment will be passed.

c. The students will show an increased sense of responsibility only if the Honor System amendment is passed.

d. The students will either not show an increased sense of responsibility or the Honor System amendment will be passed.

e. It is impossible for the Honor System amendment to be passed and for the students not to show an increased sense of responsibility.

f. The Honor System amendment will not be passed if and only if the students fail to show an increased sense of responsibility.

CHAPTER 24

COMPOUND PROPOSITIONS
IN SYLLOGISMS

24–1 MIXED HYPOTHETICAL SYLLOGISMS

Mixed Conditional Syllogisms. Hypothetical propositions often combine with simple categorical propositions to produce what is known as *mixed hypothetical syllogisms*. If the major premise is a conditional proposition and the minor premise and conclusion are simple propositions, the argument is known as a *mixed conditional syllogism*. Since the minor premise may either affirm or deny either the antecedent or the consequent of the conditional major premise, the mixed conditional syllogism has four possible moods:

p → q	If Jack's in the kitchen, then he's in the house.
p	Jack's in the kitchen.
q	He's in the house.

p → q	If Jack's in the kitchen, then he's in the house.
—p	Jack's not in the kitchen.
—q	He's not in the house.

p → q	If Jack's in the kitchen, then he's in the house.
q	Jack's in the house.
p	Jack's in the kitchen.

p → q	If Jack's in the kitchen, then he's in the house.
—q	Jack's not in the house.
—p	Jack's not in the kitchen.

It needs but little thought to see that only the first and fourth of these moods are valid. Jack's presence in the kitchen is a sufficient condition for his presence in the house, so the first of the above moods is valid. This mood is known as the *modus ponendo ponens,* the mood which by affirming (the antecedent) affirms (the consequent), or more briefly *modus ponens.* And since Jack's presence in the house is a *necessary* (though not sufficient) condition of his being in the kitchen, the fourth of the above moods is also valid, for the absence of what is necessary guarantees the absence of that for which it is necessary. This mood is known as the *modus tollendo tollens,* the mood which by denying (the consequent) denies (the antecedent), or more briefly *modus tollens.* But the second of the above forms is invalid since the absence of one sufficient condition (Jack's presence in the kitchen) does not guarantee the absence of that for which it is sufficient (his presence in the house), for there may also be other sufficient conditions (such as his being in the living room) for that consequent. And likewise the third of the above moods is invalid since a necessary condition (Jack's being in the house) is not necessarily a sufficient condition for that for which it is necessary (Jack's being in the kitchen).

Thus the mixed conditional syllogism is valid when we proceed from affirming the antecedent in the minor to affirming the consequent in the conclusion *(modus ponens),* or when we proceed from denying the consequent in the minor to denying the antecedent in the conclusion *(modus tollens).* The other two possible forms are invalid, and their respective fallacies are called the fallacies of *denying the antecedent* and *affirming the consequent* (in the minor premise).

It should be clear from the above examples that "mixed *hypothetical* syllogism" is a misnomer, for once the minor premise and the conclusion are asserted categorically there is no longer anything hypothetical about the syllogism at all. In fact, *modus ponens* simply transforms a conditional proposition into its corresponding *causal* proposition—since the connection between premise and conclusion is always an implicative one and since the minor premise and conclusion are asserted categorically. Thus *modus ponens* consists in transforming p→q into ⊢p→⊢q: "*Since* p (in p→q), then q." Hence it is patently and intuitively valid. And *modus tollens* simply transforms the major premise's *equivalent* conditional proposition into a causal proposition: "*Since* −q(in−q→−p which is equivalent to p→q), then −p." Furthermore, since we have already seen that many causal propositions are simply enthymemes or enthymematic sorites (the others being inductive arguments or transformations of propositions), the so-called mixed hypothetical syllogism is also very often simply one or more categorical syllogisms. Note the following equivalences:

(JaK) → (JaH)			(KaH)	(Everyone in the kitchen is in the house.)
(JaK) ⎫	⊢ (JaK) ⎫		JaK	Jack's in the kitchen.
⎬	→ ⎬			
(JaH) ⎭	⊢ (JaH) ⎭		JaH	Jack's in the house.

The validity of mixed conditional syllogisms may also be easily tested with truth-tables if we will but transform the syllogism into a single conditional proposition whose antecedent is the conjunction of the two premises and whose consequent is the conclusion: [(p→q)·p]→q. Note, however, that this conditional proposition is not completely equivalent to its corresponding mixed conditional syllogism, for in the former p and q are asserted only hypothetically while in the latter they are asserted categorically. Still, such a transformation is acceptable when we are concerned only with the *validity* of the argument and not with the *truth* of the propositions, for validity means only that *if* the premises *were* true then the conclusion *would* also be true—and this is what the corresponding conditional proposition says. For the same reason we may also use the shorter truth-table—since the validity of the conditional syllogism abstracts from the question of the actual truth of the implicative assertion in the conditional major premise and requires only that *if* it (and the rest of the premise) *were* true then the conclusion would also be true. Hence the validity or invalidity of the four possible moods of the mixed conditional syllogism can be demonstrated as follows:

$$[(p \to q) \cdot p] \to q$$

T T T	T T T T
F T T	F F T T
T F F	F T T F
F T F	F F T F

$$[(p \to q) \cdot -p] \to -q$$

T T T	F F	T F
F T T	T T	F F
T F F	F F	T T
F T F	T T	T T

$$[(p \to q) \cdot q] \to p$$

T T T	T T T T
F T T	T T F F
T F F	F F T T
F T F	F F T F

$$[(p \to q) \cdot -q] \to -p$$

T T T	F F	T F
F T T	F F	T T
T F F	F T	T F
E T F	T T	T T

The validity of the first and fourth moods (*modus ponens* and *modus tollens*) is demonstrated by the fact that the truth column under each of their major connectives contains all trues, showing that the antecedent always suffices for the consequent. And the invalidity of the second and third moods is demonstrated by the presence of a false in each of their major truth columns, showing that the antecedent sometimes does not yield the consequent.

There is also an interesting short cut that may be used in testing such arguments by truth-tables. We know that p→q means −p∨q; that is, p→q is true whenever the antecedent is false or the consequent is true or both. Hence if we abstract from the question of the truth of any implicative connections in the antecedent and consequent, we know that every conditional proposition will be true whenever the antecedent is false or the consequent is true or both. This being so, we may save time by working backwards on the truth-table from the consequent to the antecedent, immediately putting a T under the major connective whenever the consequent is true and going back to the antecedent only in those cases where the consequent is false. Furthermore, since the occurrence of even one false under the major connective proves the argument invalid, we may save more time by trying to produce that false situation as quickly as possible. This we do by beginning with a false in the consequent and trying to produce a true in the antecedent—a situation which would place a false under the major connective. Notice this short cut applied to the same four arguments we have just tested:

$$[(p \rightarrow q) \cdot p] \rightarrow q$$

TF F FT T F
       T T
     FF T F
       T T

$$[(p \rightarrow q) \cdot -p] \rightarrow -q$$

FT T T T   F F

$$[(p \rightarrow q) \cdot q] \rightarrow p$$

FT T TT F F

$$[(p \rightarrow q) \cdot -q] \rightarrow -p$$

TF F FT T F
        T T
      F F T F
        T T

Since we at once produce an F under the major connective in each of the invalid moods, they are immediately shown to be invalid so we need go no further. Notice also that as soon as we know that the simple conjunct in the antecedent is false we know that the whole antecedent is false—since the truth of a conjunctive proposition requires that both conjuncts be true—and we therefore do not need to explore the conditional conjunct. And observe finally that we do not need to use the same truth symbols in all four propositions (p in the consequent of the third proposition does not have to be true just because —p in the consequent of the fourth proposition is false, etc.), since we are here not comparing the four propositions with each other.

This truth-table test may be abbreviated even further, to produce a neat and simple one-line test of any argument involving compound propositions.[1] The principle of this test is that *all those and only those arguments are valid whose assumed invalidity involves a contradiction.* (Thus this test is an example of indirect argument.[2]) The justification of this principle is that by an argument's being invalid is *meant* that it is not *self-contradictory* for the conclusion to be false while the premises are true. Thus to test an argument involving compound propositions we first begin a truth-table on the assumption that the argument is *invalid:*

$$[(p \rightarrow q) \cdot p] \rightarrow q$$

T   TTF F

$$[(p \rightarrow q) \cdot -p] \rightarrow -q$$

T   TT F F

Notice that this assumed invalidity means that the consequent (or conclusion), e.g. q, is false; that the conjunctive antecedent (or premises), e.g. (p→q)·p, is true; and that therefore both conjuncts are true. Now, since p (or —p) has

[1] This test was suggested by Richard Kelly, a student of the authors.
[2] See pp. 309–310 above.

already received a truth-value in one of its occurrences, it must receive a consistent truth-value in its other occurrence; and the same is true of q (or −q):

$$[(p \rightarrow q) \cdot p] \rightarrow q \qquad\qquad [(p \rightarrow q) \cdot -p] \rightarrow -q$$

T **T** F (**T**)T (**F**)F	F T T T T F F
F (F) (T)	
Valid	Invalid

When we thus assign the remaining (underlined) truth-values in the first case, however, we find that p→q must be false instead of true, as was required by our original assumption that the argument is invalid. Hence our original assumption that the argument is invalid involves the contradiction that p→q is both true and false, and the argument is therefore in fact not invalid, but valid. (Notice that this is substantiated by the required parenthetical changes in the rest of the truth-table.) When we assign the remaining truth-values in the second case, however, we find that p→q is true, as required by our original assumption that the argument is invalid. Hence this argument is indeed invalid as assumed. Notice this short-cut test applied to the other two moods of the mixed conditional syllogism:

$$[(p \rightarrow q) \cdot q] \rightarrow p \qquad\qquad [(p \rightarrow q) \cdot -q] \rightarrow -p$$

F T T T T F F	T **T** F T T F F
	F
Invalid	Valid

Specific linguistic conditional arguments may also be evaluated in this way. All that we need to do is to formulate the argument symbolically as one conditional proposition and then use one of the truth-table tests. Let us evaluate the following argument:

    i → f   "If (war is imminent,) he contended, ("the UN has failed,") whatever its
            accomplishments in the fields of economic and social aid. But he insisted,

    −i   −f
    ────   (this is not the case;) (there are at least five major occasions when a
    −f   −i

            world war seemed probable or possible and . . . did not actually break
            out.) (from *The Haverford* (College) *News*)

$$[(i \rightarrow f) \cdot -i] \rightarrow -f \qquad \text{Invalid;}$$
          F T T T T F F   fallacy of denying the antecedent

Notice that the clause "this is not the case" in this argument is ambiguous; it may be the denial of either the UN's failure or the imminence of war. This ambiguity is immediately removed, however, by the fact that the last proposition clearly means that war is not imminent and the fact that it is offered in evidence as a premise. Hence the former proposition must be a conclusion concerning the other one of the two component propositions.

Mixed Alternative Syllogisms.   The conditional proposition is not the only one which determines a mixed hypothetical syllogism, for the other kinds of hypothetical proposition also do. An argument whose major premise is an alternative proposition (either inclusive or exclusive) and whose minor premise and conclusion are simple categorical propositions is known as a *mixed alternative syllogism*. Since the minor premise may again either affirm or deny either one or the other of the two alternants, there are four possible moods of the mixed alternative syllogism. When the "or" is *inclusive*, two of these moods are valid and two of them invalid:

pVq	pVq	pVq	pVq
p	−p	q	−q
−q	q	−p	p

$[(pVq) \cdot p] \to -q$	$[(pVq) \cdot -p] \to q$	$[(pVq) \cdot q] \to -p$	$[(pVq) \cdot -q] \to p$
TT TT F F	FFF F T T F	TT TT F F	FFF F T T F
	T T		T T
	F F T F		F F T F
	T T		T T

or:

$[(pVq) \cdot p] \to -q$	$[(pVq) \cdot -p] \to q$	$[(pVq) \cdot q] \to -p$	$[(pVq) \cdot -q] \to p$
TTT TT F F	F̶T̶F T T F F	TTT TT F F	F̶T̶F T T F F
	F		F

Notice in the first truth-table that since the truth of one alternant is sufficient for the truth of an inclusive alternative proposition, we can stop as soon as we have one alternant true. The fact that the second and fourth of the above moods are valid while the first and third are invalid can also be easily seen by remembering the meaning of "V." Since the inclusive "or" means that one or both of the alternants are true, we may validly argue from the falsity of one to the truth of the other, but we cannot argue validly from the truth of one to the falsity of the other—since they may both be true. Hence the mixed inclusive alternative syllogism has two valid moods—those whose premises deny—and two invalid ones whose fallacies are known as *affirming an alternant* (in the premise).

When the "or" is *exclusive*, however, all four moods will be valid:

p Ⅴ q	p Ⅴ q	p Ⅴ q	p Ⅴ q
p	−p	q	−q
−q	q	−p	p

$[(p \veebar q) \cdot p] \rightarrow -q$ $[(p \veebar q) \cdot -p] \rightarrow q$ $[(p \veebar q) \cdot q] \rightarrow -p$ $[(p \veebar q) \cdot -q] \rightarrow p$

```
TFT FT  T F      FFF FT   T F     TFT FT  T F      FFF FT   T F
        T T               T T             T T               T T
 FF T F           FF  T F           FF T F           FF  T F
        T T               T T             T T               T T
```

or:

$[(p \veebar q) \cdot p] \rightarrow -q$ $[(p \veebar q) \cdot -p] \rightarrow q$ $[(p \veebar q) \cdot q] \rightarrow -p$ $[(p \veebar q) \cdot -q] \rightarrow p$

```
TⱵT TT F F       FⱵF TT  F F      TⱵT TT F F       FⱵF TT  F F
F                F                F                F
```

Observe that we cannot determine the truth-value of an exclusive alternative proposition until we know the truth-value of both the alternants. The validity of all four moods of the mixed exclusive alternative syllogism can be seen intuitively by remembering that "Ⱶ" means "exactly one true," so that we may argue either from denial to affirmation or from affirmation to denial.

Since alternative propositions may contain more than two alternants, it is possible to have, correspondingly, a mixed alternative syllogism whose major premise contains three or more alternants. But such arguments are handled just like those with two alternants, except that their truth-tables need a column under only one of the "or" signs. The inclusive alternative proposition will be true whenever one or more of the alternants are true, and the exclusive alternative whenever exactly one of the alternants is true.

Mixed alternative syllogisms are not in fact any more hypothetical than mixed conditional ones, since, again, the minor premise and the conclusion assert the two alternants (or their negations) categorically. Furthermore, since alternative propositions are equivalent to conditional ones—exclusive alternative propositions being equivalent to two pairs of conditional ones—mixed alternative syllogisms may always be transformed into mixed conditional syllogisms. Consequently, since mixed conditional syllogisms are equivalent to causal propositions, and since many of them are in turn equivalent to categorical syllogisms or sorites, the same is true of mixed alternative syllogisms. Notice the following transformations:

$$
\left.\begin{array}{c} (SaP) \vee (SaQ) \\ -(SaP) \\ \hline (SaQ) \end{array}\right\}
\quad
\left.\begin{array}{c} -(SaP) \rightarrow (SaQ) \\ -(SaP) \\ \hline (SaQ) \end{array}\right\}
\quad
\left.\begin{array}{c} \vdash -(SaP) \\ \vdash \;\; \overset{\rightarrow}{(SaQ)} \end{array}\right\}
\quad
\frac{\begin{array}{c}(\bar{Q}aP)\\ SoP \end{array}}{SoQ}
$$

The minor premise of the categorical syllogism is an O proposition in order to be equivalent to the antecedent of the corresponding causal proposition, for the latter is the contradictory of an A proposition. Observe also that the conclusion of the categorical syllogism must therefore be not only obverted in order to give a negative conclusion but also limited to a particular proposition in order to match the particular negative premise. If the term "S" is singular, however, then the minor premise could be SeP and the conclusion Se$\bar{Q}$.

All the other moods of the inclusive alternative syllogism, and all the moods of the exclusive alternative syllogism, may also be transformed by the same type of procedure, as you can see for yourself by trying it out.

Particular linguistic examples of mixed alternative syllogisms may be tested in exactly the same way as conditional ones, as in the following example:

r
Either (Russia will remain a member of the UN, in spite of her revolutionary

rVc
        V   c
ideology,) or else (the UN will collapse.)

r   r
Now the Kremlin has officially announced that (Russia will retain her member-
——   ship) in order to work for world peace.

—c   —c
Hence it seems certain that (the UN will remain intact.)

$$[(r \lor c) \cdot r] \to -c$$
$$\overline{\text{T TT TT F F}}$$
                                   Invalid;
                                   fallacy of affirming an alternant

Mixed Disjunctive Syllogisms. Such a syllogism is an argument whose major premise is a disjunctive proposition and whose minor premise and conclusion are simple categorical propositions. Since the minor premise may either affirm or deny either one or the other of the two disjuncts, there are four possible moods, two of them valid and two invalid. As a check let us use here, and from now on, only the shortest of the truth-table tests:

$-(p \cdot q)$ $-(p \cdot q)$
p $-p$
$\overline{-q}$ $\overline{q}$

$[-(p \cdot q) \cdot p] \to -q$ $[-(p \cdot q) \cdot -p] \to q$
$\overline{\text{T T}\cancel{\text{F}}\text{T TT F F}}$ $\overline{\text{T FFF TT   F F}}$
  T

$-(p \cdot q)$ $-(p \cdot q)$
q $-q$
$\overline{-p}$ $\overline{p}$

$[-(p \cdot q) \cdot q] \to -p$ $[-(p \cdot q) \cdot -q] \to p$
$\overline{\text{T T}\cancel{\text{F}}\text{T TT F F}}$ $\overline{\text{T FFF TT   F F}}$
  T

The validity of the first and third moods can also be seen intuitively by remembering that a disjunctive proposition says that both disjuncts cannot be true. Hence if either one of them is true the other one must be false. And the second and fourth moods are invalid precisely because they argue from the falsity of one of the disjuncts to the truth of the other, when in fact they might both be false. The fallacies of these two invalid moods are known simply as the fallacy of *denying a disjunct* (in the premise).

Like alternative syllogisms, disjunctive ones may also have a major premise with more than two components. Such arguments are handled in exactly the same way as two component disjunctive syllogisms, except that we need a truth column under only one of the "ands." The whole proposition will be true whenever one or more of the disjuncts are false.

Like mixed conditional and alternative syllogisms, mixed disjunctive syllogisms are not actually hypothetical at all—again since their components (or their negations) are asserted categorically in the minor premise and conclusion. Hence they too (unless they are inductive arguments or consist of merely equivalent propositions) are equivalent to one or more categorical syllogisms. This can be shown by effecting the same sort of transformation we performed with alternative syllogisms:

$$
\left. \begin{array}{l} -[(SaP) \cdot (SaQ)] \\ (SaP) \\ \hline -(SaQ) \end{array} \right\}
\left. \begin{array}{l} (SaP) \to -(SaQ) \\ (SaP) \\ \hline -(SaQ) \end{array} \right\}
\begin{array}{l} \vdash (SaP) \\ \\ \vdash -\overset{\to}{(SaQ)} \end{array}
\begin{array}{l} (Qe\underline{P}) \\ \underline{\underline{S}aP} \\ SoQ \end{array}
$$

Here again the conclusion must become an O proposition, since the contradictory of an A proposition is an O, thus producing a weakened syllogism—since the same premises warrant the conclusion SeQ. But once more if S is a singular term the conclusion may be SeQ. It would be good practice to transform the other moods of the mixed disjunctive syllogism into their corresponding categorical syllogisms by following the same procedure.

Let us use our evaluation procedure to test one concrete example:

$$-(m \cdot i)$$ The government cannot (continue its program of military spending)

$$-m$$ and yet (expect the country to improve its standard of living.) But since

$$i$$ it now appears that (military spending will be decreased,) (we can look

forward to an improved standard of living.)

$$\frac{[-(m \cdot i) \cdot -m] \to i}{T \ \ FFF \ TT \ \ \ FF}$$ Invalid; fallacy of denying a disjunct

24-2   PURE HYPOTHETICAL SYLLOGISMS

Instead of having compound and simple propositions mixed together, we sometimes encounter arguments in which all of the propositions are compound ones. These are called *pure* compound arguments. If the component propositions are conditional ones, the argument is called a *pure conditional syllogism.* The following are valid examples:

$$p \to q \quad \text{If (folks get pessimistic) (they want to quit,) and if}$$

$$q \to r \quad \text{(they want to quit) (they get reckless;) so if (folks}$$

$$\overline{p \to r} \quad \text{get pessimistic) (they get reckless.)}$$

$$p \to q \quad \text{If (folks get pessimistic) (they want to quit,) and if}$$

$$q \to r \quad \text{they want to quit) (they get reckless;) so if (folks do}$$

$$\overline{-r \to -p} \quad \text{not get reckless) (they do not get pessimistic.)}$$

It is easy to see that the principle governing this type of argument is the same as that operative in mixed conditional syllogisms, namely, that the antecedent is a sufficient condition for the consequent and the consequent a necessary condition for the antecedent. Whenever a pure conditional syllogism violates this principle it is invalid, as in the following example:

$$p \to q \quad \text{If (the proletariat arises) (the politicians will quake,)}$$

$$q \to r \quad \text{and if (the politicians quake) (there will be a revolution,)}$$

$$\overline{r \to p} \quad \text{so if (there is a revolution) (the proletariat will arise.)}$$

This argument is guilty of the fallacy of affirming a consequent. The shortest truth-table test can be used on pure hypothetical syllogisms also:

$$[(p \to q) \cdot (q \to r)] \to (p \to r) \qquad [(p \to q) \cdot (q \to r)] \to (-r \to -p)$$

T **T** F	T	F	T F	F	T F F		T **T** F	T	F	T F	F	T	F F
F							F						

$$[(p \to q) \cdot (q \to r)] \to (r \to p)$$

F	T T	T	T	T T	F	T F F

Notice here that since the consequent is itself a conditional proposition, its falsity (as determined by the assumed falsity of the total conditional proposition) determines the truth-values of its two components; since (in the first example) p→r is false, then p is true and r is false. Notice also that the same is true in the antecedent of the total conditional proposition; any letter whose truth-value is not immediately known receives its truth-value from the context. Thus in the first example since q→r is true and r is false, q must be false.

A pure conditional syllogism may contain any number of conditional propositions; for example: "If a nail is lacking the shoe is lost, if the shoe is lost the horse is lost, if the horse is lost the rider is lost, if the rider is lost the army is lost, if the army is lost the kingdom is lost; hence, for want of a nail a kingdom is lost." When such an argument contains more than three conditional propositions, it might better be called a pure conditional *sorites,* after the analogy of the regular, categorical sorites.[2]

Unlike the mixed conditional syllogism, the pure one is truly hypothetical, for it contains no categorical assertions except, of course, of the implicative connections. Hence it is not properly equivalent to any set of categorical syllogisms. However, since each of its conditional propositions *corresponds* to an enthymeme, a pure conditional syllogism *corresponds* to at least as many enthymemes, and hence at least as many categorical syllogisms, as the number of propositions it contains. And since the pure conditional syllogism links these corresponding syllogisms together into a single argument while yet remaining hypothetical throughout, it is in fact a hypothetical sorites. This can be seen in the following transformation of our first example, where F = folks, P = pessimistic, Q = quit, and R = reckless:

$$(\underline{P}aQ) \longrightarrow (\underline{P}aR)$$

$$
\begin{array}{ll}
\left.\begin{array}{l}(FaP) \\ \rightarrow \\ (FaQ)\end{array}\right\} & \begin{array}{l}?\underline{F}aP \\ \overline{} \\ ?\underline{F}aQ\end{array} \qquad
\left.\begin{array}{l}(FaP)\end{array}\right| \qquad ?\underline{F}aP
\end{array}
$$

$$(QaR)$$

$$\rightarrow$$

$$
\begin{array}{ll}
\left.\begin{array}{l}(FaQ) \\ \rightarrow \\ (FaR)\end{array}\right\} & \begin{array}{l}?\underline{F}aQ \\ \overline{} \\ ?\underline{F}aR\end{array} \qquad
\left.\begin{array}{l}(FaR)\end{array}\right| \qquad ?\underline{F}aR
\end{array}
$$

By the same token a pure *causal* syllogism, such as "Since friends are pleasant they are much to be desired, and since they are much to be desired they are worth working for; hence, since friends are pleasant they are worth working

[2] Pp. 325–329 above.

for," is equivalent to a *categorical* sorites containing at least as many categorical syllogisms as the causal syllogism contains causal propositions.

Pure alternative and pure disjunctive syllogisms are quite rare in everyday life, but their structure is strictly parallel to that of the pure conditional syllogism: $-p \lor q$ and $-q \lor r$ therefore $-p \lor r$, and $-(p \cdot -q)$ and $-(q \cdot -r)$ hence $-(p \cdot -r)$. Consequently they may be tested in the same way as pure conditional syllogisms.

24–3 DILEMMAS

The number of arguments involving compound propositions is limited only by our energy, but one last type requires special attention because of its frequency and rhetorical efficacy. This is the *dilemma*.

The philosopher Thomas Hobbes, some critics have said, is in the following dilemma: "If Hobbes' natural laws are constantly changing then they cannot be laws, for laws are constants. And if they are not constantly changing then, according to his metaphysics, they cannot be real. But they must either be constantly changing or not. Hence they are either unreal or else not laws." This argument may be formalized as follows:

$$(c \rightarrow -1) \cdot (-c \rightarrow -r)$$
$$\underline{c \lor -c}$$
$$-1 \lor -r$$

Notice that the "or" of the minor premise would seem to be exclusive in meaning, but that the argument is valid whether or not this is so.

Thus the dilemma is an argument whose major premise is a conjunction of two conditional propositions and whose minor premise is an alternative proposition. This structure may be understood better by examining the four valid moods of the dilemma:

Simple Constructive

$$(p \rightarrow q) \cdot (r \rightarrow q)$$
$$\underline{p \lor r}$$
$$q$$

Complex Constructive

$$(p \rightarrow q) \cdot (r \rightarrow s)$$
$$\underline{p \lor r}$$
$$q \lor s$$

Simple Destructive

$$(p \rightarrow q) \cdot (p \rightarrow r)$$
$$\underline{-q \lor -r}$$
$$-p$$

Complex Destructive

$$(p \rightarrow q) \cdot (r \rightarrow s)$$
$$\underline{-q \lor -s}$$
$$-p \lor -r$$

A simple dilemma is one whose conclusion is a simple categorical proposition, and a complex dilemma is one whose conclusion is an alternative (and thus a compound) proposition. A constructive dilemma is one which affirms, and a destructive dilemma one which denies, in the minor premise and conclusion.

It can be seen from the above forms that the dilemma is really simply an alternation between two mixed conditional syllogisms, and thus is not really an essentially new form of argument. When we use a dilemma we are not prepared to make any categorical assertions about the components of the major premise, but we are willing to make a hypothetical assertion and hence to draw a hypothetical conclusion. Since the dilemma is simply an alternation between two mixed conditional syllogisms, the principles governing the validity of the former are the same as those for the latter, namely, that one may validly proceed from affirming an antecedent to affirming a consequent *(modus ponens)* or from denying a consequent to denying an antecedent *(modus tollens)*, but not from denying an antecedent to denying a consequent or from affirming a consequent to affirming an antecedent. Furthermore, since the dilemma is an alternation between two mixed conditional syllogisms, it can easily be shown to be transformable into an alternation between two categorical syllogisms or sorites by using the procedure followed on p. 355.

In actual use dilemmas are often enthymematic, the speaker or writer leaving the listener to supply the tacit propositions. Most frequently it is the alternative minor premise which is omitted, as when the ambitious businessman, trying to impress his son with the supreme importance of industry, argues that "If a man has money then friends are superfluous, and if he doesn't then they're useless; so friends are either superfluous or useless." Here it is to be understood that "a man either has money or he hasn't." But sometimes both the minor premise and the conclusion remain tacit, and the listener or reader is left to draw his own conclusion: "If a man has money friends are superfluous, and if he doesn't they are useless."

The validity of dilemmas may be tested either by applying the rules for valid conditional inference or by using truth-tables. The shorter truth-table may again be used, since validity abstracts from the question of the actual truth or falsity of the component propositions and any implicative intentions they may contain; and once more our shortest truth-table test will save time:

$$(m \rightarrow s) \cdot (-m \rightarrow u) \quad \text{If } \overset{m}{\text{(a man has money)}} \overset{\rightarrow}{} \overset{s}{\text{(friends are superfluous,)}}$$

$$(m \lor -m) \quad \text{and if } \overset{-m}{\text{(he doesn't)}} \overset{\rightarrow}{} \overset{u}{\text{(they are useless.)}}$$

$$\overline{(s \lor u)}$$

valid

$$\{[(m \rightarrow s) \cdot (-m \rightarrow u)] \cdot (m \lor -m)\} \rightarrow (s \lor u)$$

T	Ⱦ F	T	F	T	F	T	T	F	F	F F
F										

The minor premise may be an exclusive instead of an inclusive alternative proposition, but you can easily prove for yourself that this would not affect the validity of this dilemma.

Invalid dilemmas are usually rather easily detected with the result that they have little plausibility. Hence most dilemmas encountered in ordinary life are formally valid, and since they can be quite plausible it is important to know how to deal with them. There are three different ways of replying to a dilemmatic argument:

a. **"Escaping Between the Horns."**   The "horns" of a dilemma are the two alternatives contained in the minor premise. Hence to "escape between the horns" of a dilemma is to deny the alternative minor premise by asserting the existence of a third alternative. Thus we might answer the dilemma we have just been considering by arguing as follows: "Of course if you want to be pedantic about it, it's technically true that a person must either have some money or else not any at all at a given time; but "having money" usually means having a lot of money, and it's certainly not true that a person must either have a lot of money or else none at all. In fact, most people fall in between these two alternatives, so the conclusion doesn't follow." Yet this answer is a little precarious, for the first speaker might in turn reply: "But even on your definition there's no third alternative, for it's surely true that a person must either have a lot of money or *not* have a lot of money. If I had said that a person must be either rich or poor you would be right, but I didn't. Hence my argument still holds." Thus it is often difficult to escape between the horns, and, indeed, it is impossible if, as is frequently the case, the alternants are true contradictories. So in our earlier example about Hobbes' natural laws there would seem to be no third alternative between their being in constant change and their not being in constant change. In such cases we must try some other way of answering the dilemma.

b. **"Taking the Dilemma by the Horns."**   To take a dilemma by the horns is to accept the truth of the alternative premise and to deny one or both of the conditional propositions in the major premise. Thus we might stand up for the value of friendship as follows: "It's false that friends are superfluous if a man has money, and it's also false that they're useless if he doesn't. Even a rich man needs and wants friends, and, to accept for a moment your own ignoble principles, friends may be extremely useful to a poor man if those friends have money or influence. So you're wrong about friends being either superfluous or useless." The principle operative when a dilemma is taken by the horns is of course simply that a true antecedent does not produce a true consequent, and a false consequent does not produce a false antecedent, when there is in fact no implicative connection between them.

c. **Rebutting a Dilemma.**   Rebutting a dilemma consists in constructing a counter-dilemma whose conclusion denies the original conclusion. This is done by simply negating the conclusion proposition or propositions in *the major premise,* and, in *complex* dilemmas, also by *interchanging* them. Since the alternative minor premise remains the same, the conclusion will then deny the original conclusion. In constructive dilemmas it will be the consequents of the original major premise which are interchanged and negated, while in destructive dilemmas it will be the antecedents:

	Simple Constructive		*Complex Constructive*	
original	rebuttal	original	rebuttal
$(p \to q) \cdot (r \to q)$	$(p \to -q) \cdot (r \to -q)$	$(p \to q) \cdot (r \to s)$	$(p \to -s) \cdot (r \to -q)$
pVr	pVr	pVr	pVr
q	$-q$	qVs	$-sV-q$

	Simple Destructive		*Complex Destructive*	
original	rebuttal	original	rebuttal
$(p \to q) \cdot (p \to r)$	$(-p \to q) \cdot (-p \to r)$	$(p \to q) \cdot (r \to s)$	$(-r \to q) \cdot (-p \to s)$
$-qV-r$	$-qV-r$	$-qV-s$	$-qV-s$
$-p$	p	$-pV-r$	rVp

The actual plausibility of a dilemma, however, depends as much upon its linguistic phrasing as upon its embodiment of one of the above logical forms. To rebut the dilemma posed by our pecunious friend by saying that "If a man doesn't have money friends are certainly not superfluous, and if he does have money then they are certainly not useless" is not very persuasive. But the plausibility is increased if we rephrase the same counter-dilemma as follows: "If a man doesn't have money friends are necessary, and if he does they are still useful. Hence friends are either necessary or useful or both." A classic example of a plausible dilemma and equally plausible rebuttal concerns a legendary argument used by a mother in ancient Athens to try to persuade her son not to go into politics: "If you tell the truth men will hate you, and if you don't tell the truth the gods will hate you, so you won't be able to avoid being hated." The son's rebuttal was as follows: "If I tell the truth the gods will love me, and if I don't tell the truth men will love me, so I can't help but be loved."

But notice that the son's rebuttal does not really contradict or deny the mother's argument, for it is of course possible for a person to be both hated and loved—or neither hated nor loved, for that matter. Indeed, even if the son's rebuttal were changed to read that "either the gods will not hate me or men will not hate me," it would still not contradict the mother's conclusion, for we know from De Morgan's law[3] that $-ghV - mh$, the son's conclusion, is not the contradictory of $ghVmh$, the mother's conclusion. To contradict a hypothetical proposition we must always have a categorical proposition, here $-gh \cdot -mh$. Hence a rebuttal can never contradict a complex dilemma since the latter always has alternative conclusion. But it is possible for the rebuttal to contra-

[3] P. 346.

dict a simple dilemma, as can be seen from the above table of forms, since both it and its rebuttal have simple categorical propositions for conclusions.

Since the construction of a counter-dilemma involves an alteration in the major premise, the rebuttal is actually a variation of "taking the dilemma by the horns"; and this latter technique is in any event probably the most basic way of dealing with a dilemma.

Summary of Deductive Argument. We have now completed our survey of deductive argument. Our basic deductive tool is the syllogism, an argument with three propositions containing three terms, each occurring twice. Once they have been logically formulated, syllogisms may be evaluated in various ways, such as by axioms or by Venn diagrams. But we also use many variations of the syllogism. Enthymemes and sorites, as soon as their tacit propositions are supplied, may be immediately evaluated just like ordinary syllogisms. Compound propositions and arguments built out of them may be either translated into syllogisms (or their denials), tested by rules of their own, or evaluated by the use of truth-tables. By using any of these deductive arguments we can obtain certain and exact knowledge *provided* that our premises are true. But no deductive argument establishes the truth of its own premises. For this we need another form of argument, inductive argument; and we must now continue our earlier investigation of it.

EXERCISES

1. Formulate and test each of the following arguments involving compound syllogisms, and translate each into the other types of compound syllogism (conditional into alternative and disjunctive, etc.).

   a. *Othello* was written by Shakespeare or Francis Bacon or Edward de Vere. But it couldn't have been either Shakespeare or Bacon, because Edward de Vere wrote it.

   b. "Any cars around?" "Kelly said there wasn't, that he didn't see any, and couldn't of missed seeing it if there'd been one." (Dashiell Hammett, *The Continental Op.*, from Donald Williams)

   c. "Choice between good and evil implies that there is morality and immorality. Therefore if freedom of choice is denied, you deny the existence of the good life." (student essay)

   d. If the objective of marriage were bliss then its disagreeableness to either party would be a sufficient reason for dissolving it. But since it is not, the object of marriage is not bliss.

   e. You can't continue the G.I. bill without further increasing the national debt. Hence we will simply discontinue all veterans' benefits and this will enable us to keep the national debt from increasing, at least.

   f. If he were a serious suspect in this embezzlement case he would certainly not have been allowed to keep his job in the office. But since he has the job, he is obviously not a suspect.

g. Either you study hard or you fail the examination. You say you have studied hard? Then you will not fail it.

h. The fact that the leaves have turned earlier than usual this fall may be due to either cold or drought. Now we've had a lot of cold weather lately, so the turning of the leaves cannot have been caused by drought.

i. If he had been seeing ten movies a week we might safely infer that he is not a serious student. Since he has in fact seen less than two a week, however, he must be sincerely concerned with his studies.

j. The Democratic party cannot at the present time both write UN admission of Red China into its platform and still hope for success in the fall election. So the dropping of this item from the platform permits us to infer that the Democrats will win.

k. If the colleges and universities are to maintain their standards and still accommodate the coming wave of students, they must either make the teaching profession more attractive financially or else discover means of widely extending the use of audio-visual aids. With the recent reservation of certain TV channels for educational purposes it therefore follows that the institutions of higher education will in fact be able to accommodate the great influx of students without lowering their standards.

l. It's impossible to be an orthodox Soviet biologist and still admit the Mendelian principles of hereditary transmission of traits. Zhebrak, former president of the White Russian Academy of Sciences, defended the Mendelian principles against Lysenko. Zhebrak is therefore not an orthodox Soviet biologist.

2. Formulate, test, and answer in the three ways described on pp. 367–369 each of the following dilemmas:

a. Not wishing to pay for his daughter Penny's college education, Patrick Pinchpenny argued thus: "If a woman is good-looking higher education is superfluous, and if she is not it is pointless."

b. If freedom of speech is restricted to thinkers, we will cease to be a democracy; and if freedom of speech is granted to all, we will be exploited by fanatics. Hence it appears as though we shall either cease to be a democracy or else be exploited by fanatics.

c. If the revolution fails, you will be hanged as a traitor. If it succeeds, you will be assassinated as a martyr. So in either case you're going to get it.

d. Protagoras agreed to teach rhetoric to Euathlus for a fee to be paid when Euathlus won his first lawsuit. Taking no chances on losing his fee, however, Protagoras immediately brought suit for payment, defending his case by arguing before the jury as follows: "If Euathlus loses this case, he must pay me by the judgment of the court. And if he wins he must pay me by our agreement. Hence in any case he has to pay."

e. "In the debates between Lincoln and Douglas, in 1858, when Douglas, then Senator from Illinois (and a Democrat), was a candidate for reelection and Lincoln was the opposing Republican candidate, Douglas promised to give definite answers to any questions (not exceeding a certain number) that Lincoln might ask him. One of Lincoln's questions was: 'Can the people of a United States Territory, in any lawful way, against the wish of any citizens of the United States, exclude slavery from its limits, prior to the formation of a state constitution?' If Douglas answered this question in the affirmative, he would please the voters of Illinois, both Democrats and Republicans, and could be reelected to the Senate; but if he answered it in the negative, he could not be reelected. On the other hand, Douglas hoped to be the Democratic candidate for the Presidency in 1860, and if he answered this question in the affirmative he would offend the Democrats of the South, and could not obtain their support, and so could not be elected President. Moreover, if Douglas should be defeated in his own state for the Senatorship he could hardly hope that the Democratic party would nominate him for President. So Lincoln's question put Douglas into a dilemma: If he answered the question in the negative, he would be defeated for the Senatorship, and could not become President; if he answered the question in the affirmative, he would lose the support of the South and could not become President. But he had publicly promised to answer the question, so he could not be elected President." (from Bode, in A. M. Frye and A. W. Levi, *Rational Belief*, Harcourt, Brace, 1941, p. 316)

3. The following is a mixed list of various types of deductive argument. Put each argument into logical and symbolic form (supplying tacit propositions where necessary), name the type of argument, state whether it is valid or invalid (using an appropriate test) and if invalid name the fallacy.

a. "So the body is not the soul, for if the soul is an attribute of a living thing, then those things which are not living cannot have souls, and this we assume to be correct." (student essay)

b. "First we must prove whether there is knowledge in God, and the extent of such knowledge. Now the knower is naturally adapted to possess the form of some other thing, while the non-knowing being possesses only its own form. Hence it is manifest that the nature of a non-knowing being is more contracted and limited: whereas the nature of knowing beings has greater amplitude and extension. Now, the contraction of a being comes through matter, and since God has no matter, he, in no wise, can be contracted, and in fact he must have the greatest amplitude and extension, because he is pure actuality. We may therefore say that in God is the greatest knowledge." (a student's paraphrase of an argument from Thomas Aquinas)

c. "If any interaction between what we call mind and what we call body is to be accounted for, they cannot be completely separate. If they are not completely separate—then they can be regarded as variations of something which is essentially one. If they are one—the one is either physical in character, mental in character, or like something which we can't conceive of in character. If the latter were to be true we couldn't begin to conceive of a solution. Thus, within the scope of this paper, the two alternatives for the nature of the one are mental and physical. One of the realms we imagine as separate is mythical and has its nature contained by the other." (student essay)

d. "Therefore, if we do not wish to waste our one chance to reach the supreme, or, positively, if we want to get the most out of our existence and approach the supreme as closely as we can, we should try to develop our potentiality to its fullest extent."

"Any righteous man, regardless of his standard of right or his definition of virtue, believes that virtue is *what we should do*. Since, by our last conclusion, we should try to develop our potentiality to its fullest extent, this development is virtuous. Since we have established that anything which is virtuous is good, *everything which we do to develop our potentiality is good*." (student essay)

e. "Did you say in your evidence, 'I didn't want to do Drage any harm, provided he didn't do her any harm'?" "Yes, I think I did." "Was I correct in assuming that [this] meant, 'If Drage does Miss Yates any harm, then I want to do Drage some harm'?" "Well—I suppose I meant something like that." "Can you think of any other interpretation of the words in question?" (Jefferson Farjeon, *The Judge Sums Up*, from Donald Williams) (In addition to following the above instructions, answer the judge's question.)

f. "Assume that the universe is static. Then within it there are no relationships. Because there are no relationships there are no functions. But if there are no functions there is no unequivocal being. And if there is no unequivocal being the universe does not really exist. But to say that the universe does not really exist implies that there is something which is really nothing, and this proposition is self-contradictory. Therefore, logically at least, the universe is dynamic." (student essay)

g. If we want lasting peace we must have international inspection and control of atomic energy. But if we retain the tradition of national sovereignties we leave ultimate control of atomic energy in the hands of the individual nations. Hence if we retain the tradition of national sovereignties we cannot have lasting peace.

h. "However, rational evidence will not prove the existence of God for the nature of God transcends the boundaries of reason itself. If such were not the case, He could only be known through a logical structure, He would only be able to be known by the intellectual." (student essay)

i. "Touching upon the implicit claim of infallibility on the part of the Anglicans, he [Penn] advances this cogent argument: The Scriptures, you see, cannot determine the sense of itself; it must have an interpreter; he must either be fallible or infallible; if the first, we are worse than before, for men are apt to be more confident, and yet are still upon as uncertain grounds; if the last, this must be either an external or an internal judge; if an external, you know where you are without pointing, for there stands nothing between you and Popery in that principle; if an internal judge, either it is ourselves or the spirit of Christ dwelling in us; not ourselves, for then the rule is the thing ruled, which cannot be; and if it be the spirit of Christ Jesus, then is the neck of the imposition broken, and what shalt thou do to judge me? Let me stand or fall to my own master. And upon this foot went Luther, Calvin, Melancthon, Beza abroad, and Cranmer, Ridley, Hooper, Jewel, Bradford, Philpot, etc. at home, and as good men and constant martyrs in ages before them.

"This argument proves two truths to Penn; namely, that the Quakers are right in acting according to the spirit of Christ in them, 'that of God in every man,' and secondly, that in so doing they belong to the line of recognized

Protestant theologians." (W. W. Comfort, *William Penn*, University of Pennsylvania, 1944, p. 123)

j. "I am sure that you have read the charge that I, Senator Nixon, took $18,000 from a group of my supporters.

"Now, was that wrong? And let me say that it was wrong. I am saying it, incidentally, that it was wrong, not just illegal, because it isn't a question of whether it was legal or illegal, that isn't enough. The question is, was it morally wrong. I say it was morally wrong—if any of that $18,000 went to Senator Nixon, for my personal use. I say that it was morally wrong if it was secretly given and secretly handled.

"And I say it was morally wrong if any of the contributors got special favors for the contributions they made.

"And now to answer those questions let me say this: Not one cent of the $18,000 or any other money of that type ever went to me for my personal use. Every penny of it was used to pay for political expenses that I did not think should be charged to the taxpayers of the United States.

"It was not a secret fund. As a matter of fact, when I was on Meet the Press—some of you may have seen it, last Sunday—Peter Edson came up to me, after the program, and he said, Dick, what about this fund we hear about, and I said, well, there is no secret about it. Go out and see Dana Smith, who was the administrator of the fund. And I gave him his address. And I said you will find that the purpose of the fund simply was to defray political expenses that I did not feel should be charged to the Government.

"And third, let me point out, and I want to make this particularly clear, that no contributor to this fund, no contributor to any of my campaigns, has ever received any consideration that he would not have received as an ordinary constituent.

"I just don't believe in that, and I can say that never, while I have been in the Senate of the United States, as far as the people who contributed to this fund are concerned, have I made a telephone call for them to an agency, nor have I gone down to an agency in their behalf.

"And the records will show that, the records which are in the hands of the administration." (from a speech by Richard Nixon during the 1952 campaign)

CHAPTER 25

VERIFYING HYPOTHESES:
FORMAL ASPECTS

Review. In deriving conclusions from our deductive arguments we have so far merely assumed the truth of the propositions which we have used as premises. With such assumptions we can validly establish our conclusions as true *if* our assumptions are true. But just as a chain is no stronger than its weakest link, so also a conclusion is no stronger than its premises. Validity is not the same thing as truth, and even though a conclusion is valid it may still be false if the premises from which it was derived should happen, some or all of them, to be false. How, then, can we arrive at knowledge which is not only valid but true? Only by insuring the truth of our premises. We have already discussed at some length the ways in which this may be done,[1] but we must now return to this topic and examine it more fully, first briefly summarizing the conclusions which we have already achieved.

How can we establish the truth of the propositions which we use as premises in deductive arguments? We have seen that any proposition is either immediately (self) evident or else mediately evident. Now the premises of deductive arguments cannot always be mediately evident by *deduction,* for no deductive argument evidences its own premises; and if the premises are established by some other deductive argument then the premises of that argument need to be established, etc., until sooner or later we reach a deductive argument whose premises are not established deductively at all. Furthermore, as we have also seen, at least most of the premises of deductive arguments are not immediately evident either; we have relatively few fruitful self-evident propositions at our disposal. But how then can the premises of deductive arguments be established so as to make their conclusions true as well as valid? It is at this point, we have seen, that we must have recourse to an entirely distinct mode of mediate evidence or argument: inductive argument.

This distinct mode of argument, we have noted, consists in a return to experience, in the drawing of conclusions from observed particulars instead of from intellectual concepts. We earlier described the process of knowing as a with-

[1] Chap. 19.

drawal and return,[2] but the particular practical techniques we have so far been studying have been in the withdrawal stage. We first withdrew from concrete experience to form abstract, universal concepts, and we clarified them in divisions and definitions, thus taking the first step on the road to knowledge. Then we found that we could freely combine and separate these concepts in propositions, determine the interrelations of these propositions, and use them as premises to deduce valid conclusions—all of this entirely on the intellectual level without any necessity to return to actual experience. But now, when we want to establish these conclusions as being true as well as valid, we are compelled to return to the world of actual experience once more. This time our traffic with the world of experience has a different motive and a different character. This time we are not trying to answer the question "What?"; we are not abstracting essences to form universal concepts. Rather this time we are trying to answer the questions "Whether" and "Why?" and we do it by abstracting from experience existents and causes.

So we establish the truth (or falsity) of our deductive premises by inducing them from immediate experience, by observing that the connections which these propositions generalize are embodied in actual individuals. Thus we establish the truth of the proposition that "The earth attracts bodies" by inducing it from observations that the earth attracts this apple, and that airplane, and that man, etc. This process of induction tells us *whether* something is so— it establishes the truth or falsity of a proposition. It also tells us *why* we should *believe* that it is so—it gives us a reason for *believing*, a *cognitive* cause. But it does not tell us why it *really is* so—it does not present us with a reason for the *fact*, with an *ontological* cause. For example, it has been inductively established, by observations made in many places over many years, that the coldest night of the month usually coincides with the full moon, regardless of cloud or climate. But no one so far seems to have explained *why*. The fact is induced from observations, but this induction does not establish the *reason* for this fact, nor is the reason self-evident. To give the reason for this fact we must find another proposition from which we can deduce it. And when this other proposition is neither deductively nor immediately evident, we must establish it, as we have seen, by the use of a distinct type of induction, an induction of a whole causal or explanatory order. This type of induction is explanation by hypothesis. We have already examined its nature theoretically in some detail,[3] and we must now turn to the logical techniques for formulating and testing hypotheses.

Explanation by Hypothesis.   Let us begin our examination by a consideration of an actual example of explanation by hypothesis:

---

[2] P. 281.
[3] Chap. 19–3.

. . . Several scientists, working with sonic equipment in deep water off the California coast, . . . discovered a widespread "layer" . . . which gave back an answering echo to the sound waves. This reflecting layer, seemingly suspended between the surface and the floor of the Pacific, was found over an area 300 miles wide. . . . . . . Martin W. Johnson, . . . of the Scripps Institution of Oceanography, . . . found that whatever sent back the echoes moved upward and downward in rhythmic fashion, being found near the surface at night, in deep water during the day. This discovery disposed of speculations that the reflections came from something inanimate, . . . and showed that the layer is composed of living creatures capable of controlled movement. . . . With widespread use of echo-sounding instruments, it has become clear that the phenomenon . . . occurs almost universally in the deep ocean basins. . . . [Though] no one is sure what the layer is . . . there are three principal theories . . . the sea's phantom bottom may consist of small planktonic shrimps, of fishes, or of squids.

As for the plankton theory, one of the most convincing arguments is the well-known fact that many plankton creatures make regular vertical migrations of hundreds of feet, rising toward the surface at night, sinking down below the zone of light penetration very early in the morning. This is, of course, exactly the behavior of the scattering layer. . . . Those who say that fish are the reflectors of the sound waves usually account for the vertical migrations . . . by suggesting that the fish are feeding on planktonic shrimp and are following their food. They believe that the air bladder of a fish is, of all structures concerned, most likely from its construction to return a strong echo. There is one outstanding difficulty in the way of accepting this theory: we have no other evidence that concentrations of fish are universally present in the oceans. . . . If the reflecting layer is eventually proved to be composed of fish, the prevailing views of fish distribution will have to be radically revised. . . . Proponents of [the squid] theory argue that squid are abundant enough, and of wide distribution. . . . Thor Heyerdahl reports that at night his raft was literally bombarded by squids. . . . But equally spectacular displays of shrimp have been seen. . . . Direct sampling of the layer is the logical means of discovering its identity, but the problem is to develop large nets that can be operated rapidly enough to capture swift-moving animals. Scientists at Woods Hole, Massachusetts, have towed ordinary plankton nets in the layer and have found that euphausiid shrimps, glassworms, and other deep-water plankton are concentrated there; but there is still a possibility that the layer itself may actually be made up of larger forms feeding on the shrimps—too large or swift to be taken in the presently used nets.[4]

Here the author begins by citing a fact whose truth has been inductively established; the fact that the sea contains a widespread layer which rises at night and sinks during the day. She then continues by discussing three hypotheses which have been advanced to account for this fact, the hypotheses that this layer consists of planktonic shrimp, of fish, or of squid. And finally she presents the evidence for or against each of these three theories. Using this example as a guide, let us first examine in general the method of explanation

[4] From *The Sea Around Us*. Copyright 1950, 1951 by Rachel L. Carson. Reprinted by permission of the Oxford University Press, Inc.

by hypothesis, then the procedure of formulating hypotheses, and finally, in the next chapter, the techniques which may be used to determine which of these formulated hypotheses is to be accepted.

25–1 THE HYPOTHETICO-DEDUCTIVE METHOD

If we formulate the argument offered for the first hypothetical explanation of the ocean's phantom bottom, we have the following:

1. If the layer is composed of planktonic shrimp, then it will make regular vertical migrations, it will occur almost universally in the deep ocean basins, and shrimp will be caught by nets towed in the location of this layer.
2. The layer does in fact make regular vertical migrations, it does occur almost universally in the deep ocean basins, and shrimp are caught by nets towed in the location of this layer.
3. Hence the layer is composed of planktonic shrimp.

The logical structure of this argument may be seen more clearly by formulating it symbolically:

$$p \rightarrow (v \cdot u \cdot c)$$
$$\frac{v \cdot u \cdot c}{p}$$

The argument is formally a mixed conditional syllogism, and from our study of this type of argument[5] we see immediately that it commits the fallacy of affirming the consequent, and that it is therefore invalid, for it is possible for the layer to occur almost universally in the oceans, migrate vertically, and have shrimp caught by nets towed in its location even if it is not itself composed of shrimp. In short, as we already know, the truth of the consequent of a conditional proposition does not insure the truth of the antecedent because the consequent is only a necessary, not a sufficient, condition of the antecedent.

If, however, the situations affirmed in the minor premise composed the *antecedent* rather than the consequent of the conditional major premise, then the argument would be perfectly valid:

$$(v \cdot u \cdot c) \rightarrow p$$
$$\frac{(v \cdot u \cdot c)}{p}$$

The argument would be valid because now the fact that planktonic shrimp migrate vertically, occur almost universally in the deep ocean basins, and are caught by nets lowered in the vicinity of the layer is asserted as a *sufficient* condition for the truth of the hypothesis that planktonic shrimp actually compose that layer. Yet it takes but a moment's reflection to see that this doctoring

[5] Pp. 354–359.

of the original argument has not really cured it, since the conversion of the premise p→(v·u·c) into the premise (v·u·c)→p is just as invalid as the original argument. From the fact that planktonic shrimp behave in the same way as the mysterious layer, it does not necessarily follow that they compose the layer, for other things, such as fish or squid or something else, may also behave in the same way. More generally, we know that the simple conversion of a conditional proposition, like the simple conversion of an A proposition, is invalid because the truth of the former leaves the truth of the latter undetermined.[6]

What then are we to do? Unfortunately, there is nothing else that we can do to increase the validity or certainty of this argument. And this is true of all explanation by hypothesis, for it always has the same form:

$$H \to (p \cdot q \cdot r, \text{ etc.})$$
$$\underline{p \cdot q \cdot r, \text{ etc.}}$$
$$H$$

There is no valid way to demonstrate a hypothesis, *if* we mean by "demonstrate" to *deduce* with *certainty*. The reason for this is that a hypothesis always possesses formally the status of the antecedent of a conditional proposition, and the only evidence that we have for it occupies the position of the consequent of that conditional proposition. To say the same thing in other words, hypotheses cannot be evidenced strictly or properly because, as we have seen,[7] they are themselves the ultimate evidence for other propositions.

Yet this does not mean that hypotheses cannot be evidenced at all, that they constitute an unlawful form of argument. This conclusion follows, on the contrary, only if we insist on regarding hypotheses as *deductive* conclusions. But this attitude is, as we have seen, quite mistaken. Although there certainly is a deductive element in explanation by hypothesis, as will become more and more apparent in the following pages, hypotheses themselves are inductions, not deductions. Hence it is incorrect to apply the criteria of deductive validity to them. Since explanation by hypothesis is a form of inductive argument, we must think in terms of probability rather than certainty. Consequently, even though any attempt to demonstrate a hypothesis commits deductively either the fallacy of affirming the consequent or that of simple conversion, a hypothesis may still be affirmed with some degree of probability. Since the source of the invalidity of the demonstration of a hypothesis, from a deductive point of view, is the failure of its evidence to rise from the status of a necessary condition to that of a sufficient condition, any hypothesis will fall short of certainty in the same degree that its necessary conditions, taken jointly, fall short of sufficiency. Thus the *probability of any hypothesis, H, equals the degree to which the conditions necessary for the truth of H are also sufficient for the truth of H.*

---

[6] See pp. 190–192 and the appropriate truth-table on p. 356.
[7] Pp. 290–293.

If we possessed *all* of the conditions necessary for the truth of a hypothesis, they would also be sufficient, and our mixed conditional syllogism would then be deductively valid:

$$\overset{\leftarrow}{H} \to (p \cdot q \cdot r \cdot s \cdot t \cdots n)$$
$$\text{necessary} \to \text{sufficient}$$

$$\frac{(p \cdot q \cdot r \cdot s \cdot t \cdots n)}{H}$$

But in practice we can never be sure that the known consequences of any hypothesis are in fact all of the conditions necessary for its truth.

Thus no hypothesis can be affirmed with certainty. But if we are unable to affirm hypotheses with certainty, may we at least *deny* them with certainty? To examine this question, let us consider the argument advanced concerning another one of the theories about the composition of the mysterious ocean layer. If we assume that the prevailing views of fish distribution are substantially correct, the argument concerning fish as the composition of the layer might be formulated as follows:

$f \to (e \cdot v \cdot r)$	$\overset{f}{\text{If (the layer is composed of fish),}}$ then (it will cause a strong
	$\overset{e}{\text{echo,}} \cdot \overset{v}{\text{(make regular vertical migrations,)}} \text{ and } \overset{r}{\text{(be restricted}}$
$e \cdot v \cdot -r$	to certain areas of the oceans.) (The layer does in fact cause
	$\overset{e}{\text{a strong echo)}} \cdot \text{and } \overset{v}{\text{(it makes regular vertical migrations,)}} \cdot \text{but}$
	$\overset{-r}{\text{}}$
$-(e \cdot v \cdot r)$	(it occurs almost universally in the deep ocean basins rather
	than being restricted to certain areas.)
	$\overset{-f}{\text{}}$
$-f$	Hence (the layer is not composed of fish.)

Notice here that the denial of one conjunct of a conjunctive proposition implies a denial of the whole conjunctive proposition, since the truth of a conjunctive proposition requires the truth of all of its conjuncts.[8] And observe that this argument is deductively valid, since the conjunctive proposition which is denied is the consequent, rather than the antecedent, of the conditional major premise. Thus it would appear that a hypothesis may be falsified with certainty even though it may not be verified with certainty.

Correct in theory, in practice this conclusion must be qualified so much that

[8] See p. 333.

it is actually never true. Since the demonstration of the truth, as distinguished from the validity, of the conclusion requires that the premises be true, a hypothesis may be falsified with certainty *only* when we are *certain* of the truth of the premises. There are two explicit premises in our above argument, and the certainty of the conclusion requires that both of these be certainly true. If we are certain that fish are restricted to certain areas of the oceans and that their constituting the mysterious layer implies that they are almost universally distributed, then the hypothesis that the layer consists of fish is, so far, certainly refuted. But as a matter of fact, we are told, we are not certain of the minor premise; though the prevailing views of fish distribution indicate that they are restricted to certain areas, it is possible that these views require revision. The truth of the major premise, that the fish theory implies the almost universal distribution of fish (as well as their vertical migrations and strong echoing properties), since the layer has been recorded almost universally, seems more certain from the evidence cited; but since it is also inductively arrived at it can be no more than highly probable and therefore could conceivably be false. Hence the falsity of the fish hypothesis is in fact only probable, even though it follows from the evidence with complete validity.

But these two explicit premises are not the only ones present in this argument, for as a matter of fact there is a whole host of tacit assumptions underlying and determining the argument. There are, among the more obvious ones, the assumptions that the air bladder of a fish is more likely to return a strong echo than other relevant structures, and that fish follow their planktonic food in the latter's vertical migration. A little less obvious but just as important are the assumed reliability of the echo-sounding instruments and the assumption that the layer is indeed composed of living things rather than inorganic substances moved by external forces. No hypothesis is advanced in a vacuum; every hypothesis carries with it a variety of beliefs ranging from ultimate metaphysical convictions constituting a world-view down to propositions about particular matters of fact. And all such tacit assumptions function as premises just as much as the explicit ones. Hence a refutation of any explicit hypothesis is never a refutation of that hypothesis alone; it is a refutation of that explicit hypothesis *together with* all the relevant tacit assumptions. If we symbolize the sum of such relevant tacit premises as T, then the structure of arguments falsifying hypotheses appears as follows:

$$(H \cdot T) \rightarrow (p \cdot q \cdot r, \text{ etc.})$$
$$\underline{-r}$$
$$\underline{-(p \cdot q \cdot r, \text{etc.})}$$
$$-(H \cdot T)$$

Thus we have denied, not the hypothesis taken alone, but rather the hypothesis conjoined with the totality of relevant assumptions. Now the fact that these relevant assumptions, T, are almost all of them tacit is an indication that we are ordinarily convinced of their truth. And if T is in fact true, then we can validly deny the explicit hypothesis

$$\frac{\begin{array}{l} -(H \cdot T) \\ T \end{array}}{-H}$$

because we know that a disjunctive syllogism is valid when the minor premise affirms one of the disjuncts and the conclusion denies the other.[9] Since as a matter of fact, however, T may be partially or even wholly false—since some or all of the relevant tacit assumptions are only probable and could therefore conceivably be false—we cannot in practice affirm T with certainty. Hence it follows that we cannot in practice actually falsify H, the explicit hypothesis, with certainty even though that falsification is, from a deductive point of view, entirely valid.

Thus no hypothesis may be verified with more than probability since the evidence for it consists only of its consequences, which are only necessary conditions. A hypothesis may *theoretically* be *falsified* with certainty if and only if we are certain of all of the premises, both the explicit and the implicit ones; but since in practice we never are completely certain of all the premises, in practice a hypothesis may be falsified only with some degree of probability. Still, the falsification of hypotheses is usually sounder and more reliable than their verification since the former procedure is formally valid whereas the latter procedure is not, or because, in other words, we can usually be surer of the truth of our premises than of the exhaustiveness of our list of consequences of the hypothesis. For that reason we usually find it easier to reject than to accept hypotheses.

But if sound procedure usually requires that we falsify rather than verify hypotheses, how can we arrive at an acceptable hypothesis? We can do so, at least in principle, by a process of elimination. For if we began with all the possible hypotheses explanatory of a given fact and then falsified all but one of them, this remaining one would have to be true. This argument, you will at once see, is formally a mixed alternative syllogism:

$$\frac{(H_1 \lor H_2 \lor H_3 \lor \cdots H_n) \rightarrow F}{-H_2 \cdot -H_3 \cdots -H_n}$$
$$H_1 \rightarrow F$$

And it is valid since an alternative proposition asserts that at least one of the alternants is true, so if all but one of them is shown to be false then the remaining one has to be true.

Once again, however, we must modify our optimism. In the first place it is often the case that we are unable to falsify all but one of the hypotheses under consideration. In such cases we can of course validly assert that one or the other of the remaining, unfalsified hypotheses is true; but we cannot say which one of these it is. Even more important, we are in practice never sure that we have considered all of the possible hypotheses which could explain the given fact. For this reason any hypothesis remaining after such a process of elimination may still not be the true, or the only true, explanation of the fact under consideration, for there may well be others which we have not even considered. Yet this somewhat modest result is still important, for although we can still not be sure that we have reached the true explanation, we can know that of the hypotheses that have been considered our remaining one has stood the tests while the others have failed them, and that this remaining hypothesis is therefore *so far* true. And the only way this conclusion may be validly criticized —provided, of course, there has been no mistake in our reasoning—is by proposing a new alternative hypothesis which can stand the tests as well or better than the one that we have so far accepted.

How then do we proceed to explain a given fact? If it is not deducible from an immediately evident proposition, we proceed as follows: We first formulate hypotheses which imply, and therefore explain, the fact. We then falsify as many of these hypotheses as possible by showing that one or more of their deducible consequences fails to jibe with experience. And finally we accept any remaining hypothesis as so far true, that is, true with some degree of probability and until a better one comes along. This type of argument, this method of explanation which involves both induction and deduction, is known as the hypothetico-deductive method. With this background about its general nature, let us now proceed to examine in more detail its three phases: in this chapter the formulation of hypotheses, and in the next and final chapter the evaluation and acceptance of hypotheses.

25–2 THE FORMULATION OF HYPOTHESES

In order to use the hypothetico-deductive method we must first have a number of hypotheses which we can reduce to an acceptable one by a process of elimination. But how do we get the hypotheses with which we start? This is "the $64,000 question" and it has no clear answer, for the formulation of good working hypotheses is an art that defies clear statement. How do you know when to begin your swing at a ball coming over the plate? What rule can you give for always getting the point of a joke? There is no definitive rule for such things. They are skills compounded of native talent, feeling, intuition, hunch, creative imagination, etc., and above all a familiarity with the subject at hand which comes only with experience.

Familiarity with the subject under investigation is necessary even for the recognition of a problem in the first place. Thus the question of the nature of the ocean's phantom bottom would not even have arisen if oceanographers had not already known that the ocean is really deeper than indicated by these particular echo soundings. Once the problem has arisen, experiential familiarity with the subject permits a perception of analogies between the situation being investigated and other previously known facts; and this perception of analogies or similarities between the unknown and the known is probably the most basic source of hypotheses. The similarity between the vertical migration of the reflecting layer and the migrations of living things, for example, immediately suggests that the layer is itself composed of living things. Furthermore, to those who know the relative distributions of the various forms of marine life the similarity between the distribution of the layer and that of shrimp and squid at once suggests that one or the other or both of these forms of marine life may well actually compose the layer. Again, the similarity between the echoes received from the layer and certain other echoes received by the same apparatus in other situations may lead one acquainted with these facts to suppose that the cause of the one is similar in structure to the causes of the others—thus the fish hypothesis. And so on.

Yet the number of similarities between the problematic situation and previously known situations is practically unlimited, and we cannot test, or even formulate, an unlimited number of hypotheses. How do we limit the number of similarities, and hence the number of hypotheses to be formulated? Simply by declaring, either consciously or unconsciously, that many of these similarities are irrelevant to the phenomenon under investigation. The layer goes up and down and so do birds and airplanes, the layer is thick and widespread and so is the earth's insect population; but such similarities as these are declared on the basis of other knowledge or belief to be irrelevant to the explanation of the fact at hand. The determination of the relevance or irrelevance of any particular analogy is, however, a fallible process; similarities which are believed irrelevant may later turn out to be relevant and important, and vice versa. But there are certain criteria of relevance that we employ as guides in both common sense and science, and these criteria form a standard by which the number of possible explanations of any given fact may be reduced to a workable number. Let us now examine briefly some of the more important of these criteria of relevance.

1. *A relevant hypothesis must explain the fact under consideration.* This is obviously so since the very purpose of any hypothesis is to explain some fact. Such hypotheses as "The ocean is homogeneous" or "Rational beings live on Mars" would fail to explain the fact that there exists in the ocean a distinct layer subject to vertical migrations. It is true, at the same time, that hypotheses which are irrelevant as explanations of one fact may still be true, for the failure to explain a given fact does not prove that hypothesis false as an explanation of

other facts. Furthermore, hypotheses which are irrelevant with respect to one phenomenon may be extremely relevant to others and also prove useful as instruments of discovery. Someone interested in the second of the above hypotheses might, for instance, be led to make certain important discoveries about the planet Mars. But it remains true that we immediately discard such hypotheses as explanations of the particular fact under consideration.

2. *A relevant hypothesis must be logically possible.* We of course immediately reject any hypothesis which directly or indirectly involves a contradiction. The reason for this requirement is so obvious that it hardly needs mention. Since any actual truth must be self-consistent, any hypothesis capable of serious consideration must also be self-consistent. Consequently the failure to satisfy this second requirement establishes a hypothesis as certainly false.

3. *A relevant hypothesis should not contradict other knowledge.* The hypothesis that the mysterious layer consists of fish is an example that fails to satisfy this criterion, for, we are told, present knowledge indicates that fish are restricted to certain parts of the oceans while the phantom layer has been recorded almost universally. Yet it is extremely important that this third criterion not be thought of, like the second one, as absolutely binding, for accepted beliefs may sometimes be false. In the phantom layer case, for example, the present views of fish distribution are thought of as an "outstanding difficulty in the way of accepting" the fish theory, yet the possibility of the falsity of those views is admitted: "If the reflecting layer is eventually proved to be composed of fish, the prevailing views of fish distribution will have to be radically revised." Indeed, many outstanding advances in human knowledge have involved the repudiation of previously held "truths"—at one time almost everyone "knew" that the earth was flat and yet it turned out to be round. So acceptable hypotheses should accord with existing knowledge, but the absence of such accord is not necessarily proof of the falsity of the hypothesis. The degree to which we are willing to abandon a hypothesis which conflicts with existing beliefs is proportional to the degree of evidence in favor of those existing beliefs plus the absence of acceptable alternative hypotheses.

4. *A relevant hypothesis must be really possible.* Let us imagine that some oceanographer with more imagination than sense suggests that the reflecting layer consists of mermaids. We would immediately retaliate that this is silly because it's not really possible—even though it may be logically possible, even though this hypothesis may not involve any internal contradiction. We are convinced that mermaids are biologically impossible, and even if they should really be possible it would still be impossible for them to compose the phantom layer because that layer always remains under water and mermaids have no gills. Such a hypothesis is not even worthy of consideration because it is not really possible. Yet note that the reason we believe it is not really possible is that it conflicts with present knowledge—our present knowledge of the types

of marine life, the submarine character of the layer, and the necessity of special biological organs for underwater living. So in practice this fourth criterion reduces to the third. And consequently it is subject to the same qualification, namely, that it is possible for us to be mistaken in any claim that a hypothesis is really impossible. Again, the extent to which we are ready to abandon such a hypothesis is a function of the extent to which we are reluctant to abandon our other beliefs and to the availability of acceptable alternative hypotheses.

5. *A relevant hypothesis must have experiential consequences.* From a strictly logical point of view this requirement is probably the most important of all, because the only evidence we can possibly have for any hypothesis is, as we have seen, its consequences; and in order for the consequences to function as evidence they must be available for our inspection. On this count we would reject a hypothesis asserting that the reflecting layer consists of Poseidon's halo, for instance, for since Poseidon is a mythical being such a theory would make no difference in our actual observations. Or to take a better example,[10] the hypothesis that the universe is shrinking in such a fashion that all lengths contract in the same ratio has no testable consequences, because our measurements would be the same whether or not this were true.

A hypothesis which lacks experiential consequences is simply untestable, and it is therefore impossible to produce any evidence in favor of it. Another way of saying this is that an acceptable hypothesis must *predict* certain specified experiences. Notice also that this means that any acceptable hypothesis must be such that it is possible to produce evidence *against* it; any acceptable hypothesis must be falsifiable as well as verifiable. The reason for this is that no hypothesis is self-evident; indeed, if we could deduce the fact under consideration from an immediately evident proposition we would have no need of a hypothesis.

Hypotheses need not, however, be directly or immediately verifiable. Sometimes we cannot test a direct consequence of a hypothesis but only a consequence of a consequence, etc. Or the conditions necessary for the test of certain consequences may not be present at a given time. The experiential verification of certain consequences of Einstein's relativity theory, for example, required observations possible only during a solar eclipse. Again, the verification of many theories has had to await the coming of certain inventions—more powerful telescopes and microscopes, for instance.

It is also very important to note that this requirement applies more accurately to the way in which a hypothesis is *formulated* than to its essential idea, for essentially the same hypothesis may be formulated now so as to have experiential consequences and now so as not to have. Thus a defender of the Poseidon theory of the phantom layer might retaliate to our earlier criticism by saying

[10] From Cohen and Nagel, *An Introduction to Logic and Scientific Method*, Harcourt, Brace, 1934, p. 207.

that certain propitiatory rites, such as scattering flowers on the water, will cause the vertical ascent of the layer. Thus formulated the hypothesis is testable, and if this consequence fails to be confirmed in experience the hypothesis is rejected. And of course if this consequence is confirmed, other hypotheses may still be considered because, as we have seen, they may also imply the same consequence and, besides, some of the other consequences of the Poseidon theory may be falsified. If, however, when the layer fails to rise upon the performance of the specified propitiatory rites the advocate of the Poseidon theory should reply that this is only because the sea-god was indisposed at that particular time, we should have to answer that his hypothesis is not formulated in such a way as to be clearly testable.

In brief: Any significant working hypothesis must predict experiences which are capable of clear confirmation or falsification. A hypothesis which fails to do this could conceivably be true, but there is no way of establishing its truth.

These five criteria of the relevance or significance of hypotheses are preliminary to their actual test and form a way of eliminating certain hypotheses from further consideration—at least temporarily. Such preliminary elimination is necessary in practice because, as we have seen, the number of hypotheses which could conceivably explain a given fact is practically unlimited. Yet it is extremely important to note that no one of these criteria, nor all of them together, can establish the truth of a hypothesis, for verification requires actual tests of the consequences of that hypothesis. Furthermore, only the second of the requirements is capable of establishing the falsity of a hypothesis: if a hypothesis is logically impossible then it is also false. And finally, a hypothesis which is temporarily eliminated from consideration by its failure to satisfy one or more of these criteria may later have to be reconsidered, and it could even turn out to be actually true. Thus a hypothesis which conflicts with present knowledge, for example, may be set aside temporarily, but in the end it may be the conflicting hypothesis rather than the extant knowledge which is actually true. In short: These criteria are tentative procedural guides necessitated by the exigencies of actual experimental procedure, not (except in the case of logical possibility) conclusive tests of the truth or falsity of hypotheses. For such testing we must turn to the deducible consequences of our hypotheses and see whether those consequences jibe with actual experience.

CHAPTER 26

VERIFYING HYPOTHESES: EMPIRICAL ASPECTS

Once we have tentatively reduced the possible hypothetical explanations of a given fact to a number which may be experimentally handled, we are ready to test the truth-value of the remaining hypotheses. What is the nature of this experimental testing?

26–1 EXPERIMENTAL METHODS OF TESTING HYPOTHESES

A hypothesis is the intention of the presumptive cause of some induced effect, and the nature of its test is determined by this fact. Since a true cause of any effect must always accompany this effect, we naturally—even unconsciously in everyday life—reject any presumptive cause or hypothesis which at any time fails to accompany its presumed effect. In other words, since a true cause must be necessarily and invariably linked with its actual effect, any presumptive cause which is ever absent when its supposed effect is present or present when its supposed effect is absent cannot be the actual or true cause of that effect. The relevance of this invariable or necessary connection between a cause and effect, or hypothesis and fact, to the actual truth or falsity of the hypothetical explanation may be demonstrated with a truth-table:

	$\vdash c \rightarrow \vdash e$			hypothesis $\rightarrow$ fact cause $\rightarrow$ effect		
1.	T	T	T	1.	present T present
2.	F	F	T	2.	absent F present
3.	T	F	F	3.	present F absent
4.	F	F	F	4.	absent ? absent

You will remember[1] that a causal proposition is true whenever both of the components are true—provided also, of course, that the asserted implicative connection actually exists—because it asserts those components categorically. Since the experiential meaning of truth is presence in experience and the experiential meaning of falsity is absence from experience, we may translate

[1] Pp. 333–334.

"true" as "present" and "false" as "absent" to make a truth-table for the experiential truth-values of any explanation by hypothesis. Inasmuch as such an explanatory proposition asserts the actual existence of both the fact and its explanatory hypothesis, it also will be true only when both components are true, or present in experience. Notice, however, that when both "cause" and "effect," or hypothesis and fact, are absent, the whole hypothetical or explanatory proposition is more properly unknown or unverified than false; it might be either true or false, but it cannot be asserted to be either one *experientially*.

Our procedure for testing hypotheses consists simply in determining which of these situations is the case with respect to each of the deduced consequences of each of the hypotheses under consideration. If either situation 2 or 3, in the above truth-table, is the case, then the hypothesis is rejected as false. If situation 1 is the case the hypothesis is so far confirmed. And if situation 4 is the case, the truth-value of the hypothesis is of course simply unknown. Letting "c" = cause and "e" = effect, this principle governing the experimental testing of hypotheses may be expressed formally thus:

$$(c \rightarrow e) \leftrightarrow [-(-c \cdot e) \cdot -(c \cdot -e)]$$

$$-(c \rightarrow e) \leftrightarrow [(-c \cdot e) \lor (c \cdot -e)]$$

These formulas may be read as follows: "c is the cause of e if and only if it is not the case that c is absent when e is present (situation 2) and it is also not the case that c is present when e is absent (situation 3)"; and "c is not the cause of e if and only if either c is absent when e is present (situation 2) or c is present when e is absent (situation 3)." Thus to test any hypothesis we try to determine whether the situation which it asserts invariably accompanies each of its supposed consequents. Of course, as we have seen, it is important to deduce from each hypothesis under consideration consequences or effects other than and in addition to the original fact or effect for which we are seeking an explanation. It is important that as many consequences as possible be deduced from the hypothesis, and also that these consequences be, so far as possible, independent of each other, so that the evidence for the verification or falsification of that hypothesis will be as complete as possible. And each of these other consequences, as well as the one which instigated the investigation, must also be shown to be experientially true, if the hypothetical cause is to be the true one.

With many important hypotheses, however, it is impossible by the very nature of the case to have the hypothetical situation directly and immediately present in experience. For example, the Copernican hypothesis of the earth's orbit around the sun cannot itself, at least as long as we are earthbound, ever be immediately present in experience. In such a case our evidence is restricted to the presence or absence of the consequences of the hypothesis; if the consequences are present (situations 1 and 2) the hypothesis is *so far* verified, and if any of the consequences is absent (situations 3 and 4) the hypothesis is falsified.

These ancient common-sense principles for the testing of supposed hypotheses achieved their first systematic formulation in the famous "tables" of Francis Bacon (1561–1626) and their best-known statement in the methods of experimental inquiry of John Stuart Mill (1806–1873). Hence they are known best as "Mill's methods." Let us now turn to a detailed examination of these methods for the experimental verification and falsification of hypotheses.

The Method of Agreement (Bacon's "Table of Essence and Presence"). Mill's own statement of this method is as follows: *"If two or more instances of the phenomenon under investigation have only one circumstance in common, the circumstance in which alone all the instances agree, is the cause (or effect) of the given phenomenon."*[2] In the case of the phantom ocean layer,[3] for example, since every time a net is dragged in the vicinity of the reflecting ocean layer shrimp are caught (so we are told), then it may be concluded, according to the method of agreement, that shrimp are causally connected with the reflecting layer. Symbolically:

$$\left. \begin{array}{l} (a \cdot b \cdot c \cdot d) \rightarrow e \\[2ex] (c \cdot f \cdot g \cdot h) \rightarrow e \end{array} \right\} \quad c \rightarrow e$$

Since c, shrimp, is the only factor which, so far, invariably accompanies e, the reflecting layer, then c must be the cause (or effect) of e. We all use this method more or less consciously almost every day. If everyone at a picnic gets sick, for instance, we immediately look for the food or drink which everybody consumed.

In spite of the frequency with which we rely upon this method it is extremely important to note that it is rather precarious in several respects. In the first place, this method of agreement, as stated by Mill, requires that the instances of the phenomenon under investigation "have *only one* circumstance in common," "the circumstance in which *alone* all the instances agree." But in actual practice this is rarely if ever the case. More frequently the instances of the phenomenon in question will agree in a number of respects so that, according to the method of agreement, all of these respects would have to be causally related to the phenomenon under investigation. One additional set of factors always present in every instance of the phenomenon is the observer and his observational apparatus. In some cases this set of factors is so important as to be directly connected causally with the phenomenon in question. One important instance of this is the disturbance of very small physical particles by

---

[2] *A System of Logic*, Harper, 8th ed., 1891, p. 280. (Italics altered by the present authors.)
[3] See pp. 375–376 above.

the apparatus used to observe them—a situation recognized and formulated in the Heisenberg uncertainty principle. Another is the influence exercised by the psychologist or social scientist on his subject. Furthermore, in order to be certain that the instances of the phenomenon agree in only one respect, it would be necessary to consider every last one of the constituent factors composing each instance of the phenomenon—for example, the size of the holes in the net, the size of the rope, the characteristics of the boats and fishermen, etc., etc. But this is not possible in practice. Finally, it is always possible that other instances of the phenomenon may fail to contain the agreeing factor—the next dip of the net, for example, may fail to raise any shrimp. In principle, therefore, we would have to exhaust all possible instances of the phenomenon in order to be sure that the agreeing factor is always and invariably present with the phenomenon—an impossible task.

Thus the validity of the method of agreement is limited in two respects: internally by the actual or possible presence of agreeing factors other than the supposed cause, and externally by the actual or possible absence of the supposed cause in other instances of the phenomenon. Hence the effective use of the method of agreement requires the use of other auxiliary hypotheses, and these are of two kinds: hypotheses of *relevance* and hypotheses of *sufficiency*.

We need hypotheses of relevance in order to eliminate all but one, or at least some, of the agreeing factors as irrelevant to the effect under investigation. Thus we assume, consciously or unconsciously, that such agreeing factors as the fishermen's breakfast coffee or the similar structure of their boats are irrelevant to the composition of the phantom layer. But often we are not very sure whether a certain factor is relevant or not, a situation humorously exemplified in the following news note: "We are asked to state that Harrison Sexton, whose sudden death occurred on Tuesday morning at 7:30 on South Henry Street, had not eaten breakfast at Jack's Cafe as stated in Tuesday's issue."[4] Indeed, our evidence for declaring such additional agreeing factors irrelevant may range anywhere from practical certainty to considerable doubt, as we have seen, so that agreeing factors which are declared irrelevant may in fact be relevant to, and hence causally connected with, the phenomenon in question. Thus the fact that all of the shrimp catches agree in using nets falling within a certain size range may, we are reminded, be extremely relevant to the fact that no fish are caught, and hence to the explanation of the composition of the mysterious layer.

In the second place, we also require hypotheses of sufficiency in order to decide that the instances of the phenomenon which we possess are sufficient for determining its cause. We must in practice make the assumption, that is, that further samples of the phenomenon would not appreciably alter our

[4] From the *Morristown* (Tenn.) *Gazette and Mail*, reprinted in *The New Yorker*.

evidence—that it is unnecessary to lower the net any more because the contents found in further dips would not differ significantly from those already found. This assumption may be more or less justified depending on the nature of the situation and the number of samples already on hand, but it can never be absolutely certain.

Finally, it is important to realize that even after all these assumptions are made the agreeing factor which we finally select may contain the true cause of the phenomenon as a part, or be a part of the true cause, rather than being itself the true or proper cause of the phenomenon. In the example of the phantom ocean layer, for instance, the shrimp may attract fish which are themselves the actual cause of the echoes, and likewise water drunk by everyone on a picnic may contain some noxious substance which is itself the cause of the illness rather than the water of which it is a part. Hence the method of agreement, even after all the auxiliary assumptions are recognized, can assure us at most only that we have found something which is somehow causally connected with the phenomenon; it cannot guarantee that this factor is the true and proper cause.

So the acceptance of any hypothesis by the use of the method of agreement is fraught with danger. Yet the situation here is more hopeful than we have so far indicated, for even though this method is shaky when used to verify hypotheses it can be extremely reliable when used to falsify them. *Anything absent when the effect is present is not the cause of that effect* (situation 2 in our above truth-table). Thus the absence of fish from those ocean areas where the reflecting layer is present requires us to reject the fish hypothesis. But notice that the certainty of this rejection of the hypothesis is also based upon other assumptions which may in fact be false; in this case the absence of fish from certain areas where the reflecting layer is found is not certain, although it is believed to be true. Still, to the extent that we are sure of our facts we can use the method of agreement more reliably negatively for the rejection of hypotheses than positively for their acceptance, for whatever constantly accompanies a phenomenon may not actually be its cause, but whatever fails to accompany it is surely not its cause.

The Method of Difference (Bacon's "Table of Absence in Proximity"). Mill states this method as follows: *"If an instance in which the phenomenon under investigation occurs, and an instance in which it does not occur, have every circumstance in common save one, that one occurring only in the former; the circumstance in which* alone *the two instances differ, is the effect, or the cause or an indispensable part of the cause, of the phenomenon."*[5] For example, if an instance of the presence of the reflecting layer and an instance of its absence differed only in the presence of shrimp in the first case and their

[5] *Op. cit.*, p. 280. (Italics altered by the present authors.)

absence in the second case, then we might conclude that shrimp are causally connected with the reflecting layer. Symbolically:

$$(a \cdot b \cdot c \cdot d) \rightarrow e \atop (a \cdot b \cdot \bar{c} \cdot d) \rightarrow \bar{e} \Big\} \; c \rightarrow e$$

Since the presence or absence of c, shrimp, is the only difference between the positive and the negative instance of e, the echoing layer, then c must be the cause of, or causally related to, e. Again, if some people at a picnic get sick and some do not and the only difference between their diets is that the former drank tequila and the latter did not, then we conclude that tequila must have been the cause of the illness.

The method of difference is just as commonly used, and just as subject to restrictions, as the method of agreement. The method of difference requires that the positive and the negative instance of the phenomenon differ in *only* one respect, that all of the factors connected with them be alike save one. But this is almost never actually true—the sick and the well people at the picnic differ in many other respects besides their like or dislike of tequila. And even if it should be found to be true so far as we can tell, it is always possible that there are other differences which we have not discovered, and also that other instances of the phenomenon will be found to agree, rather than to differ, in the respect under consideration. Thus large groups of shrimp might be found tomorrow in the absence of the reflecting layer, and someone not taken ill at the picnic may secretly admit under pressure that he did drink some tequila after all. The disregard of these actual or possible situations requires the use of auxiliary assumptions in the method of difference, just as it does for the method of agreement; we need to assume that the differences in barometric pressure when the reflecting layer is found and when it isn't, or the differences in musical taste between the ill and the well people at the picnic, are irrelevant to the respective phenomena. And, once more, these auxiliary assumptions may possibly be false, even though some may be better founded than others. Hence the method of difference can be no more reliable than these auxiliary assumptions.

Again, however, the method of difference may be used negatively for the rejection of hypotheses with more confidence than it can be used positively for their acceptance. For *anything which occurs without the occurrence of a given phenomenon cannot be the cause of that phenomenon* (situation 3 in our above truth-table). But even this negative use of the method of difference cannot be absolutely conclusive, for we may be mistaken in our failure to discover the phenomenon—the echo-sounding apparatus may have gone bad, for example— or the rejected cause may be causally connected with the phenomenon as one of a number of necessary conditions even though it is not the sole or sufficient cause. Still, the actual presence of a supposed cause in the teeth of the actual absence of its supposed effect is impossible if the supposed cause is truly the cause of that effect, and we may therefore use the method of difference negatively to eliminate hypotheses.

The Joint Method of Agreement and Difference. Here is Mill's formulation of this method: *"If two or more instances in which the phenomenon occurs have* only one *circumstance in common, while two or more instances in which it does not occur have* nothing *in common save the absence of that circumstance, the circumstance in which* alone *the two sets of instances differ, is the effect, or the cause, or an indispensable part of the cause, of the phenomenon."*[6] For example, if two or more dips of the net into the reflecting layer agreed only in the presence of shrimp, if two or more dips outside of the layer agreed only in the absence of shrimp, and if these two sets of instances differed only in the presence or absence of shrimp, then we would conclude that shrimp compose the reflecting layer. The structure of this type of argument is as follows:

$$
\left.
\begin{array}{ll}
(a \cdot b \cdot c \cdot d) \rightarrow e & (a \cdot b \cdot d \cdot \bar{c}) \rightarrow \bar{e} \\
(c \cdot f \cdot g \cdot h) \rightarrow e & (f \cdot g \cdot h \cdot \bar{c}) \rightarrow \bar{e}
\end{array}
\right\} \quad c \rightarrow e
$$

c is the only respect in which the positive instances agree, the absence of c is the only respect in which the negative instances agree, and the positive instances differ from the negative ones only in the presence of c in the former and its absence from the latter.

It is clear that the joint method is merely a combination of the methods of agreement and difference, and not an essentially distinct method. But it might at first be thought that the joint method at least has the advantage of being twice as strong as either of the other methods used separately. That this is in fact not the case may be illustrated by a familiar barroom ditty noted less for its logic than for the spirit with which it is composed:

Liquor and Longevity

The horse and mule live thirty years
    And nothing know of wines and beers.
The goat and sheep at twenty die
    And never taste of scotch or rye.
The cow drinks water by the ton
    And at eighteen is mostly done.
A dog at fifteen cashes in
    Without the aid of rum or gin.
The cat in milk and water soaks
    And then in twelve short years it croaks.
The modest, sober, bone-dry hen
    Lay eggs for nogs, then dies at ten.

[6] *Ibid.*, p. 284. (Italics altered by the present authors.)

> All animals are strictly dry;
>> They sinless live and swiftly die.
> But sinful, ginful, rumsoaked men
>> Survive for three-score years and ten;
> And some of them, a very few,
>> Stay pickled till they're ninety-two.

This "argument," if it may be dignified by that name, illustrates that the joint method combines the weaknesses of both of the other methods. The argument is based on the assumptions that the short-lived animals mentioned have nothing, or nothing relevant, in common save their membership in the WCTU (animal division), that long-lived men have nothing in common save the lack of such membership, and that the only relevant difference between the men and the animals is the presence or absence of such membership. But these assumptions are of course blatantly false. And even if it were true that all long-lived humans were drinkers and that no animal ever tasted a drop, this fact would still not be the cause of the difference in their life spans, for there are other differences between them which are more relevant to this difference in life spans. Thus the joint method requires the presence of each of the practically impossible situations required separately by the other two methods: that the members of each set of instances agree with each other in only one respect (method of agreement) and that the two sets differ from each other in only one respect (method of difference). But since, as we have seen, these two requirements are almost impossible to realize in practice, we must eliminate certain of the factors as irrelevant, and this requires additional assumptions which may or may not be true.

In using the joint method—and also the method of difference—we must be very careful that the negative instances are ones in which the phenomenon under investigation is expected, or at least possible. Otherwise we might have such absurdities as a set of instances of the absence of the reflecting layer including anything from angels to zeppelins, as well as ocean areas, since in none of these cases is the reflecting layer present. And surely not even the wildest astrologist would maintain that these heavenly bodies have any relevance to the composition of the submarine reflecting layer. Mill's formulation of the method covers this point since it stipulates that the supposed cause be "the circumstance in which *alone* the two sets of instances differ," and of course if this be so then it naturally follows that the phenomenon under investigation is possible and may be expected. Even though this stipulation is, as we have just seen, practically unrealizable, it is important that the negative instances be relevant to the determination of the cause of the phenomenon in question.

The joint method is better adapted to the handling of group phenomena than are the methods of agreement and difference, but it is just as fallible as they are—if not more so. If a supposed cause should satisfy the conditions of the joint method, it would indeed be causally connected with the phenomenon under investigation, but this situation is so "iffy" as to be almost unrealizable in actual experience. Yet a supposed cause often fails to conform to these conditions, and when this does happen the "cause" may be eliminated as false —provided, again, that we are sure of our facts. But this elimination procedure is nothing more than the combined use of the other two methods.

The Method of Concomitant Variations (Bacon's "Table of Degrees and Comparisons").   It is frequently the case that the phenomenon under investigation is not the simple presence or absence of an event but rather the *degree* of its occurrence—its intensity, magnitude, or some other such variable factor. This is usually true in the domain of astronomy, and often in other sciences as well, for it is frequently impossible to remove totally the phenomenon in question. Since the first three methods concern themselves with simple occurrence or non-occurrence, we need a different method in order to evaluate causal explanations of variable phenomena. Mill formulated this as "the method of concomitant variations": "Whatever *phenomenon varies in* any *manner whenever another phenomenon varies in some particular manner, is either a cause or an effect of that phenomenon, or is connected with it through some fact of causation.*"[7] Notice the application of this method toward the explanation of the reflecting layer: "As for the plankton theory, one of the most convincing arguments is the well-known fact that many plankton creatures make regular vertical migrations of hundreds of feet, rising toward the surface at night, sinking down below the zone of light penetration very early in the morning. This is, of course, exactly the behavior of the scattering layer." The structure of the argument from concomitant variations is thus the following:

$$[(c_1 \cdot c_2 \cdot c_3 \cdot \text{etc.}) \rightarrow (e_1 \cdot e_2 \cdot e_3 \cdot \text{etc.})] \rightarrow (c \rightarrow e)$$

Yet this method, like the others, especially on Mill's formulation, is quite unreliable if we attempt to use it positively to establish the truth of explanatory hypotheses. For it says that anything whatsoever that varies in any manner at all at the same time that the phenomenon in question varies in some particular manner is causally connected with that phenomenon. But if this is so then the present movement of your eyes is causally connected with the President's decisions, because as the one movement occurs the other changes also; and everything in the world of nature is causally connected with every other thing, since everything changes at the same time. All this may of course be true, but it does little to tell us what we want to know, namely, which one of nature's multitude exercises the most important, significant, or direct influence on the particular phenomenon under investigation?

Hence the method of concomitant variations is not sufficiently discriminating to establish with reliability any particular significant explanation—unless we

[7] *Ibid.*, p. 287. (Italics altered by the present authors.)

can eliminate many of these co-variants as irrelevant or insignificant on the grounds of other facts or beliefs. Even though the positions of the New York City subways may be correlated with the positions of the reflecting layer, we declare the former to be irrelevant as an explanation of the latter. But such elimination of certain co-variants as irrelevant is not obtained by the use of the method of concomitant variations; on the contrary, it is derived from other facts or assumptions. So this method, like the others, requires auxiliary hypotheses obtained from other sources if it is to yield any significant, positive conclusions. And, once more, these auxiliary hypotheses are themselves always less than certain.

When used negatively, however, the method of concomitant variations, like the other methods, may be a reliable way of eliminating certain hypotheses. For *any hypothetical cause which in fact fails to vary concomitantly with its supposed effect cannot truly be the cause of that effect.* Thus the discovery of failure of concomitant variation, provided again that we are sure of our facts, is ground for dismissing the corresponding hypothesis.

The Method of Residues.   To the above four methods Mill added a fifth which functions as a blanket clause for anything not covered by the other four methods. Here is Mill's formulation: "*Subduct from any phenomenon such part as is known by previous inductions to be the effect of certain antecedents, and the residue of the phenomenon is the effect of the remaining antecedents.*"[8] For instance, any aspects of the phantom ocean layer not explained in terms of the plankton theory must be explainable in terms of other factors in the total situation. Or, to turn to the classic example of the use of the method of residues, when the observed motions of the planet Uranus could not be completely explained in terms of the then-known solar system alone, the unexplained residue of these motions was attributed to some other factor not as yet isolated, its probable position was calculated, and thus the planet Neptune was discovered.

It should be perfectly obvious that the method of residues is not itself an experimental method at all, although it may be preliminary to experiment and discovery. Rather it is simply a recognition and formulation of the method of proceeding by elimination, and is thus purely deductive: "Either c_1 or c_2 or c_3 etc. is the cause of e. But neither c_2 nor c_3 is;[9] hence c_1 is." When interpreted in this way the method of residues is, as we have seen,[10] the very keystone of the hypothetico-deductive method, for it authorizes our affirmation of any hypothesis remaining after we have eliminated all of the alternative ones. And still more generally, the method of residues is a recognition and formulation of a guiding principle in all of our attempts to understand reality:

[8] *Ibid.*, p. 285.
[9] Notice that "neither p nor q" means "−p *and* −q."
[10] Pp. 381–382.

"Whatever has not yet been explained must be explainable in terms of other aspects of reality."

26-2 THE ACCEPTANCE OF RESIDUAL HYPOTHESES

We began our search for the explanation of a given fact by formulating a number of relevant hypotheses, each of which would explain that fact if it were true. We then subjected these alternative hypotheses to experiential tests and eliminated all those which were falsified in actual experience. Any residual hypothesis which has so far been confirmed by experience may now be asserted to be "so far true" by a formally valid process of elimination:

$$(H_1 \lor H_2 \lor H_3 \lor \ldots H_n) \to F$$
$$\frac{-H_2 \cdot -H_3 \cdot \ldots -H_n}{H_1 \to F}$$

Having done this, we have completed our hypothetico-deductive argument and have established for the fact in hand a causal explanation which is more probable than any other hypothesis we have considered and will therefore stand as the true explanation until a better hypothesis comes along.

It sometimes happens, however, that more than one hypothesis remains after the process of experiential elimination has been completed. In this situation we may sometimes be compelled to accept both hypotheses as equally true, alternative explanations of the fact. Yet we should prefer to know whether one of these hypotheses is better than the other, and if so, which one. Is there any way we can choose between rival hypotheses which have received equal experiential confirmation? There are doubtless a number of ways, but one very important criterion for preferring one of two or more equally verified hypotheses is the extent of its explanatory scope. *Of two or more equally confirmed hypotheses, that one is to be preferred which has the greatest explanatory scope.*

Of two or more hypotheses which are equally satisfactory in other respects, that is to say, one may be better because it explains a larger domain of facts. A classic example of the operation of this principle may be found in the sixteenth-century conflict between Ptolemy's geocentric theory and Copernicus' heliocentric theory of the solar system. At that time the Ptolemaic theory could be made to explain the same observed facts as the Copernican theory—and the former even had the advantage of being psychologically simpler, or more familiar, since it is in conformity with our everyday experience of seeing the sun rise and set. Yet many of the relevant observed facts could be explained by the Ptolemaic hypothesis *only* with the addition of many special *ad hoc* assumptions logically independent of the basic hypothesis itself—the addition, for example, of "epi-cycles" and "epi-epi-cycles." But the Copernican hypothesis could explain these facts without any special, auxiliary hypotheses. Thus the Copernican theory could explain the same facts as the Ptolemaic theory and more; it possessed a greater scope or range of explanatory power, and this led Copernicus and many of his contemporaries to prefer it to the geocentric view.

This greater generality or scope of a hypothesis is often called its logical or systematic simplicity.[11] Simplicity in this sense means the unification of a great range of facts under one central idea or hypothesis, and must not be confused with *psychological* simplicity, that is, with ease of comprehension or credibility. As we have just noted, the heliocentric view of the solar system is certainly much less simple than the geocentric one in this sense, for it is more difficult to reconcile with our sensory experience. So also modern relativity physics is certainly more complicated and less familiar than classical Newtonian physics psychologically, yet it has a greater explanatory scope and thus is logically or systematically more simple.

It is important to remember, however, that a hypothesis may be true even though it has a very small explanatory scope. Furthermore, it is sometimes extremely difficult or even impossible at a given time to tell which of two rival hypotheses in fact has the greater explanatory scope. Sometimes we can get no further with a problem than to offer two or more hypotheses which, so far as we can then tell, equally satisfy all our criteria. Yet we always keep seeking for broader and more complete explanations and generalizations, so we always keep trying to explain more restricted hypotheses in terms of more general ones. Thus the desire to achieve broad explanatory hypotheses is more properly a desire to integrate our knowledge into a more and more coherent system than a desire simply to achieve true propositions.

In this way, by the use of explanatory hypotheses, we can give the "whys" of propositions which cannot be explained in terms of self-evident propositions. Such hypotheses can be no more than probable, and the same is therefore true of all the propositions derived from them. Yet they satisfy our desire for explanations, and in many areas of human knowledge hypotheses are, in the last analysis, the only type of explanation that we can hope to achieve.

EXERCISES

Analyze the following examples of explanation by hypothesis, stating (a) the hypothesis or hypotheses, (b) the method or methods used, (c) any additional assumptions made, (d) the validity of the procedure, and (e) ways of increasing the validity:

1. Seeking to discover the probable cause of my occasional indigestion, I recorded everything eaten at meals which were followed by illness: (a) carrots, milk, beef,

---

[11] For an excellent account of this criterion in these terms see Cohen and Nagel, *An Introduction to Logic and Scientific Method*, Harcourt, Brace, 1934, pp. 212–215.

bread, ice cream; (b) cabbage, milk, beef, bread, ice cream; (c) cabbage, coffee, beef, bread, peaches; (d) carrots, coffee, lamb, bread, ice cream; (e) cabbage, milk, beef, bread, cake; and (f) carrots, coffee, lamb, bread, cake. After that I laid off bread.

2. Swishy dental cream will prevent tooth decay! In a recent survey conducted under the strictest scientific conditions, one hundred students at a large midwestern university were divided into two groups of fifty each. One group followed the Swishy plan in which each person brushed his teeth with Swishy dental cream after each meal, while the members of the other group followed their previous dental hygiene routine, not using Swishy dental cream. Inspection of the teeth of the members of the two groups at the end of a year showed that the members of the Swishy group had 50 percent fewer cavities than the members of the non-Swishy group.

3. "Commercial preparations of chlorophyll cannot do all that advertisers claim they can do and possibly they are dangerous if over-large doses are taken, Dr. Alsoph H. Corwin warned last night. . . . Commercial preparations are not the chlorophyll of nature, he said; they are copper derivatives of the natural substance. Tests at Johns Hopkins indicate that some preparations contain considerably more copper than can be found in the amount of derivative in the sample, and this suggests that an overdose would lead to liver damage. . . . The commercial preparations cannot be distributed throughout the body via the bloodstream in amounts sufficient to affect perspiration odors, Dr. Corwin added; if they were, those who eat too many pills would become light-sensitive and would perish upon exposure to strong light, he explained. Since this has not happened, the blood must be free of chlorophyll." (from *The New York Times*)

4. The height of the hemline of women's dresses is caused by general business conditions. That is, dresses are short during periods of prosperity and long during depressions. Thus the 1920's, a period of prosperity, was also a period of short dresses. The 1930's, mostly a time of depression, saw long dresses. During the period of war and immediate postwar prosperity they were short, but with the succeeding minor recession the "new look" of long dresses came in. Finally, with the boom of the early and middle fifties they became shorter once more.

5. ". . . The ocean dominates the world's climate. Can it also be an agent in bringing about the long-period swings of climatic change that we know have occurred throughout the long history of the earth . . .? There is a fascinating theory that it can. . . . It was developed by the distinguished Swedish oceanographer, Otto Pettersson. . . . In his laboratory atop a sheer cliff overlooking the deep waters of the Gulmarfiord, instruments recorded strange phenomena in the depths of this gateway to the Baltic. As the ocean water presses in toward that inland sea it dips down and lets the fresh surface water roll out above it; and at that deep level where salt and fresh water come into contact there is a sharp layer of discontinuity, like the surface film between water and air. Each day Pettersson's instruments revealed a strong, pulsing movement of that deep layer—the pressing inward of great submarine waves . . . moving . . . to the ever-changing cycles of the tides. . . . From the submarine tide waves, Pettersson's mind moved logically to another problem—the changing fortunes of the Swedish herring fishery. . . . All

through the thirteenth, fourteenth and fifteenth centuries this great sea fishery was pursued in the . . . narrow passage-ways into the Baltic. . . . Then suddenly the fishery ceased, for the herring withdrew into the North Sea and came no more into the gateways of the Baltic . . . why did the herring cease to come? Pettersson thought he knew, and the reason was intimately related to . . . the pen that traced on a revolving drum the movements of the submarine waves far down in the depths of Gulmarfiord.

"He had found that the submarine waves varied in height and power as the tide-producing power of the sun and moon varied. From astronomical calculations he learned that the tides must have been at their greatest strength during the closing centuries of the Middle Ages—those centuries when the Baltic herring fishery was flourishing. Then sun, moon, and earth came into such a position at the time of the winter solstice that they exerted the greatest possible attracting force upon the sea. Only about every eighteen centuries do the heavenly bodies assume this particular relation. . . . The great under-water waves pressed with unusual force into the narrow passage to the Baltic, and with the 'water mountains' went the herring shoals. Later, when the tides became weaker, the herring remained outside the Baltic, in the North Sea.

"Then Pettersson realized another fact of extreme significance—that those centuries of great tides had been a period of 'startling and unusual occurrences' in the world of nature. Polar ice blocked much of the North Atlantic. The coasts of the North Sea and the Baltic were laid waste by violent storm floods. The winters were of 'unexampled severity'. . . . From this . . . Pettersson . . . evolved a theory of climatic variation . . . [which] showed that there are alternating periods of mild and severe climates which correspond to the long-period cycles of the oceanic tides. The world's most recent period of maximum tides, and most rigorous climate, occurred about 1433, its effect being felt, however, for several centuries before and after that year. The minimum tidal effect [and mildest climate] prevailed about A.D. 550, and it will occur again about the year 2400.

"[To substantiate this theory, Pettersson showed that in the early Middle Ages] snow and ice were little known on the coast of Europe and in the seas about Iceland and Greenland. . . . What of the previous era of cold and storms, which should have occurred about the third or fourth century B.C., according to the tidal theory? There are shadowy hints in early literature and folklore . . . the Fimbul-winter or Götterdämmerung, when frost and snow ruled the world. . . ."[12]

6. Duke cigarettes are definitely less irritating! You can prove this to yourself by taking the famous Duke nose-test. First light up a Duke and one of your own brand of cigarettes. Next take a long puff of the Duke, letting the smoke come out through your nose. Then do the same thing with your own cigarette. Feel that harsh burning? This proves that Dukes are definitely less irritating.

7. "On Friday, September 9, 1949, at 10:25 A.M., an eastbound Canadian Pacific Airlines DC-3 left Ancienne Lorette, the airport of Quebec, on a scheduled run more or less following the course of the St. Lawrence River. The flight, known as Flight 108, had started at nine that morning in Montreal, and its ultimate destina-

[12] From *The Sea Around Us.* Copyright 1950, 1951 by Rachel L. Carson. Reprinted by permission of the Oxford University Press, Inc.

tion was Seven Islands, a fishing village on the north shore of the St. Lawrence, opposite the Gaspé Peninsula and three hundred miles from Quebec. (Seven Islands has since become a much more thriving community, for it is being made ready to serve as a port for iron ore extracted from the Ungava region, to the north.) On board were nineteen passengers, including three small children, and a crew of four, all of them Canadians except for three men from New York— E. Tappan Stannard, Arthur D. Storke, and Russell J. Parker, who were the president, the president-designate, and a vice-president, respectively, of the Kennecott Copper Corporation.

"The next scheduled stop on Flight 108 was Baie Comeau, a paper-pulp center two hundred and twenty miles northeast of Quebec. Several of the passengers planned to get off there, among them Mrs. J. Albert Guay, a twenty-nine-year-old Quebec housewife whose husband, a jewelry salesman, had asked her to pick up two suitcases containing rings and watches that he had put in storage there three weeks earlier, and to bring them back to Quebec. On occasion, Flight 108 also put down at Forestville, a lumber town halfway between Quebec and Baie Comeau, but this was just a flag stop. Ten minutes out of Quebec, the pilot, Captain Pierre Laurin, who was a veteran of seven years' flying and whose wife was expecting a baby at any moment, was advised by radio-telephone from Ancienne Lorette that he could skip Forestville. Laurin acknowledged receipt of the message. That was the last word ever heard from him. Ten minutes afterward, at ten-forty-five, while the plane was cruising serenely, in fair weather, it was ripped by an explosion. The sound was audible to some people in and near Sault au Cochon, a fishing village forty miles northeast of Quebec, and also to an officer aboard the St. Laurent, a Canada Steamship Line boat en route from Montreal to Bagotville. Those who heard it looked up and saw a puff of white smoke billow out of the left side of the air liner. Then the plane veered sharply to the north, and, within a few seconds, went out of control and plummeted almost straight down onto the spruce- and balsam-covered side of a steep hill called Cap Tourmente. Everybody on board was killed instantly. In the number of fatalities, the accident was the third worst in the history of Canadian aviation, and because of this, as well as the fact that three of the victims were prominent industrialists from the United States, the incident attracted considerable attention. 'What made it crash?' mused a reporter for the Montreal Star. He added, referring to the pilot, 'The man who can best answer is among the dead.'

"The man who could best have answered, and who, along with two accomplices, was to hang by the neck until dead in consequence of this knowledge, was at the moment of the disaster wandering around Quebec—just where, no one is certain, but there is reason to believe that he was on Dufferin Terrace, which adjoins the Château Frontenac and from which there is a magnificent view of the St. Lawrence to the east. If the man was there, he was undoubtedly gazing intently toward Cap Tourmente, for he expected the plane to blow up and had a pretty good notion when and where this would happen. He was J. Albert Guay, the thirty-one-year-old husband of the housewife on the plane, and a man, who, though fond enough of his wife—'The last thing between us was a kiss,' he said later while recounting how he had ushered her into an airlines limousine at the

Château Frontenac on the fatal morning—had no compunction about murdering her, as well as twenty-two people who were strangers to him, because he felt she complicated an affair he was having with a teen-age waitress."

[The preceding and the following passages were not printed consecutively in the original article.]

"During the first weekend after the disaster, Bélanger, whose headquarters are in Montreal, sent one of his staff, Andrew H. Stott, out to the scene of the crash. Bélanger did not think it was necessary to go himself, having no suspicion that anything extraordinary had taken place. On Monday morning he sent two more of his assistants to Quebec to work on the case. One of them, Jules Perrault, telephoned him that afternoon. 'All he told me was "I don't like this," ' Bélanger recalled recently. 'But Perrault has the faculty of conveying whole ideas in a few words, so I knew something was up.' Bélanger left for Quebec at once, and established himself in a suite at the Château Frontenac, which his company owns and operates. By then, Francis, who had arrived from the West Coast, and a number of other investigators had poked through the wreckage and had become convinced that the plane had blown up before it crashed. They had talked to a couple of the local folk who had heard what sounded like an explosion while the plane was still in flight, and had seen objects tumble from it before it fell to earth. There was evidence that the plane's engines were still turning over when they struck the ground; the tips of both propellers were bent forward, which to engineers meant that they had been spinning when they hit. Furthermore, although the plane had gone down nose first, which would normally have flung the people in it toward the front, bits of flesh had been spattered against the back of the passenger compartment, indicating that there had been some violent rearward thrust.

"So the question was: What had made the plane explode? There were still traces of gasoline in its battered tanks and there had been no fire, which eliminated its own fuel as the cause. Could it have been a defect in some piece of the plane's accessories—radio batteries, carbon-dioxide fire extinguishers, and so on? Enough traces of each were discovered to make it fairly certain that none had exploded. One thing that particularly confounded the investigators was that the first people to reach the spot reported having smelled something that reminded them of dynamite, which was most certainly not an accessory on any plane, and which, indeed, the Aeronautics Act of Canada forbids any plane to carry as cargo, except under very rare and controlled circumstances. No authorization to carry dynamite had been granted for Flight 108.

"The condition of the wreckage left little doubt as to where the explosion had occurred—in the forward baggage section, known as the No. 1 compartment, on the left side of the aisle leading from the cabin to the control room. The seat closest to this compartment was found a quarter of a mile from where the plane crashed, a fact leading to the inescapable conclusion that it had been hurled out while the plane was still in the air. Bélanger and his men began checking on the contents of No. 1. Their task was fairly simple, owing to the fact that the compartment had been emptied at Quebec, after the first leg of the flight, and that everything in it had been put aboard there. The airline's cargo manifest showed that in No. 1 there had been eight pieces of hand luggage belonging to passengers who had been killed in the crash; three valises and two typewriters belonging to passengers who had made the same flight two days earlier, when there was not enough space for all the baggage; and three air-express packages. One of these contained automobile parts, another contained lingerie, and the third was a twenty-five-pound parcel, contents unspecified, that had been shipped, according to the manifest, from Delphis Bouchard, of St.-Siméon, to Alfred Plouffe, of Baie Comeau.

"It didn't take long for the investigators to focus their interest on this last parcel. Nobody named Alfred Plouffe was known in Baie Comeau. A man named Delphis Bouchard, who was a resident of St.-Siméon and a night watchman on a bridge, said he didn't know anything about any such shipment. Nor did Mrs. Delphis Bouchard, a resident of Montreal who summered at St.-Siméon and who was no relation to the night watchman. Neither of them could throw any light on the identity of the person the baggage clerk at the Quebec airport said had brought the parcel there—a dark-haired woman in her forties, who had arrived by taxi shortly before the plane was scheduled to take off and had departed in the same taxi. The baggage clerk recalled that the taxi-driver had lugged the parcel into the terminal for the woman, and then—proving himself a singular example of his species—had broken a ten-dollar bill for her when it developed that the clerk had insufficient change.

"Concurrently, as the evidence piling up indicated that a crime might have been committed, the passenger manifest was being carefully checked. At first, attention centered on the three Kennecott Copper executives. Although no logical motive for murdering them was unearthed, the mere fact that they were men of affairs made some of the investigators conjecture that they might have had determined enemies. While not discarding this possibility, Perrault, Bélanger's laconic operative, systematically proceeded to inquire into the background of all the other passengers, too, and by the time he finished, he had found that only in the case of a relatively obscure one, Mrs. Guay, was there a credible motive."[13]

[13] From "It Has No Name," by E. J. Kahn, Jr., in *The New Yorker*, November 14, 1953, pp. 90–118. Reprinted by permission, © 1953 The New Yorker Magazine Inc.

APPENDIX

SUGGESTIONS FOR FURTHER READING

Rome was not built in a day, nor, unhappily, is an understanding of logic built on a single textbook. For this reason we hope that there may be at least some students who will be stimulated, and perhaps even irritated, into pursuing their study of logic further in readings that will often be found to be better, and will in any case be recognized as different from the fare provided in the present book. To this end, we have suggested both items that would obviously supplement and tend to confirm the particular type of logic here developed and items—among them some of the great classics in logic—that present theories radically at variance with the one that we have put forth in this book.

I. Classical Realistic Philosophy, considered as the philosophical setting for logic as it is presented in this book.

    A. Wild, John. *Introduction to Realistic Philosophy,* Harper, 1948.

        This book is a stimulating and readily available introduction to what is perhaps the main philosophical tradition of Western thought, viz., classical realistic philosophy as it stems originally from Plato and Aristotle in the ancient world and from St. Thomas Aquinas in the mediaeval period.

        In addition to being an excellent introduction to the subject matter of this philosophy—philosophy of nature, philosophical anthropology, ethics, political philosophy, etc.—the book can also be used as a guide to a study of the texts themselves of Aristotle and St. Thomas.

    B. *Return to Reason,* ed. by John Wild, Regnery, 1953.

        A coöperative volume of essays, prepared by contemporary realists. Students might find essays I, II, IV, VI, and VII helpful and perhaps even interesting.

II. Realistic Logic, or Logic in the Aristotelian Tradition.

    A. Aristotle, *Organon,* Oxford.

        So long as one is studying Aristotelian logic, why not read Aristotle himself? In many ways this is easier said than done, particularly if one is concerned not just to read but to comprehend. For the Aristotelian texts are singularly crabbed and cryptic. Yet the student cannot help but find them rewarding, if only for the occasional luminous and pregnant sentences that he is certain to come across.

Of the various logical treatises contained in the *Organon,* the student might find the following rather more manageable: *The Categories, De Interpretatione, Posterior Analytics.*

B.   *The Material Logic of John of St. Thomas,* translated by Simon, Glanville, and Hollenhorst, University of Chicago, 1955.

John of St. Thomas was a seventeenth-century expositor of the philosophy of St. Thomas Aquinas, noted alike for his penetration and for his faithfulness to his master. His monumental *Ars Logica* constitutes a philosophical presentation of so-called Aristotelian logic that is quite unsurpassed by anything written since.

The book here recommended is a recent translation of those parts of the *Ars Logica* which deal particularly with the philosophical foundations of logic. Unfortunately, John of St. Thomas wrote in what is almost certain to strike a modern reader as being a most arid and vexatious scholastic style. Nor can it be denied that the present translation has scarcely succeeded in allieviating these rather dispiriting features of the original.

C.   John of St. Thomas.   *Outlines of Formal Logic,* translated by Wade, Marquette University, 1955.

A recent translation of certain parts of the *Ars Logica* of John of St. Thomas that pertain more to formal logic than to the philosophical foundations of logic. Students may find this helpful. But by and large, in the formalization of logic modern logicians have gone far beyond John. Where we today can learn the most from him would seem to be rather in the area of the philosophical grounds and bases of logic.

D.   Joseph, H. W. B.   *Introduction to Logic,* Oxford, 1916.

A remarkably rich and learned book, but singularly lacking in philosophical unity and perspective. It can therefore best be consulted on separate topics, which the student will find to be nearly always written up in a way that is most illuminating, particularly as regards the historical background of the topic in question.

E.   Maritain, Jacques.   *An Introduction to Logic,* Sheed and Ward, 1937.

A very stimulating book by one of the great Catholic thinkers of the modern world. Unfortunately, the book seems to be not too carefully organized and is really more valuable for its asides and supplementary comments than for its presentation of the subject as a whole. Besides, it confines itself almost entirely to so-called formal logic.

F.   Veatch, Henry.   *Intentional Logic,* Yale University Press, 1952.

This book represents an attempt to rehabilitate classical realistic logic, largely through defending it against attacks leveled against it by partisans of modern symbolic or mathematical logic. The student might be prompted at least to look at this book for the reason that hardly anyone else has even read it, much less liked it.

III. Mill, John Stuart. *A System of Logic,* Harper, 8th ed., 1891.

One of the great classics in the history of logic—clear, lucid, and, as many would say, rather pedestrian in a British sort of way.

To the modern student the most interesting parts of the book would probably be those in which Mill attempts to do down deductive or syllogistic logic in favor of the supposed panacea of British empiricism, viz., inductive logic.

For an excellent recent abridgment of Mill's great work, the student might like to use Ernest Nagel's *John Stuart Mill's Philosophy of Scientific Method,* Hafner, 1950.

IV. Bradley, Francis Herbert. *The Principles of Logic,* 2 vols., Oxford, 2nd ed., 1922.

The student inclined to believe that all logicians are dull would do well to read this remarkable treatise by one who is not only one of the greatest of English philosophers but a master of English prose.

Logic as here presented is placed in the context of idealistic philosophy. Moreover, as a possible come-on, it might be mentioned that Bradley is a master of the art of invective, and that his most merciless hostility is directed at the empiricist tradition in logic as represented by Mill. Nor would it be altogether without interest to the student, perhaps, to consider that without too much of a strain on his imagination he could fancy some of Bradley's most barbed shafts as being aimed right at the realistic tradition in logic as represented, say, by this very textbook. Accordingly, if the authors of this book have occasionally made this same student miserable, he might enjoy thinking how they in turn might be made to squirm by such famous passages of Bradley as the one on p. 171 on the inverse variation of extension and comprehension or the one on p. 175 on classes.

V. Dewey, John. *Logic: The Theory of Inquiry,* Holt, 1938.

Like so much of what Dewey wrote, one is likely to find this book somewhat dull and heavy going. But it is very meaty and suggestive. And although it seems not to have had too much influence on professional logicians, it may well be found of particular interest today because of its implied critique of extreme formalism in logic and its insistence upon constantly integrating logic with concrete human experience.

VI. Mathematical or Symbolic logic.

A. Whitehead and Russell. *Principia Mathematica,* 3 vols., Cambridge, 2nd ed., 1925–1927.

This forbidding work of huge bulk, with its quarto pages covered with all sorts of dots, wedges, wiggly lines, and other occult symbols, is still regarded by symbolic logicians much as Christians regard the Bible. The

Introduction and Russell's Preface to the second edition are at least written in English and may thus be read with appreciation for that reason if for no other.

B. Russell, B. A. W. *Our Knowledge of the External World* (especially Lecture II on "Logic as the Essence of Philosophy"), Allen and Unwin, 1922.

Russell, B. A. W. *The Philosophy of Logical Atomism,* Department of Philosophy, University of Minnesota, n.d. (first published as articles in 1919).

In contrast to the rigorous formalism of *Principia,* these two books present, in Russell's remarkably crisp and lucid English, some of the philosophical considerations that lay behind the development of modern mathematical logic. Very readable and very interesting.

C. Wittgenstein, Ludwig. *Tractatus Logico-Philosophicus,* Kegan Paul, 1922.

This extraordinary compilation of gnomic wisdom almost defies description. It is listed here not so much because its merits are likely to be readily appreciated by the student but because of the almost worshipful reverence with which its many admirers still tend to regard it. Perhaps one might best characterize it as an attempt to utilize the supposedly precise language of mathematical logic in order to formulate an utterly rigorous positivistic position in philosophy.

D. For textbook presentations of modern symbolic logic, the following might be recommended as being both competent and widely used, as well as having been written by eminent contemporary logicians:

Tarski, A. *Introduction to Logic,* Oxford, 2nd ed., 1946.

Reichenbach, H. *Elements of Symbolic Logic,* Macmillan, 1947.

Quine, W. V. *Methods of Logic,* Holt, 1950.

Copi, Irving. *Symbolic Logic,* Macmillan, 1954.

VII. Strawson, P. A. *Introduction to Logical Theory,* Wiley, 1952.

This book presents in a thoroughly competent way the most recent fashion in logical theory. In reaction against the symbolic logicians, who thought it the business of logic to provide men with an artificial and as nearly "perfect" language as possible, this new school of logicians feels that no artificially constructed language can ever rightfully claim to be a replacement for the "crude" language of everyday speech. Accordingly, the logician is now urged to direct his attention to the task of laying bare the logical uses contained in ordinary speech and language.

Although this book is an entirely capable performance and is even very illuminating in spots, it is stylistically both labored and obscure. To the student who chooses to take a crack at it, we say, "More power to him!"

VIII. Practical Logic.

Many students may find their curiosity aroused by the concrete details of various logical tricks and twists, especially as these manifest themselves in sophisms and fallacies of various kinds. There are a number of books which are comparatively rich in details of this sort, just as they are comparatively impoverished in the matter of providing the reader with a philosophical understanding of the nature of logic. Of such books we should be inclined to recommend the following particularly:

Beardsley, Monroe. *Practical Logic,* Prentice-Hall, 1950.

Black, Max. *Critical Thinking,* Prentice-Hall, 2nd ed., 1955.

INDEX